My Window on Main Street

My Window on Main Street

by Marilyn Solomon

ISBN 1-884186-24-6

Printed in the United States of America.

TABLE OF CONTENTS

Arts

Places of Worship

Community Service

INTRODUCTION

That frigid December night when Harold, my husband of six months, and I drove into town from Norfolk, Va., Nashua's quaint New England charm eluded me. "Siberia, that's where we really are," I thought as we traveled down Concord Street to the little motel, one of two in town, where we were to stay while we looked for an apartment. In those days apartments were scarce and mostly found in private homes.

After his discharge from the Navy, Harold had signed on with Sanders Associates, a new and up-and-coming electronics firm. Once winter subsided we made it through the first year quite successfully, making friends, buying a house and finding Nashua a warm and welcoming place to live.

Forty-five years later we are still here. Nashua is our home. Our three children were born and raised in the same house where we have lived for 44 years.

I owe my interest in the history of Nashua, beyond the city's day-to-day doings, to *The Telegraph*. A few years after I started working for the newspaper in 1976, the staff produced a special 150th anniversary edition of *The Telegraph* researching past editions of the paper dating back to its beginnings in 1832. It was an ambitious undertaking. Each member of the editorial staff was assigned several topics, which required us to read stories in the newspapers of the previous century kept on microfilm in the Nashua Public Library.

The more I read, the more intrigued I became. The life of a small town and how it mushroomed into the city where we lived today was fascinating. Even before I went to work for *The Telegraph*, the changes we witnessed in the short span of years since we came here were beyond imagination. A high-tech firm occupied the mill buildings on Canal Street, the cow pastures of Hayward Farms became the Nashua Mall, a hotel castle rose off the highway and a myriad of restaurants and stores displaced the tree-lined farms of Amherst Street and the Daniel Webster Highway.

The social scene of the town shifted from downtown to the Pheasant Lane Mall—only to have Main Street make a comeback in the past 10 years. The schools have multiplied and the hospitals have expanded. Yet, along with these monumental changes, the underpinnings of a caring community remained constant.

When I joined *The Telegraph* staff, the history of the town put all the changes in a more meaningful perspective. Little by little as I wrote stories about them, I began to feel a real kinship for the town and its people—Daniel Abbot, Father Millette, Mabel Chandler—to name just a few of the many imposing figures whose legacy is still with us. Whenever an opportunity to write about Nashua's past arose,

I was delighted, particularly after I became community news editor, working out of the Nashua office on Main Street and writing two columns a week. The people, places and events of the day provided ample material for those columns and the contemporary subjects often intertwined with the past.

Through those columns I became familiar with both the past and present, getting to know people in all walks of life I might otherwise never have met. Whether about the past or present, the movers and shakers of the community or the people living quietly behind the scenes, there was an endless stream of stories to be told, some sad, some happy, others astonishing, often reassuring and always interesting to me.

Several years before I retired, Meri Goyette—forever on the lookout for ways to raise money for the Hunt Memorial Building—suggested that I collect some columns in a book to benefit the city's signature landmark. For those of us who knew the Hunt Building as the Nashua Public Library, it is enshrined with memories.

I remember my first visit to the NPL on Library Hill soon after we found an apartment. It was a grand building with high ceilings and rich, dark wood furnishings. I was in search of a book I had spent six months patiently trying to find in the Norfolk library. Within minutes after I requested it, I saw the librarian climb the narrow, winding staircase to the stacks to locate it and put in my hands. I was impressed.

From that first encounter, to my library forays with my children, to my urgent calls to the library for information for my columns, my appreciation for the library staff has never ceased.

The thought of my book side by side with the thousands of others on its shelves fills me with a sense of awe and disbelief.

Choosing the columns for this book from the thousand or more I wrote—each and every one with a personal bond—was a challenge. Some were easier to retrieve from *The Telegraph* files than others. Most of the ones I selected highlight the social history of Nashua. There were not enough pages in the book to include all of my favorites.

This year Nashua celebrates its sesquicentennial and the Hunt Memorial Building its centennial.

This book is a tribute to both, with gratitude from a Nashuan by choice.

ACKNOWLEDGEMENTS

It takes many hands to produce a book. The connection to the reader has many more links in its chain than writing a newspaper column which is more immediate and direct. Each of the links, so important to the book process, deserves special recognition and a big thank you.

I begin with *The Telegraph* since without their financial support the book would not have happened. Their generous grant, together with an equally generous grant from the McLean Contributionship, started the ball rolling. From the outset, the encouragement of the boards of trustees of both the Hunt Memorial Building and the Nashua Historical Society was very gratifying. Adelle Leiblein and Georgi Hippauf, trustees of the Hunt Memorial Building, wrote the convincing grant proposal.

Since the columns were already written I assumed the hard part was done. I was wrong. Making the selections was difficult, but even more daunting was the fact that most of the columns had to be entered in the computer. Ten years of columns were kept in *Telegraph* scrapbooks since the newspaper did not start its computer library until the end of the 20th century. To locate some of the columns, organizations such as the Friends of the Symphony and the Pastoral Care Center searched their files to help me identify dates of publication. The computer savvy students in the Rotaract club at the New Hampshire Community Technical College in Nashua accomplished the overwhelming task of typing them into the computer. Under the guidance of Barbara Cleland, they adopted this job as one of their community projects.

After the columns were computerized, I had help in reading them for errors from two friends with editing expertise, Georgi Hippauf and Ruth Ginsburg. Ruth also saved me from a nervous breakdown in checking laser proofs.

Gathering pictures to match with the columns was the next giant step. Since a number of the photos that accompanied the columns in the newspaper were no longer in *The Telegraph* files, I had to call on many other people to provide photos to fill the gap.

The Historical Society offered to share the wealth of old photos from its collection. Too numerous to mention are the many friends in the community who came forward with photos. In fact they often delivered them to my house, Puritan Press or the *Telegraph* office on Main Street. Frank Mooney also made available a number of photos from his wonderful Nashua collection.

Friends and colleagues in the editorial room of the *Telegraph*, including editor David Solomon; Dean Shalhoup; photographers Don Himsel and Bob Haverstrom;

as well as editorial assistants Mary Zickus and Jennifer Regan answered my calls for help. Former *Telegraph* photographer Kathy Seward MacKay also contributed her considerable talents to the cover.

Last but not least, without my family's support there would be no columns and no book.

My husband Harold, my daughter Laurie, and my two sons, David and Michael, were always there to cheer me on throughout my career. With the book, my husband's endless patience, advice and computer expertise were invaluable. And his suggestion for the cover was inspirational. Both Harold and Laurie also volunteered hours to take many pictures for the book.

For me, it has been an adventure, one of both fun and frustration, leading to an exciting, new experience, publishing a book. Along the way, it renewed my deep appreciation for the people of our community.

∼

The book you hold in your hands, *My Window on Main Street,* exists because of the generosity and vision of *The Telegraph* newspaper, The McLean Foundation, and the unstinting efforts and talents of the author, Marilyn Solomon. As a result of the successful grant-writing that funded this book's publication, a significant portion of the proceeds benefit The Hunt Memorial Library Building on Library Hill, prominently situated at Six Main Street in Nashua, New Hampshire. Trustees of the Hunt Building wish to acknowledge the administrative assistance of the Nashua Historical Society. The attention to detail, creativity and professionalism of Fred Lyford and Karen Ewald Currier at Puritan Press, the Hollis Publishing Division, have taken the book from simple printing to high-caliber publishing of the first order.

My Window on Main Street was supported by the Trustees as a special initiative celebrating the Hunt Building's Centennial year, 2003. Vice Chairman Georgi Hippauf and Trustee Adelle Leiblein were the grantwriters and project managers.

HAPPENINGS

My Window on Main Street

"LUCKY LINDY" FLYOVER

Once upon a summer day the fabled "Lucky Lindy" flew over Nashua. He tipped his wings and tossed a small parachute from his open cockpit plane, floating a message toward City Hall. It fell at the feet of a young admirer not far from its destination.

The year was 1927 and Charles A. Lindbergh in "The Spirit of St. Louis" was barnstorming every state in the nation to promote air travel. He insisted on meeting time schedules for landing to ensure the public's confidence in the newborn industry.

Sixty-two years after Lindbergh's flyover on July 23, 1927, his cross-country route will be retraced by Capt. John Race, a latter-day hero of the skyways. Race, as his idol before him, will fly his plane over Nashua on his way to the Concord airport, where he will land for the night before heading West the next day.

The plane will have the same basic instruments that Lindbergh used. The mission of the modern-day aviator, however, will be quite different from that of the first. He will be touting the wonders of a white DC-8 outfitted as a hospital. For five years, since retiring from Pan American Airways, Race has volunteered to fly Project Orbis. The jet is outfitted as a hospital and is manned by a team of doctors, nurses and technicians. They have taught sight-saving techniques to more than 8,000 eye doctors and restored sight to more than 7,500 patients.

Lindbergh's expedition was chronicled in *The Telegraph*. The newspaper also carried an ad announcing the sale of "Lucky Lindbergh" coins for 10 cents, 2 cents off with the coupon.

On July 22, 1927, *The Telegraph* reported, "Lindbergh Greeted by Boston Throng. Thrills Watchers With Stunts Before Bringing Airplane to Landing."

The following day the bold headline spread across the page read: "Lindbergh Flies Over the City this P.M."

Nashuans who had heard the news took to the streets and rooftops, although time had not permitted an organized City Hall gathering.

Reaching back into early childhood memories, Gladys Grigas, then Gladys Cunningham, recalls waiting for Lindbergh's arrival with her sister and parents. "We lived on Perry Street and had a good view of the canal and the mills from our back porch. He seemed to be using the mills as a guideline. He came in low, so low I think I saw the lettering on the plane . . . and he tipped his wings."

Her husband-to-be Charles, remembers waiting with boyhood buddies at the corner of Factory and Main streets. "We could see the scroll coming down. I think it was on a small parachute. We followed it. We were disappointed when we didn't get it, so we took off."

"Years later I was surprised when I saw it at the Historical Society."

The scroll was retrieved by the late florist, Francis Collins. As fate would have it, it was his 25th birthday. The city fathers, aware of the occasion, allowed Collins to keep the memento, says his grandson, Peter. He grew up hearing tales about the Lindbergh from his grandfather and when he was in high school, he was entrusted with the scroll. The large sheet of parchment contained a message explaining the purpose of the 1927 trip.

"We feel that we will be amply repaid for all our efforts if each and every citizen in the U.S. cherishes an interest in flying and gives earnest support to the airmail service and the establishment of airports and similar facilities."

In the corner a handwritten note apologized for not being able to land in the city. It is signed, Charles A. Lindbergh.

The parchment began to show signs of deterioration, Peter said, and his grandfather suggested they give the scroll to the Nashua Historical Society.

"When you get up in age, you want things to go where they can be taken care of," added Peter who with his father, Francis Jr., still runs the family flower shop on Main Street. "It (the scroll) was pretty important to him. Lindbergh was one of the real life heroes of the time."

Two little girls who were taken to the Concord airport to see Lindbergh were less impressed by the historic occasion than by the breakfast they ate later. "We left so early. It was 5 o'clock in the morning and all I could think of was that I was hungry," remembers Dorothy Frost. Martha Davis agreed. It was her father, Walter Whipple, vice president of the Nashua Manufacturing Co., who drove them up at dawn in his open seven-seater Cadillac.

Hearing about other experiences relating to the Lindbergh flight was of interest to Mrs. Grigas, then president of the Nashua Historical Society. She expects to record the vignettes in an oral history she is compiling.

The historic magnitude of his trip must have pleased Lindbergh himself 42 years later as he watched Neil Armstrong, commander of the Challenger, take man's first step on the moon. The date was July 20, the same day in 1927 when he took off from a small airstrip on Bayport, Long Island, N.Y., to demonstrate the vast possibilities of flying to his fellow Americans.

July 1989

BLACK MONDAY

September 13, 1948. It was a classic autumn day in Nashua but by the time the sun had set, it would be forever branded Black Monday.

Gloom crept over the city as it learned its worst fears had been realized: the mills were closing.

The purchase of the city's textile mills three years earlier by Textron Inc., a large firm based in Providence, R.I., had created a sense of uneasiness in spite of the company's reassurances. Yet, the news of the mills closing came as a shock, shaking the city's well-being to its core. A century of stability had vanished, leaving in its wake massive unemployment.

Forty-one years later on a chilly March Monday evening, people with deep ties to the mills relived experiences at a meeting of the Nashua Historical Society.

"It was like the end of the world," recalled Bob Smith, a retired textile designer who had started his career in the bleachery.

Like others hit by the shockwaves of the closing, he had come to the Speare Building to hear a talk about the book, "A Testing Time: Crisis and Revival in Nashua." People who had played a role in more recent decades of prosperity were there, too. They had all contributed to the book.

Author Stephen Winship of Concord had chronicled the compelling story of the Nashua mills, both the rise and fall, and the aftermath when a determined city rebuilt its shattered economy.

The newly published book was commissioned by the Nashua-New Hampshire Foundation, the unifying force that turned the disaster around. The group of community leaders was so successful in its mission, in fact, that it put itself out of business last year.

Nashua's story has become a classic for business school textbooks schools, said Winship. It offers a moral today for cities losing their main source of employment.

The lesson to be learned from Nashua's revival, he said, "Is that nothing can happen unless there is a sense of social compact—and that existed here."

The community cohesiveness emerged within minutes of the news of the mills closing, according to Winship.

In "A Testing Time" he quotes the initial reaction of *Nashua Telegraph* editor Fred Dobens: "Is this a Monday morning joke?"

Dobens soon realized it was not a joke and immediately phoned Eliot Carter, the civic-minded vice president of the Nashua Gum and Paper Co. The two men

then divided calls to the Chamber of Commerce directors, Mayor Oswald, Maynard, bankers, lawyers, merchants and union chiefs.

As dusk fell on Black Monday, *The Telegraph* headline sounded a positive note:
"Ready for Challenge—City Swings into Action as Mills Announce Plant Closing."

All this was a familiar story to everyone at the meeting this month, yet they listened with the same rapt attention that children do to a repeated fairy tale. Winship
recounted how the city met the challenge, how the Nashua Foundation negotiated
with Royal Little, Textron chief, to purchase the mill buildings; how the Foundation
set out on a search for new industries, and how it had the foresight to lure new hi-
tech industry, starting with Sanders Associates Inc.

Seated in the audience were officers and members of the historical society
whose families play prominent roles in the book, which can be purchased through
the historical society.

Martha Davis is the daughter of the mill-manufacturing boss Walter Whipple
who later became a trustee in the Nashua Foundation.

Gladys Grigas, society president, is the daughter of Erin Cunningham who rose
from an errand boy to a foreman in the carding department.

Bea Cadwell's family connection to the mills runs from the late 1800s to the
mid 1900s. Father-in-law William Harry Cadwell followed his father, William Dyer
Cadwell, into the executive offices of the mills.

Bob Smith went to on to New York City to pursue the design work he had
learned at the mills and he returned to Nashua when he retired.

Telegraph Editor Fred Dobens checks the front page headline with Paul Boire, the city editor.

The link between the past and the present, the Nashua Foundation, was represented by Warren Kean, a director, and Evelyn Stoliker, longtime secretary.

It remained for Bob Tabor to cap the evening. He had worked for Sanders Associates Realty Corp., which purchased the mill property in the mid-50s.

"What a buy. For one-quarter million dollars, we got a lot of property."

And the city, in the bargain, got a future.

April 1, 1989

CHRISTMAS ON MAIN STREET

Willpower melted faster than the snowflakes when the sweet smell of fresh donuts from Brockelman Brothers Market drifted on to Main Street. Few Nashuans waiting at the bus stop in front of the store could resist the temptation, especially after a day of Christmas shopping.

Ernie Berube inhaled with gusto as if he can still catch a whiff of the aroma when he talks about downtown Nashua in the 1930s, the days of his youth. The retired vice president of NFS Savings Bank can picture the shops, the diners, the movie theaters, the restaurants, giving the name and location of each without hesitation. He mentions Bessie Bryant on the corner of Factory Street, Marsh Parsons next door and W.T. Grants across the street. Rosebud, the popular ice cream parlor, occupied one corner of West Hollis Street and the Yankee Flyer Diner an East Hollis corner. On shopping trips with his mother, they always stopped at Kennedy's Egg and Butter Store, where the cheese was scooped from big tubs.

" And my mother would not buy fish anywhere but Philbrick's Market," he said.

At Christmas time, the young Berube headed for Philip Morris, where he spent hours watching the Lionel trains whiz around tracks in the basement department. Santa presided at Montgomery Wards, and the Salvation Army brass band, tootling a continuous repertoire of Christmas carols, made the season complete.

As they are for Berube, memories of downtown Nashua at Christmas are still vivid in the minds of Nashuans who grew up in the depression era.

It was time when few families owned cars, television was unheard of and coke was something to drink. Main Street was the core of community life. The people behind the counter were as familiar as next door neighbors and the store owners sat in the next pew at church.

"Saturday night, especially around Christmas time, you couldn't move on Main Street without seeing people you know. We all did our shopping downtown. You could find anything you wanted at Speare's," says Gladys Grigas, past president of the Nashua Historical Society.

Speare's also had an intriguing attraction, its electricity money trolley, which sent the customer's cash down a tube from the point of purchase to the office. Miraculously, the container returned with the proper change.

According to Reynold Dean, the last owner of the store, the system is now in the Smithsonian Institute in Washington D.C. Affectionately called "Mr. Downtown," Dean was president of the Retail Merchants Association when the first Christmas lights were turned on in later years.

During the 30s, December signaled the opening of shops every night until Christmas Eve. Store windows were framed with laurel wreaths, the only festive touch available since Christmas lights were yet to come. Multicolored lights were later introduced to Nashua in the window of Johnson's Electric store. The tree decorations were looked upon with wonder, Grigas said. Most families cut their own Christmas tree. Some ordered one from Legasse's Market on the corner of Ledge and Pine streets. "They were not pruned liked they are today but they were fresh," Grigas said.

The grandest tree of course was the one on Library Hill. " Everybody marched up to the library to see the tree." she added.

Gifts found under the tree on Christmas morning were far less extravagant than they are today. A linen handkerchief for mother, a tie for father and small toys for the children more than met expectations.

"If you got an orange in your stocking, that was something," said Noel Trottier, retired director of the Park and Recreation Department. Fresh fruit was rare in the winter, unlike today. A childhood Christmas present Trottier still remembers was a pair of boots with a side pocket for a jackknife.

Although childhood memories are sweetened by the years, a sober note about the depression creeps into conversations.

"The depression was pretty bad. It left its mark," Grigas said, adding that she remembers her father coming home from the mill and talking about people who lost their jobs. The mills, not far from Main Street, were the gears of city life around which the stores and neighborhoods clustered.

During the Christmas school vacation, for the price of a dime, the children spent afternoons at a local movie theater. They also went sledding on Strawberry

Nashua Historical Society

A Christmas tree is decorated each year in front of the Hunt Memorial Building.

Hill in the back of the Crown Hill Fire Station, or skating on the Mill Pond, affectionately christened Little Silver Lake.

A few foolhardy souls skated on the canal on weekends, if weather was frigid enough. If you grew up on a farm in Hollis, as Audrey Mercer did, downtown Nashua was a fairyland far away. " It was a big deal. It was like coming to the big city, like going to Boston as we do today," she said. She carried the same awe of Main Street into later years when she and husband Robert Mercer were courting.

"When Bob and I were dating we'd just go downtown to watch the people go by," she said.

One Christmas Eve tradition Mercer remembers is family caroling after church services. The singers would visit the homes of the sick and the elderly on their mission of cheers.

"It was something we looked forward to doing, if it wasn't too cold. . . If it was, we went any way."

The weather took second place to holiday traditions at Christmas time.

December 5, 1992

CITY QUILT

Who would ever believe that a needle and thread would be tools of choice in the age of the computer? Or the means of creating a lasting impression in the year 2000?

The Mayor's Volunteer Recognition Committee for one. It has adapted an old-fashioned idea to an enduring tribute for the future.

A handmade quilt, the symbol of comfort and caring since colonial days, took its place in the city's millennium celebration, representing the group of Nashuans who practice the art of bringing comfort and caring to our city every day. They are the host of volunteers who give their time and energy daily to Nashua schools, hospitals, churches and agencies.

"In the past 50 years, most of the agencies have had volunteers since day one," said June Caron, chairman of the recognition committee, underscoring how essential volunteers are in the functioning of the social service network. In a survey of 45 of the city's 200 social service agencies committee members documented an average of 732,286 hours of volunteer work given gratis annually. One of the agencies responded the hours were too numerous to count.

Each year during Volunteer Week, the city plans a way to say thank you. Instead of the usual dinners, balloons tied to lampposts, and serenades from the Barbershop quartets, the city recognition committee selected a quilt for its millennium year appreciation project.

The heart of the quilt, the center squares, will be stitched with the thought, "Volunteers—the fabric of our city." Of course, the quilt makers are volunteers from a cross section of the city's social service agencies.

The committee distributed muslin squares to the women who made the quilt and. the skilled needle workers transformed the squares into decorative parts of the whole with a logo or a scene depicting the work of their agency. The squares were put together by quilters at the Nashua Senior Activity Center in time for New Year's Eve.

Gloria Kane was one of the many quilt makers who volunteered. A secretary in the criminal division of the Nashua Police Department , she made the Police Athletic League square. She volunteers for PAL whenever she can, usually making cookies.

"Children are important in the world," says the grandmother, praising Officer John Latullipe for the after school programs he runs at the Ash Street Community Center and the police department for its concern in conducting finger-printing sessions for the protection of children.

Of quilt-making, she says, "It will be the first time ever, but it's for a good cause."

Although she's never made a quilt, she knew she could get help from her daughter, Debra Ferreira, an expert quilt maker.

Once a quilt-maker, you're hooked forever, according to Charlotte Vail, who has been acting as a consultant behind the scenes to the committee. Although she sewed, mostly for her children, she had never made a quilt before she moved to Nashua in 1984 after her children were grown. While working at Rich's fabric store, she and co-workers got involved in a quilt making project for babies born with AIDS.

Now after taking making classes in designing and making quilts, and making quilts for her children, she is a member of the Hannah Dustin Guild. Vail did the blueprint for the design, determining the 12-inch dimension and number of squares to be used for the 9-by-12-foot quilt. Once the 42 finished squares came in from the agencies, she and the Senior Activity Center quilters hand-stitched them together. Each agency came up with the design for its square, the backing and sashing to be done in muted old-fashioned colors of antique blue, beige and mauve.

The signature of the quilt, "Volunteers—the fabric of the community," was executed by the members of the Recognition Committee overseeing the project. It included Jean Barrett, director of volunteer services at Southern New Hampshire Medical Center; Margo Bell, projects director at the Nashua Seniors Activity Center; Dolores Bellavance, city community services director; June Caron, Nashua-Park Recreation; Liz Fitzgerald, Merrimack River Watershed Council; Shaun Marquis, director of Information and Referral of Greater Nashua; Janice McDermott, volunteer coordinator of Home, Health and Hospice; Brian Demers of the Retired Senior Volunteer Program and Brenda Watts, manager of volunteer services at St. Joseph Hospital.

Each had a hand in the project, from McDermott who coined the volunteer slogan to Fitzgerald and Bell who picked the material for the sashing, to Bell who worked out the design and cut the squares with Vail. Marquis contacted the agencies and was surprised at the enthusiastic response.

"We expected about 20, and we got 50," she said.

Joan Lee, director of the Adult Day Health Center, was delighted with the idea. Seniors at the center had already made two quilts.

In addition to the skill it takes, she reiterated something our Pilgrim ancestors knew about quilting bees. "It's a wonderful group effort. Everyone sits around the table and interacts with each other," she said.

"And when it's done," said Watts, "it is truly a community effort. The theme says it all."

Unlike previous expressions of "thank you," said Caron, it will be tangible and lasting.

"When it's finished it won't be packed away in a box," she observed. After displaying it in prominent city buildings such as City Hall and the Hunt Memorial Building, it will make the rounds of all the agencies. Looking at the quilt will give everyone a warm feeling about what volunteers contribute to the quality of city life for years to come.

A HOT, WIND-DRIVEN AFTERNOON . . .

If you were a twelve-year-old first baseman and your team was clobbering a neighborhood rival, nothing could budge you from Nashua's North Common. Not even the Crown Hill fire.

"We watched the billowing black cloud come over the field. We could see the flames. It looked like they were coming from Main Street," said Stanley Vanderlosk, recalling the hot, wind-driven afternoon of May 4, 1930.

Of course he and the other players finished the baseball game. And by the time they went to investigate, barriers closed off the city at Canal Street and the boys were sent home.

Memories flashed back to that day in technicolor as Vanderlosk, now a state representative from Ward II, strolled Crown Hill with a band of Nashua history buffs. Historic Nashua Inc. had arranged for the walking tour to take place just a few days short of the 59th anniversary of the fire, one of the greatest disasters in Nashua's history.

Before it abated beyond the country club, the fire had destroyed one-quarter of the city. It left more than 400 families homeless and gutted six businesses and two churches. Fire trucks from 24 communities had been summoned to help during the more than six hours it raged through the city's east side.

Wearing raincoats and sneakers, the walkers met at Infant Jesus Church on the corner of Harvard and Allds streets, rebuilt in 1954 next to the parish house spared by the fire.

We were several blocks from where the fires began. History records the time as 2 P.M. and the place as the base of the Boston and Maine Railroad bridge on Temple Street.

How it started remains a mystery. Some said it was children playing with matches. Others surmised it was touched off when one of the players in the Sunday craps game under the bridge left a cigarette still smoldering.

"Imagine, if you will, a day very different from today," said our guide, Jeannine T. Levesque. She drew a picture of a lazy May Sunday, unusually hot and dry with high winds picking up momentum as the day progressed. "Nashuans who had cars had taken off for the beach," she said.

Six hundred children and parishioners had gathered in the third floor auditorium of Infant Jesus church-school to see a play.

Others were just finishing Sunday dinner. Still others were taking a snooze or listening to the Boston radio station.

At first firemen figured they could easily extinguish the flames. But the winds outwitted them, whipping sparks from rooftop to rooftop of the houses nearby. "They burned like candles from the roof down," said Jeannine, explaining that wooden roof shingles were like tinderboxes. On some streets, the fickle flames skipped one side and ignited the other. Frantic residents moved belongings into the street only to see them go up in flames.

Soon a cloud of thick, black smoke enveloped the city—the cloud that the baseball players saw at the North Common. It was reportedly visible east at Hampton Beach and south near Boston.

Zigzagging from the past to the present, the walkers followed the fire's path of destruction. There were 19 of us in the group ambling along in the gray mist of a chilly afternoon more typical of spring than the one in 1930.

The lawns of the neat homes were turning green, the tulips budding and the daffodils in bloom. A few children were riding bicycles, a few cars driving by. We walked from Allds Street to Bowers Street, on to Marshall and Burke streets and back to Allds. We passed the Marshall Street Playground, established in 1931; the Girls Club, formerly the John Collins Center, built in the late 70s; Vagge Village and the Maynard Homes, low-income housing developments dating back to the 40s and 60s.

We stopped to look at photocopies of pictures of the fire Jeannine had borrowed from the library. They reminded Paul Taylor, who had moved here from Massachusetts, of a visit here with relatives soon after the fire.

"All you could see were chimney stacks and cellar holes," he said of the aftermath, often compared to scenes of war devastation.

But, amazingly, there were few casualties and no fatalities.

Sandra Axton, Pennichuck Junior High School teacher, spoke of a colleague who had been one of the children at the Infant Jesus play. They had been calmly

Nashua Historical Society

evacuated by the nuns minutes before the church became engulfed in flames.

We returned to the new church where we had left our cars. Like the church and its school, new homes, wider streets, a more modern building code and new zoning laws had emerged from the ashes.

And the deeply rooted neighborhood spirit still flourishes.

May 1989

BEING FLOODED WITH MEMORIES

Coincidence strikes at the oddest times. On Tuesday my desk was moved back to 60 Main St. in Nashua, after six years of working out of *The Telegraph*'s plant in Hudson. I am now in an office on the corner of Pearson Avenue that is the new downtown Nashua bureau of *The Telegraph*.

The date of the move was strictly arbitrary, yet it happened on the anniversary week of Nashua's worst disasters, the spring flood of 1936. Not that I am implying my move was a disaster, quite the contrary. But the flood was to be the topic of my Saturday column and I had decided on it long before my business address changed.

Sitting in a spot that was a direct target of the flood is like riding a time capsule to the past. I can almost hear the Nashua River beating against the building, gushing into the pressroom as it did 54 years ago. When I walk out the door and watch the river run its usual course well below the Main Street bridge, I imagine its waters slapping furiously over the street, as it did then.

The late Dexter Arnold, a *Telegraph* compositor, set the scene for the drama in recollections he wrote to preserve memories of the terrible event:

"On March 13, the ice started to break up in the Merrimack River and its tributaries. At any rate, it was on the 13th that crowds of people stood on the Taylor's Falls Bridge between Hudson and Nashua and watched huge ice cakes sweep down the river and crash into the piers of the structure."

March 13 was but a prelude to the pounding in store for the city.

Nashuans were recovering from a particularly intense winter of bitter cold temperatures and severe snowstorms. It started after Christmas and the ground and the rivers were frozen deep. Unseasonably warm weather in early March unleashed a spring thaw of devastating proportions. Ice blocks careened down the river, creating jams that had to be dislodged by dynamite.

The city would have weathered the sudden spring thaw had it been Mother Nature's only assault. The downpour pelted the area for five days, ending with a violent storm from the South.

History records the actual anniversary of the resulting disaster as March 18. High winds whipped through the Merrimack Valley that day and the following morning the Merrimack River was rising at a rate of four feet an hour at the Old Taylor's Falls Bridge between Hudson and Nashua.

The Nashua River, tributary of the Merrimack, spilled over its banks and over the bridge. East Hollis Street, Union Station and the Boston and Maine Railroad tracks were soon flooded, as were homes in the area. By that evening, martial law was declared and the National Guard was called out.

Working through the night, *The Telegraph* had managed to publish a March 19th edition before the city lost its power at 2 P.M.

Writes Arnold, "All morning the river rose steadily while we rushed to get the paper out before the water might enter the press room . . . All afternoon crowds stood on the bridge gaping at the barricaded *Telegraph.*

"All night long at *The Telegraph*, they fought steadily against the rising waters, and though the water outside was above the level of the boards, a big gasoline pump was keeping the water at a low level inside.

"Before long, though, they were ordered to vacate the pressroom, for if a window should cave in, none would have a chance to get out."

Ray Russell of Hudson, now retired, started with the company in 1933 as a custodian and was promoted to composing room as an operator. He recalls the flood well.

"There was about four feet of water in the pressroom. We had pulled the motor up to the ceiling on a crane. As I was going down the staircase, the steel window opened and four feet of water rushed in."

The lower level of *The Telegraph* was inundated. Wrote Arnold, "Before the peak of the flood was reached, an all-time high, the water mark was several inches above the door leading to the press room."

But the newspaper never missed an issue. Ray Russell was one of the operators dispatched to the Milford Cabinet to handset the type. It took 5 hours to get 6,000 papers printed and ready to deliver.

By Monday the city and *The Telegraph* began to return to some normalcy. The linotypes were working again, but for six days the metal chases of each page were transported to Waltham, Mass., where they were printed by the *News-Tribune.*

Nashua Historical Society

Damage to the city was estimated at $2 million.

Lest you start worrying about the 70- and 80-degree weather of this week, take heart. That is where the comparison with 1936 ends, weatherwise.

The city also has taken flood precautions. In the 1940s, the Army Corps of Engineers built dikes to protect the lowland areas, as well as to control reservoirs in the Merrimack River. Zoning laws were enacted, such as those requiring the first floor of buildings in the flood zone to be above the high water mark.

But don't feel too secure in that cozy armchair when you read about floods in places like Charlestown, Va.

"It is the kind of thing you think would never happen—but it did happen," says Dexter Arnold's widow, reminding us that even Nashua can't always outwit the forces of nature.

March 17, 1990

HISTORIC MOMENT FOR SENIORS

Thirty years ago today, a photo appeared on the front page of *The Telegraph* and other papers that captured a historic moment destined to touch the lives of millions of Americans for generations to come. That news would be more far reaching than the Gemini astronauts orbiting in space or the Vietnam War ranging in the jungles of the Far East.

"President Signs Medicare Bill" read the caption under the picture of Lyndon Johnson surrounded by his wife, Lady Bird, Vice President Hubert Humphrey, and Bess and Harry Truman.

The bill to benefit all citizens over 65 fulfilled a mission Harry Truman had long championed. During his administration 20 years before, he had lost the battle for a similar health measure. In recognition of his role, it was signed on July 30, 1965, in Truman's hometown, Independence, Missouri.

Months later Nashua launched a crash campaign to enlist qualifying seniors before the law took effect in July 1966. The wheels of "Operation Medicare Alert" began to spin on Feb. 16, 1966. An office was hastily set up in the jury room of the then Hillsborough County Court House, now the Registry of Deeds, on Temple Street.

"I brought my own chair and my own typewriter," recalls Isabelle Hildreth, the community activist appointed to organize the effort, which was funded by the Office of Economic Opportunity.

"We had six weeks after we opened the office. I had to hire people, and the only people I could hire had to be 65 or over."

A team of nine men and women from Nashua and the surrounding towns was quickly trained to comb the countryside for those eligible to apply for benefits. They came from Amherst and Hollis, Milford and Mont Vernon, Hudson and Nashua. Working 15 hours a week, they gleaned names from nursing homes, church lists, town clerks, and senior citizen groups in the 20 communities in Hillsborough County.

"We had one car, and four or five people would pile in and go to the town," Hildreth remembers. Traveling the back roads to spread the work, the gray-haired emissaries of Medicare faced many obstacles.

"Many of the elderly, because of illness or language barriers, were ignoring TV, the radio and the press, and we had to penetrate their isolation," Hildreth told *The Telegraph* on April 2, 1966.

A full-page account of the campaign appeared three days after the office had closed. The deadline, March 31, had been met. Its success was cited by Bernard L. Boutin, the New Hampshire native serving as deputy director of the Office of Economic Opportunity. In his letter of commendation, he noted that Hildreth and her colleagues had contacted 5,000 people.

To overcome the language barrier, circulars had been printed in Polish and French as well as English. Every piece of correspondence sent out from City Hall was stamped, "Don't forget to sign up for Medicare."

Anthony Longobardi, district director of the Social Security Administration and an ally of the cause, remembers the talks he and Hildreth gave at the Nashua Public Library, before senior citizen groups and "to anyone who wanted information."

"They signed up almost 100 percent of the people on Social Security. There were not any objections that I remember," he says.

Now retired, he says, "As a consumer, I think it is one of the best-operated governmental programs we have."

His words are echoed by other Nashuans who through the years have witnessed its blessings in spite of its flaws.

From the time she retired from Blue Cross Blue Shield in 1978 until 1991, Madeline Walton worked with the late Stephen Gimber as a volunteer Medicare counselor at the Nashua Senior Center. She explained how to file for reimbursements and she cleared up many misconceptions. She measured her success in terms of the pride Medicare permitted older people to retain after a major illness.

"It's a wonderful program. It's made huge differences in older people's lives," says Pat Jeffrey, now the volunteer Medicare counselor at the Senior Center with Mary Larsen.

"I'm speaking from experience," says Jeffrey, who underwent a mastectomy for breast cancer.

"They have improved it right along. They are better at following up fraud. I think not a lot is wasted," she concludes.

Thirty years after Kerr-Mills took effect, Medicare still makes front-page headlines. There are critics on both sides of the fence: those who say it offers too much and those who say it does not go far enough.

Pat Francis, director of the Nashua Senior Center, sees the good and the bad. She is particularly troubled by the deprivations older people suffer because Medicare does not pay for such critical needs as glasses, dental care, hearing aids and medications.

Thirty years from today, what will be the prognosis on Medicare?

Will a healthy society build on the legacy of 1965? Will it endorse medical care for young and old alike?

July 1995

BLOODY MILL STRIKE OF '15

Violence and ethnic strife stalked the streets of the city leaving behind a long trail of suffering and bloodshed.

Sound like a current evening news report, maybe from Los Angeles? Think again. The place is Nashua; the year, 1915. The tragic event seldom spoken of today was the prolonged strike at the Nashua Manufacturing Co.

The story of how the stability of our town unraveled that year is chronicled in a slim volume, "Monday's Mourning," written by 33-year-old Hudson historian Kevin Goddu.

Its poetic title refers to Oct. 4, 1915, the day a black cloud of dissension arose in the dye house of the busy mill complex on Factory Street. The dark episode in the city's history was to last six moths, and before it ended, it pitted labor against management, one group of immigrants against another and co-workers against co-workers.

"The most violent strike in the history of Nashua began as a peaceful petition," writes Goddu in the 60-page paperback with a picture of the mill on its cover. He paid to have the book published himself.

"Just before seven o'clock in the morning when work was beginning in the dye house and bleachery, seven Polish and Lithuanian operatives approached their foreman at the Nashua Manufacturing Co. with a list of grievances. They asked for more money and an hour for lunch, and in return, they would work an extra hour," the book states.

The petition was ignored, and by the end of the second day 600 employees, including a contingent of Polish and Lithuanian workers from the Jackson Mills, had walked off the job. The Nashua Manufacturing Co. responded with a lockout.

When the strike ended six months later, little had been gained but much had been lost. Many workers left town. For the first time in its history, the state militia was called out to quell a riot at home. A newlywed Slavic immigrant, Jimmy Stivie, was beaten to death on his way home from work, in the skirmish near the Jackson Mills on Canal Street.

Other workers and their families were injured and intimidated by the police. The Greek and French mill workers were considered by their Slavic counterparts to be unsympathetic to the strike, and in the end, there was even a rift of distrust between union representatives and the mill workers.

Though Goddu, a history teacher at Timberlane High School in Plaistow, was born almost 50 years after the strike, he brings no romantic illusions about mill life to his book.

Not only did he hear stories of mill life from his grandparents, who worked in the mills, he experienced some of the unpleasant aspects himself. He worked in the Boott Mills in his hometown of Lowell, Mass., after graduating from high school, and he still remembers the hole in the floor exposing the river below.

"It was dark, dank and drafty," he recalls.

The brief stint in the shipping department was a turning point in his life.

"It was a great motivating factor. Any kid who doesn't want to go to college should work in the mills," he insists.

Today, Goddu's father calls him a perennial student. He holds an associate's degree in drafting from Middlesex (Mass.) Community College, and a bachelor's and master's degree in education from the University of Massachusetts at Lowell. He is now working for a master's degree in history from Salem State College.

History had always been a favorite subject, and in 1989, he joined the Nashua Historical society. A past board member and editor of its newsletter, he is now vice president of the society.

His interest in history also led to a brief stint as a freelance political cartoonist for *The Telegraph*.

Last year, while teaching special education classes at the Nashua High School, he developed an interest in the Strike of 1915. The class was working on projects related to the history of Nashua, and Goddu found little information about the strike in books.

When he told Frank Mooney, a fellow member of the Nashua Historical Society, about his dilemma, Mooney produced a scrapbook he had filled with news clippings, letters and other information about the strike.

With more research, using such direct sources as L'Impartial, the French newspaper published in Nashua, Goddu produced "Monday's Mourning" in September.

"I've just scratched the surface," says Goddu, who believes that history is more biography than bibliography. He regrets that no oral history of the event has been preserved.

To bring home the growing pains of the labor movement at the beginning of the 20th century, Goddu's U.S history class is scheduled to read "Monday's Mourning" after the New Year. It is a lesson in history all Nashuans should know.

December 16, 1995

CITY HISTORY SCRIBES

What an experience it was. Nothing in the annals of the city was quite like the project undertaken 20 yeas ago by a band of unsuspecting, well-meaning Nashua residents. They volunteered to research, write and edit a history of Nashua, aptly titled "The Nashua Experience."

"It is a story that couldn't be written," was the wry assessment of Robert Frost, assistant director of the Nashua Public Library.

Although a professional historian would have found the task of tracing the town's history through two centuries daunting, "The Nashua Experience" was produced by volunteers.

"And it was a strange story of the library doing it," observes Florence Shepard," retired NPL reference librarian.

Previous local histories were written by elderly pillars of the community familiar only with their own segment of society. The objective of "the Nashua Experience" was to reflect the lives of the whole community, a new concept aiming to flesh out the bare bones of history with stories of real people.

Shepard and Frost related their experiences with "The Nashua Experience" at a reception marking the 25th anniversary of the Nashua Public Library's move from the Hunt Memorial Building to its new home on Court Street.

Shepard, the editor of "The Nashua Experience," guided it through its many phases, pulling the book together for publication in 1978, two years after it began. Frost, then a fledgling library staffer, describes his role as a 'gofer," though he contributed several of the major chapters and eventually became the assistant editor.

Gathering their memories together in Frost's office, both agreed the history was a once-in-a-lifetime undertaking, a rewarding task neither had the stamina to repeat.

"The Nashua Experience" grew out of the city's Bicentennial celebration. Early in 1976, a committee of volunteers assembled in the library to tackle the monumental effort. Headed by library director Clarke Davis, the list of notable Nashuans included Elizabeth Spring, the children's librarian well-versed on Colonial history; English teacher, Anne M. McWeeney and Robert Haven, a Civil War buff; Thomas Greenman of Sanders Associates, who looked into his crystal ball to predict the city's future; and Ruth West, Ginny Nedved and Nyla Lipnich, who contributed hours of research.

Mayor Dennis Sullivan supported the project whole-heartedly—as long it did not cost the city any money.

Florence Shepard

"He kept us on a short leash financially," said Shepard.

Little wonder that Davis and Shepard trembled when they went before the aldermen to present the cost for publishing it— $36,000.

In 1977, however, Sullivan was ailing and had resigned. Alderman at large Donald Davidson became acting mayor.

"When we went to the aldermanic meeting with the manuscript, they approved it immediately," Shepard recalled. It was a smart move, she added, for within eight years the sale of the books recouped the cost. Sullivan died in the early 1978, but the authors were able to get that information into the book right before press time.

Funding was just one of many hurdles along the way. Even though fact drives the story, history is selective and deciding on what material to include often led to disagreements.

"I wanted to write about the Frank McKean scandal," said Shepard. It was the salacious tale of a handsome and respected banker, a former mayor, who led a double life in the 1890s. McKean had supported a secret lady love for years in Boston before embezzling funds and fleeing to Argentina.

Since the committee feared any living relatives might be hurt by the story, it was quashed.

"We did include the 1915 Strike," says Frost. He wrote the chapters on the mills, including the bloody battle between mill management and workers that pitted one ethnic group against another and enveloped the whole city.

Presenting the sensational material in a balanced style was a challenge and demanded many hours talking to living survivors.

"Florence put in hundreds of hours on her own time," said Frost, referring to Shepard's many trips to the Massachusetts Historical Society in Boston and Harvard Business School in Cambridge.

"So much of Nashua's history ended up in Massachusetts," she says.

Cartons upon cartons of valuable industrial information were found in Cambridge. The material had been given to the Baker Memorial Library by Royal Little when he moved the Nashua mills south at the end of the 1940s.

Tying the chapters together and integrating the individual styles of the authors was the editor's job. Typing the final manuscript fell to Peggy Green, another community volunteer.

"She chopped away on the manual machine in the office behind the desk," said Frost. "We didn't have computers then."

Working with the publishing company in New Canaan called for numerous trips slip-sliding up Route 89 on snowy nights. The finished volume, its cover highlighted by the charter granted to the territories by King George III, was eagerly purchased for Christmas gifts. There were 5,000 copies published in the fall of 1978—2,000 in hardcover and 3,000 in soft cover.

Now a memento on many coffee tables in Nashua living rooms and on the shelves of many business and home libraries, the hardcovers are all gone. There are still a few soft covers, selling at the library for $24.95, but to reprint the book would be too costly.

September 16, 1996

WAR'S END BROUGHT
UNBRIDLED JOY

The blast from the Central Fire Station horn on that warm, cloudy evening in August brought a multitude of Nashuans to Main Street, their supper dishes still on the table.

Without quite knowing why, they needed to touch shoulders with their neighbors and to vent their jubilation beyond the confines of their homes.

Few events in a lifetime spark a spontaneous coming together of a community. The day World War II ended was one of those rare occasions. The defeat of Japan brought to a full circle the victory in Europe three months before.

On Tuesday, Aug. 14, 1945, Julia Papadopoulos remembers driving into town with her father, the Rev. Michael Papadopoulos, pastor of St. Nicholas Church, and their guest, a visiting clergyman from Lowell, Mass. He and the Rev. Papadopoulos were going to celebrate the vesper services that evening for the Feast of the Assumption of the Virgin Mary. Their plans disintegrated when they heard the news.

"I have to get back to my parish right away," Papadopoulos recalls the Lowell priest insisting. The Nashuans understood and immediately found him a ride. Then Papadopoulos and her father proceeded to Pine Street to ring the church bells and hold the service.

That same night, Litchfield farmer Hervey Durocher and his wife, Marie, packed their five small children into the family's Willys sedan and sped off to Nashua.

So goes the story told by many families recalling their reflex reaction to the news. "We all piled into the car and crossed the Hudson Bridge to get to Main Street," remembers daughter Claudette, now the editor of *The Telegraph*'s editorial page.

"I had heard my parents talk about the war, but I was too young to know what a war was. That night was very exceptional. To drop everything and head into town was something they'd never do. You could feel a sense of relief."

Downtown was the scene of a celebration the likes of which had never before been seen in the city. Grown-ups and children danced up Library Hill, people honked automobile horns, tooted penny whistles and beat pots in place of drums. Before long, flags appeared everywhere and church bells rang throughout Nashua.

"This city went into a deliriously happy tailspin a few seconds after *The Telegraph* AP wire flash announced the end of World War II at 7:01," begins the account in the *Nashua Telegraph*. The newspaper had printed "an end of the war extra," after its regular edition on Tuesday, August 14. The bold headline read: "President Truman Says War Is Over."

In the front page account of the pandemonium, the newspaper reported, "Fire Dept. Pvt. Ralph Kelloway raced into the tower of the central Fire Station to do the job he had awaited for 192 weeks, two days and five hours . . . to sound the first blast announcing the acceptance of the official surrender terms by the Japanese."

"That was a signal that touched a city-wide demonstration unparalleled in the city's history," the paper reported.

Gladys Grigas can still picture one of the dignified town fathers giddily riding piggyback on a colleague's shoulder.

The young mother breathed a sigh of relief, however, because the news meant her husband Charles would finally be coming home. The infantry unit in which he fought in the Battle of the Bulge had been preparing to go to the Far East.

For the first time since the blackout of the war years, the factory whistles sounded and workers deserted their benches and looms to celebrate.

Roland Caron watched the passing parade from his grandparents' stoop on Kinsley Street. Like so many Nashua High School students, during the war he worked at Nashua Manufacturing Co. on the swing shift and on weekends. Mill work was a lot less stressful than the job he had before that, delivering telegrams for Western Union.

"I delivered many telegrams of loved ones missing in action, wounded in action and killed in action. We were instructed to stay if they needed help," says Caron, a past commander of the James E. Coffey American Legion Post who fought in the Korean War. Although elated by news of peace, many Nashuans still had loved ones serving in the Far East. For them the worries persisted.

"Even more than going to Main Street I can remember sitting around the radio, pre-TV, my parents and I with our ears glued to the news coming over it," says Katherine Bellefeuille Valley.

When President Truman addressed the nation they hung on every word. The family's interest was so intense because Katherine's beau, Norman Valley—later to become her husband—was serving the Far East with the Navy. In a letter she learned that the 20-year-old Nashua seaman had volunteered to go into Nagasaki the day after the A-bomb dropped to report on the devastation. His only protection was a rain slicker. Yet compelling as it was, listening to the radio, even on VJ Day, never detained Joseph Bellefeuille from his duties as a railroad man.

"I don't think anything would interrupt the railroad schedule," said his daughter. Everything else, however, came to a halt the day after the surrender was announced. On Wednesday, August 15, 1945, officially designated a holiday, the stores were closed, the banks were closed and of course, the factories were closed. The churches were open—and filled.

Despite the unbridled celebration well into the morning, there were few unpleasant incidents. The Police Department was at full staff, having canceled vacations and time off for a few days. There were five arrests for drunkenness. The only casualty reported was a serviceman who broke his leg in a melee on West Pearl Street.

Several false alarms for fire were recorded and there were two real fires, one a victory bonfire on Amoskeag Street. The perks of peace came soon. "No More Gas Rationing," reported *The Telegraph* on Aug. 15. Meat and other foodstuffs followed.

Edmund Keefe, then assistant principal of Nashua High School, had taken his son, Miles, to Main Street on the eve of the announcement, but it was a year later that he fully savored the fruits of peace.

For four years, he had watched Nashua's young men go off to war. In June of 1946, the graduation exercise included many ex-servicemen proudly wearing their uniforms who had returned to finish their senior year.

"And they went off to college on the GI Bill of Rights," observes Keefe, later the Nashua superintendent of schools.

September 14, 1995

REUNION OF THE WEST PEARL STREET GANG

It is easy to overlook. The monument on the triangle of green facing the Nashua District Courthouse seldom draws a glance from people walking down Chestnut Street or rounding the Walnut Street oval in their cars.

Yet the simple granite slab holds a slice of Nashua history, one shaped by a neighborhood rather than a single event or an individual.

They were "Lucky" and "Doc," the boys of West Pearl Street, when they bolted through the neighborhood to the ball fields. That was more than 60 years ago but the decades slip away like candy wrappers in the wind as they reminisce.

George "Lucky" Petrou came home this week for the West Pearl Street reunion, a Memorial Day weekend tradition in Nashua's Greek community, one he had a hand in starting more than 40 years ago. Now retired, he lives outside of San Francisco.

Charlie "Doc" Caros never left Nashua for long, except to serve in Europe with the Air force in World War II.

But they shared a time and place that linked them together no matter the distance in between. They grew up in Nashua.

Their parents had come to this country from Greece in the beginning of the century. The new immigrants worked in the shoe factory and the mills. They established grocery shops, barbershops and coffee shops around West Pearl Street. They lived on inner city streets from West Pearl to Kinsley streets, from Walnut to Ledge.

Their children were born in Nashua but after public schools each day, they were instilled with an appreciation of their Greek heritage at St. Nicholas and Annunciation church schools.

As first generation Americans, they were destined for better things.

"Lucky" went to Brown University on a football scholarship and became an executive with a food company.

"I haven't lived here for 30 years, but to me this is home," said Petrou, a reunion regular. "Whether I'm in California, Connecticut or New York, this is home. This is where my roots are."

Caros chimed in, "The boys come from Florida, from California—from all over, even from Greece. We're still the boys of Walnut Street, and Vine Street and Ash Street . . . "

The 1920s and 1930s, the days of their youth, produced vivid memories for the West Pearl Street gang. Unlike some gangs today, excitement then meant shooting marbles on Myrtle Street, playing ball at Textile Fields off Ledge Street and swimming in the canal.

The two men, now in there 70s, smile when they recall stories about the Greek swimming hole they built in the canal.

"There were three different swimming holes off Ledge Street. The first was the French hole; the second was the Lemon hole—it belonged to everyone but wasn't too good—and the third was the Polish hole," noted Petrou.

"I said, 'We have to make a hole of our own,'" he continued.

They recalled how Petrou "borrowed" his fathers saw to cut down the trees, how they fastened a rope to swing across the canal and how they built a platform to create the best swimming spot in town.

"Everybody swam in the hole built by the Hellenic boys. The Callahan's. The Degasis. It was a who's who in Nashua," sighed Petrou. "That's one of the memories of the West Pearl Street association. Those memories never die."

Like he did, many of the West Pearl Street buddies went to the finest colleges in the country, becoming lawyers, doctors, dentists and business executives. Many moved elsewhere.

World War II also shattered Nashua's tightly knit ethnic neighborhoods. One of the veterans who came home disabled was John Tsitsos. An older and smaller contingent of the Pearl Street gang visited him regularly at the Manchester Veterans Administration Hospital. They talked of old times on West Pearl Street.

To cheer him along, Petrou, the Floras brothers (Ted and George) and others organized an outing on the picnic grounds on West Hollis Street belonging to the Greek churches. It was strictly male, with a baseball game, a lamb-on-a-stick barbecue and camaraderie drawing back the "boys" from all over the country. The reunions continued informally every five years.

When the two churches united and built the St. Philip Greek Orthodox Church on the original picnic grounds in the 70s, Ted Floras took over the reunion and opened it to women.

"I had been a mailman for more than 30 years and I knew everybody," recalls Floras. Helen Lafazanis remembers how he compiled a lists of names and addresses of brothers, sisters, aunts and uncles who had left the area. He also spent weeks checking names on gravestones to make certain the memorial list was complete.

Since then the reunions have been held every three years and everyone takes home a souvenir of names and addresses.

John Lafazanis is chairman of the festivities, which began Friday night at the Greek Clubhouse, on the corner of West Hollis and Main streets beneath the Carvel Ice Cream store, the gathering spot that took over when coffee houses disappeared.

Tonight there will be the dinner dance and tomorrow, following religious services, the elders will be honored at a reception. Monday, many families will visit the cemetery before leaving for home.

Harold Solomon

A few may stop to read the inscription on the monument:

"This monument is proudly dedicated to all the early Greek immigrants who settled in this area and strived diligently for the future of their families, their adopted city, state and country."

May 23, 1992

'TIS THE SEASON FOR PLANTING CAMPAIGN SIGNS

Visually they are a poor match for the burnished trees, the muted mums and the orange pumpkins. Yet come fall, they spring up with random regularity on lawns all over town. Here a bright blue one, there a red one, an occasional green, orange or purple. For a few weeks, they wave in the breeze along the roadside like anxious hitchhikers trying to catch the attention of those passing by.

'Tis the season to plant political signs. In the democratic scheme of things, scenic beauty takes a back seat to name recognition. The few weeks they decorate the landscape can enhance a candidate's chances of landing an office on a local, state or national level. Or so goes popular political wisdom.

Though next Tuesday's local election is relatively tame, with many races uncontested, signs appear daily on the city's main thoroughfares. Broad Street and East Dunstable Road vie for the title of Placard Place. Yet Concord and south Main streets, choice locations usually, seem almost forgotten.

The prize for a hit-you-in-the eye, giant-size name tag in this year's lot goes to Jim Tollner, the lone entry for alderman in Ward 1. Its twin is judiciously placed on Charron Avenue, the other end of the ward. Sharing space in a strange alliance is David Deane, a newcomer vying for a seat on the Board of Public Works.

On the D.W. Highway, "Bienvenu. Welcome to New Hampshire" is the first sign greeting visitors, but down the road a mile on School House Square is a sign patch, each with a political message, flapping in the breeze as cars go by. Unless one stops for a red light, however, they are just a big blur.

Several of the other prime locations, thick with signs in elections past, go begging this year. The fence on the corner of Luke and Broad streets is not covered with signs as it used to be before the house was sold to new owners. Luckily, there's a new fence across the street on Broad and Dublin to take its place. Another spot, the long triangle of lawn between Broad Street and Pine Hill Avenue, looks desolate to the eyes of Nashuans who remember the days when it was a sea of signs.

Across the street at Berman Real Estate, Judy Berman wonders about the lawn's dry spell.

"We used to be inundated with calls, too, and this year we've had one," says Berman from her office. "I spend time driving around Ward 4 and 5 and I've noticed how few signs there are. What's worse, there seems to be little conversation about the elections. Even in the off years, there used to be a lot more," comments the two-time Ward 2 alderman.

The one sign of political life in the election, the controversy over the proposed Broad Street Parkway, shows up on lower Kinsley Street. At 38-40, along with the pumpkin decorations are home-made-looking signs big and small, proclaiming the message "Thou shall vote to ban the bridge."

It reminds Superior Court Judge Margaret Flynn of a time when political material was less slick.

When she first ran for office—the school board race in 1959—a friend made up her only sign, on big serviceable one on the Burns block on Main Street. "I wasn't well known in Nashua in those days," she says, noting candidates put posters with their pictures in some of the store windows on Main Street.

Ann Ackerman, history teacher and humanities director at Salem High School, also started out with a homemade variety in the early '80s but soon realized the more lasting value of a professional job.

From then on the former four-time Ward 1 Alderman and her husband, Phil, now a state representative for Ward 5, have gotten plenty of mileage out of their signs from one election to another. Though they have not appropriated each other's—his are blue and hers are red—their children Erin and Ruben have when they have run for office in college. They just pasted over the parts that did not apply, says their mother.

Ruth Ginsburg, former longtime member of the Board of Education, recycled hers when she ran for state representative.

"I'm cheap. I don't believe in waste and I do believe in recycling," she says.

Most of the local political signs are handled by Chuck Hodgdon of Nashua Screen Printing. He sits down at the computer with potential customers and works out an individual look. Hodgdon remembers a previous mayoral campaign when two candidates walked into his Factory Street offices at the same time.

"I was more nervous than they were," he says, adding the atmosphere was surprisingly cordial.

But the sign he will always remember is the one designed for Paul Chasse when he ran for alderman last election. Chasse wanted a map of New Hampshire on his sign without realizing the mistake; it came out printed backward. The booboo went unnoticed until a schoolboy reported that the coastline was on the wrong side. Later, *The Telegraph* picked upon the error, but by then, Chasse decided it was too late to reverse it.

"If he were running for state office, we could have said he was trying to turn the state around," Hodgdon suggests.

For local candidates the most frustrating part about putting up signs is seeing them torn down. The signs are an easy target for vandalism, so candidates are resigned to losing a number of them in the campaign.

A fan of campaign history, Ann Ackerman tells of one candidate who outwitted a slippery character who stole a sign off his front lawn several times. To foil the thief, he coated the sign and the stick with Vaseline.

Other than hanky panky with signs, both the Nashua Police Department and City Clerk Eleanor Benson report few incidents during local campaigns. "I've been on the force 20 years, and the biggest issue is signs put on private property," says police Sgt. Michael James.

Benson gives a list of electioneering rules and regulations to each candidate when he or she files for office. She bristles when she sees signs on city property or obscuring safety signs or tacked on telephone polls. The offenders are usually people who come form out of town to work in national campaigns, she observes.

"Signs do get your name out subconsciously," says Barbara Baldizar, former state representative from Ward 1. Now out of the political fray, she observes philosophically, "People can get so caught up in their signs."

She admits the mania got to her during her second election to the House when she spotted her opponent standing on Broad Street holding his sign and smiling at cars passing by. She was in the offices of Images and Ideas, a desktop publishing firm owned by the Ackermans. She ran out with her sign, Ann Ackerman followed and the three did a dance down Broad Street as the two candidates jousted for position with their signs. Thinking of it now makes Baldizar smile.

On the plus side, Baldizar credits her husband, Bob, for initiating a campaign tradition picked up by other candidates.

Soon after she learned she had won her seat in the house, he drove off to put hearts saying "thank you" on all her signs.

"He went out at 4 o'clock in the morning so that people would see them when they went to work," she says.

And some cynics say political signs get lost in the shuffle.

October 28, 1999

PEOPLE

My Window on Main Street

"MISTER RIVIER"

After a leisurely lunch at the Nashua Country Club, Carl Amelio leans back in his chair and peruses his datebook.

"There's my meetings," he says, smiling and pointing to page after page filled with commitments: to Rivier College, St. Joseph Hospital, the Community Council and St. Joseph Community Services to name a few.

"I guess I have a compulsion to do things," observes the 86-year-old, retired Air Force officer and former Federal Aviation Administration administrator.

If civilian awards were like military medals, Amelio's blue blazer would be heavy with decorations. Nashua has bestowed honor after honor on its soft spoken adopted citizen. His contributions to community life are legion, and this year they earned him the Greater Nashua Chamber of Commerce's "Citizen of the Year" Award.

"Doors open up when you're with Carl," says Seth Ames, vice-president of development at St. Joseph Hospital, recalling all the fund drives the two have been on together. They became acquainted in the early '70s when Ames started working at the hospital and Amelio was president of the hospital's advisory board. Amelio later became president of the board of directors.

"Its hard to say no to Carl," says Ames, a first-hand witness to the quiet powers of persuasion. "Carl is an ambassador. He likes to bring people together," Ames adds.

Sister Doris Benoit, former president of Rivier College, repeats the word— ambassador—when she speaks of Amelio. More frequently used by those associated with the college, however, is the affectionate title, "Mr. Rivier." Benoit understands the significance of the name; she was college president in '70s when Amelio was president of the advisory board.

"Right from the beginning he was a doer and a mover. Nobody could sleep on the board when he was there," she recalls.

Sister Doris credits "Mr. Rivier" with planting the seeds for two of the college's community resources, the evening school and the Rivier-St Joseph Hospital School of Nursing. Both have flourished. To show its appreciation for his efforts, the college has given him its two most prestigious awards, an honorary doctorate in science and the Alumni Association's Sister Madeleine of Jesus Award.

Amelio's talent for pulling together community resources began in Providence, R.I. He was 7 when the family immigrated from Calabria, Italy, a place he talks of with reverence and still visits as often as possible. His face lights up as he recalls his teen-age years in Providence where he organized the Paramount football team and later the Majestic Tigers.

"I went to talk to Tuss McLaughery, the coach of Brown University football team, and he sent an assistant coach to us. He was there every week," he says, adding that the fledgling team profited from the professional help.

After graduating from Providence Technical High School, Amelio attended Wentworth Institute but quickly lost interest in architectural construction studies. It took several years and a number of jobs, including theater usher and factory worker, before he found his career. In the mid-'30s, he joined the newly formed US Air Corps' 152nd Observation Squadron, with duty in this

Carl Amelio

Telegraph Photo Files

country. In 1943 he was sent to Officer's Training School, made a career of the service and retired as a colonel after 27 years.

Perhaps the high point of his military career came when he served in Japan during the Korean War. Gen. Douglas MacArthur, the commander of the U.N. forces in Korea, remains one of his heroes.

It was during Amelio's Air Force service that he met Mary Hansbury of Nashua. He was stationed at Fort Devens in Massachusetts, and she was one of a group of telephone operators invited to a dance on the base. The then-sergeant and his fair lady were married in June 1943, and Nashua became home.

The Amelio's three children, Kathy, Robert and Elizabeth were born at St. Joseph Hospital, where the Amelio name was to become enshrined. A plaque in Mary's name decorates the wall outside the cafeteria honoring her work as auxiliary president and another is hung in the auditorium bearing Carl's name.

Throughout the 33 years of their married life, Mary Amelio was deeply involved in the church, the hospital, and community life, and her husband says, it was she who introduced him to its many joys.

His first opportunity to act as a catalyst came during his second career when he was an FAA director of personnel for the Northeast Region. He devised an advanced study program for air traffic controllers that became the model for other FAA regions.

In 1976, two years after he left the FAA, Mary Amelio died. It followed the unexpected death of their daughter, Elizabeth. Community then became his salvation. In

1972 he had joined the advisory board of Rivier and in 1976, St. Joseph Hospital's board of directors. He often worked with women on their behalf.

"Women were so important in my life," says the grandfather of four. "Cheese and crackers, I used to get so mad when they were left out."

"'Cheese and crackers' is as peppery as his speech gets," says Ames adding that the gentle Amelio wit often diffuses tense situations at committee meetings, particularly with the irascible golf tournament crowd.

Amelio's contribution to the hospital during his 18 years on the board was recently saluted by the N.H. Hospital Association. Among his achievements cited were the union of Rivier College and St. Joseph Hospital to form a School of Nursing in 1983, the development of the continuing education program at Rivier that evolved into the college's undergraduate evening school and the development of St. Joseph Community Services, which he steered as president from 1978 to 1986. Since its inception, it has served 5 million meals to the home-bound and the elderly.

He has also served as president of the board of directors of the Community Council of Nashua and was director of the N.E. Conference of Catholic Hospitals Association, the Nashua Chapter of the Red Cross, and the Boys Club of Nashua.

"I'm energized by what I do," says Amelio "I feel good about it. That is my compensation."

November 19, 1994

SHOE MAKER'S SHOE MAKER

"See this," says Charles Boghigian, holding up a piece of leather shaped like the sole of a shoe. "It's worth money. If you cut it up and put it on a pair of women's heels it's $5. Men's heels I get $10 and a complete sole with heel $35.

"I've been doing this for 42 years," continues the affable 83-year-old Nashuan, surveying his compact shoe repair shop, "Charlie & Sons Shoe Repairing" on the corner of Harbor Avenue and Otterson Street.

"That's all I've known. Shoes."

His hands finger the piece of leather as he talks about his lifelong career. Several weeks ago he put a For Sale sign in the shop window and an ad in *The Telegraph*, but he has had no response.

"I guess no one is interested in the shoe repair business anymore," he laments.

Without customers, the shop seems cold and shabby. Boxes of unclaimed shoes fill the shelves, the front counter is lined with dozens of different kinds of shoe polish and in the back of the shop near the stitching machinery and the skate sharpener, the drawers are stuffed with hundreds of leather heels and soles.

But few shoes are now made with the care and quality they were in years gone by, observes the veteran shoemaker.

"Today it's plastic. They're vulcanized. Thom McAn used to make a good all-leather shoe for between $6 and $10," he adds. "Eighty-five percent of the people today wear sneakers."

In his time the Nashua shoemaker has made myriad worn shoes look like new again. Lawyers, doctors, nurses found their way to the shop for repairs and a weekly shoe shine, though the shop was off the beaten path downtown.

Hanging on the walls of the shop are posters that made them smile as they waited.

One reads, "I will heel for you."

"I will save your sole."

"I will dye for you."

The one in the back corner, he says, is the most important one: Its message: "If you have everything but Christ, you have nothing. If you have nothing but Christ, you have everything."

Boghigian's business card notes he is the second generation in the shoe repair trade. He followed in his father's footsteps in working at the J.F. McElwain factory. Boghigian worked at the factory for 37 years.

A native Nashuan born in St. Joseph Hospital, he grew up on Chestnut Street and went to work after he finished the eighth grade. His only work outside of the shoe business was a second job Thursday night and Saturdays in Brockleman's food market on Main Street. "In the produce department," he recalls with a smile.

At age 19, he considered himself fortunate to get a steady job in J.F. McElwain. The work was arduous but it never occurred to him to complain. He was happy to have a job.

"Jobs were hard to come by in those days," he says, remembering the factory as second home in spite of conditions that OSHA would never approve today.

"They had to keep that line going. You couldn't stop," he says without recrimination, adding, "It was all piecework." Four or five dozen shoes were produced in that factory each day.

After the Nashua mills closed in the late '40s and early '50s, J.F. McElwain was the largest employer in the state. They had two factories in Manchester and three in Nashua—one on Spruce Street, one on East Hollis Street and another on Northeastern Boulevard. Boghigian worked in all three at one time or another.

The nationally known manufacturer of Thom McAn shoes started in Nashua in 1922. One of its three founders, Francis P. Murphy, settled here and as the shoe business expanded, he became involved in state politics. In 1936, Murphy was elected governor of New Hampshire. Although he was a Republican, he supported the New Deal labor reforms. Following news of his election, according to *The Telegraph*, 5,000 shoe workers and a band marched up Concord Street to Murphy's house to show their support for their boss. Working conditions in the shoe factory were better than most.

"We never had any trouble," recalls Boghigian, an admirer of Murphy. A lifelong Democrat, Boghigian served as president of his union at his factory in the late '50s and early '60s. The only problem he encountered, besides negotiations, was a complaint from the front office about the workers: The men were taking advantage of the company by calling in sick on sunny Friday afternoons. They came to work tanned and suddenly recovered, on Saturdays, when they were paid overtime. Boghigian passed the word on to his union colleagues and the summer folly ended.

Boghigian's only time out from shoemaking came in World War II. He was drafted and served four years as a mess sergeant in the Army. Returning home, in 1947 he married Anna Jeranian in St. Vartanantz Church in Lowell, Mass. With a growing family—three sons and a daughter—the industrious shoemaker set up his own cobbler shop in 1958, at first working nights and weekends in addition to his regular job at the factory. His first shop was in a dirt floor cellar on Otterson Street.

"The other side of the shop was a guy making Venetian blinds." he reminisces.

He has moved several times before settling in his present location on Harbor Avenue. In the early '70s when the shoemaking business in New Hampshire declined, moving south and eventually overseas, Boghigian took early retirement and concentrated on building his own business.

His sons remember their father's shop fondly. It was a great place to visit after school and to do odd jobs on Saturdays. Though their father never went beyond the eighth grade, all of the Boghigian children graduated college. Daughter Linda holds two degrees, one in marketing and another in music.

"I still remember the smell of leather and the sound of the machines whirling," says son Gregory. Now a lawyer in Nashua, he stopped in regularly with coffee and doughnuts to talk about the events of the day.

"As a child, I never realized how hard he worked. I never remember him being sick or taking a day off," he says, noting his father's work ethic rubbed off on all his sons. Elder son Harry is a vice president of Roche pharmaceutical company and younger son Kevin owns Mountain Ridge, a pet supply company in Nashua. Kevin remembers the marble stand in the shoe repair shop where his father let him shine customers' shoes and often had to give them a pair of free socks to replace the ones his young helper stained with the polish.

"I had a wonderful childhood, lots of love and affection," he says. "There were tough times but we didn't know about it."

Though Kevin Boghigian owns the building where his father's shop has been for 20 years, he has moved his firm into a mill on Canal Street.

Worried that his father will be at a loss without the shop, Kevin has suggested his father work at his company a couple of days a week.

"I'll help him out if he needs me," says the elder Boghigian. For now, he is pleased to have more time to do things with wife Anna, a luxury he seldom had while working in the shoe shop.

January 13, 2001

JUNE CARON

Hats were back in style that November night. The Lafayette Club was a sea of flowered chapeaux, sombreros, cowboy Stetsons, baseball caps, even headgear topped with twirling propellers. Instead of offering a standing ovation, more than 100 Nashuans turned out to tip their hats to the woman of the hour.

What more appropriate way to pay tribute to June Caron, a playmaker for 35 years at the Nashua Park and Recreation Department—and a hat fancier of the first order.

"She has hats for every occasion and they match every outfit," says longtime friend Sue Waye, deputy voter registrar for Nashua.

Never one to show up at an event or a meeting without wearing a hat, Caron says, "When I want to go somewhere without being recognized, I don't wear a hat."

With or without her trademark, Caron has had plenty of clout in shaping the community's fun and games through the years, whether it's Biddy basketball games, the Senior Olympics, girls softball tournaments or the Fourth of July fireworks at Holman Stadium. The native Nashuan has worked at the Park and Recreation Department since she graduated from Nashua High School in 1965. Except for a second job, waitressing to make extra money for a trip to Hawaii, she has never worked anywhere else.

Ironically, she never has been athletic herself. Rather, she characterizes herself as a "bookworm." In her job, she says she is a "facilitator," one who makes things happen behind the scenes. To keep on track she keeps a well-worn volume on her desk to read before she plunges into her hectic daily schedule. The book she refers to is aptly titled, "Don't Sweat the Small Stuff at Work."

Her nights-days-weekends job involves chairing meetings for a city youth rally or making sure there are enough sites for girls and boys soccer games, planning the SummerFun events, and when necessary attending to details such as inflating hundreds of balloons for a Pride baseball celebration at City Hall. Vacation time is Christmas week when things are slow in the department. Yet, if a budget meeting is scheduled during that week, she is there.

Caron has a reputation for being organized and keeping notes on everything.

"You ask her for anything and she can pull it out of her notebook," says Margo Bell, project director at the Nashua Senior Activity Center. She worked with Caron on the Mayor's Volunteer Recognition Committee that produced a quilt, designed and stitched by volunteers, for the city's millennium celebration. Caron chaired the

City Recreation Supervisor June Caron guides David Lajoie, stadium superintendent, as he outlines the starting mark for the July Fourth road race.

committee and coordinated the project involving 42 of the city's social service agencies.

"She'd always be the one to jump up and make the phone call to the right person when we needed to get something done. She is both a good delegator and a hands-on person," says Bell.

"The human Rolodex," is what colleague Nick Caggiano affectionately calls her. He is the associate manager of park maintenance, and she is the associate manager of recreation since the department was recently reorganized under the umbrella of the Board of Public Works.

"The titles change but the work is the same," says Caron. Her responsibilities, however, have multiplied through the years as the city grew.

Growing up in a mall-free, more contained Nashua meant the tempo of life was slower and more predictable in the 1950s. Fun and games in June Bello's life revolved around the South Common near Nashua High School when it was on Elm Street, ice skating and sledding in the winter or playing tennis and swimming at Fields Grove in the summer. Thursday nights and Saturdays the whole town did its shopping and socializing on Main Street and the teenage crowd gathered for Cokes at Priscilla's or the Puritan.

In the '60s, Nashua began to mushroom and for a year, Caron's class at Nashua High School was on dual sessions. Hers was also one of the first classes to hold graduation ceremonies at Holman Stadium.

Her first job, as a high school student, with the recreation department, was as the Temple Street playground supervisor. After she graduated, she filled in as a secretary during summer vacation.

"I graduated on the 23rd (of June) and the following week I started work," she recalls.

The temporary job turned into a full-time one.

In the late '60s, the department was housed in the Palm Street School building and Noel Trottier headed the recreation division. Caron climbed the ladder from secretary to program director to his assistant.

"The Boys Club started over my head and in 1970, the Girls Club started there. Debbie Pignatelli (the Girls Club's first director. later a state senator) and I were pregnant together," Caron adds.

She had married her high school sweetheart, Gene "Pete" Caron, in 1975 and two years later she gave birth to son Jonathan. It was the only Fourth of July celebration she has ever missed.

During the Arel administration, the department moved to the city health services building on Mulberry Street and Caron continued to work as the program director under Trottier until he retired in 1985.

"He taught me a lot about my job," she says of the late recreation director.

In the '70s, Trottier and Caron responded to the times by launching more programs for girls and expanding the boys athletic programs. The city also arranged for a program for the Mt. Hope School in the Elm Street school gym. Caron volunteered to take the young athletes to the first Special Olympics in Boston.

Telegraph Photo Files

In a time when people change jobs as often as the seasons change, a refreshing exception is June Caron, who is marking her 35th year as a member of the staff at the Nashua Park Department. Caron's well-known collection of baseball caps and hats hang behind her in her Greeley Park office.

"The experience made me see how important recreation is to all our kids," says Caron.

Among her many related duties she became president of the first Girls Babe Ruth Softball League and brought the first regional girls softball tournament to Nashua.

Recreation for people of all ages became a priority as newcomers came to town with their families.

"The Senior Center, the Boys Club, the Girls Club were all coming together at the same time," she observes.

Another notch on her long list of accomplishments is a walking program started in the early '80s after the city purchased Mine Falls Park. She, of course, leads her troops through the park two days a week in the spring and fall. The 15 original walkers grew through the years and at last count numbered around 80.

"It was a group of every age, anyone who wanted to walk. You met a lot of people and made a lot of friends," says Claire Lemire, who joined the group when she and her husband moved here from Lowell, Mass. She walked with them for many years, earning a 1,000-mile plaque.

Today, the programs Caron started and shepherded continue to flourish. Biddy basketball teams for both boys and girls now number 110 in six leagues. There were about 20, and only one for girls, when she started working with the department.

"She probably knows every coach in the city—basketball, baseball, football— there's a lot of mutual respect there," says Dolly Bellavance, former director of the city health and human services department. She and Caron have worked on many projects together, including the first SummerFest. The few events of the first year took two or three months to plan, remembers Caron. Today, with more than 50 events, planning takes the full 12 months of the year and involves an active committee.

"And June is always there at the fireworks or the city's New Year's Eve Centennial," says Bellavance. Caron was at the Hunt Memorial Building for last year's millennium celebration on New Year's Eve—where the city's Volunteer Recognition Committee's quilt was displayed—in her tux and top hat.

Even after more than three decades, her energy and enthusiasm for her job never flag. "This is our most exciting year," says Caron, talking enthusiastically about plans with other agencies for before and after school and summer programs for the city's schoolchildren.

Caron shares the new public works division director George Crombie's vision for a community center.

"A place for the community, where the community can go—the community at large," says Caron.

To mark her 35th anniversary with the department, colleagues planted a tree next to the bandstand in Greeley Park, where Caron's office is now located. It is a Ginko Bilboa lobo, a hardy species known to be long lived and expected to flourish in the park for years to come.

January 6, 2001

THIS SPY CAME FROM NASHUA

"After all this time, you can still hear my hometown in my voice. The clipped Yankee tones of Nashua, New Hampshire, have stayed with me—as have many of the values and traditions that were instilled in me there."

So begins "A Spy for all Seasons: My Life Inside the CIA," by Duane R. Clarridge.

The 400-page thriller about the espionage conducted all over the world by the Central Intelligence Agency reinforces the old adage: Truth is stranger than fiction. This firsthand account by a top spy lays bare the clandestine missions of one of the most mysterious, and often suspect, organs of the United States government.

Nashua native "Dewey" Clarridge was an insider almost from the CIA's beginning. He was recruited in the 1950s out of Columbia University Graduate School of International Affairs, and he retired 33 years later as the chief of counter terrorism.

Considered one of the agency's "cowboys," or risk takers, he rose quickly through the ranks and headed operations in all corners of the globe. On his way out he was indicted by the special prosecutor in the Iran-Contra investigation for lying to Congress and later was pardoned by President Ronald Reagan.

His autobiography is a tale of foreign intrigue comparable to any novel by such master storytellers as Tom Clancy and John le Carre.

"The fun part of the book is the part about Nashua," says his first cousin, Barbara Hambleton, still a resident of the North End, where the Clarridges lived for many years.

The brick house on Elliot Street was the scene of the more conventional part of his life, a typical New England childhood. Surprisingly it became the springboard for a career plotting covert escapades in such exotic climes as Katmandu, Istanbul, Panama, Beirut and Baghdad.

Clarridge is the only son of the late Dr. Duane H. Clarridge, a longtime Nashua dentist. He and a younger sister, Cynthia, attended Mount Pleasant Elementary School and Spring Street Junior High School, where he played drums in the band.

Former neighbor Richard Carter remembers him as a shy, bookish kid across the street. Though Carter is four years older, the two boys played "soldiers" together.

"We spent hours dying in the trenches," says Carter, a former director of Nashua Corp. and a retired naval architect now living in Nahant, Mass.

It was Carter who gave Clarridge the nickname of "Dewey," the Republican candidate for president both families supported. Later, in CIA missions, Clarridge often adopted "Dewey" as part of his alias.

Clarridge's grandmother, Alice McQuestion Ramsdell, was committed to the Republican Party. She served nine terms in the legislature and was a friend of Gov. Sherman Adams. Her fondest wish was for her grandson to pursue a career in politics—as a Republican of course.

"Nobody talked about the Democrats—in New Hampshire they just didn't matter," Clarridge writers in his book.

Carter recalls the many hours he spent at the Clarridge home. The fondest memories were in the dentist's workshop, where he admired the older man's wood-working talents and ingenuity.

"Watching him was a continual lesson in problem solving," Carter says of the wonders that came out of the workshop. Many years later his son would discover the satisfaction of a wood-carving hobby.

Carter, too, muses about the wholesome New England qualities of life so characteristics of their childhood.

"Doc Clarridge was the personification of Yankee integrity," Carter says.

In the New England tradition, the younger Clarridge bowed to his father's wishes and went off to a highly disciplined prep school in New Jersey. He returned to New England for college at Brown University—an Ivy League school—but not, in his father's thinking, of the caliber of Harvard or Yale. A career as a diplomat or a college teacher of Russian studies was Clarridge's objective when he enrolled at Columbia University School of International Studies.

Before continuing for his Ph.D., he was approached by the CIA. "I would never have guessed he would end up doing what he did," Carter says.

Another boyhood friend, Dr. Jack Crisp, now a Nashua surgeon, makes the same comment. While growing up, Crisp and Clarridge were classmates, and both in Boy Scout Troop 7 at The First Church, but Clarridge was never really part of the group that hung out at Jeannotte's Market. After college, when Nashua classmates got together, Clarridge's name often came up in conversation.

"We thought he was a career diplomat," Crisp says.

It was toward the end of Clarridge's long CIA career that he sought a reunion with his childhood friend, Carter, who was vacationing in England.

"He heard about us being there and tracked us down," says Carter, remembering how pleased he was to see Clarridge.

"He told lots of stories about his work, but the thing he was most proud of was that he had no mentor, that he did everything on his own," Carter observes.

As his career in the CIA ended, Clarridge came face to face with another figure from his Nashua youth who also had become a key player on the world stage. Sen. Warren Rudman and Clarridge met in the halls of Congress. Though they, too, had been in the same Boy Scout troop, the conversation was awkward, because they had become adversaries in the Iran-Contra hearings.

Clarridge does not cover up his contempt for Congress and its meddling in the work of the CIA. Neither does he hide his admiration for such CIA principals as George Bush, William Casey or Oliver North.

What are the New England values Clarridge took with him into the dangerous minefields of spying? An independence of spirit, a stoic refusal to let emotions get in the way of reason, a loyalty to principles and inner strength to face one's critics— perhaps these are the values that sustained Clarridge through his long career and, ultimately, through the Iran-Contra hearings. No doubt, they also helped him resist an attempt to compromise his loyalties to the CIA and to his country, and to write "A Spy for All Seasons."

Since leaving the CIA, Clarridge has been the director of international marketing for an electronics firm in California. His book was published in January by Scribners and he is now promoting it across the country. He was also one of the key figures to appear on a Discovery Channel program about the 50th anniversary of the CIA.

March 3, 1997

COLLEGE PRESIDENTS

What do two college presidents talk about when they get together? For starters, swimming at Field's Grove, ice skating at Marshall Field and sipping sodas at Priscilla's after shopping downtown on a Saturday afternoon.

Bob Raiche Photograhy

Sister Carol J. Descoteaux

Both are native Nashuans. Sister Lucille C. Thibodeau, former president of Rivier College, and Sister Carol J. Descoteaux, retired president of Notre Dame College, grew up in Crown Hill.

Both are alumnae of the colleges they went on to lead. Close in age, the two women share many memories of Nashua in the '50s, though as children they knew of each other only through relatives.

"It is amazing that we didn't become friends until recently. I kind of knew of Lucille, I grew up with her cousin," said Sister Carol. Her friend would often talk about her cousin Lucille, as girls in the neighborhood do.

Crown Hill was a neighborhood of wide streets lined with neat homes and echoing with the voices of children at play. At the core of daily life for Catholic families was Infant Jesus Catholic Church on Allds Street. It had been destroyed in the Crown Hill fire of 1930 and quickly rebuilt a year later to house both chapel and school. Twenty-five years later the parish realized its dream of a spacious new church separate from the school.

"It was my parish," Sister Carol affirmed. "Mine too," said Sister Lucille.

"I was in the first class to receive communion in the new church," remarked Sister Carol.

"You mean it took more than 20 years to build the new church?" responded Sister Lucille.

"It was a blue collar neighborhood. They didn't have lots of money," the younger of the two suggested.

In the '50s, Crown Hill, on the surface, had recovered from the complete devastation of the fire, though the scars of losing their homes would never be erased for many neighborhood residents. The newly widened streets, noted Sister Carol, were a hedge against flames hopping quickly from one side to the other and sweeping through the neighborhood as they had in the fire. The newly built homes were filled with the young families of men and women who worked in the factories and mills nearby, which would soon be casualties of a changing economy.

Sister Carol, 51, is the oldest of the three children born to Theresa and Henry Descoteaux. Her parents were first-generation Americans of French Canadian descent. Her father, Henry Descoteaux, was a cabinet maker for Old Colony, one of the top furniture houses in the country. Its workshop was based on Crown Hill.

Sister Lucille, 54, is the only child of Emeline and Henry Thibodeau, who came to this country from Quebec. They both worked in the mills, and after the mills closed he became a compositor at Royal Business Forms.

Both college presidents spoke French as well as English when they entered kindergarten at Infant Jesus School. Their paths diverged after kindergarten, however, with Sister Carol progressing through the parish school to St. Louis High School for Girls, and Sister Lucille continuing her education through high school at Presentation of Mary Academy.

The influence of attending different parochial schools later affected their choice of the orders they joined when they became nuns. Sister Lucille entered the Sisters of the Presentation of Mary and Sister Carol, the Congregation of Holy Cross.

"The nuns were always kind to me. I never knew of any who rapped knuckles. And they always encouraged me in my studies," says Sister Lucille. It was not until her senior year in college that she chose to dedicate her life to the church.

"I was more mature then and the life of prayer and service, caring for others, seemed more appealing," says Sister Lucille.

Sister Lucille Thibodeau

To Sister Carol, the life of a nun was "a way to make a difference in people's lives in a free way—to advance the Gospel values of truth, love, compassion and reconciliation needed in this world."

In spite of the different paths to religious life they chose, the two educators share many of the same memories of their youth in Crown Hill.

"Remember the rag man?" asks Sister Carol. Sitting on his horse-drawn cart every Friday, he was a neighborhood character no one would forget.

"His horse's name was Molly. I loved to feed her," said sister Lucille.

"We named our dog Rags," adds Sister Carol.

The early days of television also call forth a multitude of names from the past.

"I loved the Mickey Mouse Club," said Sister Carol, "Annette Funicello was my idol." Obviously another fan, the retired Rivier College president nodded in agreement.

"And Kate Smith. She was on when I got home from school. We always had milk and cookies," Sister Carol recalled.

The Thibodeaus bought their first television set in 1949, the first in the neighborhood. Sister Carol's grandparents had the first set in their family, she recalls, and it brought the whole family to their house on C Street on Saturday nights.

"Down by the river, down by the railroad tracks, where it all (the fire) started," sighed Sister Carol.

Television just skims the surface of their storehouse of memories growing up in Crown Hill.

Shopping downtown on Main Street was a treat.

"I knew every inch of Main Street," said Sister Carol, naming shops that were household words: Speare's, Millers, Woolworth's and Jordan Luggage, the only store still there.

For recreation, there was Field's Grove, a city swimming area, to spend lazy summer days. All the children would bring a lunch and stay all day.

In winter, there was ice skating at Marshall Field and both women remember the man across the street who sharpened their skates and had a pot of hot chocolate on the stove to warm the crowd.

"You could go any place and be safe," Sister Lucille commented.

The two presidents took a few moments out of their busy schedules to revisit the homesteads of their youth on a hot day in June. Sister Lucille, born on Allds Street, grew up in a two-story house on Benson Street.

She remembers the neighbors who raised chickens in the backyard next door. Taking pity on them in the heat of one summer day, she sprayed them with the hose.

"They didn't lay eggs for a week," she said. "My parents were furious at me."

Nostalgia swept over Sister Carol as she surveyed the house on Haines Street where she grew up.

"My father bought the lot next door and planted that tree when I was 2 years old," she reminisced. The maple, grown tall and full, still provides shade for a picnic table.

After they graduated high school, the two women attended women's colleges close to home.

Sister Carol entered the order of the Sisters of Holy Cross in 1965. She studied at Notre Dame College in Manchester, receiving a bachelor's degree in philosophy and theology in 1970. She went on to receive a master's degree from Boston College in education and religious studies, and a doctorate in Christian ethics from Notre Dame University in Indiana.

For Sister Lucille, the journey to college president began at Rivier College in 1966. She received a bachelor's degree magna cum laude and a master's in English

Telegraph Photo Files

Sister Carol Descoteaux visits the house in Crown Hill where she grew up.

in 1972. She became a nun in her senior year in college, joining the Sisters of Presentation of Mary. After teaching English at Rivier, she earned a doctorate degree in comparative literature at Harvard University in 1990. Ironically, the quintessential teacher was an avid reader of comic books in her youth.

Both women note with pride that teaching—rather than administration—was their route to the president's office. Along the way, their paths have been marked with impressive credentials and many honors in the field of education. Sister Lucille became president of Rivier in 1997, after serving as special projects assistant to the president, then Sister Jeanne Perreault, for more than a year. Sister Carol left her post after serving as president of Notre Dame College for 15 years. In the next chapter of her life, she aims to use her education in Christian ethics, her service on the board of medical institutions and an unforgettable experience in Brazil working with people in abject poverty to benefit health care in this country.

"There are new vistas to explore," she says with confidence.

Personally and professionally the two college presidents have traveled far from their beginnings in Crown Hill. Yet the Nashua neighborhood will always be at the heart of their success as women, as educators and as nuns.

July 10, 1999

A LEGEND IN NASHUA – AND POSSIBLY BEYOND

Some of us still remember the man with the little black bag and the pocketful of stories who came calling when we were home in bed, too sick even to eat ice cream. He was the man who poked in our ears, jammed a stick down our throats and prodded our stomachs. Yet he made us smile and when he left, somehow we felt better.

"'Dr. Marcus Welby of Nashua,' I called him," says Roland Breault, remembering the late Dr. William Thibodeau, Nashua's version of the family doctor before TV gave him a name.

To the seven children in the Fariz family he was the doctor who ministered to all their family's ills, from mom's phlebitis to Jim's broken arm when it got caught in the wringer washing machine to Lorraine's appendix operation. Lorraine Fariz Pelletier, now a grandmother, describes herself as a sickly kid with terrible colds and ear trouble. "I thought he was the most wonderful doctor," she sighs, remembering visits to his office in the Sears Building on Main Street, always crowded with patients.

Dr. Bill Thibodeau, the man who for more than 50 years personified the caring family doctor in Nashua, died last month at age 96, leaving behind memories of a different era in the practice of medicine. He made house calls before breakfast, tramped through snow drifts in Hudson at midnight to deliver a baby and witnessed both the scourge of infantile paralysis and the wonders of its cure, the Salk vaccination. And as payment for his labors, he often accepted produce, chickens and eggs from the farm.

"They never wanted for roast chicken," said his niece Phyllis Mecheski, when she gave the eulogy at his funeral. Gathered in Nashua for the occasion were his son, William Charles of Sarasota, Fla., and five grandchildren.

In his later years, Dr. Thibodeau relished relating his medical adventures to a reporter calling for story material or to fellow members of the Nashua Rotary Club. All members of the club are asked to give a biography, but he was the only one asked to give his twice—first before he became the Rotary president in 1947 and then again almost 50 years later.

The last time he spoke he was approaching 90 and he gave a talk in two installments. Though the two-part talk was without precedent, no one complained. In fact, says Thomas Tessier, Rotary president 1990–91, the good doctor kept their interest to the last word."

Dr. William Thibodeau

They were fascinated by his stories about playing varsity football and being named all-American in La Crosse in college. He was not a big man in stature," marvels Tessier, adding, "He was always humorous, a very funny guy."

Though always one to look on the bright side of life, Dr. T., as he was fondly known, understood the value of hard work from an early age. He was born in 1902 in Newport, the third of nine children. His mother and father, a cobbler in the McElwain shoe shop, spoke only French at home, and Bill Thibodeau didn't learn to speak English until he went to school. His fluent French offered yet another comfort later to patients of French-Canadian heritage when he practiced medicine in Nashua.

The young Thibodeau's destiny to become a doctor was sealed in high school when a Newport doctor began taking him along on house calls and patients often called him doctor, a title he loved.

He started on the path to becoming a doctor at Dean Academy and Hobart College. His athletic ability brought him to a small college in upstate New York, and he earned his bachelor's degree waiting on tables and working other jobs. To pay for medical school at Cornell University he played semi-pro football. He interned in Jersey City and worked 18 months as a ship's surgeon in the Caribbean and South America.

In 1932, Dr. Thibodeau hung his first shingle at 220 Main St., now occupied by Coronis Cleaners, living in an apartment on the second floor. He was pleased to be one of the Nashuans pictured in the Yankee Flyer mural on the wall of the original site of his office.

Dr. Thibodeau's first call to deliver a baby came on Christmas Eve, and of course he immediately climbed in his newly purchased Ford and went to the expectant mother's home. There were many calls to deliver babies as well as to treat tonsillitis, measles and sprained ankles until specialists such as Dr. Charles Goyette, a gynecologist-obstetrician, came to town.

"He and his wife often invited Meri and me to their home on Elliot Street," recalls Dr. Goyette of the Thibodeau's hospitality. The Goyettes were also invited to the Thibodeau home in Maine, where the doctor delighted in taking his guests on walks along the beach of the Miracle Mile.

In spite of a thriving practice, Dr. T. and his wife, Edna, enjoyed a busy social life. Waltzing was among his pleasures, says his niece, Phyllis. In fact, her uncle Bill taught her to waltz as a young girl. The lesson transpired during her visit to Nashua. He had come home for lunch, as he usually did, turned on the record player, and proceeded to show her dance steps.

As a general practitioner, Dr. T. was always in constant demand any time of the night or day, and conversations between doctor and patient were often carried on in French.

In addition to keeping a busy practice, he served 25 years as the parochial school doctor, administer ing the first polio shot in Nashua. He also served as president of St. Joseph Hospital Staff and president of the county medical society. During World War II, his practice was interrupted by three years of service as a Navy lieutenant commander.

But of all the civic endeavors he supported in Nashua, the one to which he was most committed was the Nashua Rotary Club. Nashua dentist Dr. Adrian Levesque was his sponsor when he joined in 1940 and from then on, the two waged a friendly competition to earn the club's attendance record. According to Rotary lore, even when they were sick in the hospital, they each arranged for meetings to be held at their bedside instead of the Nashua County Club.

Even when living at Aynsley Place, a retirement home, in the 1990s, Dr. Thibodeau faithfully attended the weekly Monday Rotary meetings, taking his seat next to the head table next to Dr. Robert Levesque, Adrian's son. Tina Andrade, the then-administrator of Courville, and Jill Elaqua, the director of assisted care, were also Rotarians and gladly chauffeured him to meetings, which he never missed until his health started failing this summer.

"He never thought of himself as old and was always open to new ideas," offers Andrade, whom he encouraged to become the chapter's first female president.

"He loved being a doctor, he loved Nashua and he loved being involved in the community," says Elaqua.

Former patient Roland Breault, also a Rotary member, has played piano at the beginning of meetings for years."

"'Somewhere My Love' was his favorite song and he'd ask me to play it for him when I played at Ainsley Place," Breault said.

Dr. T's humor and thoughtfulness were legendary at Ainsley Place. He would often go shopping at the supermarket—his shoplifting trips, he called them—and return with edible presents of fruit or muffins for other residents.

Even when bedridden near the end, he was quick with a quip to put visitors in a good mood.

His standard response when told that anyone had died, according to Dr. Goyette, was "they went to heaven."

In their hearts, his patients believe Nashua's Dr. T is there with his little black bag taking care of everyone and telling wonderful stories.

September 14, 1999

WIFE, MOTHER, COMMUNITY LEADER

While growing up, Margaret Flynn's favorite aunt, a career woman, impressed her as the perfect role model. As an executive in the garment industry, her aunt traveled, dined in the finest restaurants, went to shows and often took her niece with her on jaunts to Boston or New York.

To a young girl growing up in the Depression, a career woman's life seemed most exciting; yet at home, her mother extolled the virtues of marriage and motherhood.

Her mother and her aunt were the two women Margaret Quill Flynn adored in her youth and the two strongest influences on the path she chose to follow.

"I decided to put the two together and do both," she says of the two options. And she did.

More than 50 years later, the wife, mother and retired Superior Court judge has also earned just about every honor there is for her contributions to civic life.

In recent years she added the Marguerite d'Youville Humanitarian Awards from St. Joseph Hospital to her many tributes. Among admirers at the awards reception were her husband, retired Superior Court Judge Charles Flynn, and their two daughters, Katherine Elizabeth Flynn, a Tewksbury, Mass., lawyer named for her mother's favorite aunt, and Dr. Margaret Crimmins Flynn, a medical doctor and research fellow at Deaconess Hospital, named for her great-grandmother. Both daughters were born in the old St. Joseph Hospital, replaced in 1967 by the modern medical complex for which their mother had led the fund drive.

Margaret Quill Flynn grew up in Stoughton, Mass., in the days when mothers stayed home and the fisherman, the baker and the milkman delivered to the door.

"I had a happy childhood; we were a close family," she recalls, adding, "It was Depression days and money was tight." The family included three brothers and her father, a factory foreman.

"I would have loved to go to Mount Holyoke like my daughter," she muses, but instead she considered herself lucky to attend Boston University with help from her aunt. She graduated with honors and also earned a Phi Beta Kappa key.

Teaching history was her original plan, but a career in law crept into her life unexpectedly when a friend told her about the new summer semester at BU Law School. She enrolled and one course let to another, though she admits, "I had no great desire to be a lawyer."

Telegraph Photo Files

Retired Superior Court Judge Margaret Flynn

In 1944, after a stint as editor of the school's law review, she graduated magna cum laude.

At law school, the second part of her life also began to take shape. She met fellow law student Charles Flynn of Nashua. It was wartime, however, and he was called into the Navy and eventually served on a PT boat in Okinawa.

The war ended and in 1950, they were married after he finished his law degree and hung up his shingle in Nashua. She had already begun her law career serving as a law clerk to justices of the Massachusetts Supreme Judicial Court.

"In no way did I feel any discrimination because I was a woman," she insists.

The war had been the great equalizer for women and in 1946, after law clerking, she broke the male, prep school, Harvard barrier when she was hired by a prestigious Boston law firm.

"When I graduated, the men were just coming back from the service. There were opportunities for women that didn't exist before," she says, dismissing the fact that she was only one of two women on the staff.

The young lawyer commuted from Nashua to Boston until 1958, when she became pregnant with her first child. To be closer to home, she joined her husband in the firm of Earley and Flynn becoming the second practicing female lawyer in the city at the time. It was the ideal arrangement for the new mother.

"I could take the baby out and wheel her around in the daytime and work at night. I never really had to give up anything. Charlie would bring things home from the office," she says.

Four years later, another daughter was born. Since the Flynns lived with his mother, they also had a built-in baby sitter. After his mother died, her mother came to live with them in the brick ranch they built in the South End.

"I had grandparent baby sitters. Women working today have a lot more burden than I did," says Flynn.

Using every moment, she combined marriage, motherhood and a career with ease. Her office was five minutes from home and the girls' schools, whether Sacred Heart School of St. Patrick Church in the early years, Sunset Heights Elementary, Fairgrounds Junior High or Nashua High. There was always time for parents' night, school plays and afternoons with the girls at Camp Sargent in the summer.

"She was a lunch monitor when I was at St. Pat's," recalls daughter Katherine. "Everybody liked her the best; she always brought in snacks. She was always home for dinner, then running out to do things. But we never felt we were second."

"Things to do" included serving on the St. Joseph Hospital board of directors for 20 years, as the only woman on the Nashua Police Commission for 12 years, on the Rivier College Advisory Board and board of trustees for 22 years, on the Daniel Webster College Advisory Board for five years and on the Nashua Board of Education for 16 years.

Her tenure on the school board, 1960 to 1975, came during a tumultuous era when a burgeoning Nashua had its first teachers strike, hired a new superintendent, and experienced schools bursting at the seams. Elm Street High School was on dual sessions, affecting hundreds of households, including the Flynns, and the building of a new high school on the west side of the highway was fraught with controversy.

A power struggle between the Board of Aldermen and the Board of Education, over who should set salaries for school personnel, erupted in a lawsuit, Sullivan vs. Flynn. Former Mayor Dennis Sullivan, representing the city, was the plaintiff, and she, as the school board president, was the defendant. The courts upheld the sovereignty of the school board.

"Margaret was always looking out for the best for the schools. She knew when to fight and when not to fight," says Selma Pastor, a school board member at the time. "She was a balancing force, a moderating influence on some of the members," offers attorney Gerald Prunier, another school board colleague.

Through nonchalant about her contributions, the approachable ex-judge with the dry sense of humor has been showered with awards for her community service. She has also received several awards for her contributions to state education.

In 1984, the YMCA ushered her into its Hall of Distinguished Women Leaders, and in 1992 the New Hampshire Bar Foundation conferred on her the honor of judicial fellow.

The Marguerite d'Youville Humanitarian Award is the culmination of a 30-year association with St. Joseph hospital and its founders, the Grey Nuns. It is the one community tie she still maintains since she retired from the bench. She has been the chairwoman of Marguerite's Place, a transitional shelter for women and children, since it opened in 1993.

Flynn has yet to find a place for the newest award but, no doubt, it will be an inconspicuous one. A clay model of the bust she received when she was the recipient of the Robert Frost Contemporary American Award from Plymouth College is tucked in a corner on the top of a bookcase in the Flynn sunroom. The plaque she received in 1991 as Citizen of the Year from the Chamber of Commerce is barely visible on the lower shelf of the bookcase, one of many in the house crammed with hardcovers and paperbacks well-worn from years of use in Great Books discussion groups.

Since she retired in 1992, the inveterate reader has added volumes from courses she has taken at Rivier College, where she has also been a founder and an active participant in RISE . . . Rivier Institute for Senior Education. Often she drives two other women to class so they, too, can monitor a course as senior citizens or attend RISE.

"That's Margaret," says teacher and longtime friend Sister Marjorie Francoeur.

"She's a people-centered person. She is always trying to find something good in the characters we read about, even characters that are not so good. Her philosophy is based on the goodness of people."

October 21, 1995

MASTER CRAFTSMAN WITH WOOD

NASHUA—ELF is the signature of the man who carves peach pits into whimsical pendants, drills square pegs with a recycled egg beater and fashions tree limbs into Indian walking sticks. And these creations just scratch the surface of his woodworking magic.

Ernest Louis Foisy is a master craftsman, a cabinetmaker more typical of a bygone era. The small house where he lives with his wife, Rita, abounds with his magnificent creations.

His hand is seen in each room, from the handmade pine and maple cabinets in the kitchen to the 18th century-style mahogany bedroom set with the pineapple poster bed. Statues of wood decorate the tables, carved plaques of animals hang on the walls and a handsome clock he made from a tiny illustration sits on the mantle.

At Christmas time, a 22-piece nativity scene is displayed on a table, and choirboy candlestick holders light the windows.

Except for an electric table saw, Foisy uses old-fashioned hand tools, many of them antiques dating back to the Civil War; others he makes himself.

Take the drill with egg-beater wheels. He turns it manually into a square hole in an old sink washer he found around the house. He produces the square peg he needed for an old door.

"The modern carpenter doesn't even know what they are," he says of the tools hanging on the wall of his workshop. Foisy works in a small garage workshop behind his neat white house near Kinsley Street, and nothing seems beyond his ability.

He does not own a lathe, so he turns spindles on his table saw. His wooden plane is one he made himself. Another tool he made measures perfect angles of all sizes. He could not afford an electric drill because it was too expensive, so he made a hand drill.

"A cabinetmaker has to make a joint that's airtight. That's the difference between a cabinetmaker and a carpenter. It's a long road," he says, holding up a giant-size mug called a "pig." It was used to drink rum by maties on old sailing ships.

He saw the original container made of two-toned strips of wood on a TV program about raising an old Navy schooner and copied it. "I figured out a way to fit the wood together at right angles," says Foisy.

Square pegs, spindles, airtight angles, whatever the challenge, he studies it and comes up with a solution. "Impossible is just a word. Nothing is impossible. If you haven't got a way to do it, make it yourself," says the 82-year-old Nashuan whose ingenuity has amazed engineers and fellow craftsmen alike.

"I was a child of the Depression," says Foisy. "We didn't have electricity until I was 23 years old. That's why I use hand tools."

Foisy was born and raised in Claremont, working in the mills after finishing eighth grade. During World War II, he joined the Air Force, serving as a bomb deployment specialist in North Africa, Sardinia and England. It was harrowing duty, and few walked away unscathed.

Foisy was classified disabled when he was discharged after the war. He came to Nashua in 1946 in search of a job.

He found a career, and married Rita Cote of Nashua in St. Francis Xavier Catholic Church. The couple lived on Chandler Street with their two daughters until they bought the house they now live in 40 years ago.

They recently celebrated their 52nd wedding anniversary, and their eldest, Pauline Caron, is principal of Elm Street Junior High School. Her sister, Doris Kenney, is a computer specialist in Manchester and is the mother of the Foisys' three grandchildren.

Foisy's career as a cabinetmaker began as an apprenticeship at Old Colony, a shop specializing in high quality furniture sold in the finest stores in New York and Boston. He made 50 cents an hour when he started, but he acquired an invaluable trade.

"I learned from an 84-year-old Englishman. Nobody else wanted to work with him. He was too slow, but I didn't care. I told him I would pick his brain."

Foisy has never forgotten the two characteristics the Englishman said he needed to be a good cabinetmaker: "Patience and the love of wood, and I had both," says Foisy.

He learned so well, he became the head supervisor of the cabinet-making department until the company closed 18 years later and he went to work for other companies.

In 1960, while working at Old Colony, a colleague at the shop asked him for advice on woodwork he was doing in the new Temple Beth Abraham. Foisy offered to help build the enclosure for the Torah, the sacred scrolls and other wood projects in the sanctuary. Edward Rudman, the owner of Old Colony, was the chairman of the building committee for the new synagogue on Raymond Street and Max Silber, the president of the congregation, supervised the progress each day.

"He is a guy that has hands of gold," says Silber of the work Foisy did.

Foisy remembers working nights and weekends, painstakingly crafting the ark, following the architect's edict that no nails should be showing. "I didn't want anybody there but me and my table saw. I worked all night."

Though Temple Beth Abraham is being enlarged and remodeled this summer, the beautiful woodwork will remain intact, says Elaine Brody, chairman of the building committee. The old sanctuary will be used as the small chapel for daily prayers.

Daughter Pauline Caron remembers her father's pride in his work for the synagogue and in whatever he was doing. On Saturdays he often took her into the Old Colony shop while he worked.

"I still remember the smell of wood—the cherry, mahogany and rosewood," she says.

Even on summer vacations at Silver Lake or Wells Beach, her dad was busy working on his projects, carving the ball and claw feet for the bedroom set or making one of his many statues, originals of Indian chief Sitting Bull.

A college art teacher watching him was so impressed, he bought several of his statues to bring back to show his students.

Always itching to make things, Foisy often carved monkey pendants out of peach pits to give to children at the beach, something he still does to delight children in the neighborhood.

"I don't throw away anything," he says. He even saves openers from soda cans to use to hang his plaques on the wall.

A master artist who works with wood is never without a project. He recently restored an antique kitchen table for a neighbor. When she bought it at a flea market, it was too battered to see its beauty until Foisy worked on it.

"He's always been generous with his time and talent," says Pauline. Both her home and her sister's are filled with ELF creations, including the 42 handmade cabinets in her kitchen. She drew up the blueprint for her kitchen under her father's watchful eye. When the architect marveled at how perfect the plans were, she remarked, "I had a good teacher."

Thinking of his teacher, the old Englishman who taught him his trade, Foisy says, "I have become the old Englishman, teaching people what I know."

June 30, 2001

"QUEEN MUM" OF MAIN STREET

The "Queen Mum" of Main Street—if such a title were proclaimed in Nashua—would surely be confirmed on Ethel Fokas. True to legends of royalty, Ethel Scontsas Fokas represents the union of two popular Main Street dynasties reigning over the downtown mercantile kingdom for almost a century. Thinking of Main Street without the presence of either family is asking the impossible.

But Ethel Fokas' claim to the title goes deeper than bloodlines. Nobody knows Main Street better than Martha's candy lady. A native Nashuan, she spent her early years not far from Main Street. She started working on Main Street as a teenager. She met her husband, Mitch Fokas, on Main Street. In fact, he courted her on Main Street and when they married, they worked side by side on Main Street for 40 years. Today their two sons, Billy and Chris, are carrying on the family tradition at Martha's Exchange Restaurant and Brewery, now a Main Street landmark.

"Main Street, that's been my life. I love it," says the youthful grandmother who can still be seen behind the candy counter at Martha's on days when her health permits. Few downtown shopkeepers have equaled her 60-year career or made as many friends on the city's main thoroughfare.

The natural-born saleswoman was the second youngest of eight children of "Zeffie" and George J. Scontsas, Greek immigrants who planted deep roots in Nashua. She was born on Jan. 4, 1925, on Walnut Street.

Her first effort in selling was at the age of 11, working in her Uncle Tony's fruit store on West Hollis Street. "I didn't get paid but I loved it," she recalls. At 15, her first job on Main Street was working after school at J.J. Newbury, a job she held until she graduated, often selling in the candy department.

In 1942, when she graduated Nashua High School on Elm Street, the country was at war and her brothers were called into military service.

"In July of 1942, I was actually thrown into my father's business," she recalls. He ran a barber and shoe repair shop, she continues, and it also had a hat cleaning service and sold magazines. The Scontsas family owned part of the Merchant's Exchange Building on Main Street, occupied by the store.

"I shined shoes, cleaned brown and white spectator shoes, blocked hats and helped my father run a very busy store," she says.

After the war, the barbershop—but not the shoe repair service—was replaced with a card shop, Nashua's first complete Hallmark store. The new business allowed Ethel to use her more feminine talents, such as buying merchandise and giving gift-wrapping demonstrations. She often went to Boston gift shows to stock the store with a variety of new and interesting items for home decor.

When her father died in 1956, two brothers, Peter and Achilles, took over the store, but she continued to add her touch.

"I loved everything I sold. If I didn't like it, I wouldn't buy it," she says.

During the post-war era, a new face appeared on Main Street. Mitch Fokas took over his uncle's candy store, Martha's Sweet Shoppe, in the same building as the Scontsas store. In 1956, he added a luncheonette and it soon became a gathering spot for local politicians and downtown merchants, a place where news was often heard before it appeared in *The Telegraph*. Along the way, Mitch Fokas became a Main Street personality. The handsome young bachelor also found time to charm the pretty brunette two stores away.

"He came in often for a shoe shine whether he needed one or not," recalls the object of his affections.

No one was surprised when the Main Street romance bloomed and the couple became engaged. Ethel Scontsas and James B. Fokas exchanged marriage vows on April 27, 1958, in St. Nicholas Church on Palm Street, the congregation her family belonged to for many years. When he came to Nashua from Milton, Mass., Fokas had joined the Annunciation Greek Church. Twenty years later, the couple would become one of the founding families of St. Philip Greek Orthodox Church, unifying the city's two Greek congregations.

Ethel Fokas

Telegraph Photo Files

After their wedding in Nashua, the newlyweds honeymooned in Bermuda, and when they returned they moved into an apartment above Martha's Sweet Shoppe and Luncheonette. Ethel, of course, left the Scontsas' card shop down the block to work with her husband at Martha's.

"He married me because he needed a clerk in the candy shop," she tells people with a smile.

They lived above the store when Kathy, their first child, was born. But by the time Billy and Chris came along, they had bought a spacious two-story home in the South End, where she still lives today and entertains her four grandchildren.

The house holds many memories, including their 25th anniversary party for 200 of their friends and family given in the backyard garden by their children.

"I knew it was coming but I didn't know where or when. When I saw Chris sweeping the driveway, I knew," she confides.

The couple would have celebrated their 40th anniversary when Mitch Fokas died four years ago on April 10—Good Friday. It was always his favorite candy season. Chocolate Easter bunnies big and small and Easter baskets made in the shop quickly disappeared from the shelves.

Ethel talks of their many years as partners in marriage and in business with a sense of pride and satisfaction. Soon after she became a part of the business, she put her buying skills to work in the candy department, bringing two famous makers, Barton's and Barricini's, to the store. When Martha's started a food catering service, her talents were visible in the touches she added to the elegant presentation.

"I sewed lovely white chiffon table skirts and arranged luscious French pastries on silver trays," she says.

Through the years, Martha's catered functions from wedding dinners to receptions for political candidates. During primary season, presidential candidates including Jimmy Carter, Gerald Ford and Al Gore were feted at Martha's and a stop there for lunch was a must on the campaign trail.

"I've met them all," says Ethel.

Primaries may bring celebrities to Main Street but sidewalk sales bring out the local crowd. Each spring and fall, Nashuans flocked to Martha's outdoor table for Ethel's baklava, pita and words of good cheer.

Along with their business and family, both of the Fokas shared a strong civic commitment. They were active in downtown affairs and in the 1970s, when the Greek community built St. Philip Church and united the two Greek congregations, both generously gave their support. He was elected the first president and served for many years on its board.

And in 1988, when the economy on Main Street was at a low, the family embarked on a costly and ambitious project to restore the historic Merchant's Exchange to its original 1870s charm and to open a full restaurant, with, of course, a candy shop.

"Everyone told us we were taking a big chance," she recalls. The two longtime restaurateurs stepped back to let their two sons make the major decisions and take charge of the business.

Down came the orange tiles from the front of the luncheonette, allowing the gracefully carved window designs to dominate the historic building. The inside decor features Nashua pictures and memorabilia.

Spearheading the revival of Main Street, the restaurant and brewery is still a gathering place for downtown diners. Although she and Mitch had flirted with businesses in other towns—Goodwin's Seafood in Hudson and a candy store in Concord—Main Street in Nashua is home.

"We're all close," she says of all the merchants on the street. "We appreciate each other and how hard we work. People are friendly. It is a pleasure being here."

And where else but from Main Street would she get a Mother's Day card signed with loving sentiments from each member of the Martha's Exchange staff?

June 16, 2002

FRANCO-AMERICANS

A recently published book about Nashua families is a summer best-seller, fast becoming a collector's item. There are the Arel, the Bellavance and the Chagnon families, for example. And also the Cotes, Francoeurs, Gravels, Levesques, Lozeaus, Ouellets and Thibaults.

They have been friends and neighbors in Nashua for many years. Their grandparents and parents came here from Quebec, sometimes by way of France. Their children grew up in Nashua, went to the same schools, played together, worshipped together and often intermarried. Together with other French Canadian families, they established churches, schools, hospitals and businesses in the town they chose to call home. Though the first generation seldom finished high school and spoke little English, the second and third generations went to college and became lawyers, doctors, teachers, and civic leaders.

The stories of these families are among the 52 highlighted in "The Third Century: A Recognition of Franco-Americans," but there are thousands of Nashua families who contributed to the saga. It is, in fact, the story of America and the myriad of enterprising newcomers who immigrated from other lands. They planted roots here and in turn contributed in many ways to the life of their community.

"It was up to us to acknowledge the richness of previous generations," says Georgi Laurin Hippauf, who compiled and edited the 155-page book with tender loving care. "In every story, the spirit is so vibrant."

Typical is the story of Alphonse and Apolline Chagnon. The young couple settled in the rural village of Nashua at the end of the 1800s, holding firm to the traditions and values they brought with them from Quebec. While she raised the children, he started a construction business, Chagnon Construction Co., and went on to build the original St. Joseph Hospital and St. Joseph Orphanage.

The Chagnons' son Emile, educated at St. Louis de Gonzague School, Nashua High School and Nashua Business College, married a Canadian girl and brought her to Nashua. They were married 68 years and had two daughters and three sons, all college graduates. One son was a lawyer, another a doctor and the youngest, Emile Jr., joined his father in the family business, as did two of his sons, Emile III and Charles, in later years.

At the end of the 1900s, a century after his grandparents came to Nashua, Emile Chagnon Jr. became a key figure in the mounting enthusiasm of the Franco American community to establish a lasting tribute to the generations preceding them and paving the way for their accomplishments.

Led by Georgi Hippauf and Maurice Parent, a committee spearheaded a celebration to honor French Canadian heritage, and Chagnon was named its finance chairman. His committee raised $85,000 for the festival, in the newly named Le Parc de Notre Renaissance Francaise, and for a bronze 6-foot statue to permanently adorn the park.

Georgi Hippauf

Andruskevich Photography

To cap the festivities, Hippauf proposed something tangible for people to take home as a keepsake. A handsome hardcover book, designed on archival paper with a fleur de lis motif, was the answer.

Producing the book with the festival as the deadline, however, took know-how and determination. Hippauf had both, as well as a deep personal interest.

The book had been part of the proposal package for the celebration drawn up Feb. 22, 1999. Between that date and the May 19 celebration, there was money to be raised, a site for the park to be chosen, a sculptor named to create the statue and a program to be arranged. In addition, there was a book to be translated from an idea to a reality, a book reflecting the proud heritage of the Franco-American community in the Merrimack Valley.

Fortunately, Hippauf had years of experience with publications to fall back on. A veteran of many political campaigns in New Hampshire, she has collaborated with former Gov. Hugh Gregg on several books about New Hampshire political history.

To accomplish her objectives, she also recruited Franco-American scholars such as Dr. Eric Drouart, a professor at Rivier College; Lee Caron, president of the Richelieu Club; and Paul Adelard Jacques, a French teacher at Bishop Guertin High School.

Originally, the book was to be published by L'Association Canado-Americaine but a change in plans required finding a new publisher. Hippauf took the project to Fred Lyford of Puritan Press in Hollis, with whom she had worked on the political books. He accepted the job enthusiastically since he knew many families in the book.

"Families were the crux of the book," says Hippauf.

Contacting the families and collecting their stories was another hurdle. Since few people knew where to begin to tell their family stories, she devised a set of questions to serve as a guideline. When necessary, Lee Caron, proficient in French, made a house call. Hippauf is also proficient in French, a second language spoken since her childhood, and could translate with ease.

"I came to know each family personally—in French and in English," she says, noting that she sent a handwritten note to each family she contacted with a sample of the layout of a page in the book and a contribution scale.

Though the stories were the meat of the book, many hors d'oeuvres are served throughout, such as "At Home in the Merrimack Valley" by Jacques, setting the scene for French Canadian immigration and tracing the immigrants' successes in the United States. Other pieces follow the progress of Christopher R. Gowell in sculpting the "Lady," the statue that stands over the newly christened park.

The book is also replete with photographs of families and of businesses in Nashua that exemplify the Franco-American entrepreneurial spirit. Retold for the education of the younger generation is the history of St. Joseph Hospital, Infant Jesus, St. Francis Xavier and St. Louis de Gonzague churches, the Millette Court of the Nashua Chapter of the ACA and Le Club Richelieu of Nashua.

There are bon mots such as the tribute to the local French press, L'Etoile and L'Impartial, written by Martha Biron Peloquin, daughter of the editor Louis Biron. For frosting on the cake there are favorite French recipes, songs and stories to be enjoyed. Also, there are vignettes from the works of Jack Kerouac and a biography that tells of his strong link to Nashua. The book ends with a poem, "A Nos Aieux," ("To Our Ancestors") by native Nashuan Jeannine T. Levesque.

Once all the material was in house, the editor's work began. Before editing, some of the stories had to be typed into the computer, hundreds of names checked for spelling, the proper accents put in the right places and photos identified.

"I'd get up at 5 in the morning, work through lunch and spend the afternoon organizing. That was the only way I could get things done by the dedication," says Hippauf, who thrives on writing projects and holds bachelor's and master's degrees in English.

"The Third Century" rolled off the presses two days before the dedication. The coffee table tome, beautifully covered with a portrait of the mills on the river, was printed in a limited edition. Copies sell for $24.95 and may be purchased at Absolutely New Hampshire on Main Street, by e-mail at georgi@empire.net or by calling Hippauf at 888-0957.

Writes Hippauf in the introduction of the book, "We grow the future from the present; the past becomes the roots from which it germinates."

July 28, 2001

"MRS. NASHUA" GETS THINGS DONE

Downtown Nashua has been chief beneficiary of Meri Goyette's dynamic talent for organizing and promoting.

Not one to wait patiently, Meri Goyette moved into her summer office on Main Street in the middle of the spring. An umbrella table for a desk, she sat in front of the Coyote Café greeting passers by and inviting them to join her. Mayor Donald Davidson is a favorite schmoozing partner.

"I can talk about things better here than in the mayor's office," she said with a smile. Since the restaurant was owned by her daughter and son-in-law, Meri and Don Reid, she was always welcome and her guests are usually offered something to eat or drink.

"Whenever she sees me, she says 'Sit down and have some chips,' and she always has a smile," said the mayor, who affectionately called her "Mrs. Nashua."

Whatever business is on her mind is certain to be about Nashua and more specifically about Main Street. She is never short of ideas to promote either. Just to name a few, she has had a hand in staging a wing-ding in Greeley Park to celebrate Nashua's No. 1 status, orchestrating fund-raisers for the Hunt Memorial Building, and in the beautification of Downtown Nashua.

As these ideas are put into effect, they often improve the city and produce a sense of pride among participants. For example, the Broom Brigade of teen-agers she recruited called attention to the careless littering of Main Street, and at the same time gave the sweepers a feeling of contributing to their town. She has even been seen picking up debris and sweeping on Main Street.

"With her persistence, she gets things done," said Davidson, citing the park bordering the Yankee Flyer as an example. Even after the bank sold the property at the corner of Main and West Hollis streets, she refused to surrender the spot before adding a bench, proper lighting and some landscaping. And after the mini-park became a reality, the bank and City Hall officials all agreed it provided the right touch for the mural.

"I call it Meri's Park," says Davidson, referring to the Yankee Flyer oasis across from City Hall.

The idea for a mural of the town's memorable diner on the site where it flourished originated with Goyette, and she proposed employing an artist who had done similar works in Boston. On behalf of the N.H. Council on the Arts, Nashua artist James Aponovich objected to the project going outside the state. Goyette immediately pulled back, a competition of area artists ensued and Aponovich's rendition was chosen the winner. The project proceeded on course and Goyette steered the fundraising to the finish, even convincing her husband, Dr. Charles Goyette, to sign and sell copies of his memoir to benefit the privately financed art work.

Though her relationship with Aponovich started off on a rocky road, it ended with a solid friendship. "We're in touch all the time," said the Nashua artist, adding that the families are friends and he has offered to supply some of his prints for another pet project, a show at the Hunt Memorial Building.

"She has a knack for persuading people to work with her," Aponovich observed, speaking from experience.

When the mayor formed an official board of trustees to oversee the management of the Hunt Memorial, he appointed Goyette the chairwoman, and since the once-vacant building has come back to life, its warm oak walls and high ceilings are now seen and appreciated by all as they were when it was the city library. From the bell tower of the stately Gothic building, chimes—installed, thanks to Goyette—ring out every day on Main Street.

The Hunt Memorial Building has been the scene of many city events she has inspired including concerts, flower shows, a board of aldermen at a buffet dinner before its regular meeting, and on the first Thursday of every month a native Nashuan speaking about "Growing Up in Nashua" in the old reading room.

Displayed on the room's old oak shelves have been household products invented and made in Nashua from the collection of Frank Mooney, an authority on Nashua memorabilia. On Saturdays, Mooney has been there to fill in visitors on the history of the Dunlap Seed Co., White Mountain Freezer ice cream makers, the Purrey blankets, and Indian Head cloth made in the Nashua mills, Shepard door locks, the paper boxes made with machines created at International Paper Box, and bread wrappers made by Nashua Corp.

On the wall of the sitting room is a plaque dedicating the pleasantly furnished room to the memory of Robie Goyette. The Goyette's youngest son was killed one evening in March 1991 in a random shooting on Main Street. For many families, the senseless tragedy would engender a terrible resentment for the place where it happened. Instead the Goyettes have turned the tragedy around, creating a brighter vista.

"It was a dark street on which Robie was killed. I vowed I would light it up. I didn't set out to do these things, but I was impelled to make it a better, happier place," says his mother.

Though she now proclaims Nashua home, the former Meri Zanleoni was born and brought up in Barre, Vt.

After graduating from LaSalle Junior College in 1946, she married Charles Goyette, the son of a family friend. He was in his last year at the University of Vermont Medical School. During his internship and residency while serving in the Army at Fort Devens, Mass., they had four children. Two more children, son Robie and daughter Robin, were born after the Goyettes settled in Nashua in the summer of 1955.

Telegraph Photo Files

Meri Goyette stands in front of her favorite Nashua landmark, the Hunt Memorial Building.

Soon after that Charles Goyette opened an obstetrics and gynecology practice, and his wife demonstrated her flare for public relations. She had her husband paged at Holman Stadium during the Fourth of July celebration. No, a baby was not due to be born; instead, it was her way of getting his name known around town.

Whether or not that was the reason, he went on to deliver thousands of Nashua babies during a 40-year career, and when he retired, to the delight of all his patients his wife threw him a birthday party in Greeley Park and invited the town. Now he gets involved in her projects, whether it's vacuuming the Hunt Memorial or dressing in costume to greet children at the Holiday Stroll finale, a part in the city's magnificent landmark.

For many years, the city has been the beneficiary of Meri Goyette's talents for organizing and promoting events. Soon after her youngest child went off to school, she joined the fledgling Nashua Arts and Science Center, working as a volunteer and a member of the board from 1966 to 1979.

After getting a taste of promoting the art world locally, she reached out to Boston and became an artist's agent, convincing the elegant Meridian Hotel to stage Saturday afternoon salons in its foyer for individual artists. She also managed to sway the Prudential to hold shows, too.

"I had the gutsy energy and I wasn't doing it for myself, so I didn't mind asking for things. People usually came through," she said.

Daughter Meri is continually amazed at her mother's never-ending vitality and creative instincts. "She's a dynamic lady and she's always doing things for other people," she marveled. Twelve grandchildren have now been added to that list of "other people."

Focusing her efforts on Nashua in the '90s, Goyette has played a key role in the revitalization of downtown and the restoration of the Hunt Memorial.

A project she spearheaded was collecting old photos from the attics and albums of long-time Nashuans to be compiled in a book. To do this she has formed the

Hunt Heritage Book Committee and "Nashua: Then and Now'" can be found on many Nashua coffee tables and on the shelf of the Nashua Public Library.

Little wonder that she has earned outstanding citizen awards from the Nashua Exchange Club and the Nashua Foundation.

To keep the momentum rolling well into the 21st century, the indomitable dreamer has a wish list to work on. It includes a home for the performing arts, a classic movie theater, more friends and volunteers for the Hunt Memorial and more benefactors to contribute to its restoration.

Only energetic, civic-minded people need apply.

May 2, 1998

ADELLE LEIBLEIN

Shakespeare, poet extraordinaire, is said to have spoken and written the language of the common folk, but somewhere along the way to the 21st century, poetry-making was relegated to the realm of oblivion.

Nashuan Adelle Leiblein protests and she intends to do something about it.

"Poetry is everywhere . . . and nowhere," she says, watching a squirrel nibble at the bird feeder in her backyard. She should know. She is a poet by profession; an award-winning, much-published poet and creative writing teacher.

Leiblein understands the paradox of poetry in the contemporary world. For most people, reading or writing a sonnet or an ode is removed from the business of everyday life.

"You should get a poem delivered every day with the newspaper," she says. To bring poetry down from the lofty to the more accessible, she is working on a project to print a series of postcards with poetry messages that can be mailed to family and friends. The poetry postcards will be marketed through "The Empress of Hyperbole Press," a Leiblein enterprise, and will feature both Leiblein's works and the poems of other writers and contemporary poets.

"Poetry is as natural as breathing," observes the writer who has even had one of her poems, "Amaryllis," translated into Mandarin.

For Leiblein, writing poetry is neither a hobby nor a pastime. It is a vocation and she finds material for poems everywhere she goes: flea markets, the town dump, the corner grocery store or even trash cans by the side of the road. Ordinary things often trigger special memories. Remembering a dear aunt to whom she was like a daughter, she wrote the poem "Auntie Joan." It relates the older woman's struggle to free herself from the binds of a tight girdle, capturing the eternal agony women endure for the sake of appearance.

"My Aunt stood before me half in and half out of one incredible, rubberized foam, long-leg, Playtex full figure girdle. She couldn't get it on or off."

The poem ends with the young niece helping her aunt to cut off the girdle.

Leiblein writes, "I put the scissors in the drawer where they belonged. I did what any daughter would. I never mentioned it."

Memories intertwine with things Leiblein sees around her. She is continually taking notes, scribbling ideas and thoughts on bits of paper or in a notebook. Sometimes three or four poems will emerge months later from something she sees or smells or hears.

Telegraph Photo Files

Adelle Leiblein

"I think of poetry as my job. I can't wait for inspiration," she says. When faced with writer's block she gives herself an assignment. "I just write. I go down every blind alley."

Sometimes, the free association may not be writing a word but rather drawing a self-portrait.

While living at an artists community in Taos, N.M., on a fellowship she received, she found the unfamiliar surroundings were not conducive to writing, so each day she drew a self-portrait. When she returned to New England, the visual studies of her moods were later translated into poetry.

Leiblein was not born a poet, but she hastens to mention she was born in Worcester, Mass., the home of Stanley Kunitz, the 96-year-old named the country's poet laureate.

Quincy, Mass., is the city where she was raised, in what she identifies as a working-class family. Neither she nor her twin sisters thought much about poetry in their youth, but their father was a wonderful storyteller and their mother, a creative housewife, provided the perfect soil for a poet in the family. Their eldest daughter, Adelle, was the first in her family to go to college, attending the University of Massachusetts in Amherst. She dropped out in her junior year but while working she earned her bachelor's degree nights at UMass Boston, where she discovered her medium for telling stories—poetry.

She continued taking workshops and was accepted in the prestigious creative writing program at Boston University for a master's degree. In the '80s, she met the group of friends and fellow poets who formed the Every Other Thursday Poets (EOTP) to support, encourage and critique each other's work.

"It is one of these serendipitous things," she says of the group's meeting. "We speak the same language. We understand what we go through." They have been meeting for 20 years at each other's homes and under EOTP Press have published several anthologies.

After working full time as an administrator at computer companies for a number of years, Leiblein decided the time had come to be a full-time poet and teacher.

Since poetry is not the road to riches, she is quick to add that her husband, David Tracey, is a "computer genius." He works at Sun Microsystems as the technology liaison with AT&T. He is also her first reader and she relies on his reaction to a first draft.

Married 27 years, the couple came to Nashua in 1988. The house they own is set back from Concord Street in an unexpected woodland. The dining room is decorated with a mural dedicated to poetry, and it is where Leiblein often writes at night. All the classic motifs of poetry adorn the walls, along with ribbons of words by Nobel prize-winning poet Derek Walcott, a former teacher of Leiblein's at Boston University.

The couple has just returned home from a two-year sojourn in Boulder, Colo., a business experience for him and an award-winning one for her. While there, she was named a recipient of an individual artist fellowship in poetry from the state of Colorado.

In spite of the honors, Colorado was a great place to visit but Nashua is home. "We came back with 800 boxes to unpack," says Leiblein, a flea market antique collector.

Not only does Leiblein combine found objects in her home decor, but she fashions jewelry out of bits and pieces with the same flair. A pearl, a snippet of a painting and a piece of metal become a lovely romantic brooch. Whatever objects she chooses to decorate her home, her pins or her poetry, they tell a story.

When the couple and their truckload of boxes returned to Nashua, Leiblein resumed teaching at the Worcester Museum of Art, the DeCordova Museum and the New Hampshire Institute of Art in Manchester, as well as privately in her home. She is also preparing her first book of poetry, "No Ache But Love," for publication. She is even contemplating writing a script for a movie.

"I want to write the great American screenplay—to go Hollywood," she says.

She has developed the story line, given it a title and put it on the list of future projects. Recently named to the board of directors of the Hunt Memorial Building, her appointment augurs well for poetry readings to come in Nashua.

When she returned home, the multi-talented Nashuan was also able to pick up where she left off with the River Rising Poets, a poetry workshop group of nine writers in the Nashua area. In spite of the move, she never had really left the EOTP, checking into meetings by telephone.

Both groups of dedicated poets have been meeting at each other's homes for years. The River Rising Poets also give readings at cafés and bookstores in the area.

"Adelle is one of these people who embraces others and makes them feel good about their work," says Rae Bruce, a retired Merrimack High School English teacher and member of the group.

Near the end of the evening, it is not uncommon to hear Leiblein offer, "Maybe you'll think I'm crazy but," says Bruce, adding her comments are always on target.

"She has a sense of where people are going with their work."

Bruce also studied with Leiblein at the Studio School in Nashua and admires her imaginative approach to teaching, her way of taking unexplored paths to writing poetry.

"She stretches your mind," says Staci Milbouer, another member of the River Rising poets.

Whatever she does, Leiblein aims to get people to see the world more vividly.

"Poetry is a window on the world, a shared humanity," says the Nashua poet.

April 21, 2001

MISS NOVEMBER

Fame finally caught up with Juliette McDonald 50 years after the fact.

In May 1944, soon after joining the Women's Army Corps, the 20-year-old brunette from New Hampshire posed for a recruiting poster.

"I thought, Why me? There were a bunch of beautiful girls on the base, " she says, recalling the day when the commanding officer sent her to the photography studio at Chanute Field in Illinois.

She never saw the results until the winter of 1994.

"I thought it ended up in the wastebasket," she says nonchalantly about the photo.

Last winter she received a newsletter from WIMSA (Women in the Military Service for America) reporting on the plans for the memorial to service women, to be erected at the gateway to Arlington Cemetery. Along with a donation for the project, McDonald sent in her name for the memorial's registry of service women.

While scanning the newsletter, she spotted a picture of a poster. It looked hauntingly familiar.

"That looks like me," she told herself. To confirm her suspicions, she sent for a copy.

"It was worth five bucks to find out."

Together with the poster, WIMSA mailed a calendar used as a fundraiser for the memorial. Illustrating each month is a poster issued in World War II to recruit women to the various branches of the military. She was Miss November.

The vivacious grandmother with the keen sense of humor promptly ordered seven more posters, one for each of her sons. She never told them. She just waited for their reactions.

"I didn't fool one of them. Even my youngest son, Brian, knew right away," she says with a smile.

The eldest, Nashua Police Detective Richard McDonald, agrees. The unexpected parcel delivered to his house last winter never raised a question about identity.

"Gee, that looks like my mom, I thought. I was pretty sure it was her even though she had never mentioned anything about it," he says.

When she posed for the camera in May 1944, she was Juliette Lacoursiere. Dressed in Army khaki, she is shown peering soulfully into the distance. Behind her, lending a wartime drama to the picture, are shadowy figures of soldiers engaged in battle. The inscription at the top of the poster reads "Mine Eyes Have Seen the Glory."

Actually, she remembers two Army blankets as the backdrop. She never heard anything about the photo and never saw the finished poster.

"There were no recruiting offices on the base and I never had any reason to go into one off the base," she says.

Six months before she became poster girl, Julie Lacoursiere was working in a defense plant in Franklin making airplane parts for the war effort. Her goal was to join the Army.

"Everybody was doing it."

She enlisted on Jan. 24, 1944, her 20th birthday. Women had to be two years older than men, who could enlist at 18. After she was trained as a cryptographic technician and Teletype operator, she was assigned to the North Atlantic Division of the Army Airways Communication System.

It was her job to code and decode messages sending planes overseas and bringing them into the fields where she was stationed. The WAC with a penchant for traveling served at Grenier Field in Manchester; at Presque Isle, Maine, and at Goose Bay, Labrador.

When the war ended, she was discharged as a corporal. Returning to New Hampshire, she managed a Sears Roebuck Catalog Store in Manchester and lived in Nashua. Like so many who had served in the war, she joined the James E. Coffey Post of the American Legion. It was there that she met another former Army corporal.

"I saw Mr. McDonald at church and at the Legion and he looked like a nice fellow," she recalls of their early courtship.

Richard McDonald and Julie Lacoursiere were married April 7, 1951, in Franklin. He worked at Sanders and in 1969–70, served as the Coffey Post commander.

"He was a dedicated legionnaire," she says speaking about her late husband. He was made a lifetime member and served as treasurer for many years, she adds.

Raising seven sons was her full-time job and one for which Army training came in handy.

"When you have a lot of kids that close, you have to run a tight ship. I can't stand disorder," she says.

MINE EYES HAVE SEEN THE GLORY

WOMEN'S ARMY CORPS

ARMY   OF   THE   UNITED   STATES

Despite sewing all their suits and shirts, umpping their games and doing all the other things mothers do, she still found time to paint.

She credits her interest in painting to a neighbor, who introduced her to the Nashua Artists Association. Her first show was an annual outdoor exhibit at Greeley Park.

"I brought nine paintings and sold several," she says. Her son built her a studio in their house on Lincoln Avenue and she entered many art shows. For several years she was in charge of the Nashua Artists outdoor show. She still has vivid memories of hanging paintings on the fence at Greeley Park and worrying about the weather.

The exhibit is an annual event at the end of August in Greeley Park but in recent years she has been unable to return to see old friends in Nashua since she now makes her home in Orange, Florida. Six of her seven sons, however, live in the Nashua area, and son Mark lives in Hawaii.

McDonald's Army poster now hangs in the back hallway of her Florida mobile home.

"There is not much wall space," she gives as her excuse for relegating it to an out-of-the-way spot.

It was, after all, just a fleeting moment in a full life.

FIRST HOSPITAL LAB TECHNICIAN

Her life was a testimony to the Yankee principles of thrift and hard work. She walked to work, wore sensible clothing and did her won laundry on a scrub board in the kitchen sink. Unmarried, she lived with her mother and dedicated herself to her family, her church and her job.

Mildred Felker was the first laboratory technician at Nashua Memorial Hospital, the core of her life for more than 40 years. When she died a year ago, at age 96, she bequeathed the hospital the sum of a half-million dollars to be used for the benefit of the laboratory personnel.

"She was a piece of gold. You could not find a better person. She was well-educated. She was unselfish. She did not work for the money. In her later years, she did not need the money but she was attached to the hospital," says Dr. Nicholas Marcopoulos, retired chief of pathology.

The woman he speaks of so fondly was his secretary when he was head of the hospital's first pathology department in the 1950s. It was her last official post at the hospital before she retired at the end of the 1960s.

Felker was born in 1897, when Nashua's city hospital leased the Collins house on Spring Street. It would be several years before the first Memorial Hospital was built on Prospect Street.

She grew up on the family "farm," at 32 Montgomery Ave., the only daughter of the late Alvin and Alice Felker. Her father was a wholesaler of country produce. Felker attended Nashua public schools and graduated from Nashua High School with honors in 1915, and from Simmons College for Women in Boston in 1919, the year women won the right to vote.

She went to work at the Boston Dispensary for Dr. William Hinton, black pathologists know for his research on syphilis. After brief employment with the Mayo Clinic in Rochester, Minn., she returned home to live with her mother when her father died in 1921. While in Nashua, she resumed her association with Hinton, helping him to write a book "Syphilis and Its Treatment," published in 1936.

Throughout the 1920s and '30s, Felker alone presided over the Bunsen burners and test tubes in the tiny basement room in the Nurses' Home across the street from Memorial Hospital. She was the only X-ray technician.

A long working day left little time for anything else. She worked Monday through Friday from 7 A.M. to 7 P.M. with three hours off and was on call from 7 P.M. to 7 A.M. every other night.

Early in the morning on the way to work each day she passed neighbor John P. Sullivan, then city assessor. His daughter, Claire Sullivan Schultz, remembers how her father would chide Felker to buy a car.

"I've got two strong legs, why do I need a car?" was her stock reply, say Schultz. It was always followed by the remark, "My taxes went up 31 cents and I want to know why."

Neighbor Thelma Rolfe remembers the sheets hung out on the line after they were washed by hand on a scrub board in the kitchen sink.

"She could afford a washing machine, but she never had one. She could get along with nothing," observes Rolfe.

Mildred Felker

SNH Medical Center

Yet as frugal as she was with her money, she was generous with her time, says Rolfe. She recalls Felker's Sunday visits to her invalid mother to report on services at the Unitarian Universalist Church.

To all the neighbors, the Felker home was known as a collector's paradise crammed with stacks of correspondence, newspapers, family memorabilia and old books she bought on weekly trips with a cousin to the antique dealers.

"She was not much of a housekeeper but she was interesting to talk to," says Rolfe.

The Felker family regarded cousin Mildred and her squirrel-like habits with awe as well as tenderness.

Patricia Walsh of Pepperell, Mass., whose husband, John, was the executor of Felker's will, calls her "the consummate preservationist."

In a remembrance of the woman she grew to love, Walsh writes, "You felt it was a personal trust to protect all letters, cards, bills, papers, and anything that came through the mail, to preserve them forever.

"Your favorite saying was, 'Well, it has to be here somewhere, for you know I would never throw it away.'"

True to form, on John Walsh's 60th birthday, cousin Mildred presented him with a postcard that his grandmother had sent from Europe in 1931.

In 1985, when Felker moved to the Hunt home, the family farm and many of the family belongings were auctioned off; however, the proud Nashuan took as many of her personal treasures to the nursing home as possible.

Family investments had multiplied over the years to $1 million. About the only recognition she made of her wealth was her failed attempt to refuse Social Security checks. She wrote the government to tell them she did not need the checks but they kept coming.

On June 9, 1993, Felker died at Memorial hospital after a brief illness. She was buried in the Felker family lot in a small cemetery overlooking land along the Merrimack River where her grandfather Felker had his farm.

In her will, she left half of her estate to Memorial Hospital. The other half she bequeathed to the family church and cemetery in Stafford and to her next of kin.

According to Bernard Streeter, then vice president of public affairs and development of Southern New Hampshire Regional Medical Center, a plaque to Felker will be placed in the modern hospital laboratory complex adjacent to the emergency department. The monies from the bequest will be used to buy the latest laboratory equipment.

Without a doubt, the sophisticated apparatus would astonish and delight Mildred Felker.

June 1995

HERB MILLER LOOKS BACK

Come spring Herb Miller will still meet midmorning coffee cronies at Martha's Exchange as he has done for years. But instead of returning to Miller's department store for business as usual, he will head for his new office on Daniel Webster Highway.

The store will be darkened, the shelves emptied and the silver letters above the door—"Meet you at . . . Miller's"—a reminder of the past.

His new working address will be the Saab-Subaru dealership he owns on Daniel Webster Highway, where he plans to set up a small office to pursue business interests. If it is anything like the cramped quarters he occupied for more than 30 years on the second floor of Miller's, the only decorations on the walls will be family photos and plaques representing years of community service. His real office was the store itself.

"Meet you at Miller's," was more than catchy slogan to both customers and the man who originated it. It was the byword of an era when Main Street was the core of community life.

"I don't remember how I thought of it. I probably stole it from somewhere," says Miller, making light of an achievement advertisers would envy. Since he coined it more than 30 years ago, the phrase has become part of the Nashua vernacular, just as the store has been a downtown landmark for nearly three-quarters of a century.

And the boss took the slogan to heart as much as the customers did.

Ask Miller what he will miss most about the store and he says, "People always knew where to find me. If anyone came back to town for a visit, they came to the store."

The returning Nashuans might be here to attend such functions as a NHS reunion Miller helped to organize or the West Pearl Street Reunion. He is one of the few non-Pearl Street residents invited to the Greek get together.

Contrary to what most friends and acquaintances believe, the merchant synonymous with Main Street is not a native Nashuan. He was born in Massachusetts where his father owned a number of "ladies waist" (blouse) stores. Julius Miller started his Nashua store in 1925 on Main Street, where Cardin Jewelers is now located.

In 1931, he moved his family to Concord Street. The Nashua store was the only one to survive the Depression. His oldest child and only son was 10 years old and enrolled in the sixth grade at Mount Pleasant School. Though it often dominated

the dinner conversation, Herb had little to do with the store, even in his Nashua High School days.

"I was too busy playing football, dating, doing all the things the kids do in high school," he says, adding, "In those days if a guy wanted to be real daring, he'd drink a bottle of beer."

In the Tusitala, the 1939 NHS yearbook, under the photo of Herbert Miller is a long list of extra curricular activities including fullback on the football team, tennis, track and business manager of the senior class.

Following the yearbook aphorism, "Reputation is more than money," are these remarks: "Herbie's good disposition makes him one of the most popular boys in his class, liked equally by both girls and boys."

College years at Boston University were interrupted by World War II and Miller joined the Air Force. He piloted B-17s in Europe before returning to finish his senior year at BU.

"His father was thrilled when he received a letter from Herbie saying he wanted to go into the store," recalls longtime Miller employee Evelyn Magee.

"When I was in the service I covered a lot of territory and there was never any question of wanting to come back here," says Miller. He did resist getting back in a plane for many years after the war however.

During the year in which the decorated Air Force Lieutenant finished BU, he met his wife Jean, a student at the Massachusetts College of Pharmacy. They married and returned to Nashua to raise a family of five children. Later she used her medical knowledge to set up the Nashua Memorial Hospital Library.

Although never pressured by his father to join the store, Miller says his return was the determining factor in expanding the business. In 1954 the store moved to

West Pearl Street and in 1968 expanded to the Main Street block. To its bridal department and women's and children's wear, it added a men's shop and a shoe department.

"I learned more from my father than I ever did in college," says Miller.

As a lasting memorial to his parents, he helped to establish the Alice and Julius Miller Building at Temple Beth Abraham in the late 1980s.

The dreams of Julius Miller were carried on by his son, but there was one big difference between the two. At the end of the day, the youngest Miller left the business at the store.

Yet for employees or associates, he was always there and he knew everyone by name, says Magee. Miller characterizes his management style as loose, not making a federal case over mistakes and trusting the sales people to use their judgment in waiting on customers.

"People would come into the store just to schmooze with the girls," he says.

Community work went hand in hand with business. He was the first president of the Heart of Nashua, chairman of the drive to expand the YM and YWCA, and in 1989 was named the Citizen of the Year by the Greater Nashua Chamber of Commerce.

From the 1960s through the early 80s community life revolved around Main Street. There was camaraderie among the merchants and the stores flourished. Miller's Department Store even survived the coming of the malls, says Miller. But when the region's economic bubble burst, the hassles began.

"It wasn't fun anymore," he says.

He talks philosophically about all the established stores throughout New England whose doors have closed in the past few years.

But about Miller's, he says, "I'm getting a lot of sympathy I don't need. It's time. That's the way it is."

February 6, 1993

BELOVED PRIEST

He was the kindly white-haired figure who regularly visited their classroom. He gave the children hugs, teased them if their penmanship was not perfect and always handed out report cards with words of encouragement.

Larger than life in his priestly garb, he never missed an opportunity to quiz them about the differences between Mr. Wright and Mr. Right.

The commanding figure of whom Sister Alida Houde speaks is the Rev. Monsignor Jean-Baptiste-Henri Victor Millette, then pastor of St. Louis de Gonzague Church. With great affection, the 93-year-old Holy Cross nun summons memories of Father Millette and the roll that he played in her student days at St. Louis de Gonzague Elementary School.

"The children loved him. He had a great sense of humor . . . He was like a father to us," recalls Sister Alida. A native Nashuan, she later taught at the school and became its principal after taking her vows.

Father Millette, the prelate regarded as the founder of the first French-Canadian Catholic church in Nashua, left behind more than many fond memories when he died in 1917. His legacy reached far beyond the congregation; it enriched the city.

Among the monuments to his humanitarian concerns were a hospital, an orphanage, and one of the first "safe houses" for single women. When Le Foyer first opened at the turn of the century, it was a place where women could live when they came from Canada to work in the mills.

"He was a man who was always thinking creatively, always attentive to the needs of his people," said the Rev. Roland Cote, pastor of St. Louis de Gonzague when it marked its 125th anniversary.

Generations of Nashuans educated in the three parish schools of St. Louis de Gonzague Church gathered for a once-in-a-lifetime occasion.

The reunion of all those who ever attended St. Louis Elementary School, Sacred Heart Academy for Boys or St. Louis High School for Girls culminated a year of festivities celebrating the anniversary.

Coming from all corners of the country for the reunion, the men and women are living reminders of the lasting influence on the city of one of its most respected and dynamic clergymen.

Though another pastor preceded him briefly, Father Henri Millette is credited with establishing the St. Louis de Gonzague Church in Nashua. The year was 1871, when the young priest from Canada arrived at his second ministerial post in the bustling New Hampshire mill-town. Though the congregation he was to lead met at St. Luke Episcopal Church on Temple Street, land had been purchased to build its own church.

By 1873, Father Millette was conducting services in the congregation's own house of worship. Built on the corner of West Hollis and Vine streets, the handsome brick edifice was dominated by two towers. Inside stained glass windows cast a soft light on a richly decorated sanctuary and its marble altar.

Only two years later the rapidly growing parish spawned another French-Canadian congregation, St Francis Xavier Church north of the Nashua River.

Taking root in the community under the leadership of Father Millette, St. Louis de Gonzague Parish started its own school in 1883 in the basement of the church. Four Sisters of the Holy Cross from Canada were sent to teach classes in both English and French. The school's enrollment soon soared, demanding more teachers and more space. Ultimately a separate facility was built on Chestnut Street.

From the single elementary school emerged two more schools, Sacred Heart Academy for Boys in the upper elementary and junior high years taught by the brothers of the Sacred Heart, and St. Louis High School for Girls.

The schools outlived their founder by many years. Not even a fire interrupted the rhythm of classes for long. When the Academy was destroyed by fire in 1965, it was quickly rebuilt, and the new St. Louis de Gonzague Academy opened in 1967 on Vine Street behind the church.

With declining enrollment in parochial schools and rising costs of education the past few decades, the Girls High School closed in the late '60s, and the other schools were absorbed by the Catholic Regional School District.

Telegraph Photo Files

The Rev. Roland Cote, pastor of St. Louis de Gonzague Church, stands near a portrait of the Rev. Monsignor Henri Millette in the church rectory.

At the turn of the century, however, the outlook was different. Confident that the parish education system was established and its schools flourishing, Father Millette turned to other needs in the parish. In 1901 he bought property on Main Street to convert into an orphanage for 40 children who were left homeless when millwork took its toll on their parents. A year later a new home to house 175 children was built and expanded with the Sisters of Charity, the Grey Nuns, ensuring a caring atmosphere.

Though the children were tutored in the early grades at the orphanage, they went to the parish schools afterward. In keeping with Father Millette's philosophy, they were treated the same as other children, wore the same type of clothes and received the same attention. Thousands of children found a home at the orphanage until it closed in 1963, and many, now parents and grandparents, were at the reunion.

Perhaps Father Millette's greatest legacy to the community was St. Joseph Hospital. Construction of the facility, ultramodern for the time, began in 1906 and was completed in 1908. When it opened, patients were admitted without regard to race or religion, according to Father Millette's wishes.

Of the oft-told tales about Father Millette's dedication to his mission of helping others, many were spun from his daily walks to the hospital while it was under construction. A favorite is about a parishioner who, worried about the priest's health during the cold weather, gave him a horse and buggy. According to legend, says Sister Alida, he sold them both and put the money into the church charity fund, continuing his daily visits on foot.

In an editorial on the dedication of the hospital, the *Nashua Telegraph* called it "the crowning achievement in the career of one of Nashua's most beloved clergymen."

When he died nine years later, his death overshadowed news of World War I in *The Telegraph* that day. The bold headline on the top of page 1 on Feb. 23, 1917, proclaimed to a shocked city. "Msg. Millette Dead."

The subhead filled in the facts: "Nashua's Honored and Venerable Priest Who Observed His Golden Jubilee A Year Ago Died at the Rectory—Conscious to the Last." He had a stroke that morning while saying mass and died that afternoon.

On Feb. 27, the day he was buried, the whole city mourned. Adhering to his wishes there was no eulogy, no grand procession to his burial in the church cemetery, one of the first things that he had secured for the church. A special children's Mass preceded the High Mass of Requiem, with Bishop George Guertin, a native of the parish, officiating.

Almost 80 years later, the Sunday Mass before the reunion was celebrated by priests who received their early education at the parish schools begun by Father Millette.

The church's motto for its milestone year was "I Remember."

"We remember our roots as an immigrant church," said Father Cote, the 12th pastor of the congregation, now encompassing the most recent newcomers to the city, the Vietnamese and Portuguese populations.

Its roots so firmly planted by Father Millette more than125 years ago, allowed the church to flourish, to overcome the tragedy of fire in the summer of 1976, to rebuild and to meet the future.

September 14, 1996

GUARDSMEN RECALL "LONGEST YEAR"

A small red flag bearing the motto "A Bas l'Avion," (Down With the Plane) will herald the honor brigade of a former antiaircraft detachment next Saturday morning in the Veterans Day Parade. With their guidon held high, a part of the contingent will strut along Main Street to City Hall while others will ride a bus behind them.

As badges of identification, all will sport red caps with the same insignia, the emblem of the 197th Coast Artillery (Antiaircraft) Regiment of the New Hampshire National Guard.

The men of the regiment have been designated grand marshals of this year's parade, saluting the soldiers who served in World War II and marking the 50th anniversary of the victory they helped achieve. The guardsmen count the liberation of Bataan and Corregidor among the battles in which they earned their stripes.

Khaki was the color they wore 55 years ago when Nashuans turned out to cheer them on their way Sept. 26, 1940, at 6:40 A.M. Wives, parents and girlfriends huddled misty-eyed on the platform of Union Station. Among the Nashuans waiting to wave goodbye were Lawrence and Gertrude Hodge.

"They walked all the way from Lake Street," recalls their son, Lester, one of the soldiers aboard the train.

This week, Hodge, Warren Rollins, Frederick Larocque, Albert Coffey, Albin Tamulonis and Raymond Kulas met at the James E. Coffey American Legion Post to discuss plans for the parade and, inevitably, to recall old times and what they jokingly call the "longest year" of their lives.

"We were in for a year and were there for five," Kulas said sarcastically. At the time he was working in his father's store, Philbrick's Fish Market.

"I was just married two weeks when I left," quipped Larocque.

"We all thought it was going to be like summer camp at Rye Beach," offered Coffey, whose father, a dentist, was also in the National Guard.

Rollins, Larocque and Kulas served with E Battery; Hodge with Headquarters Service Battery; Tamulonis with the 197th regimental bank and Coffey with the Medical Attachment.

New Hampshire's 197th Coast Artillery was activated by President Franklin D. Roosevelt on Sept. 16, under a national emergency act passed after the Germans invaded Poland.

"One hundred and thirty answered the roll call," said Warren Rollins, historian of the group.

The New Hampshire military detachment was one of the first in the country, organized in 1922 from existing infantry companies. During peacetime it was called into service when the state was threatened by floods, fires or civil disturbances.

Although the U.S. had not yet entered the war in the fall of 1940, Hitler's rampage through Europe provoked the president to mobilize resources at home. The New Hampshire National Guard was one of the first called.

"Gov. Murphy Reviews National Guard," reported *The Telegraph* on the front page Wednesday, Sept. 25. The article also announced the arrival time in Nashua of the four trains departing Concord from early morning to evening for a training mission in Texas.

"Present plans call for a year's training at Camp Hulen," the follow-up article stated the next day.

The unit's official history records a far more intense experience than summer camp duty for the young men, many away from home for the first time.

"The next three months provided as severe a test as ever imposed on citizen soldiers, Mud, snakes, lack of basic equipment, but no lack of guts and determination to make the best possible mess out of a mess," the entry reads.

What they lacked in equipment was offset by the skilled instruction of old guard soldiers such as Sgts. Adrian "Red" Belanger, Mike Patinsky, Stanley Vanderloss and Chester McKuskie, the six ex-guardsmen who met this week at the Coffey Post all agreed.

"None of the other batteries could come anywhere near the record time of field-stripping a machine gun blindfolded as could Chet McKuskie and Roger Grandmaison," Rollins recorded in his historical account.

Conditions improved little in Louisiana, the next assignment, and many of the older instructors were sent home.

"We used two by fours for guns," said Kulas, recalling maneuvers in the hot sun.

"It was like boys playing cowboys and Indians," added Coffey.

Training at MacDill field in Tampa, Fla., reinforced the company's military role to support the troops involved in combat. It was their job to sight the enemy and repulse its forces on land, sea and in the air.

In Florida, a year after they left Concord, the real danger of their duty hit home.

"We all remember what we were doing on Dec. 7, 1941, on a weekend pass in Miami and seeing the sights on a tour bus when we heard the news of Pearl Harbor," Rollins wrote.

When they returned to the base, there were orders to proceed to the New York-New Jersey area. It was their job to set up the first antiaircraft defense of New York City, positioning guns on the rooftops of factories to protect against enemy planes.

"Little did we know this would be the last time for four years we would have a roof over our heads," Rollins said, referring to their barracks quarters. Once overseas, they slept in tents.

In March 1942, the 197th landed in Australia, sailing from San Francisco and surviving a typhoon along the way. They were assigned to the Fremantle-Perth field in the southwestern part of the country, which was thought to be most vulnerable to a Japanese attack. From there they were sent to Iron Range field, a recovery base in the northeastern region closest to New Guinea.

Iron Range Air Field seemed like another world to the men of Battery E. "It rained every day, the food was not very good and the mail was always late. The surrounding jungles were crawling with large snakes, crocodiles, wild boars and all kinds of wild birds that never seem to keep quiet," wrote Rollins.

"He played the trumpet and I had to climb trees to put up communication lines," Kulas chided Tamulonis. During his stay in Australia, the Nashua musician courted and married his wife, Penny, bringing his bride back to Nashua after the war.

In his campaign to recapture the Philippines, Gen. Douglas MacArthur recruited the 197th to join his forces advancing through the Solomons, New Guinea and other islands enroute to the Philippines.

In New Guinea, they learned to eat coconut and bugs and took medications to combat malaria. In October 1944, as they entered Leyte Harbor, Japanese planes attacked and sank many ships before they landed on the beach. Foxholes were their home away from home.

From Subic Bay, they watched the shelling of the road to Manila. "After the liberation of Bataan and Corregidor, there were 40 men left from E Battery," the regiment historian adds. They cleared the way to victory in Luzon and the Philippines.

Yet, life in the South Pacific in the thick of battle was not without its rewards.

"Nights in the South Pacific were beautiful. You could see the Southern Cross in the sky," Rollins wrote.

The "longest year" of service ended with V-J Day, and the men of the 197th returned home, a few at a time rather than as a unit.

The 197th Regiment was disbanded after World War II, but New Hampshire still supports units of the National Guard. They have served in Korea, Vietnam and the Persian Gulf—later wars in which the N.H. National Guard served.

Although the regiment is gone, its theme song lives on. As the veterans march in the parade, they will step to the tune of "A Bas l'Avion," written by Warrant Officer Irving Pelletier of Nashua, leader of the 197th Coast Artillery Band.

November 11, 1995

INSTRUCTOR OF OLD SCHOOL

In the Nashua of not so long ago, teachers earned $1,800 a year and had no benefits, and females had to resign when they married. That clause was in the teachers contract well into the 1950s.

Yet the school system was a fine one in which to teach, according to Mabel Noyes, both a product of Nashua schools and an English teacher at Nashua High School for several decades.

"I never earned what a beginning salary is now," she said without rancor. In fact, when she began teaching here in the '30s she took a cut of $500 in her yearly salary of $2,300 in Acton, Mass.

"I felt poor, even though I lived at home," she said with a smile. Her father had retired as superintendent of schools and no longer hired teachers, so she could come home to teach. "We didn't believe in nepotism," she says, referring to her early career elsewhere.

Mabel Noyes, wearing a red paisley skirt and bright green blouse, sat in the wheelchair in her room at the Hunt Community, where she has resided for three years. The room is decorated with furniture from her family home, "25 Auburn St.," and paintings she has gathered from trips to just about every corner of the earth. Retired for almost 20 years, she still relished a conversation about teaching. Speaking with animation, her words skip from colleagues to classes at Nashua High School, from her high-school and college days to comparisons to today.

"Martha Cramer was head of the English department. She was one of the best minds I've ever known. Anne McQueeney and the Lord sisters were colleagues.

"We taught the standards, Scott and Shakespeare, but we always had up-to-date material, modern novels like 'Cry the Beloved Country.'"

She was pleased that she taught high school at Elm Street rather than at the new facility.

"It has rooms that don't have doors. I like to close doors."

Returning to her student days at Nashua High School—then on Temple Street—she said, "We were not trying to educate everyone in those days but we did a good job with those whom we did." Nashua High graduates went on to good colleges or to good jobs in banks and offices.

She graduated in 1919, receiving the Noyes Prize awarded to outstanding students in English. Her father, who presented it to her in his capacity as superintendent, explained that it was given in the memory of Colonel Leonard Noyes, no relation, who fought in the Civil War. She donated her gold medal a few years ago to the Nashua Historical Society.

From Nashua High School she went on to Wellesley College.

"I took it for granted that I would go on to college," she says. "All my friends did."

Her brother's tuition at Dartmouth together with hers at Wellesley "was more than my father earned in a year. It took quite a lot to send a child to college in those days."

She managed with a small scholarship, help from her parents and an uncle and summer jobs to pay the tuition.

"I waited on tables and lived in the self-help dorm, not the ones that had maids," she recalls of the campus days.

She remembered as if it were yesterday the thrill of traveling on the train to Boston from Amherst to see plays and ballets with such stars as Anna Pavlova for 65 cents a ticket.

When she began teaching, a career she says she would choose again, she rejected private school.

"I always wanted to teach in a public school because I did not want a select group that was privileged. My own experience was in public schools."

Nashua schools had many first-generation students whose parents had come here to work in the mills. Nashua excelled in educating students who spoke English as a second language. Many went on to college, noted the educator who also holds a master's degree in English from Harvard University.

Writing was another sphere of concentration in the high school, said Miss Noyes. Former students such as Vito Stoncius remember her daily 20-minute writing exercise. She would give a topic and in return expect a clearly written, page-long paragraph.

"She set high standards, but she prepared us very well for college," says Stoncius, a history teacher at Fairgrounds Junior High School. Awkward sentences would be put on the board and analyzed the next day.

Miss Noyes, who ended her teaching career at the age of 70 in Hamilton, Mass., distills her philosophy of education with the same clarity she demanded from her students.

She made certain that her students knew "enough about grammar not to make egregious mistakes; enough about writing to sound literate; and enough about literature to determine whether they've read a good book (one of lasting value) or a time waster."

"Students don't remember most of the things you've taught them but most know if they've had a good teacher," she added.

And she, said Stoncius, was the best.

January 20, 1989

NURSES SHEA AND KILL KELLY

It was a story from the past she relished repeating. For a month, she had to endure the most embarrassing punishment of all. She was not allowed to wear her white cap on the hospital floor. For a nurse, the starched white cap was a badge of professionalism to be worn with pride.

Agnes Kill Kelly smiled recalling that day in May 1930, the same day as the Crown Hill fire, when she graduated from St. Joseph Hospital School of Nursing. Without telling her supervisor, she went off with a friend to see the fire and consequently she had to work for a month sans cap.

Savoring the memory like vintage wine, Kill Kelly related the incident to friend Margaret Leola Shea during one of their frequent chats in the living room of the Mary Sweeney Home.

"We call each other on the phone every day and talk for half an hour," Shea observes.

Nothing pleases the two longtime Nashua residents more than reminiscing about their nursing careers. Both women recently celebrated their 90th birthdays at the Mary Sweeney Home, the retirement home where they live. Since both started their nursing careers in Nashua during the Depression years, they share a wealth of memories. Their careers also took similar paths, for both became nurses in industry when that was a relatively new field.

Kill Kelly, then Agnes Davin of Manchester, graduated from St. Joseph in 1930, the same year Margaret Leola Hurley of Wilton entered the Memorial Hospital School of Nursing. Her middle name was so unusual it became part of how she was known.

It was an era when student nurses at both hospitals got hands-on training as floor nurses under the watchful eye of a supervisor. At St. Joseph Hospital it was always a nun.

Patients frequently hired a private duty nurse to care for them since hospital stays were lengthy. Both Kill Kelly and Shea worked as private duty nurses in the early years of their careers, as did most nurses of the time.

In 1938, Kill Kelley worked for a year as hospital supervisor in Haverhill, Mass., and Shea was the night supervisor at Memorial Hospital for six years after graduation from nursing school, and then she became the day supervisor in the emergency surgical ward for four years. Memorial, now Southern New Hampshire Medical Center, was then a small brick building on the corner of Prospect and Tyler streets.

Since there was no doctor on duty at night, one had to be called at home in an emergency. A critical accident or mother about to give birth brought the doctor to the hospital immediately, since all lived nearby.

A regular birth meant two weeks in the hospital, with the baby tucked away in the nursery most of the time. Of course, dads never got near the delivery room.

"If you had your appendix out it was a big deal," says Shea, "And for a gall bladder you went to Boston or had a Boston doctor come here."

"You were in at least 10 days and if you had your appendix out you didn't put your foot on the floor for days. For a gall bladder you stayed a month and didn't get off the bed for two weeks," adds Kill Kelly. Instead of the up-the-next day philosophy, patients were eased gently into mobility, first dangling their feet over the edge of the bed, then sitting in a chair before attempting to walk.

A long hospital recuperation did not send people to the poor house, however. According to the two women, a good private room cost $1.50 a night, a more luxurious room, $3, and a bed in the ward, $1.

MRIs, CAT scans and other medical miracles to come were unheard of. The newest initials in the medical lexicon were IV. Before that, fluids were given to patients through a catheter in the groin.

"The first time they gave a blood transfusion, everybody ran to see it," recalls Shea.

When fractures were involved, patients would be surrounded with sandbags to keep them immobile while they mended. Oxygen was administered through a tent covering the patient's bed. A nurse trained at Massachusetts General Hospital was called in to do it.

"It had never been done at St. Joe's," notes Kill Kelly.

Just as the patient of yesterday would be astonished by the hospital procedures of today, so would the medical staff charged with their care. While nurses today shoulder much of the responsibility for daily care, in the '30s the doctor had to be consulted for every move.

"Doctors took blood pressure until late in the '30s when they decided nurses were smart enough to do it," says Kill Kelly.

"The Doctor was God," adds Shea. "You couldn't give any medications until the doctor signed the book."

As much as they applaud the nurses of today, the two women miss the professional look of the crisp white uniforms with starched collars and caps. The upkeep was expensive but it was worth it.

"It cost 20 cents a cap and the Chinese laundry on West Pearl Street was the only one in town that did it," says Kill Kelly.

When they married, both nurses hung up their caps temporarily, though during World War II they were recruited by the Red Cross, the schools or hospitals as many single nurses joined the service. Until World War II, when the rules changed, nurses who married were not hired on hospital staffs.

Agnes Davin married Nashua attorney Leonard Kill Kelly in 1941 and they had one daughter and three sons. Her husband died in 1957, leaving her to raise four children, ages 8 to 13.

To support them she returned to work four years later as the nurse at J.F. Elwain, a position she held for 14 years.

Margaret Hurley wed Bartholomew Shea in 1939 and had one son.

She too became an industrial nurse in the early '40s working at Doehla Greeting Cards for 23 years, before retiring in 1974. In 1975, after her husband died, she returned to nursing at the Hunt Community, a job she held for eight years.

"I always kept going," says Shea.

As industrial nurses, they were on the cutting edge of a field that would grow increasingly important after the mills closed and high-tech companies took over.

"Today they are called occupational health nurses," says Shea, indicating how much more emphasis has been given the job today.

In the mill years, though, much of their work was routine: treating headaches, stomach aches and bandaging bruises.

But the company nurses were also on the front lines if an accident occurred. They often had to deal with such things as a hand caught in a machine, a back injured by lifting or a worker overcome by fumes. Issues of worker's compensation became an increasingly important part of their jobs. At the same time, they were the friend, the mother figure, whom fellow workers appreciated and remembered.

"I couldn't believe how many called or showed up at the birthday party," says Kathryn Shea, wife of Shea's son, Paul.

At 90, both women still keep up on the latest medical advances through newspapers and magazines. Thankfully, neither have been patients in the hospital in recent years.

What Kathryn Shea says of her mother-in-law applies to them both:

"She is just a nurse. It is still a part of her. It will always be a part of her."

August 7, 1999

PAT MANDRAVELIS

Vintage Nashuans wax nostalgic when they speak of Memorial Hospital, and they stumble with resentment over the no-longer new name, Southern New Hampshire Medical Center. "Ridiculous," "a mouthful," "too wordy" are the typical criticisms.

Patricia Mandravelis is the exception. For more than 35 years she has played a major role in the hospital's development, yet she whole-heartedly endorses the new identity.

"There has been a tremendous change in medical care and the hospital has always kept up. Memorial is a throwback to the old days. We are still community oriented, but Southern New Hampshire Medical Center sounds like what we are doing behind the scenes—very advanced technology," she says.

If anyone is qualified to assess the evolution of Memorial Hospital to SNHMC, it is Mandravelis. She is the consummate insider, rising from nursing student through the ranks of nursing to the top administrative offices in her long association with the hospital. It is the only place she has ever worked and she has cared for hundreds of patients on the day shift and night shift—patients in the emergency department, the maternity ward, the endoscopy unit. She has set hospital policy in her role as a supervisor and later as vice president in charge of nursing. In May, she retired as vice president of Community Health and Wellness, overseeing community health programs and serving as the hospital's link to the community. Through the years, she has seen a lot of change in the medical field and personally has instituted many of those changes. Nonetheless, she has remained consistent in her straight forward approach to all who worked with her.

"I can remember her as a student here. Pat always stood up for what she thought was right—and in no uncertain terms," says Dr. Sydney Curelop, who started practicing at the hospital in the '50s and later became chief of staff.

Candid about her candor, Mandravelis responds, "I told it like it was. You always knew where you stood with me." From student nursing days to retirement, she refused to waver in her convictions. Patricia Bartis Mandravelis' family roots run deep in Nashua. One of her uncles was a dentist, another owned the Rosebud, the ice cream parlor and restaurant that was a gathering spot on Main Street. She grew up on French Hill and attended the Crowley Street School, Mount Pleasant School and Spring Street Junior High School. When her family moved to Connecticut, she came up to spend summers at her grandmother's house on the corner of Main Street.

"Her basement is where the emergency ward is today," Mandravelis reminisces. "If anyone has not strayed far from her roots, it's me," she adds in jest.

After she graduated from high school in Connecticut, she returned to Nashua to attend Memorial Hospital School of Nursing. "Nursing was one of the few careers open to women," Mandravelis says. Early in life, she developed the nurturing instincts she needed. "As the oldest of five girls, I had plenty of experience," she observes.

In starched white cap and uniform, Patricia Bartis graduated from Memorial Hospital School of Nursing in 1959. It was the same year she married Nashuan Anthony Mandravelis, and was hired by the hospital for its nursing staff.

In the late '50s, the city's doctors practiced at both Memorial and St. Joseph hospitals, and specialists were beginning to fill the ranks. Today, Mandravelis notes, each hospital has its own medical staff, but specialists continue to work in both.

Two years after she joined the nursing staff, the hospital rules called for her to resign when she was in the seventh month of her pregnancy.

Today the rules are quite different: A nurse can work until the day she gives birth. The Mandravelis' son Michael was born in 1961 in the original brick building on Prospect Street, and after he was a few months old, the young mother was rehired as a nurse.

"There was no such thing as maternity leave in those days," observes Mandravelis.

Daughter Tracy was born in the new maternity wing in 1965 and the mother of two took off a few years from work, the only interruption in her 37 years with the hospital. During her hiatus, she continued to work at home, keeping the books for two doctors and for her husband's hair salon business. In 1969, she returned to the hospital as a nurse in the maternity ward, and with the opening of a new unit in endoscopy, Mandravelis signed on as the only nurse in the unit working with Dr. Nasory Stefan. The following year they were joined by Dr. David Golden, a new physician in town. "Pat did it all. She admitted the patients, took care of them and discharged them. She also had to keep the doctors happy—not always an easy thing to do," says Dr. Golden, a gastroentologist.

Pat Mandravelis

SNH Medical Center

When she became an assistant nursing supervisor a couple years later, and then supervisor, her skill in defusing a situation and calming doctors' concerns came to the fore. "No matter what it was, I used to say I'll take care of it," she recalls. It worked, for she did as she said, to the satisfaction of both doctors and nurses. "Pat knew every nurse between Manchester and Massachusetts. She was a good leader," says Dr. Curelop.

"She knew everybody in the hospital by name. She had a great following," recalls Karen Slawsby Stone, then the public relations director. At the nurses station, Stone often ate her lunch with Mandravelis because "we had a blast."

The hospital recognized her people skills, too, and, in 1980, Mandravelis was named director of nursing and later vice president of nursing.

During her nursing career, she continued her education, earning her bachelor's degree from New England College, and in 1990, a master's degree in business administration from New Hampshire College. Throughout her career, Mandravelis was never timid about making changes during her watch as supervisor and director. Caps were shelved, and starched uniforms and white stockings were replaced by comfortable pants and tops.

It took her a while to trade her professional nurse's attire for a business suit, but she did eventually after becoming the representative of the hospital in community affairs in the 1990s. Uniforms were the least of the changes. Under Mandravelis' supervision, nurses were given increasing responsibilities. She gave the head nurses more autonomy in making decisions and in planning their budgets. At the same time, she made them more accountable for those decisions. It was a new era. Nurses

SNH Medical Center

Memorial Hospital

were no longer without authority. Previously they had to get permission from the supervisor—even to call a physician.

When asked if nurses are better educated today than they were in the past, Mandravelis concedes they are more highly trained in technology and in specialty areas. But the bottom line of the profession is still compassion, especially in today's more mobile society, where relatives are not often not nearby to offer support while a patient is in the hospital.

While technical procedures have multiplied and the scope of the hospital has expanded, she notes, the number of beds in the hospital, 180, has remained the same since the 1980s due to shorter stays and outpatient care.

"Years ago, open-heart surgery was scary and now it is routine. Colonoscopy is not what it used to be, either," she marvels. Short stays and outpatient treatment has changed the care of patients for better and for worse. Longer stays permitted nurses to spot conditions—such as postpartum depression—at the onset. "Are we a healthier nation, today?" she asks and quickly responds, "I don't think so."

Yes, children are more involved in sports, she continues, but today it is organized sports. Kids played pick-up games in their own back yards and instead of exercise clubs, people walked more rather than depending on cars.

Without reservation, however, she adds, "We're lucky Nashua has two good hospitals."

Although she will no longer be paged in the SNHMC hallways, Mandravelis intends to maintain her ties with community organizations such as the Rape and Assault Support Services Committee and the United Way.

Always positive about change, she takes delight in the time she now has—time to spend at the family summer home in York, Maine, time to play with her grandson and, simply, "time to smell the roses."

July 29, 2000

CLOSE-UP SHOT AT HISTORY

Few people get a close-up shot at history in the making. Mike Shalhoup can claim that distinction many times over. Leaning on nothing more high-tech than the telephone and a large-format Graflex camera, he has recorded the tragedies and triumphs of Nashua in the 20th century.

Harry Truman and daughter Margaret waving from a train in Union Station in 1952 as they campaigned for Adlai Stevenson for president; John F. Kennedy mobbed on Main Street in 1960 as he launched his campaign for president; fire engulfing the Armory on Canal Street in 1957; the pileup of the Montreal Red Eye in 1954 when it jumped the railroad tracks at Union Station. The whole country saw that photo—it appeared on the front page of The New York Times. Nashuans have been with him at the scene of the city's excitement thanks to his gripping photographs of fires, murders, natural catastrophes, visits of presidential candidates and sports celebrities.

As a *Telegraph* photographer, sports editor and managing editor, Shalhoup has captured city history as it happened for the daily pages of the newspaper. And now future generations as well will be able to witness the drama of their city as it played out in the latter half of the 20th century.

Shalhoup has donated the body of his work to the Nashua Historical Society to inaugurate MAPP (Millennium Photo Archive Program). With its professional know-how, the society will organize, preserve and file his photos for posterity. From the Shalhoup collection the society aims to build an index of 20th-century photos contributed by the people who lived here. It will be readily available to all.

Shalhoup has been sitting on his goldmine of photos since he retired in 1985.

A few years before, when *The Telegraph* moved from Main Street to Hudson, he had rescued them from the trash heap. "I dug into the pile like a pack rat. I salvaged what I could," he recalls, watching with dismay the newspaper's photo files being discarded during the relocation process. Hundreds of the photos were his.

Shalhoup came to the *Nashua Telegraph* as a photographer and sports reporter in 1952. He and his wife, Barbara, still reside in the same house they bought at the time, the house where they raised their two children, Dean and Karen.

Born in Sanford, Maine, Shalhoup began his 60-year career as a newsman on the Sanford Times after graduating from high school. He was a proofreader, sports editor and photographer on the town weekly. To improve his photography skills the publisher suggested sending him to a YMCA camp offering a course in how to use the camera.

Telegraph Photo Files

Mike Shalhoup

"It was the only schooling I've had. The rest was trial and error," he says with a smile. Zazu Pitts, the movie star, was the first of many celebrities he was to shoot in his long career.

The only interruption in his newspaper career was a tour of Army duty in Europe during World War II. Shalhoup came to *The Telegraph* at the urging of Albert Spendlove, publisher of *The Telegraph* and a former Sanford resident. " At *The Telegraph*. I bounced around from desk to desk," says the veteran *Telegraph* newsman. But whether regional editor, city editor or managing editor, his camera was always at hand. "I never had a scanner—I couldn't afford it. Today, photographers have a lot of high-tech stuff. I just had the telephone." And next to the phone, he had a long list of contacts from police and fire chiefs to dog catcher. They would also call to alert him to picture possibilities. Whether it was the Gagnon murder, suspected to be a Mafia job; a fire on Main Street or a hometown visit by baseball great Birdie Tebbetts, Shalhoup was there. Returning from the assignment, he also did his own photo engraving.

"The train wreck is one I'm most proud of," says the self-trained photographer of the local catastrophe in which one person was killed and a number were injured. Through the Associated Press wire, his photo appeared the next day in papers around the country, including The New York Times. At the time, there were no computers, so he had to ship the film to the Boston AP office by bus. "I've covered a lot of disasters but that's No. 1," says Shalhoup.

What is his reaction when he walks into a fire or a train wreck? "I don't think," he observes. "I say this is great picture possibility. I survey the land and pick the best vantage point." He has been known to hang from a rooftop to get a good shot, but one of the scariest assignments, he will tell you, is the time he climbed the circular staircase in the Hunt Memorial Building to get a sweeping view of Main Street. When it was the library, the tower of the building housed books and he marvels that the librarians bravely ascended it daily.

Disasters, however, were not a daily diet and more ordinary happenings called for more imaginative treatment. When the city installed new meters on Main Street, Shalhoup placed a man's fedora between the twin meters to achieve an eye-catching composition. His photos of high school sports earned him a special award in 1993 from the NHS Athletic Hall of Fame.

With a photographer's eye he also spotted scenic shots for interesting, artistic pictures in the newspaper. One winter's day on the way to work he was struck by the sight of an unusual snowdrift landscape created by a blustery wind. On another day, it was the arresting sight of an apple orchard in Hollis.

And of course holidays had to be observed with a picture in the paper. One photo of son Dean posed next to a pumpkin lantern was good for a smile on Halloween. Both were equally toothless.

It was inevitable that younger Shalhoup would follow in his father's footsteps as a *Telegraph* photographer. When he received calls at home, his father would often take him along on assignments. "I carried his equipment so I could get close to the fire or whatever," recalls Dean, who started working full time at *The Telegraph* after he graduated from Nashua High School.

Mike Shalhoup

Only Nashua's oldtimers will remember this train wreck at Nashua's Union Station in November 1954, but this photograph of the extent of the damage, taken by Michael Shalhoup, will live on forever with the Nashua Historical Society. The photo appeared nationwide, thanks to the Associated Press, most notably in The New York Times, on Nov. 13, 1954.

"He never really told me what to do. I learned by watching him," says Dean, whose career at *The Telegraph* has almost equaled his father's in years.

The elder Shalhoup, now 81, had begun thinking about the historic value of his collection. Several of his pictures are featured in the Hunt Memorial Building book of photos, "Nashua in Time and Place." When he received a letter from the Nashua Historical Society about MAPP, he knew he had found the place where the collection would receive TLC. "I was becoming a little concerned about what was going to happen to the stuff. Now I've found a good home," he says.

Frank Mooney, a member of the Historical Society, notes, "This is only the second collection of Nashua photos. The first is Frank Ingalls, and they are mostly glass negatives." Mooney and Donald Pickering, also a member of the Historical Society, are serving on the MAPP committee. Helping with the project are RISE (Rivier College Institute of Senior Education) volunteers recruited by Cal Knickerbocker, originator of the project. "Just getting Mike's collection makes it really worthwhile," says Knickerbocker.

At a recent meeting in the Speare building to discuss the progress made in cataloguing the photos were Shalhoup, Mooney, Pickering, Beth McCarthy, curator, and Jodi Lowery-Tilbury, the society's new geneaologist, who is in charge of the project.

During the conversation about old Nashua houses, Shalhoup mentioned a Saturday series he had done for the paper. "Both the exteriors and interiors. Would you like to see them?" he asked. The response was immediate. The committee was elated. The photos will be included in MAPP.

The priceless value of a photographic history of Nashua will soon be at hand and the community at large will be able to see it, too. An exhibit of the Shalhoup photos is planned for late spring or early summer, once the photos are preserved and catalogued. The title of the exhibit has already been decided. It will be one familiar to many Nashuans: the credit line, "Mike Shalhoup photos courtesy of *The Telegraph*."

January 20, 2001

PRESERVING THE PAST

Five days a week, Linda Willett lives in the past and she loves it. From 5:30 A.M., when she leaves Nashua for Boston, her thoughts dwell on oak beams, cooper nails, iron hinges and slate roof tiles—the raw materials of history. All day she works with contractors, carpenters, painters, masons and other building craftsmen as knowledgeable about the past as she is.

From the bids to the budget, she juggles all the intricacies of restoring priceless landmarks.

Willett wears the heavy title of curator of buildings for the Society for Preservation of New England Antiquities with the astonished enthusiasm of a lottery winner. She is responsible for the care, the maintenance and the documentation of 33 house museums and 10 other historic New England properties from Connecticut to Maine. The houses sweep the pages of history from the Pierce House, circa 1652, in Dorchester, Mass., to the contemporary Walter Gropius House, built in Lincoln, Mass., in 1937.

"I have a bunch of architects looking over my shoulder," says the bemused curator, undaunted by the challenge of supervising work on the home of the high priest of 20th century architecture. Next month she will speak about the restoration of the Gropius house to a builder's convention sponsored by the Boston Society of Architects.

Tracing the path of her own career from Nashua to the SPNEA never ceases to amaze her.

"What I do really grows out of living in the Haunt," says the native Nashuan.

The 1740 center chimney saltbox on Davis Court has been her home since 1968. She and husband Henry Willett moved into the fabled Deacon Cummings House as newlyweds, and despite its ghostly reputation raised their three children there.

Remembering the day in 1981 when the alderman, later the mayor, called at her home and sparked her fascination for old houses, she says, "Jim Donchess walked up to my front door and asked me if I'd be on the Nashua Historic District Commission." She accepted the volunteer appointment and, as the pundits say, the rest is history.

The civic-minded homemaker was elected secretary of the newly organized commission dedicated to preserving Nashua's past, and during her three-year tenure, served as project director for the cultural resource committee. With the help of Brian Pfeiffer, the Boston architectural historian who is her boss today, she directed the survey of the 256 buildings from Greeley Park to City Hall, ultimately defining the city's National Historic District on Concord Street.

Three buildings had previously been named to the National Historic Registry. They are the Abbot Spalding House at Abbott Square, the Stark House on Concord Street, and the Hunt Memorial Building at the crest of Main Street. That building would later benefit directly from her expertise.

"I'm very New Hampshire, but I see these buildings from a perspective of philosophy, art history, and sociology," she observes.

Nashua had always been the center of Willett's world. The oldest of three sisters, affectionately know as the "Gibson Girls," and two brothers, she graduated from Nashua High School in 1965.

After high school she managed the office of Dr. Marion Fairfield, obstetrician and pediatrician. In addition to a full-time job, she traveled each day to Durham to take classes at UNH. She majored in philosophy, a broad study providing the perfect springboard for her multifaceted career today.

In 1974, she earned her bachelor's degree. It was a year she will always remember, because Dr. Fairfield, one of Nashua's first female physicians, died before Willett received her degree. She was then in her last months of pregnancy and Dr. Fairfield was scheduled to deliver the first Willett child.

"It was to be her last delivery. She was a good friend and I learned a lot from her," Willett says wistfully.

Until Donchess knocked on her door, she was a stay-at-home mother. Son Colin, daughter Meg Elizabeth and son Jack rounded out the family. Husband Henry is a mail carrier in Hollis with a penchant for antique cars.

For Willett, the Historic District was the stepping stone to a brief, frustrating foray into politics and a more fulfilling career. To ensure better zoning laws she ran for the Board of Aldermen from Ward 3 in 1983 and served two terms, serving as chairman of both the Planning and Economic Development Committee and the Elementary School Coordinating Committee. The renovation of Mount Pleasant School was the project of the hour.

"I think it was the best thing I ever did," she says, adding that her own children were among those who benefited since they attended the school. Her bid for Alderman at Large in 1987, however, failed.

In 1989, when an opening occurred on the SPNEA, Pfeiffer remembered her thorough efforts directing the Nashua Historic Commission's survey. In addition, she had on her resume the job as a Northeast field representative for the National Trust for Historic Preservation. Her credentials also included assisting Inherit NH, the statewide preservation organization, with its education program. She also served as the chairwoman of its board of directors as a member of the board of WEVO, NH Public Radio.

To Willett, the offer of the position of SPNEA Stewardship manager was a dream come true. It was her job to monitor the condition of properties protected by preservation restrictions and to prepare related historic documentation. A year later she was tapped for amore responsible job, and in November 1994, she assumed her present post, SPNEA's curator of buildings.

Who better to serve on the newly organized restoration committee when, during the Wagner Administration, the city decided not to sell the Hunt Memorial Building? She was also a natural choice for chairwoman in the committee's infancy. Since 1993, she has contributed many hours and much professional know-how to the city's efforts to restore the prominent building designed by Ralph Adams Cram.

"It's Nashua's Web Page," she says. "The Hunt Building is a window on the world of art, history, architecture, politics and social values of the times. It is like getting in touch with the ideas of 1903," she continues.

Mayor Donald Davidson endowed the committee with a more permanent status naming a board of trustees headed by Meri Goyette. Despite a full workweek, Willett still lends her expertise as chairwoman of the building committee and treasurer. She is as much a stickler for authenticity in her volunteer efforts as she is in her work for SPNEA.

"In the main reading room, there are two coats of plaster, not dura-board or sheet rock," she is pleased to point out as a major victory. To duplicate the reading rooms' windows, which had begun leaking, she recommended a company of craftsmen in Vermont specializing in milling the proper panes of the period. The windows were replaced this summer.

Surveying the new windows in the worm oak-paneled reading room, she offers, "It's inviting to be in." Of the building itself, she observes, "It's beautifully designed, beautifully crafted, and it's public."

Linda Willett served two terms on the Board of Alderman.

Telegraph Photo Files

McQuestin House, built in 1887, located at 51 Concord Street. It is one of the grand homes in the historic district, and now the home of the Wilbert family.

And the woman who launched her career from the study of Nashua landmarks intends to see that the city's most precious architectural jewel gets the tender loving care it deserves.

September 6, 1997

STRAWBERY BANKE PRESERVES FAMILY'S ROOTS

They were the Pilgrims of the early 20th century, wending their way to America in search of a more secure life. To enjoy the fruits of the promised land, they labored and saved to bring loved ones from across the seas and from Canada.

This is an American story celebrated on Independence Day.

Instead of fireworks, the rollicking music of a klezmer band sounded the theme for the Fourth of July festivities yesterday at the Strawbery Banke museum in Portsmouth. Among the host of people celebrating the holiday in the historic Puddle Dock neighborhood were Nashua attorney Leonard Shapiro, his wife Charlotte, their three daughters, four grandchildren and many relatives.

And Shapiro was the name being honored that day, since the Fourth of July marked the official opening of the 10th restoration project at Strawbery Banke: the house where the family's roots were planted in this country. A tribute to the immigrant experience, Abraham Shapiro's modest two-story home, with an attic room for two boarders, represents a page of history from the early 20th century.

It takes its place amid the homes of earlier eras documenting daily life in America from Colonial days. The sprawling outdoor museum overlooks the Portsmouth Harbor, the commercial engine of the city through the centuries.

"It's pretty cool," said 13-year-old grandson Ben Drouin, looking at a family picture in front of the house. One of the young people in the picture is his great-grandfather, Maurice Shapiro, shown at about the same age as Ben. His brother Matt, age 10, had just visited Strawbery Banke with his fourth-grade class at Birch Hill Elementary School before the house was open. On the return visit yesterday he could walk through the rooms and see how the family lived many years ago.

The American story of the Shapiro family begins with Shepsel Millhandler, the eldest in the family. He came to this country at the turn of the century of Annapola, Russia, to escape a 25-year army hitch ordered by the czar for all young Jews.

Hearing about the family history, granddaughter Becky Dedousis, 7, said it reminded her of "Fiddler on the Roof," the musical which takes place in the same area of Russia.

Shepsel left a wife and small child behind, making his way first to Germany then to England, where he worked for a man named Shapiro. With the money he saved in England, he purchased a ticket to America and, out of gratitude, he adopted the Shapiro name, passing it on to his four brothers, whom he brought to America.

Mr. and Mrs. Maurice Shapiro who ran Shapiro's Drugstore on Main Street.

When they went through Ellis Island, they all wore a tag inscribed Shapiro to identify the person who was their sponsor. As was common among immigrants, Shepsel sent money for his wife's family to emigrate as well as his own.

Though Shepsel originally settled in the Boston area, he visited Portsmouth and decided the small prosperous New Hampshire town was the place to start a business as a junk dealer and to raise his family. He bought a house in Puddle Dock and took in boarders to help pay the way. His brother Abraham joined him in Portsmouth and married the sister of Shepsel's wife in 1905. History records that is was the first Jewish wedding in Portsmouth.

For a while the two families lived together until Abraham's family moved to Jefferson Street. It is Abraham's house that has been restored in Strawbery Banke.

In the 1920s the Puddle Dock neighborhood, where all the Shapiro's lived, was a true melting pot of immigrants from many lands. The 600 residents came from Canada, England, Ireland, Scotland, Germany, Italy, Russia and Poland. Puddle Dock was the Shapiro Family's starting point. From there later generations ventured forth.

The Nashua connection begins with brother Simon. He had his own home on Jefferson Street with his wife and four children, too.

His son Maurice was educated in the Portsmouth Schools and like the rest of the Shapiro offspring left the junk business behind to pursue another career.

Maurice studied to be a pharmacist at the Massachusetts College of Pharmacy. There he met another student, who was to become his wife. He and Hannah Goodman of Nashua were married here in 1923 and opened Shapiro's drugstore, a landmark on the corner of Hollis and Main Street from 1923 to 1965.

Their two sons, Leonard and Sumner worked in the store and graduated from Nashua High School.

In the more recent chapters of the American Story, both of the young Nashua Shapiro's were accepted at U.S. military academies, Sumner graduating from Annapolis in 1949 and Leonard from West Point in 1951. Leonard also earned a law degree from Boston University and Sumner, now a retired admiral, rose to director of naval intelligence.

Both brought their families to Puddle Dock yesterday for the dedication of the Shapiro house. Laurie Shapiro, Leonard and Charlotte's daughter, traveled from Sierra Vista, Ariz., to join her parents, her two sisters, Margery Droin and Barbara Dedousis, and their families. Retired Admiral Sumner Shapiro and his wife Jimmy, traveled from Washington, D.C. , and their son, Dr. Stephen Shapiro and his family from York, Penn.

"You'd still be in Russia, if it wasn't for your great-great-great uncle Shepsel," Leonard said to his grandchildren.

"It's exciting to fill in the pieces of the family history," and Barbara Dedousis, one of the fourth generation of Shapiro's in America.

The Fourth of July festivities at Strawbery Banke celebrated the realization of the American Dream in typical American style. U.S. Sen. Judd Gregg spoke at the opening ceremony. There was a barbecue, music and entertainment.

But a special event set the program apart. Fittingly Puddle dock was the scene of a naturalization ceremony—and a group of new citizens embarked on the American Dream.

July 5, 1997

Telegraph Photo Files

Attorney Leonard Shapiro surrounded by his grandchildren, from left to right, Ben Drouin, 13; Becky Dedousis, 7; Matt Drouin, 10, and Michael Dedousis, 8 months.

DENTISTRY OF OLDE

Take away the novocaine, the high-speed drill, the antibiotics and what do you have?

A bad day at the dentist's office?

On the contrary, filling cavities without novocaine or extracting molars without antibiotics was routine at the dentist's office in the late '40s, when Dr. Boyd Weston began practicing in Nashua. Neither novocaine nor antibiotics were perfected yet and the drill was far less sophisticated.

"Today the high-speed, air-drive drill takes a feather touch. There is no grinding away," he said, speaking of one of the greatest technical advancements during his career. After a half-century of caring for teeth, the Nashua dentist turned over his practice to Dr. Todd Pollack this spring.

The Weston name was already linked with dentistry when Navy Lt. Boyd Weston completed his tour of duty after World War II and joined his father's office at 6 Concord Street.

"I practiced there my whole career," he said.

As a boy, he remembers skipping over trolley tracks when he visited his father's office. Before the construction of the F.E. Everett Turnpike, Concord Street was the central artery to Manchester, and on Sundays the street was so clogged with cars, it was tricky to cross.

Looking back, the native Nashuan said with pride, "There's been a Weston in practice in Nashua since 1903."

Dr. William Harry Weston's two sons followed in their father's footsteps. For Boyd, the elder son, there was no question about careers, even in high school at Nashua High. After earning his bachelor's degree at the University of New Hampshire, he went on to the Harvard School of Dental Medicine. In June he attended the 50th reunion of the Harvard school's Class of 1944.

World War II was still raging across Europe and the South Pacific when he joined the Navy after dental school. Military duty provided Weston with his first opportunity to practice dentistry at Sampson (N.Y.) Naval Base, where he was stationed for 3 years.

"I never went to sea; they needed me there. There were a lot of bad teeth in those days. The dental needs of the young boys was tremendous," he recalled. Of course, the work was done without novocaine, which at the time was restricted to medical use. Even after his discharge and his return home, dentists did not use novocaine often, Weston recalls, since the effects were often deadly.

Telegraph Photo Files

Dr. Boyd Weston

"It was used in surgery but not for general dental work. You got used to working without it," he said.

For the dentists as well as the patient, it was often a nerve-racking situation, Weston remembers. About patients' reactions in the dental chair, he could write a book. "There were those who were so afraid (of visiting a dentist), they only came when they were in absolute agony and they would never come back again," he said.

Generally, women were more stoic, more even-tempered in the chair. Men, however, tended to fall at the extremes. They either qualified for a medal of bravery or turned to mush.

"I never had a women grab my hand or get out of the chair and run," he said with a smile.

Weston also had some stubborn young patients, recalling, "Kids just shut their mouths down. You can't do any work."

Much to the relief of patients and dentists, a revolution has removed much of the tension on both sides of the chair during the past 25 years. Weston attributes happier visits to several factors: the improvement of the drill, the refinement of novocaine, the advent of X-ray and the development of antibiotics.

Penicillin and its sister medications have made it possible to treat an abscess and to perform a host of special treatments. Hand in hand with the use of antibiotics is the growing numbers of dental specialists, including oral surgeons, periodontists, endodontists and implantologists.

"When I started practicing, every dentist did everything, orthodontics, oral surgery. There were no specialists in town," he says, and adds there were about 20 dental offices from here to Peterborough. Now he estimates there are well over 100.

Occasionally dentists made housecalls to see elderly patients, and all worked together to spell each other on weekend emergency calls.

Another significant improvement in dental care today that he mentions is the use of fluoride to reduce decay. It is prescribed for pregnant women and for children from infancy, and is applied topically by dentists at annual check-ups.

"Kids properly cared for don't have any decay." said Weston, estimating that the use of fluoride would mean an 80 percent to 85 percent reduction in cavities.

Weston's one regret, however, is that Nashua never approved the addition of fluoride to its water so that everyone can benefit.

"It was the dumbest thing they every did," he said bluntly.

He and many dentists in town fought for it for several years only to see the effort defeated.

"It was purely political," he said referring to the scare tactics used by opponents. He points out that fluoride, a natural substance, is an element in many water supplies around the country.

Beating the drum for fluoride is just one of the many civic causes Weston has shouldered. A longtime resident of Hollis, he served as chairman of its Planning Board and its Zoning Board of Adjustment. He was also treasurer and clerk of the School Board when the budget topped $1 million.

A charter member of the Nashua Exchange Club, he was the year's chairman of the Bucky Snow Memorial Fishing Derby for foster families, Big Brother/Big Sisters and handicapped children. The annual outing at Sullivan Farm is also sponsored by the Nashua Flycasters Association, of which Weston is also member. Not only did he organize the event and round up the food for the barbecue, he also took his weed trimmer to use on the growth around the pond.

"Why not? I have the time," he said with a smile.

"He likes to keep busy," says his wife, Marjorie. Married 51 years, they are the parents of three daughters, three grandchildren, and two great-grandchildren. The Westons moved into their 100-year-old Victorian house in 1952, and he maintains the grounds, the greenery and a good-size garden of fruits and vegetables.

In the laundry room are the trappings of an avid fisherman just returned from an expedition in Labrador.

"I brought my vest and my long underwear but I never unpacked them, the weather was so warm," he says of the trip. Fit and tanned, he brags of living on the fish he and his companions caught throughout the week since the guide forgot their provisions.

In the fall he plans to take out his bow to go hunting. Bow hunting and fly fishing have been favorite pastimes for many years, though he speaks of the rustic peace and quiet of the outdoors more than the chase.

About to turn 74, the Nashua dentist has hung up his drill but he still finds his days easy to fill.

"Next week I won't be home," he said. He is off to paint his daughter's house.

August 13, 1994

LESTER WILLIAMS

Buckle up. The shuttle from New York to London will shoot off in three minutes; traveltime is an hour.

"I have no doubt the shuttle of the future will be a missile from the lower stratosphere," says Lester Williams. His air-travel predictions are not the stuff of a "Star Wars" visionary. His projections are based on solid scientific information gleaned from studies conducted by the federal government.

As a member of the project and planning department of the Federal Aviation Administration in Nashua, Williams looks into the future every day. Yet because he is familiar with the past history of aviation, his perspective is all encompassing.

"I can remember when the word radar was a secret," says the World War II Navy fighter pilot, recalling the '40s when the radio waves detection system was first devised.

At 74, Williams is the oldest FAA employee at the local facility, and, he thinks, among FAA staff nationwide. His job calls for him to zero in on plans and programs for both civilians and the military air travel in the 21st century.

"I look at new electronic equipment like satellite control and how we're going to use it," says the retired Navy lieutenant commander, with years of experience as an air traffic controller and quality assurance evaluator. His 48 years of government service, counting military service in World War II and the Korean war, would entitle him to a cushy retirement, but instead, he chooses to punch in every morning at 6:30 at the FAA complex on Northeastern Boulevard.

"There is no age limit in the government. Besides I'm in good health and enjoy working. I couldn't take a rocking chair," says the vigorous grandfather of nine who spends summer vacations laboring on a commercial lobster boat in Maine and deep sea fishing in Alaska. He still pilots a twin-engine plane out of Boire airfield several times a year for pleasure.

His wife, Diane, marvels at his boundless energy. "He's the kind of guy who snowplows five neighbors' driveways," she says.

Williams, a Down East Mainer by birth, has been fascinated by planes since boyhood. At age 17, before World War II, he enlisted in the Canadian Navy but since he was under-age, they sent him home. It was not long afterward that Pearl Harbor was bombed and Williams signed up for pilot training in the Navy.

His roommate during the six-month basic training was Ted Williams.

"He worked just as hard as the rest of us; he was a very quiet guy," Lester Williams recalls about the Red Sox right fielder and future Hall of Famer.

"Here I was a kid out of Maine, still wet behind the ears, with a pro baseball player as my roommate. I never even got his autograph."

After basic training, he went on to flight training at Pensacola, where he was commissioned an officer. During the war, he served on 12 aircraft carriers, hitting all the hot spots in the Pacific including Okinawa, Iwo Jima, Guam, the Philippines and Tokyo. He flew more than 300 missions, earning more than his share of medals and citations. He also saw more than he ever expected, and experienced things he never envisioned.

"I was a potato picker who had never been out of Maine. It opened up the world to me . . . and they paid me for doing it," he says of his military service.

After the war, he returned to Maine, finished college at UNH and turned to a more earth-bound pursuit. At the urging of an uncle, he became a licensed mortician. It was a profession he followed between stints in the service and later working for the FAA. In fact, after coming to Nashua in 1963 with the FAA, he also worked for the Sullivan Funeral Home, and in the late '70s, became its owner for a few years.

But Williams' love of flying never faded. In 1951 he was recalled as a pilot to fight in the Korean War and after the war served with NATO at the North Pole.

"I never saw Santa Claus," he quips.

After leaving the service, Williams signed on with the FAA as a traffic controller in Fort Worth, Texas. In 1963 when the FAA established its Nashua operation, this New Englander and his family were pleased to relocate here. His five children all graduated from Nashua schools, he adds.

Though often involved in highly charged situations, the stress never daunted the former night attack pilot who led squadrons on top-secret atomic missions during the Cold War.

To become an air traffic controller, it takes three years training and two years apprenticeship. The Boston area center navigates the air traffic lanes from the Great Lakes to Nova Scotia and from New York halfway across the Atlantic Ocean.

"After being a pilot in wartime, this job is a piece of cake," Williams says. He fondly remembers the camaraderie and a "wacky sense of humor" that often pulled them through many tense times.

During the Reagan years, Williams was caught in the tangled web of the air traffic controllers' strike, but he remained on the job. It demanded working 365 days straight often two and three shifts at a time.

"I stayed at work through the strike because I already had 31 years of service and I did not want to lose that," he says, adding, "Being in the military, I learned that it is futile to fight the government."

The '90s have seen some of the strikers return to their jobs, Williams is happy to say.

Since, 1988, Williams has moved from "the floor," the traffic-control nerve center, to an office upstairs, where he evaluates state-of-the-art equipment that will set the course for flying in the future.

"Les knows what works and what doesn't," says Carol Cidlevicz, the support manager for plans and programs.

As the plant's oldest employee, he is familiar with every blip of the system; it is his everyday environment. He is at home chatting with the people in the FAA's inner sanctum. To a visitor, the world behind the guarded gates is a blueprint for science fiction. To Williams it is familiar territory.

"We have our own weather bureau and our own telephone company and a whole city underneath the ground," he says adding that the building is radiation-proof.

The most familiar spot is the large dark room on the first floor where men and women track planes on computer screens.

"These are backups," he says of the row of computers lined up like sentries at the entrance to the room where the traffic controllers work. "There are backups upon backups to everything."

Inside, the controllers sit in pairs following their screens, wearing headphones and talking to the pilots flying the planes, which look like a component of a computer game.

English is the universal language of the airways, says Robert Schneller, assisting Dawna Ruiz. The two air traffic controllers point out that even with one language, understanding the accent often complicates things. Williams smiles. He knows all the ups and downs of the job.

After contemplating the stratosphere for a half-century, the senior FAA staffer has traveled through the past and is ready to plot the course of the future.

January 3, 1998

ESL MAGICIAN

How little thought it takes to sort the mail, scan the TV schedule, or sign a delivery slip. All these ordinary tasks of daily living require, simply put, is the ability to read and write. For most of us, such skills are a given. The agony and excitement of learning them is a forgotten chapter in childhood.

To eight adults in Marty Guild's Class at the Adult Learning Center, it is an adventure they never expected to have. Reading and writing is a privilege they have been denied all their lives. Now, little by little, they are chipping away at the chains of illiteracy much the same way that nursery school children do and with the same heightened sense of discovery. Yet they are too mature for child's play.

At the same time that they are learning to read and write, these eight older students are learning to speak a new language and to understand the new ways of their adopted country.

For both students and teacher, it is a Herculean challenge they meet one step at a time.

"Little miracles happen here everyday. They are reading," says Guild, speaking of the pilot program she developed after years of experience as an English as a Second Language teacher. But as non-readers, even in their native tongue, this class is even more basic than ESL.

"One only learns to read once," the center's ESL coordinator proposes. "Second language reading adapts the reading process to fit a new situation. The great majority of skills necessary for reading one language transfer to the task of reading another," whether it be Spanish, Vietnamese, Chinese or Thai.

Her students, born in Caribbean and Oriental countries, have backgrounds that are as diverse as their ages, which range from the 30s to the 70s. Even in their new country, they lead different lives. Two are grandmothers, several are mothers, another is a grandfather and two work in the restaurant business.

Yet for three hours three times a week, they come together as a unit. In class, they share each other's joys and struggles as they work toward a common goal: reading and writing in English.

"Even the 15-minute breaks are important," says their teacher.

On Monday, when the students return from vacation, small albums of class pictures will again be on the teacher's desk. Guild is always snapping pictures to record successes. It is her way of letting them hold onto the small victories that build confidence.

Marty Guild with Worapat Ngamcharoenthana,
a student from Thailand

To personalize the class, she takes down a simply biography of each student in English and includes it in a binder. Everyone in the class gets a copy to become acquainted with his or her classmates. In addition, it presents them with another valuable reading experience. One of her students, a mother of five, learned to read her children's name that way.

"She was very proud of her accomplishment," says Guild.

Hanging across the side of the room is the banner; "We can all help each other." It sets the tone for the class. Trust, patience and kindness are Guild's bywords. Without them, the learning experience would fail.

"We laugh a lot, that's part of learning a new language, too," adds the teacher.

Guild builds fun into the curriculum with class projects such as carving jack-o'-lanterns and munching on pumpkin cookies while creating a story about Halloween. At Christmas time, everyone cut out construction paper stockings and hung them on the blackboard. "The next day when they came in, the stockings were filled with candy canes," relates the teacher.

Child's play? No indeed, says the teacher. As any mother knows, cutting, pasting, involving the senses and following directions are the foundation for learning to read and write. In this class, these exercises serve double duty, for the students learn about their new country's holidays and how they are celebrated.

Other basics like telling time and recognizing colors are handled in the same lively manner. The Oxford Picture Dictionary is a well-used class reference book.

"She has material every day for them to learn," marvels Korapin Sueksagan, one of the proprietors of the Giant of Siam restaurant. She encouraged two of her employees from Thailand to take the class after seeing the success of other employees in ESL classes at the Adult Learning Center.

"I saw an improvement in their speaking and in their working," she says, adding, "Marty is so patient."

Guild is pleased with the class's near perfect attendance record. Students have to provide their own transportation, and the lone man in the class, a retiree, pedals to the ALC on his bicycle in all kinds of weather.

"These classes are free, and people will not come if their needs are not met," says the teacher about her group from many lands.

Other cultures have always interested Guild, even during her high school days in Gorham. An only child, her first introduction to customs beyond New England was through her father, a French-Canadian immigrant.

Mother, a teacher, influenced her choice of careers. After high school, she went on to Plymouth State College, graduating in 1968 with a major in French and a minor in German. She credits the college with many of the teaching methods she still values today.

While working at a summer resort during college, Marlene Lambert met Chris Guild, a Vietnam veteran, and they were married soon after graduation.

Guild's odyssey to her present post revolved around her interest in other cultures. She taught French in Dracut, Mass., while her husband finished his engineering degree at the University of Massachusetts at Lowell. After he graduated, her career followed his to Illinois, Kansas, and Nashua, but she took a hiatus to bring up their two children, Jennifer, now 25, and Edward, 20. Husband Chris is Northeast regional manager of a California semiconductor firm.

When the Guilds moved to Nashua in 1974, she heard of the Adult Learning Center through a friend in the Newcomers Club. So began a long and happy association at the center, from volunteering for the GED Program to teaching at Clearway Alternative High School. In 1988 she developed an ESL program at New Hampshire College. From 1989 to 1996, she was an ESL teacher at Nashua High School, except for 1991, when she took the year off to finish her master's degree in ESL at Notre Dame College in Manchester.

"My heart has always been at the Adult Learning Center. I love teaching at the grass-roots level," she says.

Since she returned to the center as the ESL coordinator, she has dug deeper into the needs of newcomers to this country, pioneering the literacy program she teaches today for those people who never learned to read in their own language. In April she will present the program at a statewide conference on basic adult education.

With her children grown, the teacher has time to be a student of cultures, taking summer jaunts off the regular tourist path to explore different lands. She has traveled to Ecuador, the Galapagos Islands and Costa Rico and is planning a trip to Puerto Rico and the Dominican Republic.

"I'm a student of culture if not a cultured student," she quips.

Trips are not just for pleasure. They are planned with an eye to better understanding and relating to the students in ESL classes and particularly those learning not only to speak a new language but to read and write for the first time.

"People discount those who don't read. I want them to count, and one way to count is to read."

~

The Adult Learning Center began in 1972 in the basement of the First Baptist Church, then on Main Street. It was organized by Dorothy Oliver to offer an alternative to the traditional high school education for teenagers and adults who wanted to obtain a high school diploma. Muriel Shaw was the coordinator of the first adult tutorial program.

In 1982, the Adult Learning Center was given the Crowley Street School building by the city to continue and expand its work. After Oliver retired, Mary Jordan became the director in 1986. The independent, non-profit agency on Lake Street now runs an alternative high school at the former Mt. Hope School, numerous business programs, a daycare program for infants and children and a variety of additional courses to help people of all ages further their education.

January 10, 1998

PLACES

My Window on Main Street

RESTORATION

The lamps are clustered on the floor in the library and the new shades are stacked in another corner of the room. The paintings are propped up against the parlor walls, the dining room table is piled with dishes and all the clocks are empty shells, the workings sent out for repair.

But the pine plank floors are polished. The Indian shutters work and so do the windows and old-fashioned radiators.

The Abbot-Spalding House is a work in progress, slowly and carefully being restored to its former grandeur. For two years it has been closed to the public while Beth McCarthy, the curator of the Nashua Historical Society, and the restoration committee have labored over the integrity of every detail of the restoration from wallpaper to windows to lighting and rugs.

Ever since he happened upon the Nashua Historical Society, William Ross has been the proverbial right man in the right place at the right time. "He knows how to get things done," comments Faith Flythe, committee member and a former president of the society.

For the past two years, Ross has been the chairman of the committee in charge of the restoration of the grand white house at the crest of Library Hill.

Five years ago, he was a newcomer to Nashua and a history buff who knew little about his adopted city. He had retired from the computer business which prompted his move from California. One day, rather than wait for his car to be fixed at a garage on Amherst Street, Ross took off on foot to explore the neighborhood. Around the corner from the auto shop, he came upon the Speare House, the home of the Nashua Historical Society. He rang the bell and Bea Cadwell, a longtime member, happily introduced him to the society's collection of Nashua memorabilia.

Today, as president of the board, he is a familiar figure at the Speare House, the historical society's home on Abbott Street. Almost every day he cuts through the backyard of the brick building to the Abbot-Spalding House, where he moves furniture upstairs and down or does whatever needs to be done.

The Abbot-Spalding House, a legacy entrusted to the historical society in 1978, is one of four Nashua buildings listed on the National Historic Registry

"It is the crown jewel of the society," says Ross of the home, built around 1803 and owned by several prominent Nashua families through the centuries. National figures such as Daniel Webster and Franklin Pierce often occupied the guest room when they visited the original owner, Daniel Abbot, a lawyer, legislator and the first president of the Nashua Manufacturing Co.

Of priceless architectural and historical value, the house spans the two centuries in which Nashua was transformed from the farming village of Dunstable to an industrial hub, the second largest city in New Hampshire. For the past century, it has joined with the First Congregational Church and the Hunt Memorial Building to form the trio of Nashua landmarks at the top of Library Hill.

The family of William Spalding gave its name to the house. Spalding was vice president of the Second National Bank of Nashua and later an authority on antiques. His daughter, Sylvia Spalding, was the last resident. The house was purchased by the Historical Society at the end of the 1970s and Sylvia lived there until she died a few years later.

By the 1990s, the house was showing its age, its walls crumbling, its floors worn. The lampshades were so fragile it was feared that they would disintegrate at the touch. In 1995, McCarthy applied for a grant from the National Institution for the Conservation of Cultural Properties. It provided for an assessment of the house by an architect and conservation specialist. "It really started us on the path, though we knew it was a major, time-consuming project," says McCarthy.

In the spring of 1996, the house was closed and a group of members volunteered to oversee the job. The group included Reggie Santerre and his wife, Yolanda, Mary Mason, a longtime member who died before its completion, along with Ross, McCarthy, Flythe and Cadwell.

Renovating any house is a chore, but restoring a landmark is an undertaking with an added weight of history. The job also calls for craftsmen who respect its historical value.

"You feel the responsibility of it—trying not to lose the personality of the house and the owners" says Flythe.

Because it seemed easier, they started on the second-floor bedrooms. Then, through a stroke of luck, Boy Scout Troop 250 offered to clean out tons of debris from the basement. Last but not least they tackled the first-floor living quarters.

A learning process, researching each era and each of the three owners, accompanied each step.

'You feel the responsibility of it—trying not to lose the personality of the house and the owners," says Faith Flythe, a member of the restoration committee

Flythe, Cadwell and McCarthy spent hundreds of hours choosing the appropriate wallpaper for the nine rooms and, after looking at hundreds of books in many stores, found what they wanted at Nashua Wall Paper: The blue grass cloth for Dexter's bedroom, the feminine pattern for Sylvia's bedroom and the rose damask for the hall. Sylvia's sewing room wallpaper is the original one she chose when she lived in the house. The oriental print in the dining room is also an original. The hand-painted panels imported from France and rescued from the oldest house in Nashua by Spalding still decorate the foyer.

Unlike a new house, an old house always produces something unexpected to complicate the job. No sooner had the wallpapering started on the children's room, then a rainstorm hit, causing damage to a wall from a leak in the roof. Luckily the wall had not yet been papered. The roof, the ceiling and the horse-hair plaster wall had to be fixed before the work continued.

"The messiest job was fixing the walls," says McCarthy, noting all the walls through-out the house are of horse-hair plaster. Some of the walls downstairs were in such deterioration it

Abbot-Spalding House

Telegraph Photo Files

was impossible to hang pictures. But, though horse-hair plaster is a thing of the past, all the walls have been repaired.

"There was always a stumbling block but we managed to go on—and I'm thrilled with the results," says Cadwell.

Replacing the oriental rugs was easier since the group could rely on the expert-ise of Sy Mahfuz. The owner of the Persian Rug Gallery not only cleaned and restored many of the original rugs but also contributed the large oriental rug in the second-floor hallway in memory of his father, the late Fred Mahfuz.

Visitors will soon be able to admire the rugs, the collection of Staffordshire china displayed in the dining room cabinets, the hand-crafted Chippendale high-boys, the Windsor chairs, four-poster beds and other 18th- and early 19th-century pieces. One of the antique treasures uncovered along the way was a man's wing chair, companion to the woman's wing chair. While having the handsome pair reupholstered, the committee discovered the man's chair had been signed and dated by the previous upholsterers. Donald Mavrikis, a present day upholsterer, contin-ued the cycle by adding his name.

During his many labors at the house, forever moving furniture with the help of Reggie Santerre, Ross inspected the original construction in the attic. He reported, "the beams are all tongue and groove with hand-tooled wooden pegs." Even with-out any metal, the house is as sturdy as the day it was built.

The next phase of the project is sprucing up the exterior, beginning with the brick walk at the entrance.

Come the fall and well into the 21st century, the Abbot-Spalding House will be open to visitors. Walking through its rooms, the public will experience the past, how life was lived in Nashua before the malls and the traffic jams, when Nashua took its place among the flourishing mill towns of New England.

April 19, 1999

ABBOT-SPALDING HOUSE

It has been called a priceless portrait of Nashua's past, the pearl on the rim of Library Hill, the crown jewel of the Nashua Historical Society.

No matter what the tag line, the Abbot-Spalding House is one of Nashua's grand old houses, perhaps the most grand, and as such is long overdue as a stop on the Friends of the Nashua Symphony's Holiday House Tour. Historically, its credentials are well documented. It is listed on the National Register of Historic Places.

The house tour in early December is the much-anticipated plum of the holiday season. Also festively decorated for the season will be the Florence H. Speare Memorial Museum, the historical society's headquarters next door, and three private homes of more recent vintage.

The time has come for the spotlight to shine on the house where Daniel Webster slept, where President Franklin Pierce was a frequent visitor, where political discussion sparked the conversation around the dining room table and dances graced the downstairs hallway. Pierce's portrait still hangs over the mantelpiece in the men's library off the entry.

A piece of Americana, the Abbot-Spalding House has been restored to its original 19th-century charm by the Historical Society. Closed for more than three years while members scrutinized every detail from the horsehair plaster walls to the lamp shades to the Indian window shutters, the Abbot-Spalding House is now open to visitors with a yen for knowing more about their town.

Stepping inside will take tour-goers back in time to the farming village of Dunstable on the brink of becoming the bustling mill town of Nashua. Walking through the men's library, the ladies' parlor, the dining room downstairs, to the bedrooms and sewing room upstairs offers an intimate glimpse of Nashua's early history.

"There still are no ceiling lights in the house," says curator Beth McCarthy. "At one time, the house had gas fixtures throughout and in Abbot's time there were candles and kerosene lamps."

Built at the beginning of the 1800s, the house was the property of Nashua's first lawyer, Daniel Abbot, often called the father of Nashua. The papers for the incorporation of Nashua Manufacturing Company, Nashua's first mill, were signed in the house and Abbot and his friend Daniel Webster were among the original stockholders. During his lifetime, Abbot was the first president of the Nashua and Lowell Railroad, president of the first bank, and the first president of the first Hillsborough County Bar Association. A Whig, he served in the state legislature and in 1833, he introduced president Andrew Jackson on a visit to Nashua.

The Abbot Spalding House
(Built in 1803/04)

These are just a few of the reasons the house was central, not only in location, but to the life and times of Nashua.

The exterior of the house has undergone changes but the typical symmetrical interior layout of the Federal period has remained the same. The wide pine plank floors are the originals as is the simple molding around the house's five fireplaces.

A banker and antique dealer who appreciated its history, William Spalding was the third owner of the house. He left such an indelible imprint on the house, his name has become part of its title. To do it justice, he furnished the house with fine china, rugs and furniture of the 18th and 19th centuries such as handcrafted Chippendale highboys, Windsor chairs and a four-poster bed, all maintained with great care by the historical society. Aware of its historical value, the house was entrusted to the society by Spalding's daughter, who lived there until she died in the early 1980s.

Faced with crumbling walls and leaky ceilings at the end of the 20th century, the Nashua Historical Society invested thousands of dollars and numerous hours of research and labor in restoring it.

"When we started we had no clue to the magnitude of the challenge," says William Ross, president of the society.

Authenticity was the byword. Expert carpenters, clock makers, and upholsterers were hired to do the restoration. Once the horsehair plaster walls were repaired by a craftsperson with expertise in the old building trades, choosing wallpaper was the next formidable task. The committee mandate was to keep the wall coverings in harmony with the house's history. McCarthy has preserved swatches of some the early wallpaper and framed them next to the rooms where they were removed from the walls.

"Some of them were so brittle, I had to soak them first and then piece them together," she says.

The wallpaper tour-goers will see in Sylvia Spalding's sewing room, however, is still the one she chose.

Surveying the rooms when they finished the restoration, Ross and McCarthy marveled that they "had pulled it all together," a feat that seemed impossible when they first started. In the spring, work is expected to begin on the exterior. After using a special chemical process to remove 20 coats of paint, the society is resigned to at least a three-year process, and one even more expensive than the interior.

But, thanks to the Nashua Historical Society, its crown jewel will be in good shape for future Nashuans to appreciate. Surrounded by a picket fence, the stately white house atop Library Hill will provide a path to Nashua's past in the 21st century.

Next door to the Abbot-Spalding House, the Speare House offers another historical view of Nashua. Its exhibits reveal how Nashuans entertained, how they earned a living, how their children played and the school they attended.

Handmade quilts created by Nashua women and collected especially for the Holiday House Tour will be showcased throughout the museum. Decorating the stairwell is the masterpiece made by many Nashua needle artists. The Mayor's Volunteer Recognition Quilt is a patchwork of squares designed and stitched by members of 42 Nashua volunteer organizations as a memento of the millennium.

Walking into the dining room of the Speare House, tour-goers will find a snapshot of a genteel society social, the tea party. The white-clothed table is set with flowers and an elegant silver tea service. Teapots of every description—china, pottery, pewter and silver—are displayed on shelves around the room together with teaspoons made by Nashua silversmiths. Tea parties depicted in literature—the Mad Hatter Tea of "Alice in Wonderland"—add a touch of whimsy to the scene.

The music room downstairs has been transformed into a children's playroom. The toys of years past—wooden skis, pickup sticks, painted lead soldiers, dolls and cradles—will make tour-goers smile. And the hand-cranked Victrola has a record that plays.

Upstairs, tour-goers will see a typical one-room schoolhouse in one room and an exhibit of military memorabilia including a document with the signature of Abraham Lincoln in another.

Another area upstairs houses the tools of the printer's trade, including an antique press that still works.

"You don't need to go to the gym when you use it," says McCarthy, demonstrating the muscle it takes to get an imprint.

A healthy helping of history tied with ribbons and boughs of the season is in store for people wending their way from house to house on the tour.

November 25, 2000

100 YEARS OF LEARNING

Her eyesight failed her but her instincts as a first grade teacher never did. Blind and living in a nursing home, Alice Trow devoted her waning days to teaching a Greebriar nursing home aide how to read.

That was the last memory Annabelle (Spence) Johnson had of her first grade teacher at the Amherst Street School. She had kept in touch with Miss Trow long after she herself had chosen the same profession.

Now 70 and retired from teaching, Mrs. Johnson delights in recalling anecdotes from her elementary school years at the school in the early 1930s. The former Hollis special education teacher is one of the alumni invited to share memories with the children there now through May 18, the week the school celebrates its 100th anniversary.

Names and caring qualities of teachers in the first years of school are never forgotten. Years later we can recall them as if they happened yesterday.

"She was the most wonderful teacher anybody could want," says Mrs. Johnson of the legendary Miss Trow. "I can't remember the class being noisy. No one spoke unless the teacher asked someone a question," says Mrs. Johnson, adding that at times, the ruler was used for more than pointing.

"In those days we were never allowed to touch the blackboards. The teachers were the only users. And all elementary school teachers had to know how to play the piano," she continued.

First grade scholars became well versed in the antics of Rover, the canine character in their Beacon Readers. Miss Trow was co-editor of the popular primer of the era. After the Pledge of Allegiance, the class always recited phonetic sounds from posters over the blackboard.

Exercises in the Palmer method of penmanship were a daily ritual. By third grade, pupils had graduated to the battle of scratchy pens and messy inkwells.

Each day like clock work the milkman delivered bottles of milk to the school and the trolley clanged past the door making its last city stop at the intersection of Amherst and Broad Streets.

The trollies had been retired to the past when Devita (Flanders) Barnes attended the Amherst School in the late 30s. She will tell students about the highpoint of her day—eating potatoes roasted in the school furnace for lunch.

"We could bring in raw potatoes and Mr. Bickford, the janitor would put them in the school furnace and bake them for us." She lived near the airport and was one of the few bus students who did not walk home for lunch. A large auto bused them to school from chicken and dairy farms tucked into the rural landscape between Broad and Amherst Streets.

During the century, the red brick school house has witnessed a myriad of changes in the world outside its walls and just as many within. It is mortised with memories of thousands of Nashua school children. Many will attend the official celebration, complete with cake and 100 candles, set for May 20, in the school cafeteria. It will be the culmination of a year-long celebration coordinated by Beth Bracket, former School Board president, and a committee of parents and teachers.

In 1892, when the school was built, there was no cafeteria, no library, no media center, no gymnasium. There were just four classrooms. At first the school served as an all-girl training school for teachers. It became a grammar school at the turn of the century with the two classrooms downstairs housing first and second grade, the upstairs housing third and fourth.

Until the 1965 expansion, fifth and sixth graders went to Mount Pleasant School. In the late 1979, a 1.5 million project added another wing and renovated the original building. Joan Murphy was the principal then, as she is today.

A sense of déjà vu shadows teachers Kathy (Gaudreau) Picarillo and Carol Tetler when they walk into classrooms at the school. Tetler, the reading specialist, attended the school in the 60s and Picarillo, a second grade teacher, in the 50s. Her two daughters also went to Amherst.

Recently she introduced her class to a favorite project from her third grade experience in Mae Mellon's class—making butter.

Amherst Street School

Telegraph Photo Files

Miss Mellon will always hold a special place in her heart, Picarillo says. The last day of third grade she came down with scarlet fever, missing the year's farewell festivities. Teacher sweetened the sadness of the situation by sending her a large box of candy.

Just as they have since the beginning of the century, Amherst Street School students grow a little taller each year, gaining knowledge of themselves and the world they live in.

Last Monday, fifth-grader Shelly Brown started the day speaking over the school intercom as students do throughout the year.

"Good Morning, my name is Shelly Brown," she said, continuing with a brief biography of President John Adams.

Another memory in the making.

May 9, 1992

BROCKELMAN BROS.

Mrs. Kissel was a regular customer at the store Wednesday nights, buying big bags of bakery goods for her brood. Long before he became a doctor, Normand Cote operated the doughnut machine in the big store window on Main Street. One of Ted Slosek's jobs in the dairy department was scraping the mold off the top of the tub of butter.

Supermarkets may come and go but none will replace Brockelman Bros. in the memories of Nashuans who grew up in the heyday of Main Street. Nostalgia was the order of the day when four grandparents gathered at *The Telegraph* office on Main Street recently to reminisce about the days of their youth—the 1940s and '50s—when they worked in the legendary grocery store on Main Street.

For 30 years most Nashuans shopped for the makings of their family meals in the grocery store between Factory and High streets. The forerunner of today's supermarket came to Nashua in 1925 from Lowell, Mass., and closed its doors in the mid-'50s, when it was superseded by such national chains as A&P and First National Supermarket. An old-fashioned market with sawdust on the wood floors, Brockelman's stocked everything from canned goods to heads of lettuce to legs of lamb.

It was the downtown grocery where the women shopped each week to feed the family and the men—lawyers, politicians, tradesmen and businessmen—congregated to talk shop. And for many of Nashua's young people it was a great place to work.

"It's been a long time," mused Harry Martinson when he saw Barbara Burton, both now 77, for the first time in years last Friday at *The Telegraph* office.

"We were a lot younger then," she responded wistfully.

Joining them on the trip down memory lane were Terry Haven and Armand Beaulieu, carrying a sign he had asked to keep when the store closed. It had hung at the back entrance where his first job was to load orders to be delivered by Christian Parcel Delivery. Few women drove a car. They would take the bus downtown, do their shopping and for 50 cents the delivery service brought their order to their door.

The four Nashuans assembled had plenty of tales to tell about working at Brockelman Bros. in the World War II and post-war era.

"It was the best years of my life," observed Burton unequivocally.

"It was the highest paying job in Nashua—50 cents an hour," said Haven, adding, "the girls in the 5 & 10 made 35 cents an hour."

Nashua Hitorical Society

Arnold Delinski worked in the meat department of Brockelman's store in this 1942 photo.

Haven, at 69 the youngest of the four in a group, started at Brockelman's as a freshman in high school and worked part time through high school from 1944 through '49. She worked in the grocery department and in 1950 she married fellow Brockelman employee Ted Slosek, who worked in the deli department. After they graduated, they married and opened a shop down the street—Flowers by Theodore. They ran it together until he died in 1969 and she sold her interest a few years ago.

Terry Cote (Haven) and Ted Slosek were just one of the many in-store romances. "It was a real Lover's Lane," Haven said.

All was not hearts and flowers on the job, however. The three brothers from Fitchburg, Mass., who owned the store and several others in New England hired a shopper to check on the help but the employees soon knew who they were and the spies knew it, so it was a wink-and-nod operation.

"We had to ring up the sale on the cash register, the old-fashioned kind, and if you made a mistake it came out of your paycheck," noted Haven.

Her brother, the late Dr. Normand Cote, also worked at the store making doughnuts in the window.

"After the store closed Saturday night he had to take the doughnut machine apart to clean it. When he put it back together, he always had too many parts left over. He used to say that was the reason he became a doctor," Haven related. An obstetrician-gynecologist, the boy who made the doughnuts went on to deliver many babies in Nashua.

Filling jelly doughnuts in the kitchen upstairs was one of Burton's jobs when she started working at Brockelman's as a Nashua High senior in 1941. She was Barbara Bernard then.

"Two dozen doughnuts were 25 cents and they sold like hotcakes. I poked holes in the jelly doughnuts and filled them by hand, not machine," she recalled. Employees often helped themselves to goodies such as the chop suey cupcakes, a favorite made of leftover batter.

Burton worked at Brockelman's during the war, a time of ration coupons for many staples such as butter and meat and shortages of luxuries such as silk stockings.

"We could see the long lines of women waiting for stockings in front of Marsh Parsons from our window in the store," she recalled. The bakery department was at the front of the store across the aisle from the produce department.

"Oh, those strawberry tarts," raved Beaulieu.

"And everything was made with real whipped cream," added Burton, who went from making the doughnuts upstairs to selling them downstairs in the bakery.

Mrs. Kissell was one of the bakery's customers, since she had a large family to feed. Three of her sons were high school football stars and went on to play professional football, said Burton, adding all the clerks knew most of their customers by name and usually knew just what they ordered.

All the stores on Main Street were locally owned and everybody knew everybody. On Friday nights Main Street was the community crossroads, the social center of the town. Of course, all the shops were closed Sundays.

Phillip Morris was on the corner of Factory Street and the Elks Club met upstairs. The first Wingate's Drug Store and Speare's Dry Goods store were across the street. There were four movie theaters on Main Street. Lincoln's Department Store, a bus stop, Sears, J.J. Newberry's and Woolworth's were Main Street fixtures. Priscilla's Tea Room, next to Brockelman's, was a place to relax with a Coke after shopping. Another well patronized food store was Kennedy's Egg and Butter Store, but it only sold dairy goods whereas Brockelman's was a one-stop grocery.

Beaulieu, now 77, started in Brockelman's in 1938 and worked in many departments, including cheese and vegetables, for eight years until he married. After he left, he drove a cab and became active in city politics as an alderman, a fire commissioner and county commissioner.

Martinson moved to town after serving in the Navy in World War II. He was courting his wife, the late Germaine Asselin, a native Nashuan, and needed more money to marry so he was promoted to Brockelman's meat department. To make the hamburger look red they often stirred a can of tomatoes into the meat, he recalls. After it closed, he worked at the Nashua Beef Company for more than 30 years.

In the historical accounts of Nashua, Brockelman Brothers is just a footnote, but in the minds of those who worked there—and shopped there—it was a monument to its time on Main Street. A time of handmade doughnuts and real whipped cream.

February 3, 2001

CHINESE RESTAURANT

Amystery vignette about Main Street surfaced within the Brockelman Bros. story.

Worthy of Charlie Chan, and from the same era, stories swirled about a Chinese restaurant entombed in a building on the west side of Nashua in what was originally the Beasom Block.

"Did you know about the Chinese restaurant?" Nashuans whisper when talking about the good old days on Main Street. Alan Manoian, the downtown specialist, mentions "an entombed Chinese restaurant" on his tours of historic downtown buildings.

The street lore tells of a Chinese restaurant, boarded up but still intact, its tables and chairs still waiting for customers to arrive. Sound intriguing?

The facts, as we can ascertain them, are less romantic but still interesting about the period when Main Street was the center of town, literally and figuratively.

In the 1940s-50s era the Canton Co. was a popular eatery on the second floor of 125 Main St., the building now owned by the Cardin family, proprietors of Cardin Jewelers.

Terry Haven, Barbara Burton and Armand Beaulieu remember the good food and the popular proprietor Sam Young.

"Everybody went there and everybody knew Sam," recalled Haven. "The food was good and the prices reasonable. Everybody could afford it. They had chop suey and chow mein, none of this sushi stuff they have today."

The Beasom Block, later renamed the Patriot's Block, was destroyed by fire in 1961. Three buildings remained and, says Manoian, "They are the oldest commercial buildings on Main Street southwest of the river: Cardin Jewelery, the Nashua Garden Restaurant and Tri-State Amusement Co."

But the access to the restaurant was cut off. Young moved the Canton Company to Library Hill before it disappeared into oblivion.

When the Cardins bought the building 18 years ago, a few remains of Canton restaurant were there: the tin ceiling, the wainscoting and a stack of Canton Company menus Kathy Cardin still treasures.

The Chinese and American Restaurant menus list a Porterhouse Steak dinner for $1.20 for one and $2.35 for two; broiled lamb chops for 55 cents and fried chicken for 90 cents and $1 with French fries. The wide variety of chow mein and chop suey dishes were under a dollar. "Chop Suey of all kinds put up to take out," reads the menu. "Regular dinner from 11 A.M. to 3 P.M., 35 cents; fish dinner on Friday and Special Sunday dinner."

Young was of Chinese ancestry and while the restaurant was there, according to Cardin, he lived in a small apartment on the third floor above the restaurant.

Sadly, the Canton Company is no more. The veil of mystery has been lifted but the memories of Chinese dinners still warm the hearts of many Nashuans.

February 3, 2001

CHILDREN'S HOME

The stories, passed down from father to son, sound like pages from a novel by Charles Dickens.

"Oliver Twist" comes to mind when the Rev. Donald Magnuson talks about his father's experience growing up in an orphanage.

The setting of Magnuson's stories, however, is not 19th-century London. It is Nashua at the beginning of the 20th century.

From age 4 through his early teens, Harold Magnuson, Donald's father, was a resident of the Nashua Protestant Children's Orphanage. He was one of the first to be admitted to the refuge for destitute children, which was supported by the city's Protestant churches.

Nashua was a bustling mill town when the orphanage opened in 1903 in a home on the corner of Burritt and Brook streets on land donated by Josiah Fletcher.

In 1922, the orphanage moved to a property bought for $10,000 at 125 Amherst St., where it still remains after almost a century, undergoing several name revisions and expansions.

Today it is still dedicated to the same purpose, carried out now with a far greater understanding of children and their needs.

"It was not the caring place then that it is today," says Magnuson, recalling the many conversations with his father about his 10-year stay in the orphanage as a child.

These conversations will become part of an oral history of the Nashua Children's Home when it celebrates its centennial in 2003.

To prepare for the coming celebration, the home researched its history through the people who lived it.

"We needed help in piecing together our history," said Children's Home Executive Director David Villiotti.

One of its first efforts was to run an ad in *The Telegraph*.

The first person to answer was Magnuson, the assistant part-time pastor of the Good News First Baptist Church in Wilton, where he had been the full-time pastor for many years.

His father played a dual role in the history of the home, as a child who lived there and many years later as its superintendent.

Life was harsh in Nashua when the orphanage opened. Children worked in the mills to help their families, and diseases such as measles were rampant. Life revolved around the essentials: family, work and church.

Despite the city's growing prosperity, many families barely survived on the poor wages. Both parents worked long hours of hard labor.

There was no government program offering aid to families with dependent children and ill health produced many one-parent families, often forcing a desperate parent to put the children in an orphanage.

While the orphanage's mission to care for destitute children was praiseworthy, in practice it fell short of a warm and loving home.

Its name reflected the attitude of the day. It was called an orphanage, and the children in all these institutions were commonly referred to "little urchins," Magnuson's father often said, and they were treated as a civic responsibility rather than as little human beings with needs and feelings.

The original records, which have been preserved by the home, show Harold Magnuson was admitted Oct. 6, 1906. In a brief summary paragraph, the records also reveal a good deal more, not only about the boy's plight but the mores of the times.

His mother was a young immigrant from Sweden who became pregnant while she worked as a domestic. According to the record, "she has been supporting herself and the child for two or three years by housework, keeping the boy with her when she could, and when she could not, putting him in a nursery, presumably Catholic, as they insisted upon his baptism, to which she objected, as she belonged to the Swedish Church."

The brief biography noted that "the father was unknown" and concluded, "He is bright, intelligent, fair-haired boy—has not had measles."

Daily life in the orphanage was Spartan for the dozen children who lived there and attended Nashua schools.

Harold Solomon

A matron was in charge of the home. She was strict, took the children to Sunday services at the Pilgrim Congregational Church and paid little attention to such things as a proper diet.

"She would eat roast beef in the other room while the children had bread and gravy," said Magnuson, repeating the stories his father told him.

Though committed to their civic duty of running the home, continued Magnuson, "The board of directors rarely visited the orphanage. When they did, the children were served a delicious dinner but since they were not used to so much rich food, they all got sick afterwards."

Harold Magnuson left the home when he was 14 after completing the eighth grade and in spite of, or because of, his lack of family life in the orphanage, set out to create a full and happy family life for himself in Nashua.

He married a young Nashua woman, Hazel Burrette, who as a child had also lived in the orphanage. Both he and his bride were in their early 20s when they wed. They had two children, and their marriage lasted more than 40 years.

Soon after leaving the orphanage, Harold Magnuson embarked on a career as an agent for the postal special delivery service, memorizing all the streets in the city he loved.

"There was no one more attached to Nashua than my father, but how he got here was another story," said his son.

According to the family history, his mother was pregnant and on her way to the White Mountains to work in one of the posh summer resorts. When the train stopped in Nashua, she started to go into labor.

Dr. Kitteridge, a beloved doctor in Nashua, was called to the scene and delivered the baby. The kindly doctor retained an interest in the mother and child and was later instrumental in getting him admitted to the Nashua Protestant Orphanage.

Years later, at the end of the 1950s, the elder Magnuson returned as the orphanage's administrator after working for many years as the circulation manager of *The Telegraph*.

"He wanted to make things better for the children than they had been for him," his son said.

During that time, the Magnusons were one of the founding families of Nashua Trinity Baptist Church and their son went on to study for the ministry. After their children were grown and the elder Magnuson became the administrator, he and his wife lived in the home on Amherst Street, where it is today. In the 1960s, there were as many as two dozen children in residence, with separate dormitory rooms and playrooms for the girls and boys.

"I still remember their living quarters were right beyond the dining room door," says Lori Wilshire Cardin. Today she is the business manager of the home, but in the early '60s, she and her sister were sent to live in the home for a few years after their parents divorced. There were seven children in the family, one boy and six girls.

Until her mother could provide a home for them, she and her sister—the middle girls—lived at the home for a couple of years. The changes in 50 years were many, both in the "orphanage" and in society's attitude towards the children, and Cardin's memories of her stay differ drastically from Magnuson's.

"We always had a lot of friends to play with. There were new clothes and shoes without holes and at Christmas time lots of presents from people in the community. In the summertime, we spent two weeks with a family in the country," she said.

There was also good food—except, as far as she was concerned, the liver and onions served at lunch once a week. That lunch ended up in her napkin, which she deposited in the woods on the way back to school.

She and her sister returned to the family fold when her mother could support them by working three jobs.

After graduating from Nashua High School, earning a degree from Hesser College and working for the Nashua Housing Authority, Cardin returned to the home as its business manager.

In addition to her job, she is serving her third term as Ward 7 alderman, chairing the aldermanic human affairs committee and also serving in the state Legislature.

When she came back to the home to interview for the job, she observed, "After 30 years, the dining room looks the same."

But many other things have changed. The number of children has doubled and the professional staff increased to almost 100.

There are no longer dormitories. Instead two girls or two boys share a room. There is a day school for children in the community with special needs, a fully equipped gym, a playground for the children in the home and a separate residence for teen-age girls on Concord Street.

The apartment on the adjacent property has been purchased recently and will be converted into a transitional living quarters for teen-age boys.

As the city prepares to celebrate its sesquicentennial in the year 2003, so the Nashua Children's Home gets set to mark its centennial.

The history of the city and the children's home are intertwined in the 20th century and will go hand-in-hand in the 21st century. In many ways, the evolution of the home and its care of children mirror the growth and maturation of the city.

March 30, 2002

TOURS THROUGH CHRISTMASES PAST

Visiting old houses is like strolling through the pages of history.

A view of Nashua at the turn of the century is in store for history buffs on the Holiday House Tour mapped out this year by the Friends of the Symphony. The event is one of the traditional segues into the Christmas season.

A pocket neighborhood off Amherst Street, seldom seen by city travelers, is the first stop on the itinerary.

Even before stepping inside, the view of Fairmount Street piques the imagination. Just minutes from Main Street, the secluded neighborhood rises high above the Nashua River, overlooking the mill yard on the opposite bank. At the turn of the century, when Captain Henry Atherton selected a site on Fairmount Street for his home, the smokestacks puffed continuously—for the mills dominated every aspect of community life.

Almost a century later, though mills have died, the Atherton house and its scenic view is enjoyed by the current owners, Barbara and Richard Binder, the third family to live there.

The Atherton House at 31 Fairmount, is one of the fabled houses in Nashua. Embellishing its historical credentials is the legend that it was transported in two sections form Temple Street after it was torn down to make room for the county courthouse, now the Registry of Deeds.

According to local lore, Atherton so admired the handsome house—built by Dr. Edward Spalding in the mid-1800s—that, rather than see it demolished, he bought it in 1902 and had it moved to its present setting. Supposedly the moving operation created the worst traffic jam ever seen in Nashua.

But the story of moving the house has never been substantiated. After becoming familiar with every nail and panel in renovation projects, Barbara Binder concludes that it replicated the original architecture and layout of the Temple Street home and that the captain salvaged many of the original pieces and used them in the new house.

Though there are photos of the Atherton house, Barbara Binder has searched in vain for photos of its twin, the Spalding House on Temple Street.

Atherton, a local attorney who had fought in the Civil War, was married to Dr. Ella Blaylock Atherton, the state's first woman physician. Their son Blaylock inherited the house.

The Binders bought the house in 1982 when they moved from Florida to Nashua. It had been empty for several years.

Capping the roof is a belvedere reached from a trap door on the third floor. It has provided the perfect spot for the family to watch Fourth of July celebrations and for guests to wave to Binder's daughter Kate and her husband as they took off for their honeymoon this summer after a garden wedding.

In the foyer is a fireplace of decorative brick, one of three working fireplaces in the house. The focal point of the parlor is the mahogany fireplace set with two bas-relief tiles and surrounded by polished wood paneling.

The modern kitchen is white and the old icebox in the pantry is still in use.

Richard Binder, a technical writer for Digital as well as *The Telegraph*'s music critic, has all the Christmas candles in the 45 windows controlled by computer so that they automatically switch on each evening.

The old and the new co-exist compatibly in the house down the street owned by Sarah and David Roche. According to Sarah Roche, it was a ten-room farmhouse built after Atherton's. Taking down the chicken coop in the backyard was one of their first projects.

The tall windows in the living room of 27 Fairmount frame the mill yard off in the distance. Instead of curtains, the Roches have hung colorful blown-glass discs reflecting the sunlight. The cozy room accommodates the African sculpture, gourds and artifacts collected by the Roches and a false Edwardian fireplace.

Off the living room is the tin ceiling media room dominated by a gigantic TV projection screen, which he designed. The walls are decorated with works of

Harold Solomon

Atherton House

Nashua artists. On one wall is a large acrylic landscape by Calvin Libby, on another a fabric piece by weaver Judith Kohn. There are paintings by Carolyn Clancy, Kay Kandra and Pat Lowery Collins.

An artist known for her collages, Sarah Roche has long been involved in the local art scene. In the '70s, she was the director of exhibits at the Nashua Arts and Science Center and in the '80s the co-owner of Options, a gallery on Main Street.

Her workshop off the kitchen, originally the shed, offers light and space to create.

"It is a work in progress," says Sarah Roche of her home adding, "It is not like a new house. You can't paint one room and not the others around it."

She and friend Carolyn Gaudette, a retired Nashua art teacher, will collaborate on the Christmas decorations, such as the fanciful Christmas tree adorned with seashells. The two women staged the Calvin Libby retrospective in the Swart Gallery at the Nashua Center for the Arts shortly before it was taken over by the American Stage Festival.

Fairmount Street and its environs are rich in Nashua history.

Seeing how Nashuans lived in ages past provides an enjoyable peek into the pages of the city's history.

November 25, 1995

OLDEST FIRE STATION

Bright lights flicker and an earsplitting siren bounces off the walls. The two-minute signal calls the men to action. In seconds three gleaming fire engines speed from the Amherst Street Fire Station to a crisis.

"If we're not on our way by the time the siren stops, there is something wrong," said Lester Blundon, the driver of the Engine 1 pumper. A call from the dispatcher triggers the pyrotechnics that resemble a rock music production.

A hundred years ago, a less sophisticated alert system sent three horsedrawn fire trucks racing down the same road. Since its arched doorways first opened in 1894, the Amherst Street Fire Station has not missed a beat in service to the city.

Saturday, Oct. 15, 1994, Nashua's oldest working fire station marked its centennial with a parade, an open house and a host of other festivities from 9:30 A.M. to 5:00 P.M. The granite plaque installed 100 years ago had been cleaned free of charge by the Gate City Monument Co. and hung in a prominent place for all visitors to see.

Residents of Nashua's burgeoning North End started agitating for a fire station in their neighborhood in the 1880s. The growth and prosperity of the city in the latter half of the 18th century had spurred the development of a professional fire department. In 1870 the department built the Central Fire Station, on Olive Street (the site of the Nashua Center for the Arts and later the American Stage Festival).

"With the growth of our city, the territory covered by the department has been so extended as to place much of our city outside the limits of a reasonable run from the Central Fire Station," Mayor William H. Beasom observed in 1891.

"That argument sounds familiar, the same one the fire department made about building another station on Thornton Ferry Road in the 1980s," remarked Blundon, referring to a fire station that was never built. "After five years, the Amherst Street station was built," added Blundon, the unofficial fire department historian.

The need for a firehouse in the neighborhood on the north side of the Nashua River was demonstrated by an unfortunate incident in 1888. It was March and the city was recovering from the blizzard of '88, when the Olive Street station responded to a call at 9 in the evening in Fairmount Heights off Amherst Street.

For the horse-drawn pumpers, scaling ice-coated, poorly paved Library Hill proved the first obstacle. Though they finally made it, the men realized they had another hill to climb. Since there were no fire hydrants in those days, water was in short supply. Bowing to the futility of the situation, they turned around and went back to the station.

"The fire department is always there. People today can't understand why the fire department couldn't get there," said Blundon.

The house on Fairmount Street burned to the ground but stories of the debacle set in motion plans for the Amherst Street Fire Station.

After repeated urgings from the Fire Commission, the city appropriated $15,000 to buy land and erect a firehouse on Amherst Street. The transaction was approved by the Mayor, the Board of Aldermen and the Common Council on April 25, 1893, and the cornerstone was laid soon after.

In July 22, 1893, the weekly *Nashua Telegraph* featured a front-page sketch and story about the building. "The plans for the new Amherst Street engine house were drawn by City Engineer (A.H.) Saunders, being the first public building in the city of which plans were drawn by a Nashua citizen and which is to be built by Nashua artisans . . ."

The description of the building called for a 12- by 12-foot tower extending 100 feet from the floor and with housing for a bell crowned with a weathervane. Off the entrance on Amherst Street was the machine room. In the rear was the stable with stalls for eight horses. In back of the stable was a barn with a harness and grain room and stalls for two workhorses.

One of the innovative aspects of its design was the suspension of the second floor supported by roof trusses. That section was for sleeping quarters with two sliding poles and a smoking room with a third sliding pole. The basement design revealed the building's solid brick support systems and a raised area for a coal furnace and coal bins.

On July 21, 1894, *The Telegraph* printed an article reporting that the firehouse had been turned over to the city that week. *The Telegraph* said, "It was one of the finest houses in this part of the country."

The brief story also pointed out that the final cost, $40,000, was double the original estimate. "The house is certainly very substantial and handsomely finished. A more modest and less showy building would have answered the purpose fully as well and been a savings of thousands of dollars to the city."

Like firehouses do, it became an attraction in the neighborhood. In its early years, people came to watch the horses do the practice drill at 8 each evening. Today parents and children stop by for a tour and the firefighters are always glad to oblige.

Little has changed since 1894 in the brick and stone exterior of the Amherst Street Fire Station. For safety reasons the bell tower has been removed, and the bell is now a landmark, the Firemen's Memorial on the Concord Street triangle. To accommodate the modern trucks, the three doors have been widened and now roll up automatically.

Inside, much has changed. A modern kitchen occupies the back of the station that was once used as a sick bay for horses. It is the kitchen where Boston baked beans are made on Saturday nights. In the late 1940s two famous guests, Roy Campanella and Don Newcombe came to shoot the breeze and eat beans with the firefighters after the Dodger farm team's games in Holman Stadium. Another modern addition is TV and a training room off the machine room on the first floor.

The tower still is a convenient spot to dry hoses cleaned after each use, with a pulley to string them from a hook near the roof. The machine room's wooden floor, which began to sag under the weight of the trucks in the '60s, is now reinforced cement, and in the basement an oil burner has replaced the coal furnace.

Richard Chasse, former deputy fire chief, said the sagging floor and other signs of aging led to discussion in the '70s of building a new Amherst Street station but the practicality of renovating prevailed. And, to practice what it preaches, the department has outfitted the station with a modern sprinkler system, smoke and heat detectors and a sophisticated ventilation system.

The trucks, too, have kept pace with the times. Soon after the onset of the 20th century, the horses were retired, and now as the 20th century ends, the Ahrens-Fox open cab trucks have given way to newer, safer Pierce trucks with enclosed cabs. No longer do firefighters hang precariously on the back of the truck as they go to a fire.

"The hazards are the same; they just take on different shapes," said Blundon, looking back on history. Now instead of the horses struggling on the ice to get up Library Hill, the trucks have to fight the traffic to get down the hill.

Ask Deputy Chief John Chesnulevich or any of his men, and they will say the Amherst Street Fire Station still works for what it was built to do 100 years ago.

"If we had to build it today, it would probably cost ten million dollars," said Blundon.

November 8, 1994

Amherst Street Fire Station

Nashua Historical Society

FLOWER SHOPS

Chauffeur-driven Cadillacs once parked at the door of Collins Flowers on Main Street, recalled Francis "Bud" Collins Jr., reminiscing about a bygone era in Nashua. The grand dames who alighted included Anna Stearns, Mabel Chandler, Helen Norwell and Mrs. Alfred Hills of Hudson.

It was the mid-1940s and the younger Collins was in high school. "I would get them a chair, my father would give them a flower—a daffodil, a rose, a carnation—and then show them a selection of flowers," he addeds.

Times have changed. Chauffeur-driven cars have vanished from the streets of downtown Nashua and so have the passengers, "the fine ladies" of yesterday. But the hankering for flowers, particularly on the heels of spring, is eternal.

"I came in to smell the flowers," announced Priscilla Currier, walking into Fortin-Gage Ltd. last Thursday to buy two bunches of daffodils. It is a refrain Edward "Jody" Gage III has heard often the past couple of weeks.

"After the weather we've had we won't see crocuses for a while," says the Nashua florist.

Though in many ways the flower business has changed with the times, in many ways it has remained the same for Nashua's two oldest florist shops, Collins Flowers and Fortin-Gage Ltd., both established downtown in the early 20th century. Jody Gage and Peter Collins have grown up in the business, and both have taken over in recent years after their fathers retired. Jody is the second generation to run Fortin-Gage Ltd. on West Pearl Street and Peter Collins is the third generation to carry on Collins Flowers on Main Street.

Today stopping by the florist for sprouts of spring is no longer the luxury of a few but a habit of many.

"People are more flower-conscious today," said Edward Gage Jr., Jody's father. "They often stop at a flower shop or the supermarket to buy a bunch of cut flowers or pick up a plant." And the variety of blossoms to buy these days is staggering.

"It's no longer a local market but a world market," said Francis "Peter" Collins III. For decades Nashua flower shops were supplied with the blooms of the season from greenhouses in the area and from the Boston flower market. Decades ago, the shops' stock was limited to dish gardens, plants, baby novelties and funeral baskets.

With ready access to flowers from all over the world, the seasons have blurred. Flowers from Europe are now shipped to New York and those grown in South America are shipped to Miami, the largest distribution center in the world.

Telegraph Photo Files

Tulips from Holland are available in the winter; so are Star Gazer lilies from California and roses fresh from Ecuador or Israel for Valentine's Day. The two shops average 8,000 roses each for Valentine's Day, the busiest of the year, and Mother's Day is almost as busy.

The advent of Internet has brought the world even closer, permitting the florist to order flowers from anywhere in the world and to get delivery the next day via FedEx. What cheers a friend or a spouse more than a bouquet of flowers? And flowers for corporate dinners, weddings, anniversary receptions and the holidays as well as just for the house are a must.

To handle their business, both florists rely on a staff of creative designers, salespeople and drivers. Gage's staff includes six full-time and nine part-time people. Collins has 11 people full time and a crew of 14 part-timers for the holidays.

It was 1920 when Francis Collins Sr., still in high school, started working for Powers for Flowers, the florist shop at 133 Main St. Mr. Powers, the owner, died in 1929 and the following year, Collins bought the shop from his widow. Francis Collins joined the Rotary Club and was active in civic affairs and Collins Flowers became a fixture at 133 Main St. until 1961, when the Beasom block was destroyed by fire.

The fire happened during Easter week, a busy time for florists, but without missing a beat, Collins Flowers relocated in the Whiting Building on the corner of Franklin and Main until Nashua Corp. bought the building for office space.

Though Jim and Mike's Diner at the top of Library Hill seemed an unlikely spot for a flower shop, the Collins family recognized the site's possibilities and its visible location. In 1980 the diner was torn down and a showcase with 100 feet of window space to display the blooms of the season was erected in its place. Designed by local architect John Carter, the new building is in Nashua's historic district and had to comply with its strict requirements.

"Our roots were on Main Street and we wanted to stay there," observed Bud Collins of the family decision. Now retired and living in Maine, the native Nashuan is a graduate of the University of New Hampshire and a Korean War veteran.

After the war, he returned to help his father, who was suffering from multiple sclerosis. Despite his infirmity, the senior Collins came to work each day in a wheelchair. His wife, Leona, a former teacher, also helped in the business as did one of his three daughters in later years.

Francis Collins is described by his grandson as a jovial Irishman who always had candy in his desk drawer for his grandchildren. On St. Patrick's Day there were always green carnations in the shop. Ironically, Francis Sr. died on St. Patrick's Day in 1979 and the shop opened at 9 Main St. the following year on St. Patrick's Day.

"My grandmother and I were there to sell green carnations to people passing by," recalled Peter, who joined the family business immediately after graduation from the University of Maine. He took over the business from his father four years ago and he sits at his grandfather's desk in his office on the second floor. True to tradition, green carnations filled the large containers at the shop door the day before St. Patrick's Day.

While Collins Flowers has had three addresses on Main Street, Fortin-Gage has had the same address, 86 West Pearl St., since it opened in 1931. Fortin the Florist was the name of the shop when it shared its location with an optometrist. While studying to be a history teacher Edward Gage Jr. started working for Charles Fortin in 1955. Gage became a part of the name 10 years later when he bought the business, expanded the shop to its present size and sold giftwares as well as flowers.

"I used to come in on holidays and help him deliver. I was his runner," said son Jody. His career took several detours, however, before he returned. Jody Gage studied public administration and city planning at Syracuse University. After college, he worked in Washington, D.C., and returned to Nashua to become the purchasing director for the Bahama Beach Club and the Clarion Hotel. Purchasing food is similar to the flower business since both deal with perishable products that have a short shelf life, he observes.

"Earlier I never thought I would do this," he says with a smile, surveying the flower-laden shop. In 1998, when his father talked of retiring, he had a change of heart and in 2000 he purchased the business.

Grandfather Edward Gage, an employee of Sanders Associates for many years, still lives in Nashua but Edward Gage Jr. now lives in Provincetown, Mass., returning on holidays to help his son in the shop.

"I'll be back for Easter week. Both Easters (Western and Orthodox) fall on the same day this year so it will be busy," he says. Flowers and plants are still a part of his life. Living at the tip of Cape Cod provides the right environment for growing such different flora as magnolia, camellia and pecan trees.

The elder Gage is still involved with a special interest he began more than 30 years ago—decorating the White House for Christmas. He is also there for other holidays and special occasions such as weddings and state dinners. He is the only

New Hampshire representative of the American Academy of Florists.

"I took a picture of the Truman Balcony from the roof of the White House when I was there for the Millennium Celebration," says the florist and history buff.

After years in the floral business, both Nashua families are accustomed to the hectic demands of the holidays, when all hands are called into help. Both florists mention the "time-sensitive" nature of the business. The orders must be delivered that day and often at a specific hour.

"Nobody wants their Valentine roses delivered the next day," said Jody Gage.

"The only two holidays people don't send flowers are Labor Day and the Fourth of July," says Collins. Golf and fishing are his hobbies since all but the summer months are laced with holidays. In spite of the pressures of the business, they can always count on one reward, say both florists.

"It's a feel-good business," said Gage. "You never see anyone who doesn't smile when you deliver."

"We sell feelings as well as flowers," observed Peter Collins. "Flowers are a way to send a message."

And as an added bonus, says Marc Moreau, a Fortin-Gage salesman, "It's always spring here, even when it's dreary outside."

March 24, 1981

GOV. MURPHY HOUSE A RARE GEM

It was a rainy day in November when thousands of shoe workers and a band marched up Concord Street cheering. It was 1936 and their destination was the home of the Gov. Francis Parnell Murphy, their popular boss, a founder of the J.F. McElwain Co.

A day earlier, he had been elected to the highest office in the state. Lacking a balcony, the governor climbed out the second-floor window to the roof of the front portico and waved to his well-wishers.

That day, 88 Concord St. became the Gov. Murphy House.

Today, the house is one of Nashua's historic landmarks. To Dr. Norman Kossayda and his wife Alma, it is home. The Kossaydas are the fifth owners of the house, but in the annals of Nashua history it will forever be identified as the Gov. Murphy House.

Next weekend, the Kossaydas will greet visitors in their home during the Friends of the Symphony House Tour as musicians from the Nashua Symphony play holiday music in the background. Four other homes, all of different eras, will also be on the annual fundraiser for the Nashua Symphony and Choral Society.

"You can feel the mood of the house the minute you walk in. It is an era gone by," says Shirley Haywood of Floral Finesse, the floral decorator at the Murphy mansion. "Everyone involved is hoping to bring it back for all to see and enjoy."

For the Kossaydas, the house is a daily source of delight, both as warm and comfortable home for their family and as a ready-made outlet for their interest in antiques. Yet they purchased the house more than two years ago on the spur of the moment.

The Kossaydas met while working at Elliot Hospital and after they married their work drew them to Nashua. He is the director of the emergency department at St. Joseph Hospital and she is in charge of respiratory therapy at Northeast Rehabilitation Hospital. Six years ago, they bought a home on Columbia Avenue. They liked their home, but out of curiosity they went to look at a house on the corner when they heard it was for sale. That night they made an offer and within four months they moved in.

The house, almost a century old was built to last by its original owner, George E. Anderson. It was the companion to his brother Frank's house, the Anderson House, the more opulent mansion. The two houses bracket Columbia Avenue. In contrast to the more elegant house, an example of Beaux Arts architecture, 88 Concord St. is an

Laurie Berna

Governor Murphy House

outstanding Colonial Revival design, making it less formal and more adaptable to family living for the Kossaydas, their two girls and his two grown children when they come home from college and work.

The solid underpinnings, no longer seen in home construction, extend to the interior structure of heavy solid oak and mahogany door, thick plaster walls, and leaded glass windows. The winding spindled staircase leading to the second floor is but one of many examples of handcrafted workmanship. There are nine fireplaces throughout the 2 1/2 story house and each has an individual mantle in carved oak or mahogany with tile, stone or marble inlays.

Murphy purchased the house in 1922 when he moved to Nashua to oversee his growing new shoe business.

His was a typical Horatio Alger story: He rose from a Newport shoe company's packing department to great wealth in Nashua. Born in New Hampshire in 1877, the son of a tanner, he and his brothers were not allowed to wear shoes until the first snowfall, according to a biography written after Murphy became governor. His expertise in production brought him here as one of the co-founders of J.F. McElwain, the largest shoe manufacture in the state.

His wealth permitted him to become both a philanthropist and politician. After serving in the legislature and on the Governor's Council, he was elected Governor for two terms, 1936-40, and then ran for the U.S. Senate. A Republican and the state's first Catholic governor, he switch to the Democratic Party to run for the Senate and was defeated by Styles Bridges, a Republican. The versatile shoe magnate also founded WMUR radio and WMUR-TV; he was also an ardent sports fan, sponsoring the Nashua Millionaires baseball team in the old New England League.

Another interest was the Boston Braves. Among his many accolades were honorary degrees from UNH, St. Anselm and Dartmouth colleges.

Murphy died at 81, at his home. After his death in 1958, the house, was sold to the Sisters of Mercy and used as living quarters for the sisters as well as a library for the Mount St. Mary Seminary. The house was sold in the early '90s, after the girls school was closed.

Living in the Gov. Murphy House means living with history.

"We think the house is haunted," Dr. Kossayda says.

The legacy of owning an old house is never knowing when or where a piece of its past will be discovered. The Kossaydas have found many pleasant surprises in 2½ years they have lived at 88 Concord St. They have just hung a brass chandelier found in the basement in the dining room. It has been rewired and restored with French art globes. The elegant dining room table and chairs were a consignment shop find. Two fireplaces anchor the front and rear of the room.

Off the spacious center hall, papered with its original imported wall covering, are the dining room to the right and the living room to the left. A bright sunroom off the dining room is well used as the family room, reserved for the girls' toys.

The living room has been transformed from the dark Mount St. Mary library to a bright and cheerful room warmed by two fireplaces. The walls are painted soft yellow and a crystal chandelier, found in a New Jersey antiques shop, has replaced the utilitarian fluorescent fixtures.

The governor's office is a snapshot frozen in time. It is a small chestnut-paneled room and behind the desk carved into the paneling is the state seal and the family coat of arms.

"There are hidden compartments in here," says Alma Kossadya, pressing on a panel to demonstrate. With a fertile imagination, one can only wonder the secret documents stored there.

Downstairs in the billiard room with the tin ceiling, another piece of the past came to light when Dr. Kossayda found a buzzer that magically opened the bar when it was pressed. No doubt it was familiar to the cigar-smoking titans of Nashua's mills, the members of the Chamber of Commerce and the politicians who discussed deals there.

Another treasure they found in the basement is a weathered, giant size portrait of the governor which they intend to restore and hang in the hall.

The portrait is larger than life as was the man whose spirit dominates the house.

November 28, 1998

A FIRSTHAND LOOK AT
NEW COURTHOUSE

If you are called for jury duty in the new Hillsborough County Courthouse in Nashua, bring a seat cushion. The upholstered seats in the jury box provide an unobstructed view of the witness stand. They swivel and they recline. But if you're short like me, the contours elude all the key support points.

Lawyers and litigants will fare much better with old-fashioned sturdy wooden chairs.

Never mind the comfort factor. State senator Mary Nelson was overjoyed just to see furniture of any kind in the state's newest hall of justice on Spring Street.

This year the legislature finally approved $1.1 million for furnishings only to have the contractor, the long-established Tom and Ray Office Supply Inc., go bankrupt. Even justice falls victim to the chilled economy.

Instead of Jan. 2, the facility is expected to open in mid-February, according to Marshall Buttrick, the clerk of the court. The public will be invited soon after to inspect the courthouse, designed by architects Lavalle-Brensinger of Manchester.

Buttrick, Nelson and I toured the building last Monday. We were joined by Ernest Jette, president of the Nashua Bar Association and Tony Spagnuolo, a member of Eckman Construction Co. of Bedford.

For more than a year, the Nashua Post Office's new neighbor has seemed like a stranger in our midst. It has occupied space on the corner at East Pearl Street without actually being part of the town. It promised to quicken the tempo of downtown Nashua, but without any visible signs of life, it lacked character.

The tour with people more familiar with its working made it more hospitable.

Our entourage entered through the employees' entrance at the rear and we made our way through the Probate Court quarters toward the front. The Probate Court will move from Temple Street to the new building, occupying half of the first floor. The Superior Court takes up the rest of the first floor and the entire two floors above.

Not coming in through the revolving doors on Spring Street, we missed the full impact of the entrance, highlighted by the state seal.

Inside, a circular staircase defined by a polished wooden banister is designed to lead the eye up to the round skylight in the roof. With little embellishment, the three-story architectural space conveys the uplifting feeling justice inspires.

"It is the only major feature in the building and it is at the entrance so the public can appreciate it," noted Spagnuolo, project manager.

Spagnuolo pointed out the building's cost-saving features. He noted the exterior of the building is brick veneer and the granite trim is actually made of high-density styrofoam encapsulated in a cement coating.

"If we used real granite it would have cost hundreds of thousands of dollars whereas it cost $18,000 to $20,000," she said.

He compared the Nashua structure to a courthouse built by his company in Newburyport, Mass.

"Nashua is 85,000 square feet and cost $7.6 million without furnishings. Newburyport, at 50,000 square feet, cost over $9 million. It is a lot more elegant," he added.

Buttrick, who will move from Concord Superior Court to oversee the daily operation in Nashua, was more concerned with its "functional" qualities.

To Jette, it represented "a state-of-the-art courthouse without any unnecessary add ons." One of the less obvious benefits to Nashuans, he noted, will be lower legal fees since charges for traveling time will be reduced.

Nelson was pleased with birch plywood paneling another evidence of Yankee thrift.

"We spent our state dollars well," said the 13th district senator, who championed Nashua as the location of the state's courthouse.

Security was the feature of the courthouse that struck me the most.

For starters, bullet-proof partitions are hidden in the front panels of each judge's bench in the nine courtrooms. Panic buttons are also within reach.

"What about the lawyers?" asked Nelson.

"They can talk their way out of anything," quipped Buttrick, also a lawyer.

He hastened to point out, however, that information booths in both the Probate and Superior court sections also have panic buttons.

All windows throughout the building are tempered glass, allowing those inside the building to look out but obscuring the view of the building's interior from the outside.

The nine chambers for judges are clustered together in the rear of the third floor.

"If anything it makes it more secure, more removed from the public," said Buttock.

We had made our way up to the third floor from the basement up back stairways reserved for bringing prisoners to the court. In the basement, we viewed the stark holding cells furnished only with wooden benches and toilets. There is a separate holding area for juveniles, a new feature in this courthouse.

"The courts are a commentary on our times," Nelson remarked.

We ended our tour on the third floor in the law library, illuminated by a large skylight. The room was empty except for stacks of boxes filled with the volumes recording more than 200 hundred years of New Hampshire law. Volume one is the state constitution.

In the upstairs room is found the building's true foundation.

December 28, 1991

HUNT MEMORIAL LIBRARY

Old buildings are full of surprises. Serendipity lurks around every corner in the Hunt Memorial Building. Its centennial in 2003 will coincide with the city's sesquicentennial.

As the building's 100th anniversary approaches, those overseeing the restoration of Nashua's defining landmark on Library Hill are tripping over bits and pieces of its past. Skylights blacked out during wartime, a hidden glass tile window in the floor, the original reading room lamps stored behind the spiral staircase and a circle of miniature books buried in the rim of the lantern lighting the front entrance are but a few of the discoveries.

Sunday afternoon, when music lovers assemble in the Hunt reading room to hear the first in a free monthly concert series, they will spot another find. Before or after the Hollis Choral Ensemble presents its holiday program, visitors, too, can play history detective. If they squint a little and get the right light—the strong afternoon sun is best, according to board member Nancy Bish—they will see letters carved in a cornice above the tiled fireplace. The words spell out a Latin phrase. What it means has everyone guessing, though administrator Hilary Booth has had a variety of translations and is searching for an authoritative answer.

"So far I've been told it says 'teach me to know what I need to know' or maybe, 'grant me to know what I need to know'—which makes sense for a library," says Booth. She wants to make sure the translation is accurate before any decision is made on how to use it.

The warm oak-paneled room is an ideal setting for concerts and several previous ones have played to standing room only. The acquisition of a fine baby grand piano has made it possible to launch the free Sunday afternoon series. Money to finance the initial series was raised this summer at a concert in the millyard staged as a tribute to the mill workers.

Sunday at 2 P.M., the first event in the series, the voices of the Nashua Choral Ensemble, 16 men and women, all of whom are members of the Nashua Symphony Choral Society, will fill the former reading room with music dedicated to peace. The holiday program will range from selections from J.S. Bach's Christmas Oratorio to a Hanukkah song, "Light One Candle," written by Peter Yarrow of the Peter, Paul and Mary trio. "The room is a beautiful place to sing acoustically and esthetically," Judy Greenhill, the director of Nashua Choral Ensemble, says of the Hunt reading room.

The Hunt Memorial Building, built in 1903, was a gift to the city for a library. In 1892, Mary A. Hunt and her daughter Mary E. gave the city $50,000 to build a library as a memorial to John H. Hunt, their husband and father.

After years of bickering over the site and moving a building to clear the way, it was built on the Greeley lot.

The architect was Ralph Adams Cram, a New Hampshire native who had attained national fame for buildings at the United States Military Academy in West Point, N.Y., Philips Exeter Academy and the Cathedral of St. John the Divine in New York City.

Designed in the Elizabethan Gothic style, the Hunt Memorial Building served the city as a library until it became too small for a growing, prospering city and in 1971 a new library was built on Court Street. Until the mid-1990s, the building was used by the city education department and much of it began to deteriorate.

During Mayor Rob Wagner's administration, the city landmark was rescued from sale to the private sector by the aldermen. In subsequent years, funds have been raised from civic-minded organizations, businesses and individuals for its restoration and a board of trustees was appointed to supervise the task. The goal was to open the building for civic events so that Nashuans can see and appreciate its beauty.

"It is a building that was meant to be used," says Meri Goyette, former board chairwoman. Slowly but surely, the architectural gem is being carefully restored to its original grandeur, each repair keeping true to the original. For example, the leaky windows and the broken brass fixtures were replaced in the reading room, with Bronze Craft lending its expertise to the project. To bring the building up to code, the heating system was revamped and a handicapped entrance and bathroom

Embedded in the lantern at the entrance of the Hunt Memorial Building is a circle of books.

were installed. In order to use the building for receptions, a kitchen was installed off the main foyer.

Last spring, a major undertaking financed by city block grant funds began. The copper roof, another source of much leaking, was replaced. "We couldn't do any thing until we fixed the roof," observes Booth. Its preservation depended on it.

That led to a series of revelations about the building. The first discovery was the skylights, on the roof that had been blackened, which the trustees presumed was a wartime safety measure.

During a raging wind and rain storm, as the roof work was being done, the tarp was blown off and water rushed in, soaking the carpet below. The odor necessitated its removal—which led to another discovery, an original glass tile inset in the floor.

"It was a delightful discovery. It provided more light to the office and the kitchen below," adds the administrator, noting there are 7 floors in the multi-level building leading to unexpected spaces in its recesses.

The old library's auxiliary bookshelves off the spiral staircase are still intact. One day after looking at a photo of the reading room in "Nashua, In Time and Place," says Booth, she and Alan Manoian, the city downtown development specialist and a member of the board, realized they had happened upon the room's original light fix- tures. The lamps are on the list to be repaired and restored to their rightful place.

The ultimate symbol of contemporary times—the computer—brought to light another piece of fortuitous information. While surfing the Internet, Nashua writer Adelle Leiblein, a member of the board, found the name of architect Ethan Anthony associated with the Boston firm of HDB/Cram and Ferguson, who is writing a book on the work of Ralph Adams Cram. The board promptly invited him to visit, which he did with delight.

"It was most interesting to see the building and to meet everyone involved in saving it," he wrote afterwards. "It is gratifying indeed to see the building and to meet everyone involved in saving it. It is gratifying to see how it has been cared for over the years and how it is surviving so well in spite of its age."

Since then the board sought his input on another project, restoring the tall Gothic tower windows overlooking the foyer. Shards of plexiglass used in a previous make-do repair were raining on the foyer and for safety's sake they were covered with netting. Booth has been conferring with Paul Newman, director of urban programs for the city, about funds to replace the plexiglass and with Anthony about how to do it properly.

"He can guide us to the architecturally true historic origins of the building," says Bliss Woodruff.

All the board members are pleased with the connection. Serving on the board are Elaine Griffiths, Georgi Hippauf, Frank Mellen, board president Eleanor Quinn, Larry Szetela and Mayor Bernard Streeter. At Tuesday's boardmeeting future programs for the concert series, children's events and the "Growing up in Nashua" evenings were discussed and plans were proposed for an anniversary ball.

When anyone thinks of the city, the image that immediately comes to mind is the Hunt Memorial Building on Library Hill. Its clock tower is central to everyone's view as they drive or walk north on Main Street. With the proper care, the Gothic masterpiece often called the jewel of Nashua will be treasured for many hundreds of years to come.

December 8, 2001

LOVE TURNS "DRUG" HOUSE INTO MODEL HOME

It is a fable for our times. Once upon a time, on French Hill in Nashua, there was an ordinary house with an extraordinary past. Now, through a labor of love, it is assured a shining future.

At the beginning of the century, 48 Tolles St., was the home of Sam and Ida Kessler and their seven children. Farmer Kessler had a barn in back for keeping a cow. Old-timers tell stories of son Henry, who worked in the mill and helped with the farm, leading the cows through the streets to graze by the Nashua River.

Though Sam and Henry established a farm on Amherst Street in 1938, a daughter and her family lived in the house until the '60s.

By the '80s, the once solid family home came to represent the most sordid side of the city, making headlines as a slum dwelling labeled a drug house. It soiled the whole neighborhood. In 1987, the city was stunned to read of the drug-related shooting rampage next door.

Yet at the end of the 20th century, another role is in store for 48 Tolles St. It will soon be transformed from one of the city's pockets of blight to a symbol of pride for Tolles Street, the French Hill neighborhood and the city.

By late spring the old but still structurally sound building will be renovated. Occupying the first floor will be a substation of the Nashua Police Department and an office of French Hill Neighborhood Housing Services. On the second floor will be a three-bedroom, low-rent apartment. After that, the unsalvageable buildings across the street will be leveled and replaced by duplex homes. On the lot where the murder took place, a playground will emerge.

The modern Cinderella story on Tolles Street evolves from the alliance of two community groups with the same mission, French Hill Neighborhood Housing Services and Habitat for Humanity.

"It was a match that made a great deal of sense. We bring the ability to access the loans; they provide the hard labor and the expertise to do the work," says Bob Keating, a member of the French Hill board and, for the past few weeks, part of the Habitat construction crew.

Every Saturday morning since the end of September, carloads of workers have appeared at the site ready to work.

"It's unbelievable," says David Darling, Habitat construction supervisor. It is a word he uses frequently.

"They keep coming from everywhere—church groups, high schools, Boy Scouts, men's groups, women's groups. I checked the answering service at the office the other day there were four calls, three offering to help," he adds.

All of the labor force is volunteer, including Darling. A machine-design mechanical engineer by profession, he has shortened his work week by a day and taken a cut in pay to devote some 20 hours a week to Habitat. At least two nights a week he can be found at committee meetings; Friday is for planning and Saturdays are for working.

"I work at the computer all day, and this is a welcome change. I love it," says the man who built his house in Hollis and recently renovated the one he moved to in Amherst.

Depending on a less experienced crew presents no problems to Darling, who has worked with Habitat on several projects in the area and in nearby states.

"We all work side by side, and if somebody doesn't know what to do, you are there to help them. It's not like the construction boss who leaves and comes back at the end of the day.

"And there are none of the complaints you might get from paid workers. These people are so willing to work."

Darling describes the basement as the filthiest he has ever seen and says he never expected people to come back for more; yet they did.

"We have people of all ages. Last week one of the volunteers was a woman who is eight months pregnant. She put on a mask and went right to work."

Among the regulars are employees from Fidelity, newcomers to Merrimack, and students from the Nashua High School Honor Society. At lunch time, members

David Darling, HUD supervisor, surveys work on Kessler house.

Telegraph Photo Files

of the Hudson and Nashua Junior Women's clubs arrive with sandwiches and soup for everybody.

By last week, the walls inside the boarded-up building had been torn down and all the decay removed from the basement to the top floor, and the brush had been cut down in the lot next door. In the spring the cleared space will become a playground, thanks to Anheuser-Bush.

Until the week after Thanksgiving, workers will have a respite so Darling and the Habitat committee can plan Phase II, laying out the offices and the apartment upstairs. New windows, a new roof, and space heaters will allow people to work inside through the winter. New siding is scheduled for spring.

French Hill Neighborhood Housing Services will get the financing for the few professional jobs, such as the heating and roofing, and it will pay for building materials, though some will pay for building materials, though some will be donated.

"The building has been completely gutted, and the only cost so far was the Dumpster for the 10 tons of debris," marvels Keating, a licensed marriage and family therapist, who says he is one of the "grunts" on the job.

Restoring French Hill to a safe, well-kept family neighborhood is the mandate of French Hill Neighborhood Housing Services.

"It acts as a neighborhood bank," says John Everett, the executive director. Shepherding potential owners through the maze of financial responsibilities is another one of its functions.

The non-profit neighborhood agency sprang from the seeds of tragedy. The drug-related murder on Tolles Street mobilized City Hall and home owners in the neighborhood. One of the prime movers was the Rev. Dan St. Laurent of St. Francis Xavier Church on French Hill. Other neighborhood activists were Vincent Russo and Robert Miller.

French Hill Neighborhood Housing Services was incorporated in 1991 with a board comprising of city officials, business people and French Hill residents. In its brief existence, it has helped 23 families buy homes and 17 home owners make improvements.

With the mortgages on the 48 Tolles St. property in default, the French Hill Neighborhood Housing Association stepped in to purchase it for $17,500 at a bank auction, and later bought the properties across the street for $44,000.

After acquiring the Tolles Street properties, the next question for the group, says Everett, was, "How could we deliver what we wanted without the prohibitive costs, probably around $120,000?"

In June, the French Hill Neighborhood Housing Services found the solution, joining forces with Habitat for Humanity. For several years, the Nashua Habitat for Humanity has been in the process of establishing a chapter here and earning certification from the national organization. Its first major project this year was to modernize an old home in Milford. Now it was ready for the major undertaking in Nashua's inner city.

With the Tolles Street properties the volunteer-driven organization deviated from its usual mode of doing things. Habitat usually works directly with families to make home ownership or renovation possible. However, its principle of "sweat equity" will come into play when the one or two duplexes, offering affordable home ownership to two or four families, are built across the street.

"The 48 Tolles St. project," says Rick Ruo, president of Habitat, is "kind of like a getting-to-know-you project." He added that from there, the team expects to tackle pockets of deterioration in other neighborhoods in the city.

As for French Hill, says Everett, "It is not going uphill or downhill, it is going on."

November 23, 1996

FAMOUS CATERER

For 50 years, McNulty & Foley fed mayors, presidents and ordinary folk, but after June's sale, the tables are bare.

Resting on a shelf in the home of Rita Zeloski, the rose-patterned platter is heavy with memories. The serving piece, one of the 83-year-old Nashuan's most prized possessions, is a memento from McNulty & Foley Caterers, where she worked for more than two decades.

On most nights for almost 50 years the large china plate, stacked with slices of roast beef, was passed around the table from diner guest to dinner guest. "Sometimes I just look at it. It brings back so many memories," she sighs.

"Everybody misses it. We hate to think of it being torn down," Zeloski adds, referring to the recently closed catering hall built on Amherst Street a half-century ago. This summer the familiar white house with cranberry-colored awning and black shutters will be replaced by a sprawling gas station and convenience store, thus erasing another piece of Nashua's past.

McNulty & Foley Caterers was Zeloski's second home for some 25 years. She has always lived nearby, just three doors away. In the 1950s, she started working as a waitress part time for the first owners, William McNulty and Claire Foley. Zeloski continued to waitress for John and Irene Wollen, after they bought it in the '60s, and retired in the '70s as head waitress under Barbara Dion, who owned it until its sale in June.

In fact, because she lived so close to her base of operations, Zeloski offered to have a telephone line installed in her home to take bookings for parties coming in at all hours of the day and night.

From the start, business flourished at McNulty & Foley Caterers. The new facility was built at the end of the '40s by the first owners, McNulty and Foley, who were partners in a restaurant on High Street called the Frontenac. He was the cook and she was the hostess. "She was very easy to get along with, and he never crabbed at us." Zeloski says of her two bosses.

Nashuans immediately appreciated the home cooking, the family-style service and the pleasant surroundings, a combination so successful it never changed. "The beef was the best; it came from Nashua Beef," says Zeloski. She added that there were five and six parties in the dining room a week as well as several outside functions catered and served.

Niece Rita McNulty Cross still fondly remembers her uncle's specialties: the roast beef, the chicken pie, the secret salad dressing and the Delmonico potatoes.

His recipes were passed down from cook to cook and owner to owner, and to the delight of the diners, they were faithfully duplicated to the end.

"I can still taste the lemon chiffon pie," she says of another favorite.

Uncle Bill was the twin brother of Cross' father, Harold. They were in the business of painting interiors, a talent Bill McNulty used to stenciling the rose border in the main dining room. The design forever labeled it the Rose Room, the theme repeated in the drapes and the china. Though still in the paint business, her father helped with the clam bakes, another McNulty & Foley specialty catered outdoors at people's homes.

Besides the dining facilities on the main floor, there was an apartment upstairs, the living quarters for the two owners and Foley's two brothers. Years later, long after the original owners were gone, the apartment was destroyed by a fire but the rest of the building remained intact.

"They had a long relationship, but they never married," says Cross of William McNulty and Claire Foley, who owned the catering business for 14 years.

Irene and John Wollen took over in 1963. The Wollens, the second owners, were also the proprietors of the Meadow, a well-known eatery. McNulty & Foley had changed hands soon after Beatrice Wolkowski came to work as a waitress. She stayed until it closed this spring, eventually taking over Zeloski's job as head waitress.

"Everyone was so nice to work with, that's why we worked there so long," says the 70-year-old, who worked there 36 years.

The rapport among the staff carried over to the regular diners whose groups returned year after year for meetings and other functions. Dressed in their white uniforms with deep red aprons, the waitresses greeted the steady customers by name and, in turn, customers knew them by name.

Typical of the friendly give and take is the story Wolkowski tells of Democratic City Committee dinners emceed by the late Harry Makris. Zeloski was in charge of the waitresses at the time. "He would announce, 'Rita and her lovelies are ready to serve us.' Then everyone would applaud and we'd all come out."

Wolkowski can still rattle off some of the regular dinners. "The first Monday of the month it was the Christian Women, the second Tuesday it was Industrial Management, the third Wednesday it was the Home Builders," she recounts, continuing with the list. Bronze Craft had its retirement parties at McNulty & Foley Caterers. Nashua Corp. had its Christmas parties there. The Bowling League had its annual dinners in May.

The Fish and Game Club dinners were particularly memorable since the hunters provided the meat to be cooked. Porcupine, deer and bear were some of the delicacies. Later on they settled for the more traditional meat and potatoes menu ordered by other groups.

For a myriad of Nashua families, McNulty & Foley Caterers was the place to celebrate special occasions: wedding and engagement receptions, luncheons after funerals and baptisms, anniversaries, graduations and bar mitzvah receptions.

Neither wind, rain nor snowstorms interfered with the festivities. One wedding reception on a lake in Dunstable, Mass., was accompanied by thunder, lightning and tumultuous downpours, recalls Patty Ledoux, a waitress for 23 years at McNulty & Foley.

"We were like drowned rats," she says of the waitresses who sunk into the mud when they ran from the house to the tent, getting soaked in the process. But that was part of the job.

Says Wolkowski, remembering the hot times in the kitchen without air conditioning, "Some times we were so busy, by the end of the evening we were exhausted. Then we'd get silly. Patty (Ledoux) would start and Cindy (Duby) would follow." The two waitresses started the high jinks, spraying everyone in the kitchen with the hose from the sink.

"We were such a good group, that's why we stayed together so long," Wolkowski observes.

Barbara Dion shares many of the memories of the times when she and Wolkowski worked side by side. Dion and her husband, Richard, became the owners for the caterer's last 25 years. After they divorced, she managed it by herself with the help of her three daughters, Kristen, Cathy and Lori. Running an eating establishment with a staff of 25 to 30 was second nature to her, because she was the daughter of Armand LaRose, one of the owners of the Modern Restaurant. Her mother, Gisele, baked the breads for McNulty & Foley's Sunday brunches, which Dion started in the '90s. It was the only walk-in restaurant service except for a brief flirtation with Friday night dinners.

Filed away in Dion's memories are the receptions for Nashua mayors, from Mario Vagge to Donald Davidson, and governors, congressmen and presidents. "We served Reagan three times," she says, referring to the 40th president.

But in her book, the most unforgettable people to dine at McNulty & Foley Caterers were the PSH linemen. After the blizzard of '97, McNulty & Foley was asked to feed the teams of repairmen who poured into the state to restore electricity that was off for days after the storm. For weeks hundreds of tired and hungry crews were fed from 6:30 A.M. to 11:30 P.M.

McNulty & Foley had lost its power, too, and on the first day, Dion remembers cooking by candlelight and camping lanterns. To make the workers feel at home, she made their favorite French-Canadian dishes.

Summing up a quarter-century as cook, manager and chief trouble-shooter, she says, "It was a good place. It got three kids through college."

With more hotels and restaurants moving into town and less "old Nashua" nostalgia to ensure the steady flow of parties, it was time to move on. Bottling the famous "soggy salad dressing" is one possibility she is considering. Another is opening a soup and salad bar.

At the estate sale in June, each of the staff was given a memento. Claire McHugh, one of many longtime McNulty & Foley customers, made sure she had a piece of Nashua's famous catering halls as a remembrance of times past. She bought several place settings of the rose china at the recent estate sale.

"We could have sold at least a million more," sighs daughter Kristen Dior Baker, who was the function and sales coordinator for her mother the past seven years. "People who were married there or had parties there wanted anything, from doorknobs to a fork or spoon." By owning a spoon or meat platter or a doorknob, Nashuans could hold onto the neighborly feeling McNulty & Foley Caterer knew how to create so well.

July 12, 1998

EX-MILL HOUSES

The years fade away when Pauline Raby looks at the snapshot of herself in her wedding dress, framed in the doorway of the brick apartment building on Canal Street.

She can still see workers at the Jackson Co. Mills hanging out the windows waving furiously to the bride across the street.

From 1939 until the day she married Normand Raby in 1946, Pauline Hebert lived in one of the three apartment houses facing the mill complex, now occupied by Sanders. Her mother worked in the spinning room of the mill and her father in the J.F. McElwain shoe shop.

"There was a great big tree by the side of the yard, where I parked my bike," Raby remembers.

"There are a lot of memories in that place."

She is pleased the century-old tenements will not end up on the scrap heap of time with the land leveled for parking lots as so many of the tenements were.

In December 1993, the city accepted a proposal by the Area Agency for Developmental Services of Greater Nashua to take over the property. In March 1995, the agency took ownership, and the property is now in the process of being rehabilitated as its headquarters.

Raby was one of the first to donate to the non-profit agency's fund raising drive to offset the cost of the renovations. Her reason for contributing was not simply nostalgic. The agency has been instrumental in the care of her mentally disabled daughter, offering encouragement and arranging for regular visits from a Home Health and Hospice Care aide.

The Greater Nashua Area Agency was one of 12 organizations established by the state in 1981 to make it possible for former Laconia State School patients as well as others afflicted with developmental disabilities to be integrated into the community.

The agency's mandate was to develop local support services and to coordinate the care of individuals with other agencies. In 1994, more than 700 people and their families benefited in many ways. The agency assisted the handicapped with independent living and work: it also lightened parents' loads by arranging for respite care of handicapped children and support groups to discuss similar problems with other families.

With a permanent home, the agency expects to have a more effective base of operations, and its central location downtown will make it more easily accessible than its cramped quarters at Harris Pond, Merrimack, said Beth Raymond, associate director of the agency.

Raymond supervised the transformation of the dilapidated tenements built in the 1870s for mill families into a new home for the agency, helping hundreds of families today cope with mental and physical disabilities.

Little has changed in the exterior façade of Canal Street's last remaining mill houses, though the three separate buildings have been joined together into one unit. An elevator has replaced the stairwell in the middle building and the third floor allows for space for the Early Intervention Program of Southern New Hampshire Regional Medical Center to join the agency. In the agency's new home, therefore, services needed from birth through adulthood will be under one roof.

With its space more than doubled, there is ample room for training sessions, conferences and a library with books, videos and resource material for clients. No longer will the 50 staffers need to double up for offices.

"Each of the offices has a window, and everyone would like one with a view of St. Francis Xavier Church," said Raymond referring to the prominent church atop French Hill.

Built of brick, the solid tenements have weathered the ages—even a flood and a hurricane in the 1930s—and the agency has taken care to preserve the feeling of its former life. In the entry and in rooms throughout the three floors, much of the rough brick has been left exposed. On the outside, slate will replace the asphalt tiles on the mansard roof to restore the character of the original Victorian architecture.

"I love this building," said Mario Machado, project supervisor for Brookstone Builders of Manchester. "I would like to own it myself," he adds.

During the last decades of the 19th century, a sea of tenement housing bordered French Hill. The wave of immigrants coming to work in the factories created

Tlelgraph Photo Files

a need for schools, churches, shops and living space for families. Neighborhoods sprung up around the city's mill, the Nashua Manufacturing Co. off Factory Street and the Jackson Co. on Canal Street. The Jackson Mills were where the fine Indian Head cotton cloth was made.

Until the 1920s, a canal's waterpower was no longer needed and the canal was filled in. Named for its industrial waterway, Canal Street became a broad tree-lined boulevard with shops, food markets and tenements. The self-contained community even had a cafeteria on the ground floor of a corner apartment building for the convenience of supervisors who lived only blocks away.

In the mid-'30s, the economic power of the mills began to wane. The great flood in the spring of 1936 also had taken its toll on the houses.

"My mother had to move out in 1936 because her living room was destroyed. The first floor of the building was flooded to an inch of the ceiling," recalled Ella Cloutier, an RSVP member coordinating the Area Agency's fund drive at the Coliseum Avenue residence for seniors.

The era of affordable mill housing maintained by the mill owners came to an end on Sept. 26, 1936, when the tenements were put up for auction by private bidders.

"All are equipped with city water, flush toilets, gas and electricity and many have bath and heat," advertised the auctioneer.

In the following decades, the mills were closed, the neighborhood declined and the remaining tenements became slums. With neglect of absentee ownership, the city took the buildings for back taxes in 1993. Another parking lot was one of the options for the property, but instead, the Board of Aldermen asked for proposals outlining a good use of the buildings.

"The city sold it to us for back taxes, $66,000, and allowed us to pay it in three annual installments," says Raymond.

With the move at hand, the agency will have time to raise money for outside landscaping to compliment the building.

As they drive along Canal Street in the days to come, Nashuans such as Pauline Raby and Ella Cloutier will enjoy the view as well as the memories.

December 2, 1995

SOCIETY GIVES LOCAL
HISTORY NEW LOOK

If you think packing up a household is work, try moving history.

The Nashua Historical Society has just completed a major renovation-expansion project at the Florence H. Speare Memorial Building, the society's home at 5 Abbott St., and everyone in town is invited to see the results Saturday, June 12, from 1 to 4 P.M.

Sixteen months ago, hundreds of boxes packed with fragments of Nashua's past were removed from the building. Put in storage were a chunk of Old Ironsides, the Goodrich Sisters' silver, Pvt. Amedee Deschenes Croix de Guerre medal from World War I and a document bearing the signature of Abraham Lincoln, to name a few.

Only the bright red fire engine, the pride of the town's volunteer bucket brigade in 1824, remained in the basement. It was too cumbersome to move.

The renovation and expansion of the building cost $345,000 and took three months to complete. The society's backbreaking task began after the construction was finished and a team of members volunteered to help.

"There were 20,000 items packed in boxes. We had to reverse everything and put it back," says Frank Mellen, society president, as he surveys the delicate pieces in the cabinets lining the formal dining room wall. Unpacking the many treasures and arranging them in interesting displays, has taken almost a year.

"And we're still not finished," adds Beth McCarthy, the society's first full-time curator, who was hired in March.

"I think I've found someone to fix the clocks. Clocks are so temperamental," says Mellen, referring to the many antique clocks in need to tune-ups.

Come Saturday, the Historical Society will be ready to welcome the public to show off the enlarged pine-paneled meeting room and the handicapped-access additions including an elevator. As before, however, the center of attraction will be the exhibits telling the story of how a rural hamlet called Dunstable in the 1700s became a milltown named Nashua in the 19th century and grew to a metropolis of more than 100,000 as the year 2000 approaches.

On the day of the reopening, a piece of Nashua history will be given to each visitor to take home as a souvenir of the occasion. For that one day, the old post office in the basement of the Speare House will come to life fully certified to perform its federal mailing duties.

Visitors will be able to step up to the wooden post office window—once a part of Shapiro's Drug Store on Main Street—to buy stamps and mail letters.

A machine-borrowed form the post office will hand-cancel envelops with an original stamp designed by Kevin Goddu, a graphic designer and a society member. Commemorative envelopes with the Speare Memorial Building and the Abbot-Spalding House will be sold for $3.

"Each state is allowed by the federal government to designate a certain number of temporary postal stations, and we were lucky to be chosen," says McCarthy.

Before leaving, people can pursue the collection of mailboxes including one of the oldest in the U.S., from the early, 1900s.

There are three floors of history in the Speare building, counting the basement, a treasure trove of Police and Fire Department artifacts and found objects from the mills. The most noticeable attraction is the T.W. Gillis Pumper Fire Truck, 150 years old and still in mint condition. The first end-stroke fire engine in Dunstable, it was purchased for the town by the Nashua Manufacturing Co. and named for the company agent.

In the corner behind it is an antique Nashua landmark that made headlines 20 years ago. It is the famous weathervane from Amherst Street Fire Station. A plaque tells the story of how it was mysteriously stolen from the top of the station in the '70s and just as mysteriously returned a year later, after a call alerted the police department to its whereabouts.

If anyone is tempted to get misty-eyed about the past, a look at a ball-and-chain display will quickly clear the vision.

"They used that on people locked up for the night at the poor house," Mellen points out. The Poor Farm was both the city's House of Corrections and home for the indigent from the mid-1800s to the early 1900s. It was located off Taylor Road, now the site of the Nashua Country Club, and a picture of it hangs on the wall above.

A more nostalgic remnant of the past is the whistle that sounded the change of shifts in the mill yard. It was recently rescued from the junkyard and turned over to the society for its collection.

Upstairs, a replica of a one-room schoolhouse on Coburn Avenue will take visitors back to the early 1900s. The schoolhouse was attended by children who lived on surrounding farms. Mary Sullivan, one of the pupils a the District 7 Schoolhouse, has helped assemble the classroom complete with lift-top desks, primers of the day, and most feared object of all, the polished oak paddle used to administer discipline.

Also on the second floor, now easily reached by elevator, is a pictorial history of Nashua recorded on slides as well as the military room and the Speare Room.

The military room attests to Nashua's part in the nation's wars from the Revolution to the two World Wars of the 20th century. The medals and uniforms of two Nashua heroes of recent wars are displayed side by side in the cabinet at the far end of the room. They belonged to Deschenes, who was decorate in World War I, and Navy bomber pilot Paul Boire, the city's first casualty of World War II.

Telegraph Photo Files

Florence H. Speare Memorial Building

The Speare building and its historical companion, the Abbot-Spalding House, will again be open to visitors Tuesdays and Thursdays 10 A.M. to 4 P.M., Wednesdays 10 A.M. to 3 P.M. and 5 P.M. to 7 P.M., and Saturdays 1 P.M. to 4 P.M. throughout the summer.

Weekly tours for fourth-graders who study the history of Nashua in the public schools will resume in the fall. Edmund Keefe, retired superintendent of schools, is in charge of the committee conducting the tours.

He says the budding Nashua historians "love the player grand piano and the mill fire-alarm system."

Keefe recalls one boy's reaction to a picture of the Nashua High School football team that he shows the touring youngsters.

"I taught some of those boys," Keefe told them.

A voice in the group shouted out, "Mister, that was 1934. Are you 100 years old?"

"No, but I'm getting there," Keefe responded with a chuckle.

History stops for no one, and it never ceases to fascinate.

June 5, 1993

"PEST HOUSE" COMES OF AGE

The year 1892 was a very good year.

The second year of the 1890s promised even greater growth and prosperity for the city of Nashua. The only shadow on the horizon was the mill workers' strike at the Nashua Manufacturing Company.

The Odd Fellows Building, one of the grand edifices then gracing Main Street, was dedicated that spring. The Masonic Temple had been finished the year before. Mary A. Hunt gave $50,000 to the city to erect a new library in memory of her husband John M. Hunt. YMCA members eagerly awaited a gymnasium under construction on Water Street, and ground had been broken for a new school on Amherst Street.

It was a memorable year in the city's history for many reasons but most of all because the town fathers decided it was time for the city to provide its citizens with a public hospital, as Manchester and Concord already had done.

The thriving mill town had outgrown the Pest House located near the Poor Farm, where people with smallpox and other contagious diseases were isolated at the time. Even the one-room Emergency Hospital in the basement of the new Police Station on Court Street seemed inadequate.

On May 9, 1892, doctors and civic leaders organized the Nashua Hospital Association with William Diah Cadwell, the head of the Jackson and Nashua Manufacturing companies, as its first president.

A year later the association rented the Collins house on Spring Street for $360 a year, setting up a 24-hour hospital with eight beds.

Faced with disabled soldiers returning from the Spanish-American War and more patients than the Nashua Emergency Hospital could accommodate, the association purchased the Hall House at 8 Prospect Street five years later. This 25-bed hospital was fully equipped and fully staffed with the help of a new Nursing School.

Renamed Memorial Hospital in 1913 after receiving a substantial bequest from Dr. George Wilbur, a new hospital building replaced the Hall House and laid permanent claim to the corner of Prospect Street and Dearborn Street.

Starched white caps and uniform were still mandatory when Beatrice (Michaud) Cadwell, who later married Cadwell's grandson, graduated from the hospital's school of nursing in 1934.

"The student nurses did all the work on the floor. It was a different world. We had quite a lot of responsibility but we didn't have the technology they use today.

They didn't have penicillin. Sulfa came out a year or two after I graduated," remembered the class valedictorian.

The speaker at her graduation, Dr. Frank Kittredge, noted the change in public's attitude toward the hospital through the years. The stark prison-like picture had vanished, he said.

"Today a child thinks it is a grand adventure when he goes to the hospital for the removal of tonsils and adenoids," the pediatrician was quoted in *The Telegraph*.

A century since the seeds of its existence were planted, Nashua Memorial Hospital has mushroomed, its complex of buildings overtaking the entire block on Main and Prospect Street. An east wing and a North building have been added, increasing the beds to 188, the staff to 1,000 and the specialized units to dozens, to say nothing of the labs and such hi-tech equipment such as CAT-Scans, and MRI's. Even a multilevel parking garage has been built across the street.

"The only part of the hospital that is still standing is the part that was there when I was in training and they are going to tear it down," noted Mrs. Cadwell, referring to the 1915 building which will be demolished soon to make way for a new wing.

Ask anyone associated with Memorial when the small town hospital was transformed into a modern medical facility and they focus on the year 1952. The Nutt Surgical Wing was completed with moneys from a legacy left to the hospital when the Nashua merchant, Charles Nutt, died, ironically in 1892.

Joseph Latvis helped to lay the cornerstone of the building, where he would later take charge of the maintenance department. He started working in the hospital in 1931 at the age of 19, and was then the lone member of the maintenance department.

Memorial Hospital

SNH Medical Center

Telegraph Photo Files

"We were burning coal up to the time of the Nutt building—90 tons a month and everything done by hand. My first pay was $38 a month for 60 hours-plus a week," said the man who retired in 1977 after 44 years with the hospital.

With the completion of the Nutt building the hospital converted to oil. It also entered the modern era of air-conditioning and auxiliary power.

"It is a different way of doing things today. Everybody's a specialist and I'm not talking about the doctors. There is an air conditioning man, a refrigerator man, a boiler man, painters, electricians . . . "

Yet with all the added departments and all the new medical wonders, one thing has remained about the same, said Helen Lafazanis, a member of the Women's Auxiliary since 1954.

"It is still the friendliest place to be. That hasn't changed at all."

May 1992

NASHUA PUBLIC LIBRARY

Heads bent engaged in reading a book, the figures of two children sit silently on a wooden bench in the corner of Robert Frost's office.

"People do a double take when they come in," says Frost, the assistant director of the Nashua Public Library. "I have my two children here for the winter. They are good company, nice and quiet."

In the spring, the life-size bronze sculpture of a small boy in overalls and his older sister with bangs and a pony-tail will grace a granite bench on the walkway outside of the library. They will face Court Street with the brick wall of the children's room for a back drop.

"The artist chose that spot because they are visible to people coming from every direction of Court Street," says Frost.

The sculpture, commissioned by the library's Burbank Fund, is the creation of Lloyd Lillie of Newton, Mass. Of his many sculptures of historical figures throughout the country, he is perhaps best known for the startlingly-realistic statue of Mayor James Michael Curley, sitting on a park bench in Curley Memorial Park, Boston. Another of his seated statues, Red Auerbach, is in Quincy Market Mall.

Lillie came out of retirement to create the touching monument for the Nashua Public Library and he used his two grandchildren as models for the piece.

Though the two bronze figures belong to the 21st century, they are timeless in dress, demeanor and choice of entertainment, reading a book. It is that simple pleasure that unites the past, the present and future and has made the library the social, intellectual and educational center of the city through the centuries.

Ironically, in the 20th century the Nashua Public Library was the lightning rod for controversy, not once but twice. The storm both times was precipitated by a generous monetary gift to the city from a prominent resident, specifically to build a home for the library.

When it began in 1851, Nashua's house of books was not a public library but a private reading club in a local book store. Almost a decade after Nashua was chartered, the Union Atheneum was formed. Its members were charged dues to borrow books. The reading club also sponsored lectures bringing such famous figures as Oliver Wendell Holmes and Stephen Douglas to town.

In 1867, an institution supported by taxes, the Nashua Public Library, was established by a group of young women who had organized during the Civil War to raise money for soldier's benefits. They turned over their assets to the city to start

CHILDREN READING
BY LLOYD LILLIE
DEDICATED JULY 19, 2001
FUNDED BY
LEONARD BURBANK FUND

Laurie Berna

a public library and the Nashua Manufacturing Co. came forth with the books from its collection for its employees.

Among the women advocating the public library was Mary Hunt, whose name would later be associated with the city's first library building at the turn of the 20th century. Before that time, the library's books and reading rooms were housed in city buildings, first in County Records Building and then the Odd Fellows Building.

When John Hunt died in 1892, his wife, Mary, and her daughter, also Mary, offered city officials $50,000 to build the first permanent facility as a memorial. It took 11 years filled with dissension before the Hunt Memorial Library Building became a reality. During the stormy interlude of wrangling over the site and the need for such a facility, the women threatened to take back the offer. At one point, they took the city to court for reneging on its part of the agreement.

The Greeley lot on Railroad Square was chosen as the preferred site but while the city dillydallied, it was bought by a real estate syndicate. Finally, after the case went to the Superior Court three times, the city took the land by eminent domain. In the meantime, the elder Mary Hunt died and there were further delays in obtaining the money.

At the dawn of the 20th Century, *The Telegraph* printed an editorial admonishing the city fathers.

"Any man in the business world dealing with another as the city of Nashua had with the donors of this fund would be disgraced among his fellows. Had an individual disregarded the solemn order of the Supreme Court as the city of Nashua disregarded it, that individual would be in contempt."

The object of all the contention, the distinctive building designed by architect Ralph Adams Cram, opened in September, 1903, after clearing of buildings on Main, Lowell and Clinton streets and two years of construction. Grand as it was inside and out, there was little fanfare for the opening. An announcement of the opening was printed on an inside page of *The Telegraph*. The following day a full page inside detailed the magnificent gothic design and elegant interior decor, complete with sketches.

Too many disagreements, however, had drained much of the joy from its opening. Ironically, with time the Hunt Memorial Library on Library Hill was destined to become the defining building of Nashua, the one etched in everyone's memory.

More than 60 years later history would repeat itself with the building of new and more spacious home for the Nashua Public Library on Court Street.

Through the years, the library had progressed from one where only the librarians had access to the books to a modern institution where the patrons could search the stacks. By the end '50s, the city grew at a rapid rate and the library was pressed to keep pace with its book collection and research material. Yet its space was increasingly inadequate. In 1959, the library put its first bookmobile on the road to bring books to the neighborhoods.

Also in 1959, another generous donor, Mabel Chandler, left her family home on the corner of Kinsley and Main streets, without much to-do. She also bequeathed $60,000 for its upkeep. As an ethnic center, it became an auxiliary to the Hunt Building, but it was not the solution to the crowded conditions of Hunt and not far enough from downtown to be a branch library.

The design of the Hunt Building did not allow for additions beyond the three levels and the tower, where many books were stored. Its narrow, winding staircase were a challenge to any librarian, frequently fetching books there. Several studies confirmed the need for a new library.

"We even had books in the coal bins and in the men's room" recalls Joseph Sakey of the use of every empty corner. Sakey arrived on the library scene in mid-50s and served as executive director until 1971, leaving before the new facility he fought for was opened. After years as executive director of the Cambridge (Mass.) Library he has returned to spend his retirement years in Nashua.

Sakey was the proverbial right man in the place at the right time. To get the new building built, he had to marshal all the forces in the city to overcome adversaries, including Mayor Dennis Sullivan. The former postman took the city reins in 1966 after being an alderman.

The mayor and many of the aldermen scoffed at the need for a new library even after Eliot Carter, a civic leader and treasurer of the family business, the Nashua Corp., stepped forward in 1968 to offer the city $800,000 to get the new library rolling.

His only proviso was the choice of the site. He and his wife Edith, a member of the library board of trustees, preferred the Court Street location in the heart of downtown. The mayor begrudgingly suggested the Mill Pond site on the outskirts of town.

The climax of the battle royal took place at a public hearing called to close Olive Street, the last hurdle to obtaining the Court Street site. The mayor contended the campaign for the new library was an "elitist plot," said Sakey, noting a new group of low-income people, VOICE, proved otherwise.

According to Carter's account of the event in a slim volume, "Tangled Tapes," the mayor was expected to rally his troops to defeat the resolution. Much to Carter's surprise, the politically-active group VOICE, appreciative of the Carters' work on their behalf, also turned out to register support for the resolution and the new library. And its voice prevailed.

After Sakey pointed out the need for future expansion, Carter contributed another $300,000.

Although the mayor had vetoed accepting the Carter contribution of more than a $1 million, the Board of Aldermen finally decreed that the money, along with federal funds, would be used and construction of a new library would begin.

The Nashua Public Library on Court Street was dedicated in September of 1971. Sullivan did not attend. Edith and Eliot Carter did.

The Hunt Memorial Building, designated a National Historic Monument, became administrative offices for the school department until the 1990s. During the Wagner administration it was rescued from private sale to be restored as a community center.

The staff moved everything into the new building in 1971 just like the staff of the Hunt Building did 70 years earlier. This time there were more hands but the books numbered in the thousands.

"We worked till after midnight many a day," says Frost, then a newcomer to the library staff. "We loaded the books into wooden rifle boxes and passed the boxes down a bread line. In comparison to the old building, the shelves looked empty. But not for long."

"We're at capacity now and have been there a long time," Frost said.

True to Sakey's predictions 30 years before, the space for expansion will all be accounted for in the first decade of the 21st century.

"Joe Sakey's vision was justified," says Florence Shepard, head of the reference department in the Court Street building until she retired in 1988.

According to Clarke Davis, the director since 1975, the music art and media department moved into the lower level West Wing in 1995. In addition to its circulation of tapes, painting and books, it is the scene of such special event as the summer Bach Lunch Series.

It also houses the Winer Learning Center with computer, video and study stations. The biography section was moved to the East Wing in 1989 and the fiction section will be moved to the East Wing when funded by the Capital Improvement Committee.

Today an average of 1,200 patrons visit the Nashua Public Library daily. It has the largest circulation of any public library north of Boston, circulating 500,000 volumes a year. It requires a staff of 32 full-time employees and more than 20 part-time employees.

In spite of the electronic revolution, the sculpture of two children reading a book will be relevant to 21st century not just a representation of the past, but as a symbol of the future.

"We will always continue to be a library in the print sense. We have such a large inventory in print. It is accessible, affordable and a comfortable format," Davis said.

Using a computer is handy but it can not replace curling up on the couch with a good book borrowed from the Nashua Public Library.

January 1, 2000

Florence Shepard and the histories of Nashua, "The Nashua Experience," and "Nashua New Hampshire, A Pictorial history," and the Nashua files of the library reference department were invaluable resources for this article.

LAST ECHO OF LOVE

He was a successful Nashua businessman, a member of the Nashua Millionaires Club, a three-time police commissioner and a pillar of the community. But Roscoe Proctor is best remembered as a man who loved animals. His name will be forever paired with the first pet cemetery in New Hampshire.

Proctor's will specifically called for it: In his will, he bequeathed the ribbon of land in the city's North End to the Humane Society of New Hampshire for a pet memorial ground.

Since 1930, the Proctor Cemetery on Ferry Road has been the final resting-place for some of the most beloved four-footed residents of Nashua and other New England towns.

But alas, this story is a bit of a memorial, too: The cemetery will soon close for lack of space.

When Proctor left it to the Humane Society, the 6-acre piece of land seemed more than generous for a city with 31,463 people. Little did he imagine Nashua in 1998, bulging with more than 81,000 people and little untouched land left. Today, instead of trees, the cemetery is choked by condo and housing developments.

During the past 68 years, 80,000 animals have been buried in the isolated area hugging the Merrimack border. Cats, dogs, birds, horses and even a few white rats are buried there, according to Michael Philbrook, executive director of the Humane Society. As in life, they rest in death in many different accommodations, from simple homemade boxes to velvet-lined solid oak caskets.

Last week, the weather—a gray October day—cast the perfect mood for strolling through the grounds, surveying the sea of miniature monuments and stopping along the way to read the touching memorials. A homemade wooden cross, a snapshot attached to makeshift gate, a bunch of artificial flowers mark some of the graves, though artificial flowers and fences are prohibited in Proctor's will.

"I just don't have the heart to tell people to remove them," Philbrook, the devoted owner of a toy fox terrier, Petunia Jane, says of the artificial posies. With fences, the Humane Society has been more successful, because barriers between the graves interfere with the upkeep.

There is a tomb to the Unknown Dog, hit by a car and never claimed by its owner. A celebrity dog, Paugus, is buried there. He and his master were voted "American Boy and Dog of 1931." Paugus also had further claim to fame as the grandson of Chinook, Admiral Byrd's sled dog.

A memorial to Roscoe Proctor

One of the sad stories are the many birds buried there after a fire destroyed an aviary in Merrimack.

Another victim of a fire—Nashua's Crown Hill fire—is buried there. In fact, Creampot bears the distinction of being the cemetery's first pet to be interred in the Proctor Cemetery.

She belonged to Jennie Kendall, animal activitist in the early 1900s, the founder of the NH Humane Society and the person credited with inspiring the pet cemetery.

Kendall, the first female sheriff in the state, was the friend of Proctor, a prominent Nashua businessman in the state who was active in Democratic politics. He was a Ward 7 alderman and a state representative, according to the *Nashua Telegraph*. "In his later years, he devoted his political activities to building the candidacies of Democratic office-seekers in the city and the state," a *Telegraph* news article stated.

Proctor was president of a very successful family business, Proctor Brothers, a cooperage on E. Hollis Street that *The Telegraph* called "one of the largest industries of its kind in the world today."

Unfortunately, Proctor made headlines on the front page of *The Telegraph* on Saturday, May 11, 1929, when he was stricken with a heart attack and died in Chicago on a business trip the day before. He was a bachelor, 48 years old, often pictured holding his pet Pomeranian.

According to Humane Society lore, Kendall and Proctor shared a love of animals. She helped him provide humane care to the horses he used in his business and convinced him to donate a piece of property he owned on Ferry Road for the state's first pet cemetery.

It is safe to say Proctor's and Kendall's paths often crossed in her work with the police department. That the police respected her concern for the welfare of animals and underprivileged children can be seen on the monument dedicated to her in the cemetery between two pine trees:

In loving memory of M. Jennie Kendall
Outstanding crusader for defenseless animals and underprivileged children
Devoting her life to their welfare. Founder of this cemetery in 1930 and
Faithful custodian until her death September 28, 1939.
"She was the voice of the voiceless; through her the dumb could speak
Till the deaf world's ear was forced to hear
The cry of the wordless weak."
This tablet erected in grateful recognition by
Her loyal friends and members of the Police Department, Who gave their
Constant support.

Kendall and Proctor are the only two humans with memorial stones in the cemetery.

After Kendall died, her niece, Marian Draper, succeeded her as president of the NH Humane Society, serving from 1930 to 1959. Draper built the first animal shelter for homeless animals in back of her house. A year ago, when the old yellow farm on 2 Lake Avenue was sold to the city for the new Lake Street Fire Station, the Humane Society was given some of the Draper Farm memorabilia from its original site.

The present animal shelter was built on the Ferry Street land donated by Proctor in 1978 and plans are under way to enlarge it in the year 2000, the Humane Society's centennial year.

Though the cemetery will close when the last few regular plots and 50 plots for cremation urns are sold, the cemetery will remain with perpetual care. Since the sale of the plots funded maintenance, the Humane Society of New Hampshire has started a Proctor Cemetery Animal Fund to take up the slack.

In the meantime, Philbrook will be directing pet lovers to the NH Society's recently opened cemetery in Stratford.

Landscaping to beautify the Nashua cemetery and the shelter is now under way; the Nashua Garden Club has adopted it as one of its many civic projects. Piles of rich dirt from the landfill and lilac bushes from the state have already arrived. A flagpole, beds of perennials and greenery will appear in the spring.

"We never know when they're coming but we know when they've been here," says Philbrook, pointing to some of the new bright spots.

Although he is buried in Woodlawn Cemetery, Roscoe Proctor's legacy is Proctor Cemetery. His monument at the entrance to the cemetery will be adorned with flowers.

The inscription reads:

In memory of Roscoe Proctor
Friend and lover of animals who by his will
Made this cemetery possible at his death.
May 10, 1929

October 17, 1998

CITY MONUMENTS TO REMEMBER

In the clear, cool air of the morning, Steve Walters pushed his lawn mower along Main Street, cutting the oases of greenery along the way.

After, he turned up the flowerbeds for the summer annuals, and Debbie Killmon and Mike Bonenfant followed behind, picking up the stalks of tulips that had passed their bloom.

Walters and his assistants were beautifying the memorial parks for the parade next Thursday, the day when New Hampshire celebrates Memorial Day.

When he started tending the hallowed patches eight years ago, the Parks Department horticulturist said he stopped to study the monuments.

"But, after a while you don't see them anymore," he said.

He was one of the few people in town, however, who knew where to find the Memorial to Vietnam Veterans. Most Nashuans respond to inquiries about that memorial with blank stares, even when standing 100 feet away from it. The scalloped stone, dedicated on Oct. 12, 1969, fades into a corner of the Ledge Street ballpark.

Though eyes may skim the memorials daily, the monuments meant to keep our past before us go virtually unnoticed.

How many times do we drive past the Soldiers' and Sailors' Monument on the crest of Library Hill without taking a moment to see what it is all about? Yet, together with the Hunt Memorial Building, the statue creates a scene signifying Nashua, much as the Washington Monument calls to mind the nation's capital.

Erected in 1889, the Soldiers' and Sailors' Monument is a lasting tribute to the men who fought in the Civil War. Once arguments about where to put it were settled, it was built to endure at Abbot Square. The foundation of the statue is embedded 11 feet in the ground.

Crowning the stone shaft is the figure of Victory, 9-feet high and carved from New Hampshire granite. Several bronze bas-reliefs encircle the middle. The most allegorical bears the inscriptions "with malice toward none and charity for all" and depicts the goddess of Liberty with a broken chain at her feet. A slave kneels before her and standing over him with hands clasped in peace are a Union and a Confederate soldier.

The monument's most striking features are the figures giving it its name—the soldier, with gun pointed toward Main Street, and the sailor facing Concord Street. The sailor grips a rope in his left hand, and in his right, raised above his head, is the handle of a bladeless sword.

General Foster Statue

When the blade was removed from the sailor's fist, no one knows. In face, no one noticed it was missing until it turned up one day in the late'70s on the desk of then-Mayor Maurice Arel. It was promptly restored only to have it stolen once more.

Another monument to the Civil War salutes a single hero, Maj. Gen. John Gray Foster. A statue of the West Point graduate, who distinguished himself at Fort Sumter, stands at the intersection of Locke, Granite and Orange streets—Foster Square. The statue, unveiled on Memorial Day, 1922, faces Orange Street, the site of the general's boyhood home.

At the foot of Library Hill is an island of memorials dedicated to the two world wars. Deschenses Oval, named in honor of Pvt. Amedee Deschenes, was dedicated on Nov. 11, 1920. The simple marker offers a touching biography of the soldier who was posthumously awarded the Croix de Guerre medal for bravery in the battle of Xivray, France, on June 16, 1918. Deschenes survived Xivray, but was caught in a gas attack at Saint Mihiel and died in the hospital four days later. He was buried in France on Oct. 1, 1918.

Sharing the park at Railroad Square is an imposing monument to World War II, dedicated Nov. 11, 1953. Three steps lead to a long, stone memorial. Differing from other monuments, this one recognizes the role of women in war.

A flagpole and an inscription are the solitary marker memorializing Spanish American War veteran John Lyons. Lyons did not die in the war. On the contrary, he was active in veteran's organizations and "never missed a march," according to Jeanne Johnston, longtime secretary-treasurer of the Joint Veterans Committee.

Telegraph Photo Files

He died in his 90s, and two years later on Nov 11. 1966, the playground where Allds and Marshall streets meet was dedicated in his name.

It took 200 years for men who fought in the Revolutionary War to receive their due, but in June 1976, the Rotary Club in conjunction with the city's American Revolutionary Bicentennial Committee erected a monument in the shape of New Hampshire. It honors the first N.H. Regiment.

Always on the Memorial Day parade route are ceremonies at City Hall, where the elaborate monument to Korean Veterans, the city's most recent memorial stands shaded by apple trees in an open, sanctuary-like setting.

In terms of a monument, Korean veterans fared better than their Vietnam counterparts because of the efforts of James MacDowell and Byron Buckingham, both past commanders of the Disabled American Veterans. Refusing to let the Korean War remain "the forgotten war," they secured the choice location left vacant when the John F. Kennedy bust was moved to the front of City Hall. A two-year fund drive raised $30,000 and the parapet and series of urns was dedicated on July 1, 1989.

Soccer players, hikers and runners pass one of the city's loveliest monuments, a boulder at the entrance of Mine Falls Park. It was dedicated on Sept. 28, 1986, to Allen Soifert, a U.S. Marine who died while with the multinational, peacekeeping force in Beirut, Lebanon.

The inscription on the polished face of the rock, quarried from Mine Falls, encompasses the message of Memorial Day.

"No greater love has a man than this. That he lay down his life for peace."

March 25, 1991

SWIMMERS SAW "HOLE" PICTURE

Sunday afternoons in the hollow, the air was sweet with the spicey aroma of kielbasa and the sound of polka music drifting over the Nashua River.

Those summer Sundays were reserved for St. Stanislaus Church parish picnics on "pa's land," says attorney Lucille Kozlowski, whose father owned the grove bordering the Nashua River off Fairmount Street.

As the accordions and fiddles picked up-tempo, youngsters splashed near the riverbank. The more daring teen-agers, however, swam across the river to the canal. The water was clear and cold, and the teens rode the current past the French Hole and the Lemon Hole to the Polack Hole. The Greek Hole was just beyond. The last swimming hole was the Mill Pond, known to all as little Silver Lake.

On a hot afternoon in the early 1930s, money and material things were few, but places to swim were plentiful.

"Everybody had their own swimming hole. They just cleared the brush. The mills never bothered anybody. The police never came down there. There was no drinking, and there never was any ethnic problems," recalls Charles Grigas, a Nashua native who is now retired.

In the South End, there was Field's Grove on Salmon Brook. It offered bathers the comfort of a lifeguard, the convenience of a bathhouse and access to Red Cross swimming lessons. Down the brook toward East Dunstable Road were watering spots the town folks had labeled the Baby Swimming Hole, the Women's Swimming Hole and a Men's Swimming Hole. Each was tailor-made to the size, sex and strength of the more timid swimmers.

A sharp bend in the brook near New Searles Road produced the "Suds." A favorite with the children, it earned its name from the soapy appearance of the water as it was churned up at the turn.

Through the center of the city ran the canal. It drew the more adventurous swimmers. The swift current offered more of a challenge than the calm waters of the brook, and for those who learned how to ride the rapids, a water roller-coaster sense of excitement. On the weekends, the current was more gentle since the mills had less need to generate electric power.

The shores of the Nashua River Canal were like the Northwest frontier. One by one, the city's various ethnic groups staked a claim to a piece of its territory for its share of summer fun. "All the land belonged to the mills. Whenever they needed sand or gravel, they went in and got it. There were dirt roads everywhere," says Grigas.

Nashua Historical Society

The canal was built in 1824, diverting water from the river to supply the power needs of the mills. At the turn of the century, the hydraulic power was augmented by electricity.

As the town grew around the mills, it is easy to imagine Nashuans exploring the wooded areas on the edge of the city and discovering the oasis on the banks of the canal. By the '20s, a string of man-made beaches lined its shores offering a retreat from the heat of the city. Best of all, the central swimming spot behind Textile Ballfield was free. Ledge Street School now stands where the ball field was.

Grigas' wife, Gladys, also a native Nashuan and the former president of the Nashua Historical Society, has suggested placing markers along the canal to identify the sites of the swimming holes. The daughter of Ervin Cunningham, a mill foreman, she grew up on Perry Avenue, and the canal was one of the unofficial playgrounds of the neighborhood. Another was the clay tennis court behind her house, built by her father with the help of other mill officials and used by mill families.

The paths to the swimming holes fanned off Ledge Street. The first and biggest sandy expanse, the French Hole, was enjoyed by men and women as well as families.

Next was the Lemon Hole, a secluded, strictly male enclave.

"We created the Lemon Hole. It was off-limits to women. We couldn't afford bathing suits, so we went without them. There was no fear of women going by," continues Grigas.

The topic of conversation was usually baseball, the local teams' stats and Boston's two major league teams, the Braves and the Red Sox. For an afternoon of fun, little more was needed than a Tarzan-style rope hung from a tree to swing over the water.

Beyond the French and Lemon holes, the only swimming spot with a wooden diving board was the Polack Hole.

"It was the Polack Hole, not Polish Hole," says attorney Koslowski, insisting it be called by its proper name.

Priscilla (Pawlukiewicz) Davis remembers picking blueberries and mushrooms walking up Ledge Street to the Polack Hole.

"I wasn't a great swimmer so I'd glide along the current to the French Hole. We were all friends, and we all got along," she recalls.

The last group to stake a claim to their own slice of the canal was the Greek boys who fashioned a beach near the Sandy Bank off Broad Street.

"From 6 o'clock to 8 o'clock, we'd look for work. We'd go from the Nashua Corporation to Johns-Manville to J.F. McElwain to the Nashua Manufacturing Company. There was no work, so we'd go down to the canal," says John Lafazanis.

Ed Hutchins talks about the ballgames at Textile Field. A swim in the canal inevitably followed.

"If we had a suit, we'd swim to the French Hole and the Polack Hole," he says.

Hutchins remembers the canal as the hangout for the college crowed, who had plenty of time on their hands to develop their physiques and tans since summer jobs were scarce. Savoring a sense of nostalgia for the summers of his youth, Hutchins says, "The water was so clear you could drink it."

As the '30s drew to an end, so did the popularity of the watering spots along the canal. The pollution increased and so did the awareness of it.

Looking back, Lafazanis says, "The Depression improved. People got a few bucks and bought a car. No one carried it (visiting the swimming holes) on after we left. The water got a little slimy, and there were other places to go."

August 28, 1998

TENNIS COURTS

It happened on Perry Avenue during the Depression. In the midst of the bleak economic times, a beautiful clay tennis court emerged in the neighborhood of mill owned-housing. For years to come, it provided long, golden summers of fun and games for the families living there.

Except for the wealthy, few people enjoyed the luxury of a tennis court in their own back yard. But Gladys Grigas, then Cunningham, can still picture every detail of the one behind the stucco two-story house at 17 Perry Ave., where she and her sister, Dorothy (Moquin), grew up. "The only space big enough was behind our house," recalls the 81-year-old native Nashuan, a former president of the Nashua Historical Society.

"We could see the Nashua Canal from our back porch," she adds nostalgically.

The man who made it all happen was her father, Ervin Cunningham, an assistant overseer in the carding room of the Nashua Manufacturing Company.

He and his wife, Marie, were playing their usual evening game of croquet with their neighbors when the inspiration struck: Being able to play another game, maybe even tennis, would offer a pleasant change. There was a baseball field nearby on Ledge Street but a tennis court would attract all ages, and girls as well as boys.

"At the time it seemed like a pipe dream but the idea persisted and my father elected to approach the agent of the Nashua mills, who was Walter Whipple," relates Grigas.

Much to everyone's delight, Whipple thought the neighborhood tennis court was a fine idea and offered to help with the construction. Concern for the quality of life beyond the mills—supporting churches, schools, housing and recreational facilities—was woven into the fabric of the mill philosophy. It was designed to attract workers immigrating from many countries and to keep them in the labor force.

Ervin Cunningham prepares site for tennis court.

"Deal gently with them! For behold they come from many a distant land and loving home," wrote Mary Halpin, an Irish mill worker, according to Stephen Winship in "A Testing Time: Crisis and Revival in Nashua," a history of the mills. Whipple, says Grigas, was a humanitarian and true to his agreement: The mill provided the material and the people in the neighborhood provided the labor. Soon after they heard the news, the men in the neighborhood began clearing the brush and leveling the land for the tennis court. Though they labored long hours in the mill, the men gladly pitched in after work. The mill also supplied the equipment as well as the material, absorbing all the expense. Grigas remembers horse-drawn wagons arriving at the site and dumping loads of cin-

Cunningham interviewed by WOTW

ders to prepare the court and clay to cover it. When the court was ready, there were the many eager players of all ages lined up to use it. During the day, armed with rackets and balls, the children flocked to the courts; evening hours were reserved for adults. "Anyone could play with the stipulation that those who did had to maintain it," Grigas observed. The tapes were frequently swept of clay dust and nets were tightened at the end of every day. After it rained, to smooth out any gullies the men and the boys pulled a huge roller over the court. "And," adds Grigas, "the girls sat on it to give it heft." More experienced players such as the late Walter Haven coached the novices and the late Royal Dion started a business of restringing rackets.

Grigas played all through her Temple Street Junior High School and high school years, graduating from Nashua High School on Spring Street in 1937 before the new high school on Elm Street was ready for occupancy.

Enthralled by their newfound skills, the young tennis players planned a tournament at the end of the season. The winner received a heavy white sweater. Grigas wore hers for many years. The tournament and a cookout, complete with hamburgers and roasted corn, became an annual event.

The Cunningham household was the center of activity because of its location. The racket crowd knew they were always welcome, and when he was home, Ervin Cunningham loved to entertain them with far-fetched stories.

Another draw was the batch of freshly-baked doughnuts Mrs. Cunningham made each morning. "It was like a big family. We always knew when someone was sick," says Mrs. Grigas.

The tennis courts were a boon to all but especially for the teen-age boys, since summer jobs were hard to get in the Depression years. After a close match on the courts, the canal was just a few steps away for a cool swim.

"My father didn't let us swim in the canal until we were good swimmers. There was a strong undercurrent," says Mrs. Grigas. Her husband, Charles, also a native Nashuan, notes, "All the land belonged to the mills. Whenever they needed sand or gravel, they went and got it. There were dirt roads everywhere."

Yet the mill needs never interfered with summer fun along the Nashua River Canal. It was dotted by beaches established by the youths of different ethnic groups. There was the French Hole, the Lemon Hole, a secluded strictly male spot, the Polack Hole and the Greek Hole. The Polack Hole ("It was the Polack hole, not the Polish hole," insists attorney Lucille Kosklowski) was the biggest and boasted a diving board.

A friendly atmosphere prevailed from one hole to the next with teens often swimming from one hole to another to meet a friend. "The mills never bothered anybody. The police never came down. There was no drinking problem and there never was any ethnic problems," says Grigas.

In the '30s, the mills auctioned off the houses in the neighborhood, giving first choice to families who had rented from the mills. "There was an understanding that they would give a break to the people who lived there," says Mrs. Grigas, noting that her father paid $1,900 for their house.

The off-white stucco house at 17 Perry Ave. is now painted brown, but its front porch is still intact. The neighborhood is still a quiet pocket of single family and duplex houses, lawns and trees untouched by the traffic of Ledge Street around the corner. But the back yard is overgrown with brush and the tennis court is just a memory, though Gladys and Charles Grigas' son "Pepper," the oldest of their three children, says he spotted a trace of clay still there last fall.

Perry Street is paved with many memories for the Grigas family. Looking back to the '30s, Gladys Grigas remembers the joy of summer days in Nashua.

Though it was not the best of times economically for the country or for Nashua, the young people in town never wanted for a place to swim, to play tennis or to make friends. "Our childhood was special. It is one I would wish for anyone," says Mrs. Grigas.

A LONGTIME HUB OF CITY ON THE GO

Editor's Note: May is Nashua History Month. The former Union Station was a community centerpiece in an era when passenger train service flourished. As American writer Charles Turner observed in 1982, "When the whistle and the call stretched thin across the night, one had to believe that any journey could be sweet to the soul."

Listen. Even today, we all recognize the haunting signature song of a train, blaring through the countryside. Some of us savor the sound like a piece of penny candy, remembering when trains carried passengers as well as freight to far-off places.

"I still miss it," says Catherine Valley of Hudson. She grew up on Nashua railroad time. Her father, Joseph Bellefeuille, was a railroad man until he retired in the late 1950s. By then, Nashua's passenger rail service, drained of vigor by the highways, was slowing to a halt, too.

"Dad was a track foreman, he had 18 people working for him . . . By the time he retired, he had two."

President Harry Truman and daughter Margaret

Telegraph Photo Files

From 1880 to 1965, Union Station was the nerve center of city life. It was the point of arrival for French-Canadians in search of a new life. It brought dignitaries to town, including presidents Teddy Roosevelt, William Howard Taft, Harry Truman and Dwight D. Eisenhower.

Valley was in the crush of Nashuans that greeted Truman and daughter Margaret on his historic whistle stop campaign in 1948.

"They shouted 'Give 'em hell, Harry,'" she recalls.

Business people like Marvis Mellen and her boss Max Silber took time out from the office to cheer on Gen. Eisenhower in his campaign to win the presidency in 1952. They still remember the excitement.

The platform of Union Station was the stage on which many real-life dramas were played, particularly during the two World Wars.

Years before, temperance agitator Carrie Nation took the spotlight for a moment at Union Station. She visited here in 1901, and according to *The Telegraph*, during her speech, the reformer asked a man in the Union Station crowd how many saloons there were in town. "One hundred and fifty," he answered. "Then there are 150 gates to Hell," she responded.

In the '30s, '40s and '50s, Nashua families set their clocks by the railroad schedule. Morning departure time for commuters determined the hour that families would rise, and the return trip set the dinner hour. At 6 P.M., the train from Boston made a special stop to let passengers off on Main Street behind Canal Street.

Nashua's railroad system, Valley's father told her, was unique. It had the roundhouse and the tracks that allowed trains to head east or west, north or south.

"Even Lowell didn't have that, and in Boston, you had to switch from the North to the South Station."

In Union Station's 85-year history, countless Nashua families boarded the train there for vacation adventures.

"I remember when we went off to Buffalo; I was 12. I was all excited. It was an overnight trip," Valley recalls. She can still picture the elegant dining room, the tables set with fine china and silver, the guests served like royalty by black waiters in formal white jackets.

A window seat to watch the changing countryside made the trip even more enjoyable. And with a flick of the wrist, the seats could be adjusted to face each other, making it possible to play cards or carry on a four-way conversation.

Train trips were frequent for the family because Valley's father had a gold card. Quite different from today's version, it was awarded to employees with a long service record. It was also more valuable than the plastic one of today, because it took Boston & Maine families anywhere in the country they wanted to go.

"Even better, there was no bill to pay," says Valley.

There were other perks of being the daughter of a railroad man—discounts on candy bars and comic books, for example.

"Rose ran the counter for snacks and magazines, and dad bought so many comics there, she didn't charge us when we came in. 'Your father works for the railroad,' she said."

Nashua Historical Society

Union Station

Memories lead to other memories. "On a cold day, you could hear the steam in the depot coming on," she adds, wistfully.

The one black mark during the railroads many years of operation, however, was a seven-car derailment on the morning of November 12, 1954, as the train approached Union Station. The accident created a major traffic jam in town.

Several people were injured and one died in the tragedy. The *New York Times* ran *Telegraph* photographer Mike Shalhoup's picture of the catastrophe on its front page the next day.

Even in the railroads waning years in the 1960s, when there was a single passenger car going from Concord to Boston, some Nashuans, such as Cal Libby, preferred the crowded quarters to driving on the highway. Each day a single passenger car came from Concord and by the time it got to Nashua, all the seats were taken. He stood all the way to Boston, where he worked for an advertising agency.

"Going home you had to run like hell to get to the station. If you missed the 5 P.M., you had to wait until midnight." The last train accommodated the sports and theater crowd.

In 1965, the closing chapter was written on passenger rail service, as Union Depot was razed, and the Howdy beefburger restaurant took its place. Today, the site at the corner of Temple and East Hollis Streets is occupied by Rakis restaurant.

"It's a shame they tore it down for a hamburger stand," laments Frank Mellen, speaking for many other Nashuans.

Mellen, president of the Nashua Historic Society, is still a railroad buff. For a recent vacation, he and his wife, Marvis, rode Amtrak to New Orleans instead of flying.

Ask Mellen or Libby or Valley if they would welcome the return of rail service, and they answer with an unqualified "yes."

And so did the majority of Nashuans responding to a survey taken by the city and the Commuter Rail Committee established by Gov. Judd Gregg in 1991.

J. Cameron Stuart, chairman of the now-independent committee, stresses that it is proceeding more carefully with its plans than was the case during the early 1980s when an attempt to revive the system failed.

Gregg Lantos, senior transportation planner of Nashua Regional Planning Commission, says the commission has an ongoing study about restoring passenger service to the Nashua area. He points out the obstacles include the great expense of upgrading the tracks.

"It's still down the road, but it makes good sense," he adds.

"Amen," say reluctant automobile drivers to whom the words "All aboard" sound so inviting.

May 1, 1993

WHITE WING PRESCHOOL

The aroma of soup wafted through the hallway, insulating the rooms from the winds whipping around the building. Donna Schuster's kindergarten was cooking up a savory broth of stone soup.

"I collected the stones and sterilized them and the children brought in the vegetables," she said. Of course the recipe came from the children's fable of the same name. "It is S week. We think of all the words like 'super' and 'scrumptious' that begin with the letter 'S'," she continued.

It was Friday morning at White Wing Preschool in the two-level extension of Unitarian-Universalist Church. The thermometer registered a record chill but the six classes were humming with activity.

In Rachel Quigley's kindergarten next door, the 5-year-olds had just finished concocting miniature volcanoes in empty film containers to go with the dinosaur bones they had pieced together.

Downstairs, munching on marshmallow and peanut butter snowmen for snacks were the 3-, 4- and 5-year-olds in Darlene Travis' class. Since it was too cold to go out, a big bin packed with snow occupied several 4-year-olds in Karen Trowbridge's class while Emmy Kepner, in a blue smock, painted a pink streaked design on her easel. Listening intently to a story about animals who take refuge from the cold in a mitten were the 4-year-olds in Mary Ellen Monico's and Merina Dolan's class.

"It must have been a day like today," Monico said. As she read the "The Mitten Book," the children followed along stuffing big paper mitten-shaped envelopes they had made with a mouse, a frog, fox and bear when they were mentioned in the book.

"There's always a good noise here . . . active and good," said Laurie Conrad, the director paying her morning visit to the classrooms. In the room across the hall from her office, the mixed-age class, she stopped to get a hug from Emily Arrand.

For 40 years, the classrooms at White Wing have echoed with "a good noise." The high-energy level has never abated from the first day the school opened its doors in the fall of 1959. Public kindergarten in Nashua was but a dream and there were few quality private preschools.

It was a problem the Rev. Donald Rowley and his wife, Norma, confronted when they moved to Nashua with their two small sons in 1958. He was the new minister at the church. The Rowleys could not enroll their oldest son, David, in Wintergarten, the preschool at the Good Shepherd Episcopal Church. It was filled and the waiting list was long.

With younger son, Philip, the Rowleys were to be more fortunate. Plans to remedy the situation about it were underway when the Rowleys arrived. The church had purchased the land next door when the Armory burnt down in 1957. The original objective was to build a Sunday school, according to Naomi Lyon, who was teaching Sunday school then. The Universalist Church nearby had recently merged with the Unitarian Church.

"Sunday school classes were bursting at the seams," Lyon observed.

The new White Wing of the church was designed by Nashua architects John Carter and Bliss Woodruff with church offices and the classroom furnished to scale for children. Each class had a tall window, lots of wall space for children's art work and an opening to the grassy knolls overlooking Canal Street.

Once the congregation realized the space would go to waste during the week, it organized to establish a preschool. During the week, the church parking lot made a perfect area for a playground.

"There was a group that tried to get a public kindergarten, but that was turned down," Lyon recalls.

A Nashua native, she recalls going to public kindergarten but during the Depression public kindergarten was discontinued and it would take more than 50 years before it was restored. In the '50s, the city was mushrooming, with new young families moving to town who expected kindergartens.

A private, non-profit school, with one class for 4-year-olds and one kindergarten, White Wing was at full capacity when it opened in 1959 and by the second year, there were two kindergarten classes.

The Kindergarten class of 1968 led by Barbara Parker, teacher (on right), and Sandy Linton

A separate education committee acted as the liaison between the school and church and, Rowley said, he purposely maintained his distance to preserve the nonsectarian aspect of the school.

"I only went in when something needed to be fixed and no one else was around," he says. Since his office was on the top floor of the new wing, it was a constant joy for him to see the children at play from his window.

"Although the school was financially independent, if there was a shortage the church would make it up. We never charged the going rate," he noted.

The congregation wholeheartedly supported the school and when the federal government launched its Head Start programs in the early '60s, it was welcomed by the church to use the classrooms in the afternoons until it moved to permanent headquarters in the Tacy House.

From its first days White Wing Preschool flourished in its compact new building.

"The community was ready," says Marian Woodruff who was named co-chairman the first year with Sylvia Jane Foulkrod.

Before school began the two teachers and full-time aide, who helped in both classes, were sent to Lesley College in Massachusetts for the summer to prepare for the fall opening.

"We shopped for supplies while we were there to save money on delivery so we could buy more supplies," recalls Barbara Parker, the first kindergarten teacher. Like so many teachers who followed her, she remained on the staff a long time. In recent years, her stay of 11 years was overtaken by Karen Trowbridge's 22 years teaching the nursery class.

Preparing the children for elementary school was fun.

"The children were wonderful and still are," Parker says. "The emphasis was on creativity, everything coming from the kids. It was a hands-on developmental philosophy."

One day the children were learning to walk like elephants and giraffes in a creative dance class with Rosemary Clough. The next day they were making up stories about numbers or painting cards for Mother's Day. There was a child-size organ in Parker's class and to her amazement one of the students sat down and played it. It was Philip Rowley.

Nursery school and kindergarten classes and their teachers make for indelible memories. Betty Tamposi smiles when she remembers her nursery school experience in Evelyn Quimby's class. Quimby and her husband Carl had just returned to Nashua after his tour of duty with the Army. She stepped into the nursery school class when the first teacher had to leave.

"They are such nice memories. Mrs. Quimby was so sweet and kind and the room was brand new," says Tamposi, one of two girls in a class of 14 boys.

"I brought in a paper bag full of chicken feathers from my uncle's farm and a bull horn. It still smelled like the bull."

Kindergarten and nursery school is also about families and White Wing was a second home for hundreds of siblings through the years. Hugh and Mary Phillis will soon have an album full of White Wing class pictures. Their five daughters went there to preschool and now their son Hugh attends. He is enrolled in the class of mixed ages.

"He is the big guy," says Lori Lerude, whose son Grant is one of the younger boys. "At home he is the youngest but at school he is treated like a big kid."

One of the families with a history of several generations at White Wing is the Phillips family. The late Mae Phillips, often regarded as the quintessential kindergarten teacher, taught at White Wing in the '70s. Her daughter Kathy, then attending Alvirne High School, worked by her mother's side during school vacation. Now Kathy Whitaker, the secretary of the White Wing board, and her two sons go there as another daughter and son before them. Sammy, the youngest, is in the mixed-ages class and Brad is in Rachel Quigley's kindergarten.

"I still do the paper whites (plant). The kids watch it grow and record it in their science journal," she says, revealing that her two daughters, Sara and Jackie, now teen-agers, had Phillips in public kindergarten. "And we still hatch chicks and ducks as Mae did in her class."

And the incubator in the kindergarten class was made by Brad's grandfather Richard Phillips.

In Laurie Conrad's office, one wall is lined with all the books from Mae Phillip's library on early childhood education.

In the 40 years of kindergarten and nursery school, the scholars and their teachers have changed but much about the school has remained the same. The parents still panic at registration, often waiting hours in the cold to register. When all is met with success, and their children attend, they line up each day on Grove Street for carpool. And their passengers are weighted down with all they things they have made to take home.

Since the beginning, a 3-year-old class and a mixed-age class have been added to the preschool program but the classrooms still reverberate with energy and all the classes for next year, except for a few openings in the 3-year-old class, are filled.

"We accomplished so much in three hours. I wish I could do as well the rest of the day," Quigley says.

And so it has been for 40 years. Plans are being made for a White Wing 40th anniversary reunion and celebration in Greeley Park. Alumni and teachers are all invited to attend.

January 22, 2000

YANKEE FLYER TOP CHOICE

Pick one snapshot from Nashua's past guaranteed to unleash a flood of memories. What would it be? Union Station? The Colonial Theater? The Hunt Memorial Library?

The Yankee Flyer was the choice of the Nashua High School class of 1960 reunion committee. A photo of Nashua's quintessential diner graced the cover of the class's yearbook reprinted as a souvenir at its 25th reunion. After reviewing suggestions from classmates, the reunion committee decided the diner's nostalgia quotient was tops.

"It was one of our hangouts before school and after school," said Diane O'Donnell Urquhart, remembering the daily gatherings inside and out. "We'd go there in groups. It was the place to find out what happened at St. Joe's dance or whatever else was going on in our lives."

Another Nashua High graduate of the same era applauds the choice. In fact, says Robert Chouinard, the ivory-colored diner with the green trim could easily have served as the setting for "American Graffiti," the movie celebrating youth of the 1950s.

"We'd go cruising up and down Main Street in our cars four or five times a night, and we'd always end up at the Yankee Flyer waiting for the girls to come by," recalls the 1957 NHS graduate. He was the proud owner of a 1947 two-door Ford sedan with a rebuilt engine. He earned the money to buy his first car working after school at the Yankee Flyer diner. His father also moonlighted weekends as the counter man.

In the more than 35 years that it occupied the east side of Main Street across from City Hall, the Yankee Flyer left an indelible—and a delicious—impression on the folks who lived here, worked here or were just passing through. Although gone for many years, it reappeared in the news recently when the city scrapped plans to immortalize it in a mural on the wall of the Coronis building.

"Before the highway was built, everybody stopped at the Yankee Flyer," says Mary Anne Kyriax, the last proprietor. In September 1965, after Kyriax sold the site to Tamposi real estate interests, the end for the heartbeat of hometown life was heard on Main Street.

Strictly a slice of Americana, diners blended with the landscape of the times. The exterior design duplicated the look of a dining car on a train, then the popular means of travel. Inside it offered a modern chrome simplicity rather than a mahogany luxury and the menu featured hearty home cooked meals at reasonable prices. A side order of hometown gossip added relish to the meal.

The character of the Yankee Flyer was shaped by two men from Haverhill, Mass., William Reich and Chris Kyriax. Reich, a shoe cutter, owned a billiards parlor over a confectionery store owned by Kyriax. In the mid-'20s they decided to pool their business talents. Besides a partnership of many years, they enjoyed a lifelong friendship. In fact when they moved to Nashua, Kyriax lived with the Reich family until he married years later.

According to local lore, the two men were on their way to Keene to check out a restaurant for sale when they stopped in Nashua to see Reich's friend, attorney Robert Early. He took them to the Main Street Diner near Montgomery Ward's. They never went to Keene; they bought the diner. For the first years, business was slow but their luck turned toward the end of the decade.

"Things changed when the construction workers building Presentation of Mary Academy in Hudson heard about the diner and started coming to eat there," says Eleanor Reich McLaughlin, relating the story often told by her father.

The word spread, business grew, and Reich and Kyriax decided it was time to expand. They bought the diner across the street that was owned by Arthur Ryan and continued to run the two diners for a couple of years until business warranted consolidating their efforts.

A large front-page ad in the *Nashua Telegraph* on April 17, 1930, heralds the opening of the new Yankee Flyer at 236 Main St., in front of a station of the Boston & Maine Railroad. Open 24 hours a day, the diner served fine steaks, chops, braised lamb and seafood, the ad stated.

Nashua Historical Society

The Yankee Flyer's fame traveled throughout New England when the original wooden structure was replaced by a state-of-the-art porcelain-enameled steel car, custom-built by a company in Merrimac, Mass.

The 56-foot diner, said to be the first of its kind in New England, left the J.B. Judkins Co. factory with much fanfare.

Fixtures included fluorescent lighting, chrome counter stools with red leather seats, and curved booths at each end to accommodate larger parties.

Reich's wife, Jennie, was the hostess; Reich, the business manager, and Kyriax, the night man and supervisor of the staff. If need be, the two men could bread clams or handle the counter when it was busy. *The Telegraph* Editor, Fred Dobens, wrote in his "Around the Town" column, "Kyriax was a particular favorite of ours, and we liked to drop into the place for a cup of coffee and chat with him, before we went home after working late at night. In those days it was one of the busiest places in the city, crowded day and night."

It was also an exciting place to meet celebrities of the day.

"The Yankee Flyer" was the topic of a talk Eleanor remembers giving in English class at Nashua High School. One of the regulars was Bill Cunningham, Boston sports columnist. A more unexpected visitor was Walt Disney, the Hollywood cartoonist.

As the daughter of the owner, she also had the ideal place to celebrate her 16th birthday.

The back room restaurant was more appropriate for parties and more formal dining occasions.

"Nobody ate there until they connected it with a corridor to the diner and then it was packed," says Eleanor McLaughlin with chuckle.

The meals at the diner were prepared by Neil Turcotte. He butchered his own side of beef for the roasts, the stews and the New England boiled dinners certain to draw in the hungry downtown merchants, politicians and other regular patrons from all walks of life.

"Al Robichaud, the baker, was famous for his muffins, his coconut cream pie and his fig squares; he took his recipes to the grave," says McLaughlin. Robichaud worked through the night to make his mouth-watering confections so they would be ready for the early morning crowd.

"I considered myself lucky to eat there," recalls former Alderman Adam Gureckis, who worked as a dishwasher during his high school years in the early '40s. A free meal was one of the perks of the job.

In 1942, Kyriax married, and in the early '50s, after Reich retired, he took over the business. Kyriax died after owning the diner just four years, and his widow took over the management. As the mother of two children, Mary Anne Kyriax had to learn to manage both her family and the business.

"Mother was famous for her cat naps," says daughter Cynthia Burney, now an English teacher at Elm Street Junior High School.

One of the employees was Hilda Brisebois, who worked the 6 A.M. shift from 1954 until the day the diner closed. When she started, the diner's hamburgers cost

25 cents and coffee was a dime. For policemen, a steaming mug of coffee on the house.

"Everybody knew everybody. We even knew what they would order on a particular day," says Brisebois. "We were very busy on holy days. The Catholic people couldn't eat before communion."

"The only time the place was closed was on Christmas Day," she adds.

When it closed for good and the car was removed from the site, a trail of memories were left behind. Mary Anne Kyriax says people often report seeing the Yankee Flyer elsewhere. She and her daughter checked out a diner in Salem, but it was not the Flyer. Another has been spotted in Newburyport, Mass. They plan a trip there soon but they have little hope of finding it.

A mural of the old downtown diner might remind followers of gravy days, but the daily specials and the friendly atmosphere can never be duplicated, according to Nashuans who sat at its counter for a taste of home.

February 1995

YANKEE FLYER MEMORIES

Yankee Flyer nostalgia is as rich as a slice of its coconut crème pie, the dessert Nashuans "died for" in decades past.

Like the coffee served with it, memories of the former Main Street diner seem to flow from a bottomless source. Several weeks ago, I wrote a lengthy story about its history and received a lot of calls afterward.

The new "memories" warrant a postscript, particularly because the Yankee Flyer is now destined to be immortalized in a mural. According to mayoral assistant Georgie Lyons, Nashuans can expect to see the indelible likeness before the end of the year. It will be painted on the Coronis building facing the site the Yankee Flyer occupied for more than half of the 20th century.

Where better to start on the postscript than with the coconut crème pies—or the man who made them. His name was Alphonse Robichaud. He was known to one and all as "Fred" or "Freddie," according to his daughter, Cecile Wright. She called after reading the first article on Jan. 28 to say I identified him incorrectly as Al. Several other people told me the same thing.

Wright also had another impression to set straight.

"Everybody says when he died his recipes went with him. They did not," she insisted.

"They were all in his brain, that's true, but my mother threw them away when we moved."

Though he knew them by heart, Fred Robichaud kept his recipes in a file in a closet off his oldest daughters' room and she read them often.

"The ingredients were astronomical—a 50-pound bag of flour, a 20-pound bag of sugar and 12 dozen eggs," Wright recalls with a smile.

One day, after her father died, she came home and found them gone. Her mother decided they were of no use to the average family baker and threw them away.

Fred Robichaud was the baker at the Yankee Flyer for more than 25 years. Born and raised in Maine, he began his career as a cook in a logging camp. After the death of his first wife, he and his teen-age son, Al, moved to Nashua in the early 1930s.

For a few years he worked for the Nashua Country Club. In the mid-30s he took over baking duties at the busy Yankee Flyer, which fronted the Boston and Maine Railroad stop on West Hollis Street. The amiable owners were Bill Reich and Chris Kyriax. Before long, word of Robichaud's doughnuts, muffins, fruit squares

Telegraph Photo Files

and mouth watering pies traveled far beyond Main Street and the borders of the state. He baked them fresh—by the hundreds—each day.

"You had to be invited into the bakery shop. You didn't just walk in, even if you were the owner," says Wright, the oldest of two daughters born of his second marriage to Lucienne Boucher in 1936.

She and her sister, Irene, were the exceptions to the rule. Every Sunday after attending Mass at St. Louis DeGonzague Church they walked along the railroad tracks to the diner. When they left they carried a box of raspberry squares and chocolate crème pie for Sunday dinner.

The bakery was located in the back of the diner, next to the kitchen. Robichaud worked there six days a week, 13 hours a day, starting at 1 A.M., for the grand sum of $40 a week.

The only day the diner was closed was on Christmas, and Robichaud, his wife and two daughters were invited to the Reichs' home.

"We never left without lots of presents," said Wright.

She relishes another story told of the Christmas season at the Yankee Flyer. One year before the holiday, friends and admirers stopped by to wish Robichaud a Merry Christmas. Each insisted he share a toast and by the time he made the doughnuts for the next day, he happily went about the task but left out one of the ingredients.

"It never happened again. It was the only day they didn't have doughnuts," says Wright with a chuckle.

A slight man, Robichaud was not fond of sweets himself. As he grew older, he developed a hunched back from bending over his dough day after day. In his last years at the Yankee Flyer he was not well, and his son, who by then operated a camera shop across the street, checked on him daily.

The man known for baking the best coconut crème pies in New England, died in October 1954, after four years in a TB sanitorium in Pembroke.

There are more stories to tell about the Yankee Flyer, but they will have to hold for another day.

March 13, 1995

HIGH-TECH HISTORY
IN AN ANTIQUE SETTING

If keeping tabs on family records triggers an Excedrin headache, imagine the responsibility magnified a million fold.

For the Hillsborough County Registry of Deeds, maintaining legal documents for 29 towns and two cities—Nashua and Manchester—is all in a day's work. Between 300 to 400 papers are processed daily and there are some 3 million documents indexed in its archives dating back to 1771.

What's more, all of the information can be retrieved at a moment's notice.

"We're very user friendly," says Registrar of Deeds Judith MacDonald. "All citizens have access to the material."

Come the new year, the registry will enjoy the best of the old and new worlds. A state-of-the-art optical imaging system will be in place allowing for storage capacity of information to more than quadruple.

The hi-tech heaven will be housed in the century-old building on Temple Street, now restored to its original grandeur with tin ceilings, old radiators and a magnificent wood staircase illuminated by a skylight.

Since the Hillsborough County Courthouse opened in 1903, the other major tenant in the building has been Probate Court. Last March it was moved to the new Hillsborough County Superior Court on Spring Street. A corner of its modern façade is visible from MacDonald's office, and a set of Probate files remains, since the court administering wills is closely related to the bureau recording all real estate transactions. Any related matter such as liens and building plans are also within it purview.

Spirits of the registry staff are soaring in their new-found space. Twenty-four people turn the department gears recording, verifying and processing information.

Ellen Joy, the retention supervisor, works in the basement transferring all the files to optical imaging discs, similar to CDs.

"A roll of microfilm holds three books of 350 pages and the tape holds eight rolls of microfilm," she says. Microfilm replaced the books used until five years ago.

Also downstairs, in space once used for Probate files, is the lower vault as well as the sheriff's office. As old buildings do, a steam pipe in the basement has sprung a leak and the sheriff's office is a bit damp.

County offices also occupy the upper floor. The courtroom has been converted into offices for Ellen Robinson, and her Human Services Department staff, the county attorney and the county commissioners.

Hillsborough County Registry of Deeds

The main floor, however, is now completely the domain of the Registry of Deeds.

"This is the slow time of the year," MacDonald says.

"Not today," notes Shirley Ravenelle.

She, Ruth George and Emily Tupper have been too busy taking entries to sample the department's holiday buffet spread in the next room.

The outer office leads into the upper vault, where some 50 to 75 people a day look up information about county properties. Milling about are paralegals, abstractors, surveyors, genealogists and private citizens, and many daily visitors.

The department's pride is the newly acquired room, soon to be lined with optic imaging equipment, word processors and screens operating off CD-like discs. Off to the side are two new areas for private conferences, a welcome addition for lawyers to use in closings or other quiet endeavors, says MacDonald.

Among other services, she notes, the department provides faxes, copies of deeds and plans, and information often used in court cases, or to determine town property taxes. An indication of how well it is used is the $1.8 million the service added to the county coffers this year.

In addition to her official duties, MacDonald has been overseeing the renovation project begun in 1990.

"Many a day I've come in with a hard hat on. I didn't know that was part of the job description," says the dynamic registrar of 12 years, just elected to her seventh term.

"Are the electricians coming today?" she asks Annette Jacques, deputy registrar.

The building had to be completely rewired to accommodate modern amenities and in the process MacDonald has become conversant with construction details such as outlets, vents, elevators and fire exits.

Restoring the building called for knowledge of its architecture and input from the Nashua Historical Society. Lowered ceilings were removed to expose the original high tin ones and moldings were resculpted where deterioration had set in. Throughout the building, wood was stripped of years of stain and varnish. A skylight patterned after the original design was dropped into the roof and to duplicate the original tall windows and doors, architects referred to old pictures and postcards of the building.

Beyond the building with its mysterious insignia under the peak of the roof - its significance still baffling local historians - the registry is a valuable repository of the county's history.

"These are priceless," says MacDonald, pulling out a handwritten bound volume.

"This is our history. It should be preserved. The deeds date back to 1770. Some of them mention slaves and Indian chiefs."

December 26, 1992

REUNIONS

My Window on Main Street

CLASSMATES RECALL GOOD TIMES

Friendships forged in high school may get rusty with time, but a few good memories bring back the shine.

On a sunny Saturday afternoon members of the Nashua High School class of 1931 gathered in classmate Frederic E. Shaw's back yard for their 65th reunion.

"This will be a casual affair to reminisce and remember, so bring along your favorite tape of yesteryear. No dancing, but we can tap our feet," wrote Shaw in the letter of invitation.

Twenty-five classmates and twelve spouses sat at tables with umbrellas to shade the strong sun, catching up on each other's news. Inevitably they return to the halls of Nashua High School on Spring Street, remembering the days of their youth. Though they graduated in the midst of the Great Depression and a year after the devastation of the Crown Hill fire, the good times were many.

"Next time Rudy Vallee is in Hampton Beach, I want to go," Shirley Dugas Foley sighed nostalgically as they listened to piano board renditions of "Tootle-oo, So Long, Goodbye" and "The Thrill Is Gone" popularized in the '30s by the man with the megaphone. Ralph Barr sparked many memories playing the Vallee favorites and other songs of the day in the background.

"When Rudy Vallee comes to Hampton Beach, we'll go dancing," responded Shaw, microphone in hand to welcome guests to the festivities.

At the 50th reunion, Shaw and the former Shirley Dugas led classmates onto the dance floor at the Nashua Country Club. Both had earned the reputation as smoothies on the dance floor from classmates.

"We used to have dances in the gym every Friday afternoon. The chaperones sat in the balcony," recalled Beatrice Pombrio Weisman, adding that the girls wore dresses and the boys suits and ties.

"They didn't wear blue jeans," quipped Barbara McQuesten Hambleton. Classes demanded the same proper decorum, she said, adding that the Latin she studied for four years at Nashua High School she puts to good use doing crossword puzzles.

Throughout high school, Rosalie Devereaux Bingham Stein played the piano in the school orchestra conducted by the legendary Elmer "Pop" Wilson, the Nashua High music teacher.

"Pop Wilson got the football band going in our senior year and everyone left to play in the band. We were the last class to have a really good orchestra," claims the mother of eight. She still plays piano for her church.

THE BAND

The Nashua High School Band played an important role in school activities during our years here. The band played at assemblies and athletic events, in parades, and at other school and civic functions. Only with the perseverance and good nature of our music director, C. Elmer Wilson, was such a unit possible.

Each year the band gave an annual concert with the glee club which gave the public an idea of what the students were accomplishing musically. A short concert was also given each year in the junior high school to acquaint the students with the high school music program. Another annual event was the field day in Lowell in which several high school bands from Massachusetts and New Hampshire participated. In 1950 the band marched in a parade celebrating the centennial of Clinton, Massachusetts. In 1951 the band played at the dedication of the rehabilitation hospital at Crotched Mountain. In 1950 David Bingham, who plays the baritone saxophone, was the only member of the 1952 band who went to the All-State Band. In 1951 those who went to All-State were as follows: horns, Cynthia Martin, Priscilla Wilson; tuba, Dyson Walker; saxophones, David Bingham, Normand Cote; bell lyre, Paul Josephson; drums, Normand Kimball.

THE JUNIOR RED CROSS CLUB

The Junior Red Cross Club, one of the most active clubs in high school, works for everyone in the school. In the room...

Picture of Pop Wilson in NHS Yearbook

Though the senior prom is usually the event preserved in nostalgia, it was graduation that provided Bea Weisman with a bittersweet memory.

"My parents gave me the money to buy a class ring, but I needed a pair of shoes, brown and white spectator pumps. I wore them to graduation and never got the ring."

Money was tight in most households, and buying new shoes was a major purchase. Most of the class worked to earn spending money to take a date for a Coke or to see the new talking movies such as "Cimmaron" and "All's Quiet on the Western Front." At the time, Nashua had four theaters—the Colonial, the Park, the Tremont and the State. The Colonial often featured vaudeville shows, and the Nashua Theater on Elm Street was destroyed that year by a fire.

There were 201 students in the graduating class, and many fought and died in World War II.

For many in the class of 1931, entertainment was a luxury. They had to work to help support their families.

"We came out of quite a Depression," remarked Harry Coronis, who graduated in the class with older brother Sam.

Two brothers in the same class was not unusual then, said Sam, who had to drop out for two years to help his widowed mother. While he was finishing high school, he worked behind the soda fountain of Priscilla's, the high school hangout.

The Coronis brothers are typical of the success stories born of hard times and long hours of labor.

Harry Coronis went to work for a year after graduating from high school to earn money to attend Dartmouth.

"Tuition at Dartmouth was $1,000 a year, and that was a lot of money. We had to work to earn money to go to school, and a lot of us couldn't afford it at all," he said.

After Harry graduated, he and his brother opened a pressing shop above the Scontsas card shop on Main Street, and the next year they started Coronis Cleaners, where Bagel Alley is today.

"We did pressing, cleaning, tailoring— the whole shebang," says Sam.

In 1963, Harry turned the business over to his brothers and founded Industrial Reproductions Inc., a national million dollar company.

Classmate Shirley Dugas worked part time at Speare Dry Goods Co., and saved her money to go to

FACULTY

Teaching staff from NHS yearbook

business school in Boston. When she returned to Nashua, she took over the store's bookkeeping department until she started a business with her husband in Lowell.

"My parents made plenty of sacrifices to send me to UNH," said Tom Stylianos, the retired principal of Nashua High School.

Stylianos, still looking fit at 84, was president of the class and one of the high school's outstanding athletes. He was captain of the baseball team.

Of his high school days, the man who rose to become the principal of the Spring Street Junior High and later the high school remembers coping with dual sessions in his senior year.

"Overcrowding is a perennial problem," he said.

Stylianos suggested the great strength of the class was its multiethnic mix. Many, like himself, were the children of immigrants—from Greece, Canada, Poland and Lithuania.

"School was the melting pot. That's where we all learned to live together."

Edmund Keefe, the guest of honor at the reunion, agreed.

"I taught many of these people U.S. history, and that is why they all get out to vote," he claimed. In 1931 he was in his second year of teaching at the high school.

Not only did the class learn the importance of their vote, they learned to value friendships, particularly the ones made in Nashua High School.

Just ask Madeline Walton, the class secretary, who has kept a record of classmates through the years.

"They pester me all the time, everybody wants a reunion," she said.

June 22, 1996

CLASS OF '33 HAS ROUGH START

They saved their nickels for vaudeville shows at the Park Street Theater, danced to jazz records played on the Victrola and sipped sodas at the Rosebud after football games.

Loudly they sang at the North Common next to the Amherst Street School to spur the Purple Panther football team to victory:

"Nashua's going right down the field, nothing can stop them, all have to yield . . . "

Yet life was less than idyllic for the members of the class of 1933 at Nashua High School. During the four years they spent in the brick building on Spring Street, they weathered the Great Depression and the city's own disaster, the Crown Hill Fire.

Today, class President Christo Scontsas will be welcoming about 75 alums and spouses at the class' 60th reunion at Martha's Exchange. Memories of good times and hard times were recalled at a recent meeting of the reunion committee that planned the gathering.

"What we had to worry about was to get through school," said Charles Barry.

"Everybody was poor," added Louise Kelley.

The never-to-be-forgotten stock market crash shook the nation on Black Monday, Oct. 28, 1929, a month after the Temple Street Junior High School graduates entered the high school on Spring Street as freshmen.

The specter of the Depression haunted their high school years. To make matters worse, during their sophomore year, many lost their homes in the fire that started May 5 in a Boston and Maine Railroad trestle off Temple Street and gutted the eastern section of the city.

"We had 212 graduates. Many had to drop out because of their finances, but they are still invited to the reunion," said Ruth (Bourdon) Ledoux, reunion co-chairman with Barry. Like most of her classmates, she worked after school. She was a salesgirl at Nelson's Five and Ten.

Yet despite the Depression, good times were many because pleasures were simple and expectations were far from grand.

"We made do with what we had," said Bessie Weisman. One of the favorite pastimes they all recall was watching the shoppers come and go on Main Street. Another was a nickel Coke at the Rosebud or Priscilla's. Two sipping on the same glass made it twice as good.

And the fried clams at Goodwin's were worth walking miles across the bridge to Hudson. Though buses weaved around the city, walking was the chief means of getting around, even to the junior and senior proms.

"No one even thought of limos then," says Ethel (Freeman) Tipping, chuckling.

"I wasn't allowed to date," confesses Ledoux, who chaired the 50th reunion. As a shy outsider who moved to Nashua from Medford, Mass., she had few friends in high school. She lived on Robinson Road in the South End, out of the social swim of the city, and walked to the Spring Street school every day.

"You stayed in your own neighborhood," said Tipping, who grew up on Crown Hill and was one of the lucky ones not touched by the fire.

Neighborhood "gangs"—words with a friendly ring in those days—defined the ethnic character of the city; many in the class of 1933 were first-generation Americans. There was the Greek section centering around West Pearl Street and the Lithuanian "High Rock" on High Street. Above Canal Street was French Hill, bordering the North End around Concord Street.

Diverse as the cultures were, they met and mixed at Nashua High, the center of their lives for four years. Although torn down and replaced by the Court House, the school is forever etched in their minds.

They speak of eating sandwiches in "the pit," the lunchroom that doubled as a basketball court. They had homeroom in the basement with Edmund Keefe and Henry Sharpe, both starting their teaching careers. Keefe, who went on to become superintendent of schools, will be a guest at the reunion. Another new teacher in the music department, Elmer Wilson, fondly remembered as Pop Wilson, organized the Boys Band.

And Barry can still hear history teacher Webster White insisting the proper name for the new popular music was "synchronized syncopation," not jazz.

One of the most unforgettable spots in the school was the tunnel linking the building to the Quincy Street annex, where home economics and industrial arts were taught. Remembered with smiles was the dark, narrow passage with pipes overhead. They often leaked and the dripping sound compounded the eery feeling.

"It was scary," recalls Julia (Tamulonis) Bruce.

The high school outgrew the building on Spring Street a few years after the class of 1933 graduated, but for members of the class, Spring Street High School was the bridge to the world beyond.

Louise Kelley and Ethel Tipping became teachers. Louise returned to the Spring Street facility as a teacher and later as a librarian when it became Spring Street Junior High School. Ethel, who married classmate Hobart Tipping, continued to teach at the Adult Learning Center; she retired after many years at the Charlotte Avenue School. Russ Widener became a lawyer, and for 22 years served as clerk of the Nashua District Court. Angie (Landry) Kopka and classmates Joseph Kopka married and made names in real estate.

Like many other classmates, Helena O'Brien joined the service during World War II. During her tour of duty, the graduate of Memorial Hospital School of

Nursing met and married George Shultz, who later became Ronald Reagan's secretary of state.

Ruth Ledoux fulfilled a lifelong dream after marrying, having seven children and working for an insurance agency. She entered Rivier College when she was a great-grandmother, and in 1984 completed her bachelor's degree in history at St. Anselm College. She was 68 years old.

In its diamond year, the class of 1933 can look back at the Depression as just the first of many challenges met with success.

May 29, 1993

TIMES HARD FOR CLASS OF '35

From 2 A.M. to 7 A.M., John Chesson hustled to deliver milk to his customers, driving a truck through the dark streets of Nashua and leaving bottles of fresh milk on their doorsteps before breakfast.

In good weather he finished in time for his first class at Nashua High School, but on snowy days, he often arrived well after the bell.

"Walter Nesmith never reprimanded me when I was late; he understood," says the retired Slawsby Insurance Agency executive, remembering the headmaster of the Nashua High School at the time.

Memories of their days at Nashua High School will fly faster than the golf balls at the Nashua Country Club on Sunday when 80 members of the class of 1935 gather for their 60th reunion.

Since 1940, they have met regularly every five years. "We had figured the 55th would be the last," says Edwin Steckevicz, the class business manager, who has organized reunions since 1950. Bowing to demand, he and other members of the reunion committee set about planning the 60th get together.

It was the height of the Depression years when 266 members of Nashua High School's class of 1935 marched to the stage of the high school on Spring Street to receive their diplomas. To help sustain their families, many of the 452 who entered as freshmen had dropped out of school to work in the mills.

Family consideration always prevailed. Steckevicz, like others in the class, was filled with high hopes of going on to college. Instead, he was needed to help in the family Clover Leaf grocery store in Hudson and then was called into military service.

The class of 1935 was weaned on hard times, disciplined by hard work and, several years after graduation, seasoned by fighting in World War II.

"We did not have much, yet we never felt deprived. Everybody was in the same boat. We never complained of being bored either. The word was not in our vocabulary," says Eleanor Sullivan Adams, a longtime member of the reunion committee.

Fun in high school days meant friends gathering to sing around the family's player piano on Sunday afternoon or to listen to a Rudy Vallee record on the Victrola.

For teens in the '30s, swimming in Fields Grove in the summer, ice skating on the North and South Common in the winter and roller skating at the Jack O'Lantern provided plenty of things to do when they weren't studying or working. An ice cream at the Rosebud, a Coke at the Busy Bee or a piece of pie at the Yankee flyer made any occasion special.

Saturday afternoons at the Park or Colonial theaters were a treat, and the give-away of dishes added to the thrill of a movie. Those who went regularly often collected a whole set of dishes.

"For the price of 10 cents, you'd get dishes, see a movie starring Claudette Colbert, Clark Gable or one of the Barrymores and hear a piano player," remembers Phoebe Coronis. She was the class valedictorian; her graduation speech focused on the contribution of ancient Greek society to modern life.

Among the school functions she fondly recalls were the monthly tea dances held in the late afternoon in the school gymnasium, with the Nashua High School band playing such hits of the day as "Cheek to Cheek," "Red Sails in the Sunset" and "On Treasure Island."

"Nezzy," as the bespectacled headmaster was affectionately known, and the teachers ruled with benevolent discipline. A particular favorite, English teacher Elizabeth Cornell, to whom the 1935 Tusitala is dedicated, demanded a thorough knowledge of grammar and sentence structure as well as literature. Yet, says Lester Gidge, founder and president of Nashua Industrial Machine Corp., she was willing to excuse his poor penmanship and praise his story-telling skills.

"She said my mind worked faster than my hand," he recalls. That boost to his self-confidence was never forgotten.

Dr. Maurice Chagnon remembers Cornell's encouragement as she coached the senior class play, "The First Suit," in which he had a leading role.

Sixty years after graduation, the class of 1935 remains close and the memories are sweet. Some of the class moved to other parts of the country, 89 had died, but a group of close friends see each other around town and at the Nashua Senior Center.

The hard times can now be appreciated as stepping stones to success.

"We had to make do with nothing. I guess that's what started me on my path," says Gidge. A prolific inventor, with more than 50 patents to his name, he worked after school in a machine shop from the age of 14.

Long before women's lib, Coronis learned the fundamentals of business at Nashua High School and forged a career as the executive secretary to several presidents of Nashua Corp.

Along with a successful career as a vice president and sales manager at Slawsby Insurance Agency, Chesson played a key role in Nashua community life. Raised in St. Joseph Orphanage after his parents died, he went on to head a number of organizations including the Chamber of Commerce, the Red Cross blood program and the Salvation Army. In recognition of his efforts, Chesson was named the chamber's Citizen of the Year in the late '60s.

After hanging out his single as an ophthalmologist, Chagnon, too, became active in civic affairs. He served as director of the Chamber of Commerce, a director of Rivier College, headed the Nashua Lions Club and was president of the YMCA board during its building campaign in the '60s.

Steckevicz, retired sales manager of Consolidated Foods, served 12 years on the Hudson Board of Selectmen. The class can also boast of a managing editor of the

Nashua Telegraph, the late John Stylianos, who was voted the class athlete, and a well-known Nashua physician, the late Dr. Philip McLaughlin, who was the senior class president.

"We all did pretty well," says Gidge of his classmates.

The 60th reunion of the class of 1935 took place Sunday afternoon with a social hour and a dinner. Through years of experience, the committee has learned to concentrate on the basics.

"We started out with the usual formal reunion but as we went on, we dropped the dancing, the awards and all the other things. People just wanted a chance to say 'hi' to old friends," says Chagnon.

1995

CLASS OF 1939 HAS MADE ITS MARK

History had dealt them trying times, the Depression in their childhood, a world war in their youth. Yet, they survived and prospered.

Fifty years after graduation, more than half of the Nashua High School Class of 1939 gathered at a reunion dinner in the ballroom at The Clarion. It began at 6 P.M. and at midnight strains of "Thanks for the Memories" were still drifting from the dance floor.

"You haven't changed a bit," Irene (Fortier) Levesque remarked as she checked off names of arriving classmates. It was the oft-heard greeting of the evening, a harmless opener for catching up on the years. They all knew they had added a few pounds, wrinkles and gray hairs, but they also had produced families and made their mark on the world, meeting its demands with grace.

"After graduation, I went to work for the Nashua Corporation, preparing to go to UNH, but a war came along. The U.S. Marine Corps edited my plans," said Frank Richardson, the class president.

As class orator, he recalled mentioning the growing unrest in Europe, never suspecting it would intercept his life and the lives of his classmates. "We all knew Hitler had moved into Austria and Eastern Europe, but we didn't know it was going to break out into a world war. We were thinking about moving on, going to college, getting good jobs."

The year 1939 was filled with promise. The graduates made up the largest class, numbering 356, to receive diplomas from Nashua High School and the third class to graduate from the block-long, brick school on Elm Street. Inspired by new coach Buzz Harvey and charged by classmate Louis "Doc" Daukas, the Nashua High School football team scored its first victory in many years over the Manchester Central football team.

Everybody was talking about "Gone with the Wind" and Rhett Butler's shocking farewell to Scarlet: "Frankly my dear, I don't give a damn." Long before the film arrived, the State Theater ads urged Nashuans to reserve seats.

The radio eased the silence of doing homework and it was "smooth" to dance to records of the big bands such as Guy Lombardo and the Dorsey Brothers. "Deep Purple" was the class song.

The innocent years ended on Dec. 7, 1941. The bombing of Pearl Harbor put personal lives on hold. Most of the young men and few of the young women in the class of '39 shipped off to fronts in Europe, North Africa and the Pacific. Word was received that Army Pvt. Phillip Labombarde was taken prisoner of war in Germany. Navy bomber pilot Paul Boire, for whom the Nashua airport is named, and five other men in the class lost their lives in the line of duty. A plaque inscribed with their names was presented to the high school following the class' first reunion. Usually held after five years, it had been postponed by the war until 1947.

Happy to resume normal lives, more than half of the class returned home to Nashua and three-quarters of the graduates stayed in New England, noted Richardson when he addressed the class at its golden reunion.

He had returned from the Pacific to marry class vice president and his high school sweetheart, Lorraine Sherman, and to continue a career at Nashua Corp., from which he retired recently as director of purchasing. Class business manager Herbie Miller expanded the family store on Main Street and Bernie Pastor acquired P.E. Fletcher.

Labombarde ran the family's International Paper Box Machine Co., Frank Clancy hung out his law shingle, Earl Damon pioneered real estate in Merrimack and Bob Weisman established an insurance business.

Track star Homer "Speed" McMurray opened a veterinary practice on Amherst Street and in 1976 he demolished the building to make room for a restaurant. "He started it all," joshed his wife, Dorothy, referring to the commercial development on the once rural road to Milford.

Old clips from *The Telegraph* announced that Pvt. Merton H. Caswell had married Beverly Clarkson and Claire Shea had wed Dennis Sullivan. Sullivan was destined to become Nashua's colorful mayor in the mid '60s, resigning from office in 1977 because of a terminal illness.

As the years passed, graduates of 1939 had become key players in Nashua's community life. They also established a substantial scholarship fund at the high school.

One by one at the reunion, they made their way to the table where two of their teachers, Mabel Noyes and Ruth Milan, were seated. A hug or a handshake was also in order for Olga (Tsiantas) Stephanos who had graduated a few years before them and worked in the office of Headmaster Walter S. Nesmith. "I took care of the delinquents and tardy kids like a mother. Sometimes I covered up for them," she said with a smile adding, "They were all good kids."

The "good kids" grew up in time when "coke" meant soda, when nothing was "throwaway," when TV was a fantasy. They learned about priorities from fighting a war. They achieved in every sphere. And they remained connected even as they went their separate ways after 1939. Through the years, reunions were just one of many ways to stay in touch.

1989

NHS CLASS OF '41

If someone were to compile a local "Guiness Book of World Records," the Nashua High School Class of 1941 would snare several entries. It was the first—and for many years the largest class—to graduate from the newly built high school on Elm Street, often proudly compared to a college campus and now a junior high school. It was the first class to "go on strike" for a cause, the first class to go to a junior high for a full three years, and the first class to answer the call to military service in the draft.

"We often had 35 to 40 in a class, but there was no fooling around. We paid attention," recalls Warren Rollins, a retired teacher and president of the Class of '41 Alumni Association.

It was also the class that produced such key figures in contemporary state history as Governor Walter Peterson, Attorney General George Pappagianis and Sam Tamposi, the farm boy who became a real-estate magnate.

John Kissel, the varsity athlete in the class, tackled the big time—playing football with the Cleveland Browns before coming home to teach at Spring Street Junior High School. Nick Rodis, the best athlete in class and Robert Kennedy's roommate at Harvard, became the physical fitness goodwill ambassador during the Kennedy administration.

The class has also been well represented on the downtown scene by alumni such as funeral director Leo Dumont, of the Dumont-Sullivan Funeral Home; Armand LaRose, the chef at the family's Modern Restaurant, and Main Street shopkeeper Alfred Lawrence. His high school hobby, photography, developed into a family business, Cameraland, now managed by his son.

Though many including Tamposi, are gone, the Class of 1941 gathered together for its grand reunion at McNulty Foley restaurant.

Fifty-five years after graduation, Chin Ngoon was one of the classmates looking forward to sharing memories of the high school days.

"I had a lot of friends and I haven't seen them for a long time," said the retired engineering executive, now living in Merrimack.

Prophetically, the phrase under Ngoon's accomplishments in the yearbook, the Tusitala, reads:

"Other friends may come and go
And we may like them heaps
But somehow you're the kind of friend
We like to have for keeps"

Though popular in high school and an associate editor of the Tusitala, Ngoon had little time to socialize after class—but then neither did most of the other students. They worked in the mills and in the shops and soda fountains on Main Street. Classmate Rita (Willette) Derosiers worked in her father's store, Babe's Market, on Lake Street.

Ngoon worked after school, often until midnight, in his grandfather's laundry on West Pearl Street and in the summer he had a job in the mills. He had come to this country at the age of nine, grown up in the ethnic-rich neighborhood of West Pearl Street and was fired with an ambition to achieve the American dream.

"The teachers were very good to me and, outwardly, nobody showed any negative attitudes," said the man who was the lone Asian in the class of '41.

After earning his degree in engineering from the University of New Hampshire, he served as a bombardier and navigator with the Air Force in Italy. His plane was shot down over Munich. He returned to Nashua, rising to executives' echelons in Sanders Associates.

"The company grew and I grew with it," he said of the high tech firm instrumental in restoring Nashua's healthy economy in the '50s and '60s after the mills went south.

Ngoon was one of the 505 in the class of 1941 who entered the new high school after dual sessions at Spring Street Junior High School. Appropriating a union technique more common at the time, as ninth-graders they had called a strike at the junior high to protest the crowded conditions and marched to Governor Murphy's house on Concord Street. The *Telegraph* recorded the unusual, defiant act in a picture spread.

Hard work and an ability to roll with the punches defined the students in the class of 1941. They had grown up in the depression and had weathered two of Nashua's worst disasters—The Crown Hill Fire in 1930, and the Flood of 1936. In 1941, they stepped from high school into the crossfire of World War II.

"By the year (1942), there was not a boy in town," said Glenda (Cantara) Araldi, daughter of the fire chief. On Dec. 7 1941, six months after graduation, President Franklin Delano Roosevelt had declared war against Japan and Germany.

Many of the young men in the class, like Rollins, had signed up for military duty before graduation.

"We jumped the gun," said Rollins, a Navy recruit who took part in some of the fiercest battles in the South Pacific.

"We knew something was coming. They had started the draft in 1940," chimed in John Keenan, a petty officer second class aboard an aircraft carrier in the Pacific.

In high school, many of the upperclassmen were proud to be counted among "Cheney's Boys," recruited by the NHS assistant headmaster, Cheney Lawrence, to serve in the New Hampshire National Guard. He was commander of the 197th battalion. Summers the boys went off to Citizen's Military Camp.

"It was like a vacation between school," remembers Angelo "Van" Anagnost.

But, after 1941, military service was no vacation and the young Nashuans were sent to places in the world they had never known existed.

The girls wrote letters. "I haven't written as much since," says Glenna Araldi with a smile.

"And they sent pictures of themselves in bathing suits" adds Rollins.

In the most trying hours of the war, these letters triggered thoughts of the happy times during high school days.

"We didn't have a lot of money, but we had a lot of fun," said Araldi.

There were football games at the north common and dances afterwards in the high school gym or the Spring Street auditorium. A sundae with the works cost a dime at the Rosebud or Priscilla's. The same dime bought a ticket to the movie to see the latest Lana Turner, Gary Cooper or Rita Hayworth movie and in the '30 and '40s Nashua boasted several plush movie houses.

"On Saturday you could get into Park Theater by bringing a can of beans for the Salvation Army," says Keenan who became a Nashua firefighter shortly after the war.

For special occasions, the big bands, such as Harry James and the Dorsey Brothers, could be heard in ballrooms in Bedford, Lowell, Mass., or at Canobie Lake.

"We went to Canobie Lake after the senior prom . . . but we didn't have anything to drink," says Mrs. Araldi.

Compared to that of their grandchildren, their world had built-in boundaries not to be crossed. It was an era where when traveling in the fast lane meant dancing the Jitter Bug. For thrills they listened to The Shadow on the radio or saw cowboy-and-Indian serials at the movies.

It was a time to be remembered with a smile, they all agree.

August 3, 1994

ALUMNAE REFLECT ON WAR YEARS

Read between the lines of the slim, leather-bound book on the table in the Nashua Country Club dining room. It speaks volumes about the young women who wrote it and the tumultuous times in which they matured.

The "'Messor," Latin for reaper, turns the clock back to the historic summer of 1945 when 22 hopefuls graduated from St. Aloysius School for girls, later rechristened St. Louis School for Girls.

They received their diplomas on June 10, which fell between VE day, marking an end to fighting in Europe, and VJ day, victory over Japan and the end of World War II.

On a recent June evening, the yearbook was on display with other mementos at the class' 50th reunion dinner at the country club. A dozen alums gathered around the table to share photos of grandchildren and relive the days of their youth in the brick building on Mulberry Street, now the city health department. Only one, Rita Calawa Therrien was a great-grandmother.

Looking back on graduation, Sylvia (Pelletier) Erickson quipped, "We didn't have a senior prom; there were no boys to invite. They all enlisted when they were 17. None of the schools had dances."

The yearbook reveals few after school activities except the choral group. In fact, the school day was minus a study hall because many of the girls worked four hours a day on the swing shift in the mills and full days on the weekends.

"We had to keep the blankets rolling," says Erickson.

Many of the girls earned money to pay their own tuitions, 50 cents a month for parishioners of St. Louis de Gonzague Church and a dollar for girls who belonged to other Catholic churches. All of their classes, including Latin and French, were taught by nuns except for religion, the domain of the Rev. Richard Carrigan.

In their spare moments the girls baked batches of cookies for the boys in the service and rolled bandages for the Red Cross. They sipped cherry Cokes for a nickel at the Rosebud or Priscilla's and for 15 cents savored a piece of the Yankee Flyer's homemade pies.

"Every drugstore had a soda fountain and everybody had a joke about a soda jerk," Erickson recalls.

For a list of "favorites" in the yearbook, the seniors at St. Aloysius School for Girls picked: Lowell Thomas broadcasting news of the war on the radio, Bing Crosby in the movie "Going My Way," and movie star Greer Garson of "Mrs. Miniver" fame. Their favorite saying was "Are you kidding?"

Telegraph Photo Files

St. Louis School for Girls reunion

For entertainment besides going to the movies, they enjoyed bowling, usually meeting in the alley below the Rosebud on the corner of Main and West Hollis streets, later a Carvel Ice Cream store.

Their high school years were war years, when just about everything was rationed—gasoline, shoes and all kinds of food.

"Nobody complained, not even about the stockings. They were thick rayon and made everyone look like they had wrinkled elephant legs," said Erickson, who was voted classmate with the best sense of humor.

None of the girls had a car, so they walked or rode on the network of busses threading through the city and linking with city bus lines beyond.

How they and the times changed, they reminisced. Nowhere was the difference more clearly documented than in the traditional yearbook dreams list at the back of the book.

"To be the blushing bride of a lucky Navy officer," was the dream of the class valedictorian.

"Of course, I wasn't," said Justine Malouin Cutting, retired Sunapee postmistress. Five years after graduation she had married a farmer from Sunapee.

Unable to attend the reunion, she spoke about her dream in a telephone conversation. It was just a typical response of a young girl growing up in wartime, where servicemen were visible everywhere, she said.

"I didn't feel any different from the other girls because I was valedictorian," observed the brainiest member of the class.

A nature-lover, she aspired to be a forester, a sentry in the woodlands. She applied to the U.S. Bureau of Forestry and her letter was returned. It stated the bureau did not hire women.

"I was quite disappointed. That wouldn't happen today," she said.

Classmate Erickson's dream was to "shake the hand of General Douglas MacArthur," who was voted the class hero. The yearbook also paid tribute to another heroic figure, President Franklin Delano Roosevelt, who died before the war ended.

A lighter note was the dream of class President Leatrice Parten Cardin: "To stay 18 forever."

"I think she still feels that way," offered Erickson.

"A champion ice skater" was the dream of Sister Annette Thibeault, who had traveled to the reunion from Los Angeles.

Instead she went to nursing school with the last group of women to benefit from President Harry Truman's Nursing Cadet Corps program. Also in the corps was classmate Theresa de Jardin Dube.

Becoming a nun was not what Thibeault had planned for her life when she graduated. In fact she was 28 when she took her vows in California, and for many years she continued her work in a hospital there.

The editor of the Messor was Ursula Hudon Cote. Her dream was to be the mayor of Hudson. Instead she worked for 37 years as a telephone operator, taking the job right out of high school before she married.

"Companies would call up the school asking for girls from St. Aloysius," she said adding that the school had a reputation for properly educating its students.

Of the many changes she witnessed on the job, she says, "I started with 'number please' and when I finished, we were doing directory assistance on the computer."

The one constant was the Nashua exchange, Tuxedo, which translated to 88, the beginning numbers when the dial system was installed.

While the world around careened on a head-long course, while men conquered space and women broke barriers in the business world, for the class of '45, memories of St. Aloysius School for Girls remained a constant buffer against the tide.

August 5, 1996

Telegraph Photo Files

CLASS OF 1950

"Our Hearts Were Young and Gay"

It was their class motto, their yearbook theme, the title of their senior play and their class poem.

"Gay meant happy then," observed Bob Hackett at the last committee meeting for the Nashua High School Class of 1950 planning its 50th reunion. The class business manager was master of ceremonies at the dinner, kicking off the weekend celebration at the Crowne Plaza Hotel. Festivities continued with an old-fashioned picnic at Alpine Grove in Hollis. More than 200 classmates and their spouses attended from all over the country and from such faraway places as the Philippines.

The class song, "Give Us Your Tired, Your Poor," based on the Statue of Liberty poem by Emma Lazarus, was not quite in sync with "Our Hearts Were Young and Gay." It was, however, the choice of Nashua High music director Elmer "Pop" Wilson and they accepted it.

The Nashua High School Class of 1950 had good reason to be carefree. World War II ended before they were in high school and none of their classmates was called into service before they graduated. The Depression was something their parents told them about. Nashua, population 35,000, was a quiet mill town until the late 40s. In 1950 its economy was recovering from the mills closing, jobs were scarce, but the outlook was optimistic.

When not studying or doing homework, the Nashua High seniors led the good life, attending football games on Friday night at Holman Stadium or going to out-of-town games on buses from the school. After school they met friends at the Rosebud to play the jukebox and sip cokes. At NHS, they joined the Latin or French clubs, the Future Homemakers or the Future Farmers of America. Saturday nights they danced the Lindy at "Saturday nighters" in the YMCA.

"The last city bus was at 11:15 at night. If your date didn't have car, he walked you home or you took the bus," recalls Connie (Bouchard) Erickson.

The sprawling brick high school on Elm Street, built in the mid-30s, was the next best thing to a college campus. During the three years they spent inside its halls, they stored up many memories to make them smile in the years to come.

Edmund Keefe, the genial headmaster, put up with the occasional class antics and practical jokes, such as jacking up the front wheels of his car. "He was stern when he had to be, but he was fair and had a good sense of humor," Hackett recalls.

"Miss (Helen) Coffey played golf on the desk," recalls Bea (Nadreau) Brewster of the colorful math teacher, an avid golfer. Brewster is chairperson of the reunion, the class's ninth since graduating.

"Gentlemen, open doors for ladies" was Miss (Lillian) Dowd's constant reminder to the boys in her English class, particularly the football players. Her former students remember how strict she was about assignments. "You remembered every detail of 'The Tale of Two Cities,' even the color of the horse," says June (Shaw) White.

Buzz Harvey was the venerated coach of the football team and Tony Marandos of the basketball team. Both produced many championship teams and were held in awe by the students. Basketball was one of the few team sports in which girls had a chance to excel. English teacher Anne McWeeney, the coach, never hesitated to cheer the loudest at their games.

"We traveled all over, even to Hudson," said Terry (Desrosiers) St. Laurent, one of the class' stars on the girls' team.

Friday nights in his white uniform, "Pop" Wilson led the band up Library Hill to the football games in Holman Stadium. On Saturday morning he gave piano and voice lessons at his house, remembers White, one of his pupils.

Marching up front with the NHS Band was senior Robert Plamondon, playing his horn. Referred to in the Tusitala, the yearbook, as 'Pop' Wilson's right-hand man, he would follow in his mentor's footsteps as music director of Spring Street and Elm Street junior high schools.

"Some of our memories we can't put in print," quips James Lamb, recruited for the reunion committee 10 years ago when class president Robert Dobrowolski, a football star, died.

Erickson and Nancy (Pike) LaQuerre, however, do not hesitate to talk about wearing the same dress to the senior prom and to the graduation two days later, June 23, in the high school auditorium. White gowns were the rule for seniors' prom dresses since they wore them to graduation exercises rather than black caps and gowns.

"There were 311 graduates in the class, 68 are deceased and we can't trace the whereabouts of 11," notes Brewster, who has been keeping tabs on classmates over the years. Several classmates died in later wars. The Korean Conflict began just days after graduation.

Invited to all the reunions are the few students who dropped out before graduation; several were the girls who went to Mount St. Mary Seminary for their senior year when it opened on Concord Street.

A reminder of what the country and Nashua were like in 1950 prefaces the program book for the reunion. Harry Truman was president. The average income was $3,216 and the average cost of a house, $14,500. "All About Eve" was the best picture and the top song was "Mona Lisa" sung by Nat King Cole and recorded on a 78 rpm album, of course.

"Milk was 82 cents a gallon and a Chevy, brand new, was $600," offered Tony Guertin, member of the reunion committee.

"And we couldn't afford it," responds Brewster.

Though not wealthy, few of the high school students worked after school. Some found jobs in downtown shops on weekends. LaQuerre remembers working Friday nights at Jordan's Luggage Shop and St. Laurent at J.J. Newberry's. Lamb's first job was in Kennedy's Butter and Egg Shop, scooping butter from a big vat for the customers. Hackett worked in his father's store.

"You knew everybody on Main Street and they all said 'hi,'" says Brewster, noting Wednesday nights when the shops were open. Main Street was the meeting place of Nashua.

In those days, moviegoers went to the State, the Park, the Tremont or the Colonial theaters. Few families owned a TV set and VCRs were unknown.

"We had a small black-and-white set," says Brewster. "We would go to a friend's house every Tuesday night to watch 'Uncle Miltie,'" recalls Erickson.

The yearbook notes "Connie Bouchard has hopes of being a civil servant." And she is. In addition to serving on the committee, Erickson holds a full-time job as bailiff of the Superior Court on Spring Street. During her high school days it was the site of the city's only junior high school, the one they attended for grades 7 through 9.

For the class of 1950, TV was something they aspired to buy for their homes, but splitting atoms and men walking on the moon was the stuff of science fiction. Raising families and starting careers were the primary focuses for their futures. Nashua High School sent them on their way armed with the knowledge they needed for college or vocational training and the intangibles to cope with life.

In the year 2000, computers have replaced typewriters and SUVs (sports utility vehicles) clog the highways. The world looks very different to the class of 1950 from the time they graduated from Nashua High School. Grandparents they may be, with a history of accomplishments, but their hearts are still young and gay.

September 30, 2000

NASHUA TRUST COMPANY

Families have reunions. High school and college alumni have reunions. Military units have reunions. But an annual reunion of bank personnel—and scheduled on a day once stained with tears?

As planned with good reason, the Nashua Trust Company held its 10th reunion on October 10 in 200l. That October date will forever remain a black day in Nashua banking circles, particularly for the people who worked for the Nashua Trust Company.

The year was 1991, not 1931, and the day was Thursday, not Monday, but it was every bit as bleak as the day the Depression hit the country.

On Oct. 10, 1991, the Nashua Trust Co. was a casualty of the upheavals of the banking industry in Nashua and throughout New Hampshire. In another blow to community-based banks, the century-old Nashua Trust became a page in history when it was taken over by First N.H. Bank, a subsidiary of the Bank of Ireland First Holding Co., an international financial institution.

The secure world of the Nashua Trust collapsed and reorganization was sure to follow, leaving longtime employees in limbo.

"We had to hold each other up and cry on each other's shoulder," says Mariette Sirois, remembering the day she heard the news. Like so many of her colleagues, she was a loyal employee of the Trust, having worked there since graduating high school, and she was there 30 years. When she left soon after the bank closed, she was assistant vice president in charge of loan operations.

"It was a sad day; many people were subsequently laid off," says David Bingham, then a vice president of the Trust and one of the last tenured employees to be released. "We were like a big family and we wanted to keep in touch with each other," he adds.

So on Oct. 10, 1992—and ever year since as close to the date as possible—Nashua Trust employees have held a reunion and it has become a happy time, a chance to see each other again.

There are many memories to share and make them smile in spite of the demise of the bank where they had invested many years of their lives.

A favorite unforgettable incident happened when the timing mechanism in the vault door went awry. It was discovered when the bank opened at 9 A.M., and no one could get to the money or papers needed to do business. A hurried call was placed to a local construction company to drill it open.

"If you think it inspired confidence in the customers to hear drilling when they walked in the bank . . .," says Bingham.

As he retells the story, the slim vice president, Conrad Dionne, volunteered to be shoved through the hole in the door to get inside the vault, but it took several days before access was fully restored.

Bingham himself figures in another amusing story—of East Pearl Street awash with money. He was the first teller to man the walk-up window outside on East Pearl Street, the precursor to today's ATM machine. No one had realized how windy the street was or the draft that would be created when the window was opened by a customer.

"The bills flew up on the canopy, our custodian John Boyd went up to get them but some flew out on the street," says Bingham, adding he soon realized that a weight was needed to secure the checks and the bills.

Another veteran staffer, Stella Duchesneau, remembers the cloud of tear gas that engulfed the main floor when the emergency pedal in each teller's cage was triggered by accident, and Robert Whitney recalls the telephone operator's booth above the front door protected by bulletproof glass.

"She took all the incoming calls," he noted of the era before e-mail and answering machines.

One memory they all share underscores the difference in the banking environment in earlier decades.

"Roland Burnham, a VP, was a tough guy, but if he couldn't give you a loan on bank terms, he'd give you a personal loan," says Bingham, now a financial consultant to small business.

With Nashua Trust credentials, many employees went on to new careers. "We work for our ex-customers or ex-bosses at the bank," says Jamie Pappas, an accounting supervisor for Monarch Instruments and at 40 one of the youngest on the reunion committee dinner.

The first reunion former Trust employees attended was at McNulty Foley, followed by years at the Nashua Country Club.

The 10th reunion was filled with a special nostalgia. It took place in the Villa Banca. The restaurant takes its name from its previous tenant of 90 years, the Nashua Trust Co., and the famous vault is still in view as a reminder of days gone by.

"We'll feel right at home," says Sirois.

"My office was the ladies room," remarks Evelyn Loraine.

Loraine matches the profile of the typical Trust employee. She graduated from Nashua High School in 1950. She started as a part-time teller of the new Hudson branch in 1964 when it opened. In 1985 she reluctantly parted with the bank as an assistant vice president doing commercial lending when she and her husband moved to Maine.

As did Loraine, employees could bank on 30- and 40-year careers with the Nashua Trust Co.

David Bingham's career was a typical success story. He was "16 going on 17" in 1951 when he was hired to work part time at the bank. The Trust sponsored his banking education and when he returned he climbed the ladder from teller to vice president of commercial loans.

"It was my first job and the only way they could get me out was to close the bank."

Robert Whitney and Stella Duchesneau both had the luxury of retiring before the doors closed.

Whitney worked there 42 years, under three presidents, taking leave for four years to serve in World War II. He retired in 1981 as a vice president. Duchesneau also retired in 1981 after 37 years of service to travel with her husband. She went from being the head commercial teller to settling the books.

"I had no title. I just settled the books," she says.

At the time Duchesneau settled the books, Nashua Trust was the largest state-chartered commercial bank in New Hampshire. It was established in 1889 and its first home was on the McQuestin block, now the Slawsby building on Main Street. Nashua was a thriving city of 19,311 in spite of the absence of telephones, electric lights and automobiles. By 1900, the Nashua Trust had outgrown its quarters and moved to the Masonic Building on the corner of Main and East Pearl streets. It operated as a full-service bank and played a prominent role in the city's community life, making loans for the rehabilitation of houses destroyed in the Crown Hill Fire in 1930, the flood of 1936 and the economic crises provoked by the departure of Textron in 1948. It also helped countless community businesses and provided mortgages to thousands of Nashua home owners. Its directors were pillars of the community and employees were encouraged to take part in the community.

The downhill slide began at the end of the '80s, when it was acquired by the Amoskeag Bank, which was closed in 1991 by the FDIC and sold, without losing a beat as far as depositors were concerned, to the First N.H. Bank. The collapse of the Amoskeag and the Trust, along with other troubled New Hampshire banks in the group, have been attributed to the poor economy and bad real estate loans. In 1995 it was taken over by Citizens Bank, owned by the Royal Bank of Scotland. Citizens has its Nashua headquarters in the former Trust drive-in across the street from City Hall.

But the nostalgia of remembering the good old days of the Nashua Trust Co. keeps former employees coming back to reunions.

"We knew everybody by name at the bank, the customers and all about their families," says Pappas, who now works in Amherst.

"I miss being on Main Street," she adds wistfully.

September 8, 2001

SCHOOL DAYS ON FRENCH HILL

"*A home without books is like a house without windows.*"

"*If at first you don't succeed, try, try again.*"

"These are the things the nuns taught us and we never forgot them," says Gabrielle Duperron, recalling her formative years at St. Francis Xavier School. "When we came out we knew what we were all about and what we had to do to make something of ourselves."

And the young pupils did. They grew up to be doctors, dentists, lawyers, nurses, business executives and scientists.

Memories of St. Francis Xavier School have filled the days of Gabrielle (Bleau) Duperron since she moved back to Nashua in 1987 after retiring. Her first celebration of nostalgia led to the reunion of the class of 1939. Her second, an even grander event, was to be the reunion of every class that graduated from the parochial school at the crest of Chandler Street on French Hill.

More than 100 people showed up for the first meeting in January to organize the event, says Mrs. Duperron. Since then, page by page—class by class from 1907 to 1973—the alumni reconstructed the school's 66 years of history

"Most of us were the children of the millworkers," says Muriel (Neveu) Francoeur, class of 1939. She is in charge of publicity for the reunion set for Sunday, October 4.

To preserve the heritage of its population, the school taught religion and French Canadian history along with English, history and geography. It also maintained a bilingual curriculum with half of the classes in English and half in French.

"To tell you the truth, we preferred speaking French," says Mrs. Francoeur, adding that classmates often lapse into French when they get together. She also recalls the strict rules of conduct gently but firmly enforced by the nuns. "There was an imaginary line between the girls' playground and the boys' and you didn't dare go over it." she remembers with a smile.

The original schoolhouse for children of the St. Francis Xavier Church was a one-room wooden structure with living quarters upstairs for the nuns. In 1924, it was replaced by a 16-room school with two offices and a library. The school closed in 1973 and today the building, Xavier House, is a residential facility for older people.

Though the school's records have long since vanished, Mrs. Duperron was able to find the attendance sheets. From them the retired computer programmer has constructed a filing system with all the names of the graduates. To update it, she started calling the male graduates first, reasoning that they would lead her to the women whose names had changed by marriage.

Mention the name Laura (Labile) Houle of Nashua, at 99, the oldest living graduate, for example. Referring to her files, Mrs. Duperron will tell you that she graduated in 1907 and taught for four years at the school before marrying Avery Houle.

Among the women helping her organize the reunion are Simone (Riviere) Belanger, class of '32, Gabrielle Langlais '24; Laurianne (Cote) Belcourt '10 and Laure (Scharest) Fortier, '36.

The committee has located nuns at the school, including Sister Bertha Richards and Sister Mariette Charron. They have also invited priests who attended the school to concelebrate the mass at 11:30 A.M., preceding the reception. To accommodate the huge crowd expected, it will be held from 1 P.M. to 8 P.M. at the Alpine Grove in Hollis. "Six hundred and thirteen have already accepted and we're just starting," reports the chairman.

February 24, 1992

ST. LOUIS DE GONZAGUE REUNION

When Lorraine McNally heard news of the gathering she made sure that her name was on the invitation list. "Somebody will give me a ride" says the 89-year-old great grandmother, anticipating a once-in-a-lifetime occasion.

McNally—the former Lorraine Dufour—will be the oldest graduate of St. Louis de Gonzague Grammar School at the grand reunion of the three parish schools on Sunday, Sept. 15, 1996, at Alpine Grove in Hollis.

Attending will be some 1400 alums of the St. Louis Grammar School, Sacred Heart Academy for Boys and St. Louis High School for Girls. Two dining rooms and a tent were reserved to accommodate the crowd.

"I don't think there are many of us left in the class of 1921" says McNally, who still is a member of the parish.

Though plans for the reunion quickly spread through the congregation, getting the word out to the hundreds more who have moved on presented far more difficulty, according to Beatrice Berube and Roger Cote, members of the reunion committee.

"There were no records we could put our hands on" Berube says, adding, "Now we have everything on the computer."

Since they retired, Berube and Cote do volunteer work each week at the rectory. She had been supervisor of the Hillsborough County Welfare office and he had been a vice president of the Nashua First Federal Savings and Loan Bank. It took two years to plan the reunion to cap the St. Louis de Gonzague Church's yearlong celebration of its 125th anniversary.

To dig out the records, the Rev. Roland Cote, pastor of the church, and nine committee members enlisted the help of Sister Jeannette Caron, a Holy Cross nun in Manchester who had been educated in the St. Louis parish schools. She tracked down names through the Board of Education of the Diocese. George La Voice, principal of Nashua Catholic Junior High School, also opened his files and the committee scoured the area for every resource they could find.

"We put notices in all the Catholic church newsletters, and that worked out well," Berube says. "Strange how news travels," she observes, mentioning inquiries received from Canada and other parts of the country.

As more and more names turned up one piece of the puzzle was perplexing: "We kept coming across the same address, 293 Main Street, where the Ford garage is today," Cote says.

It was not long before they realized that this was the address of the former St. Joseph Orphanage—children living there attended classes at one of the parish schools.

The first Catholic school in Nashua was established in 1883 by the Rev. Jean-Baptiste Henry Victor Millette, the beloved first pastor of St. Louis de Gonzague Church. According to "The Nashua Experience" 500 students were enrolled and eight nuns taught classes in the church basement.

Soon after, the parish built the first separate facility on Chestnut Street. It was to be used as an elementary school for boys and girls. In 1889 another facility was built on Vine Street for boys in grades 5-8; it later went up to the ninth grade. The Holy Cross Sisters taught the younger children, the brothers of the Sacred Heart taught the boys. In the late 1960s the Vine Street building was destroyed by fire and rebuilt the following year. Now empty, it was occupied recently for a year by the public school.

For high school, the boys attended Nashua High School, or after 1964, Bishop Guertin High School, which was also staffed by the Brothers of the Sacred Heart. The girls had their own high school.

St. Louis High School for Girls was established in a building on Mulberry Street bought from the city in the late '30s. It closed in 1969, with the girls going to Mount St. Mary Seminary, Presentation of Mary Academy or Nashua High School.

In 1973, the grammar school and Sacred Heart Academy were absorbed into Catholic regional schools and the schools of St. Louis Parish remained as a memory.

As they planned for the reunion of the three schools, memories of school days inevitably were stirred into the mix. Berube, for example, entered the St. Louis Elementary in 1930 and graduated from the high school in 1942.

Frank Mooney Collection

"We were from French-Canadian families," she recalls. "Our parents still spoke French and we studied French. The nuns were very strict. You had to study something until you knew it."

She smiles when she speaks of the sister who tapped students with a ruler when they did not pay attention, and when she speaks of her favorite sister, who taught religion, French and sewing.

"Sister Norbert, everybody loved her," she says.

"The brothers were from Canada and they were great hockey players," recalls Roland Caron.

By the reunion, they hoped to have every St. Louis School student accounted for and enjoying the festivities.

Remembering old times, renewing old friendships sparked the weekend with joie de vivre, and proved well worth the effort.

July 8, 1995

ALUMNI BANDSMEN
PICK UP THE BEAT

Their uniforms may fit a bit too snugly, their breath may be a bit more measured when they blow their horns and their legs less prepared to parade to Holman Stadium.

Yet their enthusiasm for drumming up the spirit at Nashua High football games remains unchallenged.

Nashua High school band alumni revisited the stadium to play at the game highlighted by a halftime ceremony celebrating 100 years of football at Nashua High.

"I'll be there," said Pete Malavich, class of '43. The sousaphone player, just recovering from triple bypass surgery, will deliver the oompah-pahs from his big brass horn as he did in his high school days.

Instead of their NHS purple and white uniforms the musicians donned black pants and white shirts that were sure to fit. Rather than make a grand entrance or do a snappy half time shows, they rallied the stadium crowd with some rousing band tunes at crucial moments in the game.

"We will be playing some of the music we played in high school . . . the Nashua High School fight song, "Cheer, Cheer for Old Nashua High," and maybe even "Beer Barrel Polka," which was popular when I was there," says trumpet player Robert Plamondon. The 1950 graduate easily recalls the words to the first verse of the fight song:

"Nashua High is going right down the field.
Nothing can stop them.
They all have to yield."

Plamondon shared baton duty for the day with Romeo Couture, Class of '39. At age 75, Couture is the senior member of the assembled alumni bandsmen.

Steve Norris, Class of '47 and conductor of the band from 1956 to 1986, had to bow out because of a prior engagement. He was rehearsing for his sons wedding the next day, and Dan O'Donnell, class of '74 and Norris' successor, took the the NHS musicians to UMass to participate in annual Band Day marches with a host of other groups in the Northeast.

Like Plamondon and Couture, many of the musical alums play in the Legion band as they did in high school. Music has always been an important part of their lives. That pattern was set in their youth when they came under the spell of Nashua's Music Man, Elmer "Pop" Wilson.

With great affection, Pops Boy's speak of the man who prodded them to practice and perform their best. And he always did it with humor.

"If he heard a sour note, he'd reach up and put it in his pocket. He'd do a lot of little things like that," said trumpet player Al Beals, class of '47.

"Pop Wilson was to music what Buzz Harvey was to football," observed Plamondon referring to the NHS football coach of the same era.

Two of Pop's boys followed in his footsteps, carrying on the band tradition in Nashua schools. Plamondon retired in 1994 after being a junior high school band and music director for 40 years, first at Spring Street and later Elm Street.

In the 50s, Norris inherited Pop's baton as director of the music and band at Nashua High School. In fact, the senior bandmaster postponed leaving for a year to make certain his former student got the job.

Like their idol, Pop Wilson, Norris and Plamondon remained active in school music after retiring.

Couture, an applications engineer, is the veteran conductor of the Legion Band, from the time it was under the ageis of the James E. Coffey Post in Nashua until its affiliation with post 48 in Hudson. He learned to conduct high school from Pop Wilson.

"When I was with the Coffey Post, the tables turned and Pop became my guest conductor," he recalled with pride. Summer concerts in Greeley Park, with Pop conducting, were a special treat.

Couture traces his love of music back to 1929, when he was 9 and joined Pop Wilson's Nashua Boys Band, the forerunner of the Nashua High Band.

In the early 1930s, while at the Spring Street High School, Wilson was discouraged by a flagging interest in the school orchestra and formed the Nashua High School Band. It was an instant success.

Pop's assistant was learning how to conduct from the master. After graduating in 1939, Couture continued to help Pop until the younger man was called into military service in World War II.

Whenever the band needed an instrument, Wilson selected a student to play it. A high school student during the war years, Malavich was Pop's choice to play the sousaphone because of his size. His older brother had also played the instrument in the Boy's Band.

"Pop got us all started," said the man who still plays the sousaphone. "In those days you were given a book and an instrument, and you learned by yourself. You practiced and you practiced."

By the 1940s, the band's first uniforms were replaced by more spiffy purple trousers with white stripes down the seams, matching purple vests and capes, topped with white garrison hats.

Before football games, the musicians gathered at Spring Street, then a junior high school and marched to Holman Stadium. Pop led the way with bobby sock fans tagging along behind.

"We will always remember him dressed in his white uniform with his white garrison hat, his curly hair snow white," said Plamondon, adding "That uniform is somewhere; we are still looking for it."

In 1946 the high school football spirit reached a fever pitch when the Purple Panthers won the state championship and were invited to play in the Gator Bowl in Jacksonville, Fla.

Determined to be there for musical support, the band launched an all-out campaign to raise money to go along.

"We played in Lowell, in Manchester, in Fitchburg, and Lawrence, but we'd never traveled that far away," said Plamondon, who shared memories of the trip with Norris, Beals and Mert Rolfe.

They climbed the steps of the Capitol at 2 A.M. and had time to take a swim in the ocean after they arrived in Florida. To keep expenses down, they bunked five and six to a room.

"When we came back, quite a crowd met us at the train," recalleds drummer Rolfe, class of '48. The Nashua High football team finished the year undefeated.

Thirty years later another crowd welcomed the band back. This time the musicians, led by Norris, had scored the victory. They placed first in the Cherry Blossom Parade in Washington, D.C. For the former Norma MacKinley, flutist in the class of '76, and Scott Smith, a trumpet player in the class of '74, those were the glory days of Nashua High School Band.

Without missing a beat at the anniversary celebration, Pop's Boys and all those who played and marched in the years since carried on the band's tradition of stirring the crowd to cheer loudly at Holman Stadium.

November 5, 1996

ARTS

My Window on Main Street

NEW GALLERY REKINDLES DREAM

Editor's Note: With a new director and its financial problems alleviated, the Nashua Center for the Arts seemingly is off to a fresh start. Today, the Sunday Telegraph *begins a series taking a look at the Center—its history and its future.*

A hum of voices rose above the balcony at the Nashua Center for the Arts as people strolled around the brightly lighted room, admiring displays of furniture, arts and handiwork. Musicians serenaded in the lobby and a festive food table was set in Carter Gallery.

If walls could talk, these would rejoice to see the room alive again.

Once upon a time this gallery had been the Children's Museum, where squeals of youngsters could be heard as they shimmied down the fire pole or tugged at the giant stuffed spider hanging from the ceiling. For the past four years, this space had been dark and empty, a reminder of bleak times at the Nashua Center for the Arts.

But by October 1991 the room was refurbished for the dedication of the Swart Gallery in honor of Margaret Swart, one of the center's founders, who died the previous year.

Among the guests commenting on how much they enjoyed the crafts exhibit were people associated with the center in days when openings were always memorable events: artist Jafar Shoja, a former director; Joseph Sakey and Morton Goulder, trustees who had led the building fund drive in the 1960s, and Beatrice Cadwell, a member of the original organizing committee.

Did the room's rebirth as the Swart Gallery auger a fresh start for the center itself?

Signs do point to a more promising future. The red ink that had dominated its ledgers for years was disappearing. A new director was about to be hired.

When the idea for the Center originated in 1959, the League of Craftsmen was notified it could no longer use a building on Arlington Street, where it held classes. "You don't move kilns and looms that easily," recalls Bea Cadwell.

Cadwell remembers that Margaret Swart called a meeting in her home to talk about the situations. One of the proposals was for the League to look into establishing permanent quarters, one that could be used by other arts groups in the city as well.

The time was right for an arts center. Local arts and crafts groups such as the League flourished.

Business leaders were enlisted for the cause and the committee multiplied. There was architect John Carter; attorney Robert Hamblett; insurance executive Archie Slawsy; merchant Leo Bergeron Sakey, then executive director of the Nashua Public Library; Goulder, one of the founders of Sanders' Associates; and other civic-minded Nashuans.

By design or by coincidence, the committee drafted a valentine to the city of Feb. 14, 1961, in the form of a declaration of objectives for the proposed center. It stated the purposed was "to create a cultural center in Nashua which will have a new main Library with a pleasant reading room, adjacent exhibit space which can be used by local industries, and art groups for exhibitions as well as traveling show from museums."

Plans also called for a theater, studio facilities and meeting rooms.

It would be an arts and science center—for, as one of its guiding forces, Robert Hamblett, was often heard to say, "There's science in art and art in science." And Nashua and its surroundings were well represented by both disciplines.

For the next 10 years, the committee offered a taste of the excitement such a center would bring to the city, intellectually and socially, staging exhibits in empty stores in downtown Nashua and at Greeley Park. People still talk about one such show: an IBM show recreating the inventions of Leonardo Da Vinci.

A weeklong festival of the arts at Bishop Guertin High School in the spring of 1966 further entrenched the idea of a need for an arts center. The festival featured exhibits by the Nashua Camera Club, the Arts Association, the Mineral Society and others. There were performances by the Nashua Symphony, Actorsingers, Theater Guild, the Barbershoppers and the Choral Society.

The response was overwhelming. It drew more than 8,000 Nashuans.

Two months later, the Center became a reality when it was given its first home, rent-free. The building at 4 East Pearl St., owned by the Hambletts, had once been a home but it needed work. To hold down expenses, the board staged a paint-in.

For five years—from 1968 to 1973—the center operated out of the old 12-room house. It was under the guidance first of Marian Woodruff as program director, and later of Shoja, who became the first executive director in 1968.

Volunteers kept the facility humming. They set up exhibits, did the publicity, created children's projects and did whatever else was necessary.

Artists Cal Libby, architect David Cheever, designers Bev Payeff and Bliss Woodruff, Nashua elementary school art teacher Carolyn Gaudette were but a few who contributed time, talent and energy. For Meri Goyette, who rounded up sculptures and paintings from artists throughout New England for shows, the volunteer work paved the way to a career as an artist representative in Boston.

There were classes for adults and children. There were shows of Picasso lithographs and Rembrandt prints, held in cooperation with the Boston Museum of Fine Arts.

Nashua residents loaned paintings and sculpture for an exhibit called "Nashua Collects"; the Camera Club staged a photography exhibit; city schoolchildren had their own exhibit; Nashua artist James Aponovich displayed his sketches in the gallery.

The board of directors began to conceive of a larger, more comprehensive Arts and Science Center, one including a 700-seat theater.

In 1968, they launched a building fund drive, hoping for a million-dollar pot at the end of the rainbow.

January 5, 1992

ARTS CENTER PLAGUED BY LACK OF MONEY

Editor's Note: With a new director and its financial problems alleviated, The Nashua Center for the Arts seemingly is off to a fresh start. Today, The Telegraph *continues its series taking a long look at the center—its history and its future.*

Three days of ceremonies and celebration, crowned by a Dedication Ball, heralded the opening of the new Nashua Arts and Science Center on Court Street in the fall of 1973.

But when the doors opened, the paint on gallery walls was still damp and the coffers were dry.

The four-year-old building campaign had raised $1.4 million, but no provisions had been made for programming or operating expenses, a fact that continues to haunt the center.

Even the theater space was not completed because the building fund had been depleted.

Several sites had been considered for the new center, but being a Court Street neighbor to the library won out. The city's price tag for purchase of the Central Fire Station was $100,000 to secure the site.

Eliot and Edith Carter, who had just donated more than $1 million toward the new library, gave contributions amounting to $300,000 to secure the site.

Eventually, their son's firm, Carter and Woodruff, would design the more than 35,000-square-foot facility.

City Hall was not as receptive to the idea of an Arts and science Center as its founders would have liked. Mayor Dennis Sullivan regarded the center with skepticism. He questioned the need for such a facility, as he had done before with the new library. He also prophesied the inability of the private institution to exist without public funds.

Unfortunately his crystal ball held more fact than fantasy.

But it didn't seem that way on opening day, when Margaret Swart, a longtime arts advocate and a member of the founding group, began her president's message by saying: "Today we realize the dream of a handful of dedicated people who present to Greater Nashua the new home of The Arts and Science Center."

In the time-honored tradition that brought benefits of all kinds to New England towns, the impetus for an arts center came from a small band of community leaders. All were well-established professionals and successful entrepreneurs: their roots in their town ran deep.

As generations inherited the family business, their children carried on the unspoken family responsibility of giving back to the community.The center grew out of this tradition. Like themes in a symphony, the names of certain families reappear throughout center's history:the Swarts, the Hambletts, the Carters and the Slawsbys.

Mrs. Swart, a potter in her own right, was the daughter of William H. Beasom, mayor of Nashua in the 1890s and the wife of *Telegraph* publisher William "Roby" Swart. Eliot Carter was vice president of the Nashua Corp. Together with his wife, Edith, they had supported humanitarian and intellectual efforts in the city since the 1930s.

Robert Hamblett, a Nashua native and attorney, became the center's legal counsel. Archie Slawsby, also a native Nashuan, owned an insurance agency.

Their children inherited their interests.

As did his father, David Hamblett served on the center's board of trustees. John Carter and Karen Slawsby, also played key roles in the development of the center. Carter headed the fund drive and served on the center's board; his firm Carter and Woodruff, designed the building. Slawsby was the director of the center when it moved into its new home on Court Street. (After five years, the original director, Jafar Shoja; had resigned to take a teaching job at Rivier College.)

Recalling the opening—"The Show," featuring the Boston Visual Artists Union—Karen Slawsby says the only expense was the transportation cost. The BVAU members even helped to hang the show in the new Nashua gallery.

Karen Slawsby welcomes U.S. Congressman James Cleveland to the Center.

Telegraph Photo Files

"We had a lot of space and we needed a big splashy exhibit. We had a very limited staff (three people), but we pulled it off. Everyone worked very hard, including the volunteers," she says.

Like all those entrusted with running the center, from Marian Woodruff in 1966 to Steve Jones in 1990, Slawsby quickly learned the ingenuity it took to juggle artistic demands and financial burdens.

"We were always playing catch-up on operating expenses," laments Slawsby, who signed for 14 months. "If I look back and think, 'Would I do it again?' the answer is 'No'" she said, recalling that her salary was $12,000. (She now owns a printing business in Hudson.)

Throughout the years, board members, particularly the Swart family, came to the rescue by writing a check to cover unpaid telephone or electric bills. Electric heat was particularly costly. Fixed building expenses, energy, telephone and security ran $8,000 to $10,000 a month.

The first of many distress flags to be raised publicly for money was reported in *The Telegraph*'s May 29, 1975, edition. The headline read: "Center in urgent need of funds; city symphony to give a benefit."

The financial problems were caused, *The Telegraph* article said, because 10 percent of the pledges on the original building fund had not yet been paid leaving a mortgage of $160,000. Start-up costs, which included moving from one building to another that was 10 times larger, left a debt of $40,000.

Bread-and-butter expenses, more than $100,000 a year, were hardly anticipated in 1968 when the building fund drive began.

Some grant money was available to offset these costs. The National Endowment for the Arts, the New Hampshire Commission on the Arts and the New Hampshire Charitable Fund were welcomed sources for programming and class expenses.

Other survival measures also were adopted.

"When classes slowed down, we had an auction or a house tour to keep things going for the summer," said Ann Carner, administrator in the late 1970s.

Phone-a-thons, honorary dinners to roast prominent citizens, membership drive and other fund-raising efforts plugged the red holes in the ledger, and business and industry continued to be generous.

At the end of the 1970s, the center ran a major fund drive. The 12-month campaign brought $255,034.87 in pledges. The funds enabled the center to reduce its mortgage to $69,641.

Through the years, the need for a stable source of income became painfully apparent. In 1983, an endowment fund was reactivated in hopes of making the future of the center more secure.

But the brighter picture gave way to a grim one as the 1980s progressed. Trustees sounded the death knell for the center more than once. Drastic economic measures were taken and the staff reduced. The Children's Museum and the Carter Gallery were temporarily closed.

As it faced the end of the decade, the center was forced to refinance its outstanding debt, enlarging its mortgage, and to sell some of its land to the Indian Head Bank (now Fleet Bank, NH) for a parking lot.

When the center defaulted on mortgage payments a consortium of banks took over its debts, which totaled nearly $300,000. Forgiveness of part of that debt was considered but never approved.

After 14 years on a roller coaster, the center's financial problems hit bottom in 1987, when the city intervened to work out a plan to save it. An attempt was made to form an alliance with the library but its board was not receptive.

Rescue finally arrived in the form of a proposal to sell the building to a private developer.

On Jan. 14, 1988, *The Telegraph* announced: "Stabile is the owner of the center."

The story reported that developer John Stabile had assumed the mortgage and leased the building back to the center rent-free. He had bought the property for one-third of its assessed value. The deal also called for the city to relinquish first right refusal should the building come up for sale again. The terms of the agreement troubled a number of residents.

As financial aid was depleted and with the ghost of Dennis Sullivan saying, "I told you so," the city voted to allot $50,000 to the center but this fiscal year marks the final payments.

January 6, 1992

VOLUNTEERS PLAY VITAL ROLE

Editor's Note: With a new director and its financial problems alleviated, The Nashua Center for the Arts seemingly is off to a fresh start. Today, The Telegraph *continues its series taking a look at the center—its history and its future.*

"There were rats and rotten food in the freezer, but we cleaned it out," recalls Bev Payeff.

The "we" were the artists, architects and designers volunteering to sanitize the former 20th Century Supermarket on High Street for a Leonardo da Vinci exhibit in the early days of Nashua Arts and Science Center.

When it came to boosting the center, there was no job too dirty and no one too squeamish to tackle it. What the facility lacked in financial resources was offset by the wealth of time and talent given by those who believed in it.

"Volunteers were the backbone of the center. They were a fantastic help," recalls Jafar Shoja, a former director and now an art professor emeritus from Rivier College. Karen Slawsby and Ann Carner, also former directors, give credit to volunteers for the work done for the center.

In the late '70s, volunteers opened the Soupcon for lunch; the center's own repertory company, CenterStage, took over the theater and the Children's Museum, had lined up projects to intrigued children and to please parents.

Guiding the volunteer groups was Carner, who worked as the administrator from 1976 to 1979 at a salary of $16,000.

Joining Carner were Sarah Roche, who took charge of exhibitions, and Nancy Stewart, who took charge of the Children's Museum. Both had strong arts backgrounds and both had started out as volunteers.

All three were well schooled in the art of tapping the community's resources and expertise.

For science exhibits such as the "Hidden Giant," an exposition on printing, Roche relied on a committee of business people headed by Morton Goulder of Sanders Associates, now Lockheed Sanders Inc.

Arts exhibits often came from the community, featuring such local artists as Cal Libby or Kay Kandra. Edith Carter's collection of Japanese art and artifacts drew viewers from all over New England. A member of the Japanese embassy in Boston attended the gala opening.

Perhaps the most successful volunteer project was the Soupçon.

In 1977, with Betty Gimber and Winifred Hersey at the cash register, the center's Auxiliary opened a lunch spot two days a week overlooking the garden. It was a simple operation, with homemade soup, salads and desserts. Members, many of whom also catered receptions at the center, made cheesecake, pies and brownies. The women employed a manager and an assistant; another member set up the professional bookkeeping system, all profits went to the center.

"We were in the black from the first day we opened," says Gimber.

Once the word spread, the auxiliary's kitchen opened a third day a week to a steady stream of diners, and the group contemplated expanding to a five-day service.

Restaurant patrons browsed through exhibits and picked up schedules for classes. The center's attendance for the 1978–79 year was 109,265.

During the same period, Carner forged a partnership between the center and the Heart of Nashua Association, getting a grant to stage a summer block party on Main Street. The street party of performing artists attracted more than 10,000 people and became an annual event during summer sidewalk sale days.

A yearlong series of ethnic festivals serving up colorful customs and food specialties also drew people to the Center.

CenerStage, the center's own theater group, had a brief but daring residency. It staged contemporary productions such as Harold Pinter's "The Dwarfs," Eugene Ionescos "The Chairs," and Jean Anouilh's "Antigone."

After half a dozen years on Court Street, the Arts and Science Center had woven its way into the fabric of the community. With fund-raising dinners, auctions and a major development drive, the center's financial picture looked rosier, too.

Things were going so well, in fact, in 1980 the board moved to hire an artistic director to replace Carner with someone who could elevate the center to a higher plane.

It was a decision that proved to be costly.

The board chose Jules Landsman at a salary of $30,000—almost double Carner's wage. He had been a director of a craft center in Lewiston, Maine, and was finishing his last year of studies for a master's degree in arts management at Boston University.

"He brought organization. Everything went through him. He was the chief cook and bottle washer," says Richard Horowitz, then president of the center's board.

Nancy Stewart soon left but Roche stayed to execute exhibits on India, Africa and other art shows aimed at attracting new audiences to the center.

"I liked working with him, but (Landsman) stepped on a lot of toes," Roche admits.

Landsman increased the center's paid staff to 12 but the volunteers decreased dramatically.

The toes of the auxiliary were vulnerable to Landsman's plan to consolidate all center activities under a central management. He moved to bring the restaurant under the management of the center. When he requisitioned the auxiliary's books, "We refused," said Gimber.

The auxiliary disbanded. Members took their dedication and fund-raising ability to the Friends of the Symphony and other organizations.

At about the same time, CenterStage's director and catalyst Bob Shea quit to pursue a master's degree. And as a grant that paid the group's expenses ran out, the theater group folded. (When Shea returned to the area, he became manager of the Palace Theater in Manchester.)

Landsman left when he completed his degree in 1981.

It would be a long time before the center recovered.

January 7, 1992

CHILDREN'S MUSEUM LOST IN SHUFFLE

Editor's Note: With a new director and its financial problems alleviated. The Nashua Center for the Arts seemingly is off to a fresh start. Today, The Telegraph *continues its series taking a look at the center—its history and its future.*

In the Children's Museum at the Nashua Arts and Science Center, youngsters met dinosaurs, teddy bears and spiders.

They learned how to crawl out of the house in a fire and how it feels to be sick in the hospital. They designed chutes for marbles and built fantasies with tumble forms.

Live lambs and other furry creatures were brought to the museum by Arthur Provencher, who later owned Benson's Animal Farm. Money was obtained from the Kings Daughters Benevolent Association, a Nashua charitable group, to bus children from Nashua schools to the center each week.

"With every child who came into the center, came parents. Membership grew," recalls Ann Carner, a former director. Funding from the New Hampshire Commission on the Arts also provided scholarships for needy children to take art classes, a practice that had been started in the center's first home on Pearl Street.

During Rosemary Clough's brief tenure as director from 1981–83, a window to the future was opened with the establishment of the Micro-computer Center. The Children's Museum under Nancy Stewart had introduced Nashuans to the tool of the future. The Micro-computer Center, a joint venture with ComputerMart, went even further, becoming the first of its kind in the state to teach complete computer literacy to children and adults.

From the beginning, children's programs had been a focal point of the center. When it was on Pearl Street, it had a grant from the New Hampshire Commission on the Arts to offer free classes to neighborhood children.

The museum had been carefully planned before the new center opened. Teachers studied and surveyed the kind of projects that appealed to youngsters.

When the museum opened, Bev Payeff, now an interior designer, put the findings to work designing and making everything from the museum's trademark, Webster—a huge spider puppet—to Grandma's Attic and challenging experiments and games.

Eventually, as debts mounted at the center, the children's museum was temporarily closed.

By the time Steve Jones was hired in 1984, the center's financial problems had become acute. The future of the children's museum was endangered.

A grant from the New Hampshire Charitable Fund provided the case for the Children's Museum to reopen. It had a new name—The New Hampshire Children's Museum—and it was no longer the same.

"It evolved into more of a baby-sitting service," Jones says candidly. The grant paid for an Enrichment Camp, a pre-school-type program for youngsters.

During 1986–87, the children's museum was rented to the Nashua School District for use as fifth- and sixth-grade classrooms while Mount Pleasant Elementary School was being enlarged.

It never again opened as a children's museum.

Lacking funds to renovate the museum, children's activities were brought in from outside sources. In the Carter Gallery, there were Stage Festival's Young Company productions and the Kaleidoscope series of Saturday afternoon entertainment programs. The shows tickled the imagination and brought in needed revenue.

Lost was the joy of young minds discovering how things worked and why.

January 7, 1992

FUTURE LOOKS BRIGHT

Editor's Note: With a new director and its financial problems alleviated. The Nashua Center for the Arts seemingly is off to a fresh start. Today, The Telegraph *continues its series taking a look at the center—its history and its future.*

The history of the Nashua Center for Arts is etched with ironies. Throughout much of the economic boom of the '80s, the center teetered on the brink of financial disaster. Yet in the bleak economy of the '90s, its financial picture now seems brighter than ever.

The center has two more years rent-free on the lease arrangement with developer John Stabile, owner of the building since 1988. "As long as the center is viable and headed in the right direction, I see no reason why the (Stabile Family) Foundation will not extend the courtesy of the lease for life," says the Nashua developer.

Just as promising is the five-year contract for Holman Stadium concerts, a rich source of revenue. The Nashua Board of Aldermen recently approved the contract for the Arts Center to rent the stadium.

But many also are still asking some basic questions: Why has it taken more than 20 years for the center to get on firm financial footing? Why were the performing arts ignored for so long? What needs to be done to make sure it doesn't fall into debt again?

Looking back to the early '80s, Peter Timms, director of the Fitchburg (Mass) Museum of Arts was struck by the "great possibilities" of the neighboring arts institution. Subsequently, he accepted a position on the center's board and was surprised at what he encountered.

"You kept hearing how Nashua was boom city. Yet you heard this litany about how the center was in trouble and the money had washed through."

As an afterthought he adds. "Each member of the board was impressive but the chemistry was lacking."

The resounding theme of statements made about the centers early years was that it lacked a unified concept of its role in the community.

"None of us really sat back and said 'How is this going to run?' until it was too late," admits Joseph Sakey, one of the founders.

Timms left the board after Steve Jones was hired. "I felt very good when he came along," says the man who has been at the helm in Fitchburg for 18 years.

Jones had a working knowledge of the performing arts. After graduating with honors from San Francisco Art Institute, he returned to New England to earn his master's degree in fine arts from the Massachusetts College of Art. During college years in Boston, he managed and booked acts for a nightclub. For three years before coming to the Nashua center, he was the director of the Newport Library Arts Center.

Jones welcomed the newly organized Merrimack Folk Association to the center. It was the baby of three Nashua men—David Larlee, Sanders computer executive; Robert Daniels, music teacher; and James Murray, printing sales representative. The folk music buffs frequented coffee houses in Cambridge, Mass., and decided the quality entertainment would fly closer to home. They rented the theater and played to enthusiastic audiences in spite of the room's drawbacks.

"The theater was freezing," recalls Daniels, acting director of the center until Reinert was hired.

With Jones' encouragement, the Merrimack Folk Association moved from the theater, which is in the lower level, to the Carter Gallery on the main floor. In 1988, the popular cabaret-style events became the Center's Downtown Live Series. It featured such folk artists as David Mallett, Tom Rush, Tom Paxton, Patty Larkin and Christine Lavin.

Trying a summer concert fund-raiser, Larlee and Jones brought Peter, Paul and Mary to Holman Stadium in 1989. The concert earned $12,000 for the center.

Last summer, after Manchester's summer concert series hit a snag, Larlee and Jones convinced the city to allow promoter Don Law to bring big-name shows into Holman Stadium. Stars such as Whitney Houston, Bonnie Raitt, Michael Crawford and the Allman Brothers brought $120,000 for the center.

"Last year we owed $60,000 in debt and $14,000 to the IRS. All have been retired," notes Larlee.

Despite some neighborhood detractors, the summer concerts left the center "with a manageable blessing" of legitimacy. Another plus in the performing arts for Jones was bringing the Nashua Theater Guild back into the fold for dinner theater performances last year and this year.

Carrying out the umbrella management plan, art classes were turned over to James Aponovich and his wife, Elizabeth Johansson, and dance classes to the Kozak Gomez School of Movement.

But Jones, drained by financial battles and criticized for neglecting the fine arts, resigned in the summer.

"There is no greater conflict than trying to please everyone when money is a problem," says Sakey.

With money burdens reduced, what challenges await Richard Reinert, the new director? Like so many well-wishers, Sakey and Carter would like to see a stronger working relationship established with its compatible neighbor, the Nashua Public Library.

Larlee's objectives include reintroducing the "science" that was deleted from the center's name in 1987. He envisions the center as a science and art resource for the schools.

Rebuilding connections to the community is another goal. He has started by enlarging the board from the seven in July 1990 to 24 this year.

With its wall of windows facing Indian Head Plaza, the Swart Gallery may prove to be a valuable bridge to the future.

The opening reception last fall for the Swart Gallery was a tonic to Larlee who had come to know the center in the troubled '80s when the atmosphere was often tomblike. He speaks with pleasure of the "warmth and sense of sociability" of the recent occasion.

Nashua newcomers George and Lisa Hammond had the same reaction. They attended the opening reception for the League of New Hampshire Craftsmen's Living with Crafts exhibit with his mother who was visiting from New York.

"The first time I went into the building. I was disappointed. The only gallery was the small one," recalls Lisa, a native of Atlanta, Ga. The craft exhibit opening made up for the initial negative experience. "I loved it. We joined that night," she said.

She hopes the center will play an important part in the developing years of her children.

The young mother wonders: "How else will my children learn to appreciate art unless it's a part of their lives just like school, work and play?"

January 8, 1992

ARTS CENTER'S DEPARTURE

Editor's Note: Unable to meet its financial obligations to the city, the Center for the Arts moved its collection out of 15 Court St., according to The Sunday Telegraph, *Jan. 1, 1995. It was briefly housed in Daniel Webster College before it dissolved.*

A corner window of the old YMCA building on Temple Street is my favorite lookout point in Nashua.

Every six weeks I sit in a chair of the hair salon on the first floor and survey the passing parade around Indian Head Plaza while I get my mop restyled. The view captures a quality of Nashua often overlooked. Encircling the modern brick-colored bank at the end of the plaza are three jewels of 19th century architecture.

Built in the late 1800s, the former Hillsborough County Courthouse, the city's first police station and the Central Fire Station were the heart of the city. A century later the buildings are still in use, though for different purposes; they are, respectively, the Register of Deeds court, the James E. Coffey American Legion Post, and, until recently, the Nashua Center for the Arts.

Last week as I looked out of the corner window, the Center for the Arts faded into the night. There was a black hole where, winter evenings before, the building was bright and alive with activity. On the second floor, the broad windows framed ballerinas in a picture reminiscent of a Degas painting. Below, the soft light of the Swart Gallery sent out a glow.

Months ago, as the city, now the building's owner, debated its fate, the Nora Gomez Academy of Movement moved out. One by one, so have many other occupants. Last week the arts center was packing to leave, too, and the new building manager has yet to be named by the city. The center suspended its daily operations Sunday while its board of trustees reorganizes its programs, staff and board.

"It is like going through the stuff in the attic you have acquired over a 22-year period," says Robert Daniels, director of the center for the past 2½ years. A large green dumpster filled with broken chairs and crumpled paper takes up most of the sidewalk on Court Street.

Decisions of what will stay and what will go are the concerns of the day. Walking through the empty classrooms on the second floor overlooking the Swart Gallery, Daniels notes the paintings of Nashua artist Rosmond deKalb, donated to the center by Margaret Swart, will go to new site. The Calvin Libby collage will go where the center eventually settles, he says.

Other center adornments such as the lobby fresco dedicated to the memory of Mrs. Swart will be difficult to move and will remain for the time being.

The plaque on the second floor installed at the dedication of the Fire Station in 1870 will stay and so will the one near the entrance marking the dedication of the then-Nashua Arts and Science Center in 1972.

"They are part of the building," says Daniels, trying to be matter-of-fact about the inventory.

Inscribed on the lobby plaque are the names of people who contributed time, money and commitment to an institution they founded and, like fond parents, hoped would serve the city well for years to come. Some of the benefactors like Eliot and Edith Carter, William and Margaret Swart, Robert Hamblett, Leo Bergeron and Archie Slawsby are dead, but many are still alive to wonder about the outcome of their efforts.

How well I remember the excitement rippling throughout the town in the '60s when more than a million dollars was raised to remodel and expand the fire station for a community arts center. It was the grandest sum of money ever raised in Nashua. The Nashaway Woman's Club sold its office building at 6 Concord St. and turned the profits over to the center campaign; the Nashua Symphony Orchestra, the Actorsingers and Nashua Theater Guild gave benefit performances. Everybody in town worked on the fund raising.

The enthusiasm was catching, the dreams engaging. The grand design envisioned the Center and its neighbor across the courtyard, the Nashua Public Library, forming a hub of cultural activity on Court Street. Not far from Main Street, it was easily accessible to all, with plenty of parking.

When it opened, the Carter Gallery provided great space for arts and industrial exhibits. There was also a small-unfinished theater later used by CenterStage, the center's own theater company. And there was the Children's Museum. Who will forget the fireman's pole to shimmy and the ceiling spider puppet with many legs to pull?

In spite of a thorny financial history, the center kept adding to its repertoire. On the cutting edge of the computer revolution, it installed a computer lab. The Center's Auxiliary set up the Soupcon—a restaurant overlooking the garden—and there were art classes of every description for children and adults.

Memories include the elaborate receptions catered by the auxiliary for openings of shows. They were warm gatherings to the last, a retrospective this fall of Nashua artist Calvin Libby. Just as memorable were evenings of dinner theater, Downtown Live concerts and original productions presented by the teen-agers in Kids Into Drama.

In the end, the vision became clouded by such things as a leaky roof, a poor heating system and a picture of the arts as struggling stepsister always on the dole.

Why was it so difficult to see Cinderella waiting in the wings?

January 8, 1995

"LITTLE" LEGACIES GO A LONG WAY

If they were alive today, two successful businessmen would applaud the way the city is spending their money. You could even say it would be music to their ears.

Moses Hunt and Ira F. Harris left relatively small legacies to Nashua, but both funds have enriched the lives of contemporary residents considerably. One of the dividends is the summer Bach Lunch concert series in the theater of the Nashua Public Library.

Had they attended the concert last Wednesday at noon, Hunt and Harris would have encountered a full house quite unlike any they had ever seen. There were music lovers of all ages, some in business suits obviously on a lunch break, others in shorts, slacks and T-shirts.

As they waited for the woodwind quartet, Infinity, to take the stage, the concertgoers pulled a variety of lunch treats out of brown bags.

Organizing their crew in the back of the 100-seat auditorium were Cindy Bannon and Pat Riley. The two mothers each had their three children—ranging from 8 years old to 21 months—in tow.

"The library has some excellent children's music tapes," said Bannon, noting they provide a wonderful introduction to the music of such great composers as Bach, Beethoven and Mozart.

"It is nice to have the children listen to tapes, but to experience live musicians playing is even better," added Riley.

Merrimack piano teacher Antoinette Lovejoy and friend Sue Hurwitz knew from attending last year's concert that their children were good listeners.

"We're all musicians. I teach them all piano, even Sue," said Lovejoy.

"When you're able to bring food, they can watch and snack at the same time," said added.

Stefan Silverston munched on a banana while he waited for the music to begin. He and his wife, Joan, attended Bach Lunches whenever their computer software business allowed them to get away.

Roberta Prokop of Hudson and her daughter, Meghan, 15, were fans of Infinity.

"My sister is Judith Teehan. She plays the flute (with the group)," said Prokop.

The woodwind ensemble also included Margaret Herley on the oboe, Stephanie Ratte on clarinet and Rebecca McCatty on bassoon.

Their lyrical, hour-long program began with a Mozart Divetimento, progressed to the 20th century, curved back to the 17th century and ended, fittingly, with "Adieu" by 20th century composer Gordon Jacob.

Each of the musicians gave an introduction to segments of the program.

Infinity was known to several youngsters in the audience. The woodwind musicians had played at 20 schools in the area during the "Music in Our School" Week, financed through the same funds.

"How many kids get to see a bassoon in action?" said Arthur Olsson after the concert. He also noted that the group had played recently at the Castle College summer series and the tickets were $25 apiece.

Thanks to Moses Hunt and Ira Harris, the Bach concerts were free.

Moses Hunt was born in Nashua but made his fortune as a businessman in Boston. He died in 1887 and left $15,000 for a free lecture fund.

Ira Harris, a clerk with the Indian Head Bank who was always involved in civic affairs, died in 1927. The 1936 will of his wife, Mary Proctor Harris, bequeathed $20,000 to the city in a fund established in his memory.

In the late '70s, Mayor Maurice Arel suggested coordinating the efforts of the two funds.

"We cooperate together, we plan together but we are two separate funds, financially. Our objectives are the same," said Olsson, a trustee of the Hunt Fund together with Ruth Gaukstern. Trustees of the Harris Fund are Donald Marquis and Florence Shepard.

The Nashua Symphony Association lines up the performers for the Bach Lunches. The series just completed its fifth season with four concerts: Alexander Henderson, tenor; Nicolai Lomov, piano; R.P. Hale, harpsichord; and Infinity, woodwinds.

"I just love the bassoon," said Jeannette Brooks of Merrimack as she left the NPL theater. She would be back next year.

THE EAST PEARL STREET GALLERY

Shopping for gifts should be fun, not an exercise in endurance. The newest wrinkle, cyberspace, satisfies itchy fingers and tight schedules, but not the soul of a true shopper. When searching for the meaningful present, the place to take a stroll during the holiday season is Downtown Nashua.

As has been said many times, Downtown Nashua is the place where the salespeople are friendly, the shoppers neighborly and the merchandise out of the ordinary. Gift wrapping often goes along with the good cheer. All together it is a recipe for an enjoyable shopping experience.

If you subscribe to the theory that bigger is better, head for the malls. If small is beautiful—and far more serene—downtown is the right direction to go.

The East Pearl Street Gallery is a perfect example.

"It's amazing in a space 7 feet by 25 feet, how visually attractive you can make it," says Mary Swanson, longtime member of the Greater Nashua Artists Association.

The artists association opened the gallery, the first in its 50-year history, in June. Displayed in the long corridor gallery, sandwiched between Charlie's Barber Shop and Crosby's Bakery, are the works of 30 artists.

Surprisingly, the narrow space gives it a warmth and a charm larger galleries lack. Yet there is plenty to see. The walls are decorated with nearly 70 original paintings, drawings and photographs, and together, with the browsers' bin, there are 100 artistic pieces to peruse: landscapes, still-lifes, portraits, pastels, watercolors, oils and prints. Although there are more than one, numbered prints are original works of art too, as opposed to mass reproductions, Swanson points out.

Together the works on the wall offer a visual feast and, individually, a study in style, color and subject.

They range in price from Diane Nichol's watercolor, "Field of Dreams," $125, to Monique Sakellarios' oil, "The Clearing," for $825. Photography is raised to an artistic level by Jack Ebel, who captures a nodding sunflower with his camera. Though in black and white, in mood it resembles a painting by Georgia O'Keeffe and it sells for $300.

"It's hard to see a new view of traditional subject," says Swanson, an artist who appreciates the unique way each of her colleagues looks at the world. She has several paintings in the exhibit and unframed works in the bin. All the paintings on the wall are beautifully framed by the artist.

Floral painting by Mary Swanson

"People will go into a store and buy a reproduction of a painting, and by the time it's framed, it's quite expensive. These are all originals, already framed," says Loretta Hubley, the president.

"We're trying to get people to realize there is a lot of good art here," adds Brenda Gabriel, the past president who campaigned for the gallery. All of the work in the gallery, except items in the bin, have been juried to insure the quality, and the artwork is rotated every six weeks.

A visit to the new gallery is a must for downtown shoppers, if only for a few moments of personal enjoyment. Members of the Greater Nashua Artists Association, who spell each other at the gallery, welcome visitors. It is open Wednesdays through Saturdays from 11 A.M. to 5 P.M., and there is ample parking in the back, off Spring Street.

December 2, 2000

NASHUA SYMPHONY OFFICE

Strains of the Liszt piano concerto drift over the rooftops of city buildings, through the trees, into the cars pulling in and out of the Nashua Library parking lot. Coming together bush by bush in the middle of downtown Nashua is an island of nature's serenity easily accessible to anyone seeking a retreat from the hustle and the bustle of the city streets.

The speakers piping music into the air are courtesy of the Nashua Symphony, now installed in its new office off the courtyard tucked behind the American Stage Festival building on Court Street.

This is a stellar week for the symphony. As the orchestra prepares to launch its 75th season, the overgrown weed patch leading to the Church Street office entrance is being restored to the flowering green space it once was 20 years ago.

Adding a new dimension to the surroundings is the music, and the selections played each day are not random. "We've been playing pieces from our concerts this season," says Roxanne Turner, the executive director of the Nashua Symphony Association.

The Liszt CD being played over the speakers won a Grammy for soloist Emanuel Ax. The internationally acclaimed pianist will bring his award-winning performance Saturday to Nashua at Keefe Auditorium at Elm Street Junior High School. He will be accompanied by the Nashua Symphony under the direction of its conductor, Royston Nash. The grand finale of the season's openings concert will be Tchaikovsky's Fourth Symphony.

Tickets for the auspicious occasion are fast disappearing, reports Turner, adding with a smile, "ticket sales are up 30 percent for the season.' When your budget of $350,000 depends on ticket sales and contributions that is good news indeed.

It is a year to sing about for Nashua's premiere professional musical organization, at 75 the oldest in the state and the only symphony affiliated with a choral society. Its more spacious, more accessible headquarters is another reason to rejoice.

"My office used to be Whisper's Café," observes Turner, referring to the restaurants occupying the lower level of the Center for the Arts before it was closed and the building was taken over by the city. In the '70s and '80s, the courtyard served as an extension of the center's restaurant with outdoor tables on the patio during the summer. As the center withered, so did the courtyard.

Laurie Berna

By the end of the week, the poetic view will be restored to go with the music played on the speakers. For this the symphony and the city can thank a group of Nashuans who truly live up to expectation. Bringing back the inner city oasis for all to enjoy is the work of the Leadership of Greater Nashua (LGN). The object of the yearlong program run by the Nashua Chamber of Commerce is to train potential civic leaders. Its participants come from all walks of life including business, industry, banking and social services. Throughout the year, they learn about the working of the city, its strengths and weaknesses, its resources and needs. Each year the group picks a project that will improve the city.

Among the 23 in the class of 1997–98 was Mary Phillis, former vice president of development on the Board of Trustees of the Symphony Association.

"Beautifying the courtyard was adopted unanimously by the group last December," she says, and the last month or two it has really come together."

The inner city courtyard project was attractive to the LGN because of the numbers of people it would benefit: Seniors living nearby, business people, library and State Festival patrons and shoppers, to name a few.

To accomplish their goal, the group—with the help of Ward 8 Alderman Maureen Lemieux—received $20,000 of federal Block Grant money for the project.

"We learned a lot about working with government money," notes the mother of six. For additional expenses, the group raised almost another $20,000. G. Frank Teas Jr. led the fund-raising effort.

When they first surveyed the courtyard, they tried to imagine its greener days.

"It looked like a secret garden. We saw so much potential for the beautification project," she offers.

By the end of the week, the rickety old wooden fence on Church Street will be gone and in its place will be a handsome, black, wrought iron fence with granite posts, the work of Gate City Fence. New granite steps will lead into the courtyard.

Fresh sod with an irrigation system beneath it has been installed by T & S Landscaping of Derry. Morin Landscaping, who did the original design, will take charge of the finish work.

On Saturday, members of LGN will take over the planting of bulbs, shrubs and annuals to ensure there will be color throughout the three seasons it can be used. On Sept. 18, it will be officially turned back to the care of the city's Park and Recreation Department and opened to the public, says Roger Hatfield, superintendent of Training for the Nashua Fire Department, and member of the LGN class of '98.

Completing the picture will be granite benches, a new picnic table, a couple of shade trees and granite posts to mark off the path to the library parking lot.

In the midst of the din of traffic and city life will soon be a pleasant place to read, to watch the birds, to eat lunch and to listen to music. Future possibilities include outdoor Stage Festival performances on the patio, concerts by small musical ensembles and NPL's Bach Lunches.

The Nashua Coalition for the Arts will get a preview at its meeting Thursday evening in the Nashua Symphony office, and creative city artists may generate even more ideas.

"It will be picture perfect," says Mary Phillis, "and the true test is when we start seeing people using it."

September 4, 1998

NUTCRACKER

Tony Cafarella has his work cut out for him.

It is 8 A.M. Saturday morning when the Nashua craftsman heads for his workshop. He sips a cup of coffee while he studies the blueprints for a magical kingdom placed in his hands this summer.

Cafarella is constructing the framework for the newly designed sets of the Granite State Ballet Company's production of "The Nutcracker." He has a month to get 48 flats ready for Thomas Shanton, the Goffstown scenic designer, to paint.

Spread out on the workshop table are the blueprints drawn to scale for four set changes. A meticulous craftsman, Tony is cutting to order each of the one-inch by three-inch sections of lumber he needs. The precut pieces, he says, are too flimsy. After each one is cut to specifications, a canvas material will be attached to take the paint.

As his jigsaw begins to buzz, Cafarella quips, "I'd rather be 'Norm Abrams' assistant than an accountant." Abrams, the master carpenter and the host of PBS's "New Yankee Workshop" is his idol. Carpentry is Cafarella's avocation. Professionally, he works for Digital Equipment Corp. in Acton, Mass.

He has also been married for 25 years to Doreen Cafarella, the founder and artistic director of the Granite State Ballet. Their home is filled with his handiwork. He just finished making a hutch for the kitchen, building an addition to their house and a shed for the back.

"He's run out of projects so he is working for me," says Doreen.

"Once they are put up on stage, you have a nice neat set that will work well in any theater in the area," she says of the wooden supports on which the canvas is mounted and the scenery is painted.

Doreen formed the Granite State Ballet in Nashua in 1986, and since, the "Nutcracker" has been the centerpiece of its season. The first year the company just presented the second act. But the next year the production was given full treatment and to keep it fresh, something new is added every year.

"This year we have another surprise so no one will get bored with our 'Nutcracker,'" says Doreen, who retired from performing two years ago.

"We are a professional company and it is important that people do not perceive us as just a local ballet school doing the 'Nutcracker,'" she adds, mentioning that some 20 professional dancers head up the cast.

Public relations volunteer Susan Gilbert-Edgett, already in the process of writing releases for the Christmas favorite, notes that for every dancer on stage, there are six people working behind the scenes.

Seamstress Lois Estabrook of Wilton is also designing several new costumes. But the major undertaking is the new set.

Shanton already has established a solid reputation with the company. Last year, he designed the intricate set for Granite State's production of "Coppelia." A dancer, too, he had performed a small role in the ballet.

"When I saw 'Coppelia' I knew he had to do the 'Nutcracker,'" Doreen remembers. She was fascinated by his method of painting the "Coppelia."

The floor of the Granite State studio on Arlington Street became his easel and with great flourish, he applied the paint with a long brush.

"My rehearsal was going on and I was watching him paint."

"He understands how to use shading of colors so when the light hits them, they stand out," she marvels.

To capture the many moods of the "Nutcracker," Shanton has designed four sets. The first, picturing a winter scene of elegant 18th century townhouses, was almost eliminated.

"It is only there for two minutes at the beginning," she notes.

It was such a perfect introduction to the ballet, the dance director decided to use it instead of the curtain. People will see it as they take their seats.

The second set is an interior of the house where Herr and Frau Silberhaus hold their Christmas party and their daughter Clara receives a nutcracker. The most elaborate scene, the third set, projects the ethereal quality of the forest during the snowstorm.

For the fourth and last scene, Shanton creates the fanciful land of the Palace of the Sweets, where Clara is greeted by the Sugar Plum Fairy and her cavalier. Dominating the set is a tall archway, the perfect entrance and exit for the dancing

confections who entertained Clara. After the colorful dance sequence, the curtain falls as Clara departs with the Nutcracker.

The story of the "Nutcracker" is a familiar one to Tony Cafarella. He has watched his wife dance the role of the Sugar Plum Fairy many times. As have his two sons, Tony and Billy, he has worked backstage and this December he will be on duty supervising the crew.

Through the years, the Christmas ballet has become a family tradition for Nashuans just as it is for the Caferellas.

Before it tackles "The Nutcracker," the company will present a Summerfest show Saturday, Aug. 20, at 7 P.M. at the Greeley Park Band Shell. It will feature a mixed repertoire ranging from classical pas de trios from "Swan Lake" to an upbeat Duke Ellington medley, "For the Fun of It." Ballet enthusiasts are invited to catch the rehearsal going on all day at the shell.

August 6, 1995

ON THE TOWN

Neither sleet nor snow will stay these pros from their appointed rounds. Nor viruses nor the flu. Whatever obstacles winter throws at them, the Nashua Actorsingers will go on with the show. The company is in rehearsals for "On the Town," opening Friday, March 9 at 8 P.M. at the Edmund Keefe auditorium and playing Saturday, March 10, at 8 P.M. and Sunday, March 11 at 2 P.M.

Spring has come a little early for the theatrical troupe. May is the traditional month for the spring show, but because of a conflict in the auditorium's scheduling, the company could not arrange for the two consecutive weekends needed to set up and present its elaborate musical production.

So the spring show will be staged in March instead of May. And the change in the date has brought with it all the hang-ups of winter. "During rehearsals, we've had a blizzard," said director Kathy Lovering. "We've all been fighting the flu and the weather," agreed stage manager Lou Duhamel. "And Sara Minerd, who plays the leading lady, slipped and twisted her ankle," Lovering added.

In spite of the mishaps, rehearsals have never been canceled. The show must go on dictum, has been the Actorsinger's rule since the group organized in 1955 at the Church of the Good Shepherd to perform Gilbert and Sullivan operettas. In 1959 the group incorporated mounting dozens of successful musicals such as "Oliver," "Camelot"and "The Sound of Music" through the years.

For "On the Town" rehearsals, the lights have been burning bright since the New Year in Actorsingers Hall on Lake Street. The building was purchased by the troupe in the early 70s to rehearse for shows and to store sets and costumes. The three floors are buzzing with rehearsals for "On the Town" and "Narnia," the Junior Actorsingers show. The young thespians began rehearsals last weekend.

Two nights a week, on Wednesdays and Sundays, when the "On the Town" cast is kicking up its heels to the tune of "New York, New York, It's a Wonderful Town," "So Long Baby" and "Lucky to be Me," the back stage crew is painting, pounding nails and working out the glitches for the sound and lighting systems. Trying to catch up after delays because of illness and the weather, the dedicated behind-the-scenes staff often stops in for a few hours on Saturday mornings. As show time approaches, the work sessions starting at 6 P.M. are more frequent and go well into the wee hours of the night.

"When push comes to shove, we can be here till one in the morning," says Larry Doiron of Dracut, Mass. A printer by day, he does carpentry as a hobby for local

Michele Bossie, taxicab driver, and Ben Esterman, her boss in On the Town

community theater companies. Last Saturday morning, the Actorsingers' master carpenter was assembling the parts of a taxi cab on the second floor of the Lake Street building, where sets are constructed. Since the play takes place in Manhattan, the action revolves around cabs. And the subway as well as the Big Apple landmarks such as Carnegie Hall and the Museum of Natural History.

The story line follows the antics of three sailors from the Brooklyn Navy Yard on leave for 24 hours in New York City. One wants to see all the sights, another wants to meet lots of women and the third wants to meet the girl of his dreams. Frank Sinatra and Gene Kelly played two of the sailors in the movie version of the Broadway musical.

Doiron's job is to create a yellow checkered cab that taxies the sailors about. The interior of the cab is easy. A black leather seat has been recycled from another show but the yellow checkered cab being built around it is just taking shape. Doiron's next challenge is to reproduce the cab's rounded fenders. Locating an old car at the landfill or around town is one possibility, he offers joking. "Don't worry, we can always use Styrofoam," assures Lovering, the show's counselor, cheer leader and jack of all trades as well as director. She has come in Saturday morning with her two daughters, Emily, 12, and Madeleine, 11, to paint panels for the nightclub scene. Carefully she fills in the colors for the Jack of Diamonds wall section. Duhamel has marked lines on the Ace of Diamonds wall section, which is propped up nearby.

"He's an ace at that," quips Lovering. The "smell of the greasepaint" keeps the backstage crew coming back year after year to volunteer their time after working at regular jobs all day. They take no bows; the applause they receive comes from each other. "You help out any where you're needed," offers Lovering, a member of the Actorsingers since high school. She and her husband, Bob, met at Actorsingers and now their daughters are involved in Junior Actorsingers.

The girls pitch in once in a while painting sets. "We're all interchangeable," says Duhamel, also a veteran who doubles as set designer. His wife, JoAnn, a hair stylist, will fashion "On the Town" '40s hairdos. She is also helping Alene Bonner with costumes. The Duhamels' daughter, Allison, is in the chorus. "For this show, they've lowered the age from 15 to 14 since they need more dancers," says Pam Gilpatrick, producer of "Narnia," adding that the teen-agers in the Junior Actorsingers have rehearsals for both shows. That means at least four rehearsals a week.

There are more than 80 people backstage and on stage in the Nashua production of the Broadway post-war hit, the first musical composed by Leonard Bernstein, decades before "West Side Story." "The music is tough . . . tough," observes Lovering. "You have to bend the notes, there are often six flats in a row and the rhythm is syncopated," she says.

There are also 17 scene changes. The show's director oversees all aspects of the production and she knows that just as much energy goes into Creating the backdrop for the song and dance routines as the routines themselves. Among the many set challenges, besides the taxicab, are the New York skyline at night and a dinosaur for the Museum of Natural History. It collapses into a pile of bones and has to be put together again before each show.

Tom Ritrovato, assistant stage manager, has devised the giant collapsible creature that was modeled after a child's toy. His daughter, Lanea, is in the Junior Actorsingers and his son, Aaron, is helping with the sound for "On the Town."

Saturday morning Lovering takes time out from painting to meet with Ritrovato and Dennis Schneider, an engineer and CEO of his own high-tech firm. The lighting director of "On the Town," he says hanging the equipment in the aging rafters of Elm Street Junior High auditorium requires some ingenuity.

Schneider got hooked on the theater backstage when he was courting his wife, Kerry, at Cornell University. Since moving to Nashua, both have been active in the Actorsingers, he offstage and she on stage, often in comedic roles. She plays the role of Madame Dilly, the inebriated voice teacher who stashes a bottle in a hidden compartment in the piano.

While they're talking, Rich Rothbell, a graphic artist by day, bursts in to show off the life-size poster of "Miss Turnstyles," the show's equivalent of Miss Subway, who turns out to be the love interest in the show. Rothbell, who has a bit part in the show, is also designer of the "On the Town" poster with the sailor and his girl dancing against the New York City skyline.

Recreating the skyline on stage is the mammoth task of Terri, the relocation manager for the Air Force at Hanscom Field in Bedford, Mass. A relative newcomer to Actorsingers, she has applied high-tech know-how to the job. O'Keefe's son, Mike, is in the "On the Town" chorus. "It's hard to put the brush down," she says, remembering running out on stage between acts to touch up a set when the curtain came down. Modern technology has made recreating the New York City skyline easier. After researching her subject, she made transparencies to project onto the wall, taking the guesswork out of outlining the buildings and determining where to put the windows. On stage, with Schneider's help, the 14-foot-high by 24-foot-wide panel will twinkle with lights.

For the week of March 2, the sets will be moved into the Elm Street auditorium, where the cast will hold its dress rehearsals. "Let's hope we don't have a snow storm when we move them in our open truck. The paint is watercolor," Lovering says.

February 24, 2001

PLACES OF WORSHIP

My Window on Main Street

FIRST CHURCH OF NASHUA

If ever a town carved the perfect spot for a landmark, it is the hilltop overlooking Main Street and the Nashua River.

Through the 1800s, it was the site of the Indian Head Coffee House. As a stop for the stagecoach and a hub of the social scene, it contributed much to the community life in a growing mill town.

In 1894, the colonial inn was torn down to make way for another landmark, a solid granite structure built to weather the centuries with grace. The land on the corner of Concord and Lowell streets was purchased for $1, and a house of worship quite singular in Nashua's architectural landscape, was erected for the sum of $123,000.

The building became the 10th home of the Congregational Church in Nashua. The history of the church reflects its deep roots in Nashua. From its first gathering place in the Meeting House in Dunstable in 1685, it moved north. Subsequent meeting places include churches fondly called Old South, Olive Street and Old Chocolate, the brown church on Main Street.

In its last home, the granite church conveys a sense of permanence. The exterior is distinguished by its bell tower, twin turrets and rose windows. Inside, a dome with another rose window crowns the semicircular sanctuary of carved oak pews. The chimes of its 15-bell tower were displayed at the Chicago World's Fair in the same year of the dedication.

A month ago at a rededication service, the parish of the First Church of Nashua celebrated its 100th anniversary in its majestic home on Library Hill. The occasion was also the dedication of a major expansion project adding 11 classrooms, a chapel and new office space.

"I still don't have any pictures on the wall," says the Rev. James Chaloner, church pastor, as he enters his corner office. On his desk is a Christmas tree-shaped container filled with homemade Christmas cookies, a gift from a parishioner.

"We even have room to spare," says Chaloner, surveying the area off the back entrance while showing the facility to a visitor. In January, it will become a second-hand clothing shop open for the neighborhood. As part of its community outreach, the church has also housed a Chapter 1 kindergarten for more than ten years. The federally funded preschool now uses the new Sunday School facility during the week.

The church and the annex, previously two separate building, were joined with a passageway, and an elevator was installed making all areas handicapped accessible. A second floor was built over Nauss Hall, and the new annex was named in honor of Dr. Paul R. Walker, the pastor with a 27-year record of service to the congregation.

Now retired, Walker is living in California. He expects to visit Nashua in the spring to give the sermon, "This Old House," which he was scheduled to deliver at the rededication. Shortly before leaving for Nashua, however, he broke his leg.

Thoughts of the Walker Building, the space needed to deliver the church into the 21st century, took shape at a church planning retreat in 1987.

"We had reached a plateau, and we had to move forward," says Chaloner. Despite the economic downturn that hit Nashua at the end of the 1980s, parishioners pledged more than $1 million to make the dream a reality.

Chaloner credits the positive attitude of Frederic E. Shaw, one of the mainstays of the church, with setting the tone for the building campaign. He also started the ball rolling with a generous gift for the chapel, which bears the Shaw name.

In contrast to the ornate 560-seat sanctuary, the chapel seats 70 people for more intimate wedding, funeral and children's services. Two stained-glass windows, removed from the original church so the two buildings could be joined, now frame the altar of the new chapel. Its simple classic décor is in the manner of Colonial New England churches much to the satisfaction of the parishioners, says Chaloner.

"It's so serene and peaceful," Shaw adds. Checking on the floral display, he asks Chaloner to call him if flowers are needed in the future.

The Church and the Shaw family share a long history in Nashua.

"My father, Elijah Ray Shaw, and my grandfather, Jason E. Tolles, belonged to the church before me. My father sang in the choir, and I was baptized in the church," says the 80-year-old Nashuan, a retired vice president of the J.F. McElwain Co. His mother's aunt, Mary Ellen Tolles, he adds, played the organ when the church opened in 1894. And many decades later, his four children attended Sunday school there.

Growing up in the church gave him a firm footing in life and also expanded his horizons, says Shaw. He relates how he met other teen-agers from different parts of the state, the nation and the world at church conferences.

Trying to understand the meaning of war was the indelible lesson that Lucille Lintott Cudhea learned in youth group discussions at the church. The native Nashuan still remembers the sessions conducted by Dr. Whitney S.K. Yeaple, the interim pastor when Dr. Earl Nauss volunteered as a Navy chaplain in World War II. The discussions were particularly helpful to the young woman who had lost her father in the war and had a brother in the service.

"During the war there was a banner with gold stars and blue stars hanging behind the pulpit," she recalls. The blue stars represented the men in the service and the gold stars, those killed in action.

There were happier times, too, says Cudhea. The youth group's weekly skating parties at Holman Stadium are among her favorite memories.

"They were all-inclusive; you could invite any friends even if they weren't members of the church." And there was always hot chocolate for everyone, back at the church.

Interior shot of First Church

Chaloner also grew up in the church, but becoming its minister was not part of his life's plan as a youth, says the 46-year-old pastor.

Attending services was part of the bargain he struck with his mother in order to play on the church's basketball team. "Some of Dr. Walker's sermons stuck without my knowing it," he says with a chuckle.

After graduating from UNH, he worked in the personnel department of J.F. McElwain. It was another minister of the First Church, the Rev. William Holliday, who urged him to try a new direction. Chaloner returned to school as a divinity student in Bangor, Maine, and unexpectedly came home to fill the post of assistant minister of the First Church. When Holliday was reassigned in 1984, the hometown parishioner became the senior minister of the church.

In the coming week, Chaloner will compose his Christmas message in his new office in the Walker Building. On Christmas Eve, he will take the corner pulpit to address the hundreds of parishioners filling the pews, the gallery and even the auditorium adjacent to the sanctuary. Music minister Robin Dinda will play the treasured Anderson organ and the choir will sing "Silent Night" as the candles are lit and cast a glow over the sanctuary. At the end of the service, the church bells will ring throughout the town, as they have for the past century.

December 17, 1994

CHIMES RING LOUD AND CLEAR

In the summer of 2001, Nashua's North Main Street was the place to see a fascinating sky show as the First Church of Nashua was in the process of being restored. It was mesmerizing to watch a cage on the needle of a crane swing through the air and graze the bell tower of the historic stone church on the corner of Concord and Lowell streets.

Scaffolding may be the way to repair factories and office buildings, but for the First Church that kind of rigging was deemed unacceptable.

"We are a church. We can't put scaffolding around and keep people out," says Betty Lou Shirley, chairwoman of the Prudential Committee overseeing the restoration of the granite grand old lady at the crest of Library Hill. "Besides, we're on a busy corner and we can't block it off."

For two weeks, at 7 A.M. in the cool of the morning, steeple jack Al Fauteux of Keene and his crew of three men positioned a crane on Lowell Street to reach the heights outside the bell tower, the first target of the church restoration project. Through the heat of the day, they erased the wear and tear of time, patching damaging leaks, replacing the broken tiles of the slate roof, remortaring the granite and even tightening the lightning rod. They continued working for another two or three weeks outside the tower but on a rope rigging instead of a crane.

Housed in the tower since it was built in 1894 are 15 bells weighing a total of 20,000 pounds. In 1893, called the Chime of 10 the bells were first heard morning, noon and evening at the World's Columbian Exposition in Chicago, when they were purchased as a gift for the church by a member of the congregation. The cost of the bronze bells was $5,000.

After the exposition closed, the Chime of 10 was returned to the Cincinnati company that made it and five more bells were added to complete the set, a Chime of 15. The largest bell weighs 4,500 pounds and the smallest 270 pounds. The bells have an octave-and-a-half range. Named the Mary Park Nutt Memorial Chime, in honor of the donor, the Chime of 15 was shipped to Nashua and in the 118-foot-tall church tower. A polished wood keyboard to play the bells was installed in the tower off the second floor of the church. It is still there today.

Since the inauguration service in June 1894, the Chime of 15 has sounded through the city on Sundays, holidays such as Christmas and Easter and special occasions such as the eve of the 21st century.

In the summer, while steeplejacks labored outside, the work of the church went on inside and the bells in the tower continued to ring. Sunday after the communion service, Jean (Strand) Lyons, one of the corps of volunteer bell musicians—many are also members of the handbell choir—began 15 minutes before services with her usual introductory hymn, "Joyful Joyful We Adore Thee" followed by a communion song and ending with a chorus of "Amazing Grace." Her repertoire often included her father's favorite hymn, a Swedish folk tune, "Children of the Heavenly Father."

"I dedicated it to his memory," she says. Chris Strand's daughter says her father was a jack of all trades who did whatever was needed at the church in his spare time. "If he wasn't working or at home, my mother knew he was at the church doing something. It was his way of tithing."

In the late 1970s, Strand and Bill Richardson, an electrical engineer, embarked on a mission to rescue the bell tower from harm. Through the years, the floor of the tower had been badly damaged by birds and bats flying in through openings. Strand designed and built a screen enclosure to keep the predators out of the four arched tower openings, characteristic of the church's Romanesque architecture. To put the screens in place, the two men devised a pulley system.

"My father was busy doing it all summer in our cellar and back yard," she recalls, noting he built a cross into the screening to enhance the enclosure.

When the screens were finished the family was recruited to clean out the debris. "The family took out 30 bags of pigeon droppings," remarks Lyons.

Almost 20 years later, it was Lyons who realized the bells needed to be repaired. She complained of having difficulty pressing the C bell, "I knew it did not feel right when it played."

Her son John, also a bell ringer, had discovered a nut holding one of the straps that hold a large bell had come loose, presenting an immediate danger because of its weight. The leaks of the tower, obvious to everyone, were another source of destruction.

In August 1998, under the supervision of George Borski, head of the church building committee, an effort to restore the bells and the tower began. The wooden beam supporting the bells for more than a century had rotted, so it was replaced by a steel beam. The leaks around the deck upon which the bells rested, necessitated the deck's replacement by one that is copper-clad and leak-proof. The work was done by the P.M. Mackey Co. in Nashua.

A new steel cable pulley system attaching the bells to the keyboard replaced the old one and the company that made the original bells, the W.E. Vanduzen Co. in Cincinnati, repaired the wear and tear.

"Now you don't have to push as hard," says Lyons, an administrative assistant in the Community Development Department at City Hall. Another improvement is that she can now hear the hymns as she plays.

"It is an honor to play the bells," she continues, "But you hope you don't hit a wrong note."

When the bells were restored, the congregation voted to spotlight its historic treasure and soon, in the dark of evening, the church will be illuminated, adding a dramatic note to downtown Nashua.

The lights, the bells and the bell tower are just the beginning of a major restoration campaign undertaken by the congregation, says Shirley. "I expect we will have to raise $850,000 to do the job."

Since the objective is to restore the antique beauty of the Nashua landmark, craftsmen who understand the character of the church are needed to do the work. With more than 50 years in the steeplejack business, 69-year-old Fauteux fits the job requirement. He and his crew, who leave Keene at dawn each day, are masters at handling the many facets of the job, including construction, carpentry, roofing and masonry. They are also accustomed to working in all kinds of weather, from winter white-outs to summer heat waves.

Roberto Serpentino of Boston, trained in Italy, is another artisan hired to clean and replace the broken shards in the stained glass window set like a jewel in the ceiling above the sanctuary. The wide solid oak door off the parking lot presents another problem, since even the doors and windows were sized and constructed differently when the building was built. Also a priority on the schedule is a complete rewiring of the church, one of the first buildings in Nashua to be electrified.

"This is about the preservation of a landmark," says Shirley, pointing to the triangle at the peak of Library Hill—the First Church, the Hunt Memorial Building and the Abbot-Spalding House. These three buildings, she observes, are at the heart of Nashua history.

"We are blessed to be entrusted with the stewardship of the church," she says, adding, "I hope the work we do lasts another 100 years."

August 11, 2001

NASHUA'S FIRST BAPTIST CHURCH

As a deacon and sexton of the First Baptist Church in Nashua, Walter Silas Jaquith took it upon himself to keep the clock in the church tower on time. Whenever it lost a few minutes, he would climb to the loft overlooking Main Street and balance precariously as he reset the hands.

"The police officer walking by would tell him how dangerous it was but he continued to do it," says his daughter-in-law, Sylvia Jaquith. He was affectionately known as "Papa Jaquith" to the congregation in the 1940s, she adds.

Sylvia and her husband, Walter F., grew up in the church. They courted when both were teaching Sunday School, and 68 years ago, they married in the church. Their three sons were baptized in the church, as their father's grandmother, Hannah Jane Pingree, had been earlier. In fact, church records indicate she was the last parishioner to be baptized in the Nashua River. The date was Dec. 2, 1866.

The Jaquiths are one of many families whose roots run deep in the history of Nashua's First Baptist Church, ABC.

Arriving at the theme for the church's 175th anniversary was an easy task for Co-chairwomen Sandy Martinson and Betty Cernuda. "Generation to Generation—God's Faithful Then and Now" perfectly suited the occasion.

Laurie Berna

To launch the celebration, a service honoring longtime members was held in January 1997. Among the more than 200 members attending was Tina Page, who joined in 1919. In February, a service honored church couples married more than 25 years. Grace and William MacDonald, who have been married 72 years, cut the cake. The year concludes with a banquet and religious celebration in October to be attended by former ministers Craig Collemer, Kenneth Fiery and Wallace Forgey and their wives. The Rev. and Mrs. W. Hubert Port; Clara Bonell, widow of the late Rev. Harold Bonell, and Dorothy Greer, widow of the late Rev. Jean Greer, have been invited to take part.

Memories of family milestones—baptisms, weddings, Men's and Women's Fellowship dinners, the church fairs, and the Children's Day festivities—will cast a glow throughout the year.

"We've been here all our lives. We were born and brought up in the church," says Martinson, president of the Women's Fellowship. She and Cernuda, vice president of the fellowship and financial secretary of the church, have been involved in church projects since their Sunday School days, when the church by the river was a landmark on Main Street. After the congregation moved to the new home it had built on Manchester Street in 1980, the two native Nashuans continued to count the church as a priority in their busy lives of working and raising families. Generations before them had done the same.

The seeds of the First Baptist Church were planted at a meeting of six men and nine women on July 10, 1822. Minutes that are yellowed with age show that the meeting took place at the schoolhouse on Stark Square at the top of Concord Street. For its first 11 years, the young Baptist Church congregation had no home, and for six years, no permanent pastor.

In 1833 it raised the grand sum of $4,000 to build its first church, though it was not a wealthy congregation and many of its members worked in the mills. Land on the corner of Franklin and Main streets had been left to the church for that purpose and members dug deep to contribute.

"Money was raised with some help coming from several rich Baptists in Hudson," writes Frank

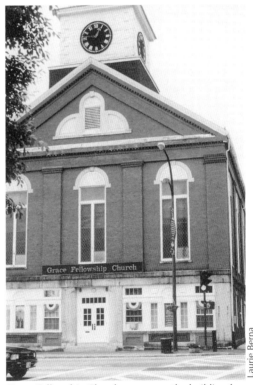

Grace Fellowship Church now owns the building formerly the First Baptist Church.

Laurie Berna

Mellen in the history he researched for the church's 150th anniversary.

Their church meeting house met a terrible fate in 1848 when the wooden structure was destroyed by a fire. It was replaced two years later by a fine Greek Revival-style structure, and this served the church for more than a century, withstanding such disasters as the great flood of 1936. This old church building still stands today as the house of worship for another congregation, Grace Fellowship Church.

Much history was to be recorded in that classic brick building with the tall, narrow arched windows. It originally housed two shops on Main Street, but they were later removed when the church needed the space to expand. The new church boasted fresco walls, a rosewood altar and fine organ built by a local craftsmen. A steeple, containing a bronze bell and clocks regulated to railroad time, added distinction to the exterior.

"For many years, Sunday mornings were always the same. At 10:30 the Baptist bell would ring first, summoning church-goers, followed by the bells on the Olive Street Church, the Pilgrim and the Unitarian, and then the sequence would be repeated,'" writes Mellen in his 150-year chronicle.

On V-E Day in the summer of 1945, Papa Jaquith ascended the steeple with his grandson, Garland, to ring the bell and proclaim to all of Nashua that the war was over.

With too many memories invested in its chimes to leave behind, the bronze bell was installed in the contemporary church when the congregation moved in 1980. It represented a piece of the past in the contemporary building; other treasures in the old building such as stained-glass windows could not be transferred.

Through the years as the church grew in membership and consequently outgrew its quarters on Main Street, it stretched its outreach to the community and beyond. It took one of its first civic stands of the 20th century in 1935, when it opposed the renewal of the franchise of Rockingham Race Track.

In 1955 when Bonell left his post in Geneva, Switzerland, as administrative secretary of the World Council of Churches, to become minister of first Baptist, he brought a new perspective to the congregation. Throughout the '60s, the church opened its doors to displaced people and refugees, often helping them start new lives in Nashua. Exchange students were also sponsored by the church and woven into the fabric of its life.

In the late '60s, led by the Rev. Kenneth Fiery, the church reached out to youth groups in the community, such as the Pine Street Youth Center and the Children's Association. Through longtime church member Isabelle Hildreth, the first woman to receive the Nashua Chamber of Commerce's Good Citizen Award, the church gave support to NEEDS, a workshop for the handicapped, and to the greater Nashua Child Care Center.

And then there was Grovesnor Martin. Branded a "town character" and often taunted by the children, he was a familiar sight on Main Street, wearing a ragged coat and toting a shopping bag.

"He was our local Rainman, a beautiful lovable man who never grew up," recalls Fiery of the man who had a talent for memorizing obscure statistics but lacked the ability to cope with daily life.

To permit him to keep his small subsidized apartment, Isabelle and Mac Hildreth organized teams of church members to regularly clean it and do his laundry. Each week he was welcomed to services. The congregation arranged for his funeral, and two collection plates engraved "In Memory of Grovesnor Martin" are used each Sunday in the services.

In the '80s, with the encouragement of Greer, the church adopted another cause. It held a tribute to the late Dr. Martin Luther King Jr., on the Sunday before his birthday. Last year Ethel Parker was in charge of the event she had proposed 15 years earlier and now is a tradition enjoyed by the community.

Parker was the first African-American to join the church in the '60s, when she moved to Nashua from the South. It did not take long for her to regard the congregation as "family," and there are now many black families active in all aspects of church life.

With the stained glass window behind her, The Rev. Dr. Margaret Hess preaches on the pulpit.

The congregation's ethnic and racial diversity was the factor that drew the Rev. Dr. Margaret Hess to Nashua in 1991. The first woman minister of the church and the first full-time female pastor in the city was readily accepted by everyone.

"The particular gift of the church is its diversity. We have to continue to cultivate that, to be intentional about it and to invite it," she says.

Sunday at 6:30 A.M., in March air chilled with the dawn, Hess will welcome early Easter worshipers to the Sunrise Service at the First Baptist Church on Manchester Street. Together with the Rev. Jeff Evans, associate minister of the First Church, and the Rev. Edward Koonz of the Pilgrim Congregational Church, she will lead those assembled on the still-frozen lawn in prayer and song.

Twenty-eight years ago, the church in the hollow was a dream. Yet the wooded site where it would be built was the setting for another sunrise Easter service. "First we had to clear the brush away," recalls Fiery, then the pastor of the church.

Later Easter Sunday morning, the faithful will congregate for Easter services in the sanctuary of the modern white church, facing a restored, century-old, stained-glass window of Christ surrounded by his apostles.

Though the building in which they worship is but two decades old, its foundation is 175 years strong.

March 29, 1997

ARLINGTON STREET
METHODIST CHURCH

A more perfect portrait of New England piety would be hard to match. In a calendar issued by the Arlington Street United Methodist Church to commemorate its 100th anniversary, Lowese and Jesse Hill are pictured in a familiar pose; prim and proper in identical black dresses and no-nonsense hair-dos. Lowese is playing the violin and Jesse, the piano.

As the church begins its centennial year with a special service dinner Sunday, the Hill sisters will be remembered for their heart-warming contribution to the story of Crown Hill's Little Brown Church on the Hill. If religion is a celebration of life, the Hill sisters deserve to be designated the unofficial historians of the Arlington Street United Methodist Church.

From their home on Williams Street, the two maiden ladies set out to record each birth in the neighborhood on the church Cradle Roll, calling on parents before and after the blessed event. Soon after the baby was born, a cradle with a pink or blue name card appeared in the church nursery, where the Hill sisters taught the little ones hymns and watched over them from infancy to kindergarten during the Sunday worship

"They always dressed alike, wore high-button shoes, carried umbrellas to keep the sun off their heads and called each other 'Sister,'" recalls Arlene Marshall Geer, about the beloved pair who dedicated their lives to church work. "We always thought of them as old," muses Ethel Freeman Tipping.

The sisters lived little more than half the church's century, their years of service totaling 119. But in that time they left a lasting imprint on the memory of long-time members of the church, such as Mrs. Tipping and Mrs. Geer.

Now grandmothers, both women moved to Crown Hill as girls. The Freemans lived four houses from the church on Haines Street and the Marshalls, just down the street. Of course both families joined the Little Brown Church on the Hill. Like so many before and after them, both women grew up in the church, raised their own families in the church and to this day are active members in the life of the church. Mrs. Geer has served as president of the United Methodist Church Women for two different terms. Mrs. Tipping is the only woman to serve as president of the board of trustees, not once but twice.

"We got such a good start," says Mrs. Tipping, recalling the days of their youth.

"And I always say, when I go there I feel like I'm home, though I don't live on Crown Hill anymore," she adds.

Many members have since moved to other neighborhoods and new members come from the outskirts of the city and beyond. Not Roger Gaskill, however. A life-long member, he still makes his home in the same house on McKean Street, where he has lived all of his 73 years. The house belonged to his grandparents on his mother's side. Both sets of grandparents, the Sawyers and the Gaskills, were members of the church and his great-grandfather, Samuel J. Gaskill, was instrumental in its beginnings. Today Roger Gaskill is the church historian and head of the Administrative Council, and his wife, Sylvia, has been the church secretary for many years.

In an era when travel depended mostly on foot power, a neighborhood church was important to Nashua families. The church was an essential part of their lives.

It was the need for a church to be within walking distance of home that gave rise to the Arlington Street Methodist Church.

At the end of the 19th century, Crown Hill residents attended the Main Street Methodist Episcopal Church. In 1892, however, its minister, the Rev. Dr. C.W. Rowley organized a Bible study group to meet in Crown Hill homes. Soon afterward the Crown Hill worshippers secured a larger, more centrally located meeting room on the second floor above a grocery store owned by S.J. Gaskill. The Thursday evening and Sunday services in the Crown Hill Chapel, above the store on the corner of Arlington and Gillis streets, were led by church members.

With Nashua prospering and many companies such as the Wonalancet Cotton Mill, and the Roby & Swart and Gregg & Son millworks locating on Crown Hill, the companies' workforce chose to settle their families in the same neighborhood. The population growth, together with the interest in the prayer meetings, underscored the need for a neighborhood place of worship, and in August 1897, land was purchased for a separate church. In March 1898, with 52 charter members, the chapel became an independent church with the Rev. C.C. Garland as pastor. By November 1898, the foundation for the new building was laid, and the following September the partially finished church was dedicated.

"The work on the auditorium was continued, much of the work done by lantern light after a hard day's work. None were too proud to work, and none too holy to shovel, to saw, to hammer or paint," it was recorded in a historical sketch, published years later.

From its beginning at the turn of the century, the unpretentious brown-shingled church was firmly planted in the life of the neighborhood. Its hilltop location on Arlington Street was to spare it from destruction in two of Nashua's historic catastrophes in the early decades of the 20th century: the Crown Hill Fire in May 1930 and the Flood of 1936.

During the famous fire, which took its name in the history books from the neighborhood it devastated, homes, businesses and churches were leveled by the raging flames. But the Methodist church on Arlington Street was untouched.

"The wind was half-way up McKean Street to Newbury Street, when it turned around. It went south—that's why the church was spared," recalls Gaskill.

Much to the congregation's relief, the new Moehler pipe organ, installed three years before, remained unharmed by either the fire, the flood six years later or the

hurricane in 1938. The organ, said to have the best tone in the city, is now being restored for the Centennial celebration.

In the '30s and '40s, the Little Brown Church on the Hill served the neighborhood as a place of worship and religious education, and also as the center of its social life. "We had no radio or television. Our social life depended on the church," says Ruth Coronis, the former Ruth Barron, whose family was among the early church members.

Junior high and high school teenagers in the youth group looked forward to meetings of the Epworth League on Sunday evenings. Presenting plays was a favorite project of both the Epworth League teen-agers and the adult groups, who often performed in productions together. Several original scripts were written and produced by a talented member of the group, Win Bailey. Members who saw or performed in it, still talk of "Down on the Farm." "There were a lot of little romances that went on," says Ethel Tipping of Epworth League days.

Among those who met their spouses at church activities was Arlene Marshall. Her future husband, Luther Geer, was a Sunday school teacher at the church and escorted her home after services.

Good friends, their romance bloomed during World War II. Throughout their romance, their marriage of 49 years, and raising five children, they were active in all the church organizations. Though "her best friend" died two years ago, the grandmother of seven is still involved in the church and the Salvation Army.

This year, with the help of family and friends, she has compiled her spiritual poems in a book, "Light on the Hill," dedicated to the church.

During the World War II years, when Luther Geer and many of his fellow churchmen fought in the war, all the women in the church baked cookies for the soldiers and met weekly to roll bandages for the Red Cross.

Looking back at the high points in its history, the congregation was jubilant in 1964 when the church's basketball team took first place in the City Basketball League.

During the '70s, under the dynamic leadership of the Rev. Edward Brown, the only clergyman to be named pastor emeritus of the church, the congregation promoted the ecumenical spirit, engaging in exchange programs with Infant Jesus Catholic Church. The two churches attended each other's services, and members even taught in each other's Sunday school classes.

"It was the first time many of us were ever in a Catholic church and the first time many of them were ever in a Protestant church," observes Mrs. Geer.

Working in the community has always been a commitment of church members who regularly volunteer at the Soup Kitchen, take part in the Crop Walk, host Boy Scout Council meetings and help with the city's recycling program. The ecumenical spirit continues with the church assisting the St. Joseph Hospital Parish Nurse Programs.

"Our church is very mission-minded—doing for others here and overseas," says Mrs. Geer.

With funds left by the family of Jesse and Fred Brown, members of the congregation have worked in Peru, Puerto Rico and Costa Rica, where they helped to build a church. Brown's daughter, Arlene Burton, at 91, is the oldest member of the congregation.

Through the century, little has changed about the church. It is still rooted in the neighborhood but with the advent of cars, the neighborhood boundaries have blurred. Church suppers and other traditions continue as they have through the years. Gaskill will play his trumpet on Palm Sunday this year as he has been doing since he was a boy.

Little, too, has changed, in the appearance of the little Brown Church on the Hill. The stained-glass window over the front entrance was installed when the church was built. The original bell in the tower is still tolled by young members of the congregation.

"All my kids pulled the rope, " says Mrs. Geer. "It was so heavy they rode up with it."

The few changes in the front entrance were made in 1950s, when the sanctuary, the choir and the organ loft were remodeled and the office, named for the Rev. Ernest Drake, the minister at the time, was added under the bell tower. The newest addition is the chimes given a few years ago in memory of Mr. and Mrs. Clarence Ware, longtime members of the congregation.

On Sunday the chimes will herald the service celebrating the 100th anniversary of the Little Brown Church on the Hill. Bishop Susan Wolfe Hassinger, head of the Methodist Church's Northeastern Jurisdiction will preach, assisted by the current pastor, the Rev. Jeffrey B. Kress, and many former pastors. Organist Anthony Schaffer will play the music he wrote to accompany a poem, "Joy in Service," composed by Arlene Geer for the occasion.

And while the congregation sings, "Having Joy in Service," the banner beneath the choir loft will ripple gently in the breeze. Made by the youth group for the church's 100th anniversary, it is a collage of the hands of all the church members stitched tightly together. The inscription reads, "None were too holy to shovel. 1898–1998."

March 28, 1998

TEMPLE BETH ABRAHAM

It was the turn of the century, the dawning of a new era and the time for a small cluster of families in Nashua to firmly establish roots in their adopted community. On July 7, 1899, the Bace Abraham Society of Nashua was officially recognized by the state of New Hampshire. It was the first synagogue to be chartered in the state.

More than 100 years later, the Jewish congregation is flourishing and firmly planted in the life of the community. The congregation capped a series of celebrations marking its centennial with a gala dinner dance preceded by Sabbath services Friday evening and Saturday morning. The weekend will wind up with a brunch Sunday at the temple.

Throughout the year members have researched and reported to the congregation how the synagogue came to be and how it has grown through the century. As so many immigrants before and after them, a handful of Jewish families found a home in Nashua in the waning years of the 19th century.

For them it was the land of opportunity they envisioned when they sailed from Eastern Europe. Nashua, a city of 24,000, was a prospering mill town, centered around the river. Jobs in the mills drew many immigrants—French Canadians, Greeks, Poles and Lithuanians.

Opportunities to make a steady living also attracted a few enterprising Jews who arrived from New York, Boston, or Baltimore. The Lowell and Nashua Railway out of Boston provided easy access.

By the early 1890s, there were 10 men, a minyan, the number necessary to conduct daily prayers, in the Spalding Building on Main Street and at the home of Aaron Borofsky on Ferryalls Court. In 1895, 15 Jewish families formed Agudas Achim Lodge which subsequently became the Bace Abraham Society.

The society was formed with "the purpose of keeping up the Jewish religion and purchasing a place of worship." In 1901, its members—mill workers and shopkeepers who had started as peddlers—had raised enough money to buy land for a synagogue and a cemetery. By 1912, it had opened its first bank account with $933.20.

For almost 60 years, the house of worship they built in French Hill, on the corner of Tolles and Locke streets and in time named Temple Beth Abraham, became the center of Jewish community life.

Services on Friday night and Saturday morning were held in the sanctuary on the second floor. On the first floor were Hebrew School classes, social events and committee meetings such as the Hebrew Ladies Aid Society and the Hachnosath Orchim, an organization to help strangers in need of food, clothing and money to get to the next Jewish community.

By the end of World War I, the membership of Temple Beth Abraham had more than tripled.

During the early decades, two dynamic figures emerged to lead the congregation in its mission to preserve its Jewish heritage. Abraham Slawsby joined the synagogue in 1906 and went on to serve as president for 26 years.

Philip Porter came to Nashua in 1915, worked tirelessly to build the Hebrew School and had the vision to purchase the land to insure the temple's future. Both successful Nashua business men, they never wavered in their commitment to the synagogue and Jewish causes throughout their lives.

By the end of the '20s, the Jewish community had grown to 50 families and most of their homes were in walking distance of the temple. Samuel Kessler's family lived at 50 Tolles St. and his son Henry kept a cow—the beginning of Kessler farm—in the backyard, letting it graze along the river. Pastor's Market on the corner of Tolles and Locke streets was one of several small family grocery stores. Matzos for Passover could be purchased at Newman's and Wolfson's bakery was the one bakery in town that sold bagels.

Bringing the old world custom of the times to the temple's sanctuary, Bernie Pastor recalls, "the women sat behind the railing and I sat with my father and four brothers in the fourth row." In the '70s when he was president of the congregation, his wife Selma, their three daughters and their son David all sat together in the sanctuary.

Through the years the congregation had witnessed many such changes as it adapted to life in this country. In the mid-'30s another key figure in the temple's history arrived on the scene, first as a Boy Scout leader and later as the president of

Laurie Berna

the congregation. Max Silber moved to Nashua from Manchester when he married Edith Kamenske in 1934 and transferred his interest in scouting to his new community by establishing the first troop at the synagogue.

The '30s were a time of progress and tranquillity on Tolles Street. The synagogue had been remodeled and was the spiritual home to more than 60 families. But the shadow of Hitler haunted Jewish families here as it did throughout the United States. It became crucial to help family members in Europe escape the spread of Nazi tyranny.

Jacob Yezerski was a typical Nashuan. With the help of relatives, he had come to Nashua in the mid-'20s and later brought his wife and children. He established a grocery store on West Hollis Street. But one daughter and a son had remained in Vilna, Poland. In 1936, before Hitler's invasion of Poland, he brought his daughter and her family to Nashua and two years later his son.

"The rest of the family died," says granddaughter Shirley Lelchuck, one of the fortunate ones to come to Nashua. She has been active in the temple since her youth and today serves on the Centennial Committee, the temple Board of Directors, is active in the Sisterhood and Hadassah, and in 1997 she and her husband, Jules, received the temple's Crown of Good Deeds award. "In the synagogue, we were all family," she recalls of early days in this country.

She was the Hebrew School teacher when the new rabbi, Bela Fischer and his wife, Edith, came to Nashua to lead the congregation. The son of a rabbi, he had fled from his native Hungary, where he had studied at the University of Budapest and the Jewish Theological Seminary.

When he arrived in Nashua, the 33-year-old clergyman had his work cut out for him. The previous rabbi, though revered by all, had resigned in frustration. Caught between the elder generation of immigrants still attached to their old world ways and their children, he felt the congregation slipping away.

To Fischer, shaping a congregation with renewed vigor was a challenge. To appeal to the younger generation, many of them college educated and World War II veterans, he injected more English and more song into the services and invited interesting speakers. He established a couples club, men's breakfast club and a choir. His wife, a musician, organized a theater group to present plays about the holidays such as Purim.

Despite the changes, Rabbi Fischer also won the approval of the older generation. His first test, he was informed by Aaron Harkaway, then president, was to impress A.J. Goodman, recognized as the congregation's Talmudic scholar. Each night the young spiritual leader received a telephone call from the learned elder statesman of the temple questioning him about the Talmud, the collection of ancient rabbis' writing on Judaism.

"My luck held out for most of the questions. I stood the test, was accepted by A.J. Goodman and from that day I could do no wrong from an orthodox point of view" Fischer says.

Under Rabbi Fischer's guidance, Temple Beth Abraham flourished. Within a few years, the social hall and Hebrew School became too small and the congregation purchased a house on Beacon Street to use as a Jewish Community Center and Hebrew School.

However, it did not take long for talks to ensue about the need for everything under one roof. To achieve that goal, Philip Porter offered the temple the land he had purchased at 4 Raymond St. and the plot across the street. He also launched the fund drive for the new building with a check of $10,000.

On a spring day in April, 1960, Fischer led the congregation in a procession through the streets of the North End to its new home on Raymond Street.

The talents of two members of the congregation, Silber and Edward Rudman, had meshed to make the dream of a new synagogue a reality. Rudman, the chairman of the building committee, was the artistic mentor of the project. His legacy is the glow of the richly polished woods which lend warmth to the interior and particularly the ark where the Torahs, the holy scriptures, are housed. Silber, the president for 16 years, longer than anyone since Slawsby, was at the site day and night to oversee each step of the construction.

"The cost, $160,000, was enormous to us but it was all paid off by 1970," he observes.

What seemed so spacious at first began to shrink as Temple Beth Abraham extended its reach well beyond its original neighborhood to families living in the surrounding towns. The membership, no longer just Nashuans, came from different parts of the country; with them came different religious experiences.

Women played a more important role on the Board of Directors and in the religious services. Girls celebrated their 13th birthdays with a Bat Mitzvah just as their brothers did with a Bar Mitzvah. Older women, once denied the ritual, also studied for the religious event.

When Fischer retired in 1981, he was named rabbi emeritus of the temple, as a tribute to his efforts to strengthen spiritual force in the Jewish community and in the community at large. He served as president of the Nashua Ministerial

Laurie Berna

First synagogue on Locke Street

Association, on the board of the Salvation Army, in the Friendship Club and working with city leaders on multi-cultural efforts.

Fischer had also set in motion plans for a separate Hebrew School building. It stands as a memorial to Alice and Julius Miller, parents of Herbert Miller, the largest donor, and it was built in 1986 on Hattie and Philip Porter Park. Heading the building committee was Alan Silber, son of Edith and Max, and a graduate of Temple Beth Abraham Hebrew School.

Since 1990, Rabbi Mark Finkel has been leading the congregation. With a membership of 348 families, Temple Beth Abraham embarked on a $2.2 million project to enlarge and renovate the building on Raymond Street.

Under the direction of building committee co-chairmen Elaine Brody and Dick Horowitz (who died soon after its completion) the new Temple, a replica of European synagogues of old, still anchors the end of Raymond Street.

In its newly refurbished home, Temple Beth Abraham embarks on its second century in the city of Nashua.

March 4, 2000

CHRISTIAN SCIENCE CHURCH

Her beeper never leaves her side. Whether flying cross-country in the family plane or suddenly awakening at home, June Austin responds immediately. As the only practitioner for the First Church of Christ, Scientist, in Nashua, the caring Nashuan ministers to callers with prayer. She has hundreds of stories of how she has helped the healing of broken limbs and broken spirits, of common illnesses and cancer.

"There is no need to be physically present. It's the prayer that does the healing and nothing is beyond its reach," she says unequivocally about all crises. "I raised four kids and I never had any medical help."

The Nashua grandmother has belonged to the Christian Science Church since she met her husband, Charles, and she has lived by the teaching of Mary Baker Eddy for most of her life. She and her husband have been members of the Nashua church for 42 years; Charles is a member of the board of directors.

"I've had each of my four children and 13 grandchildren in Sunday school," she says with a smile.

The Austins will be on hand to welcome visitors to the reopening of the Christian Science Reading Room next Saturday at 115 Main St. In the newly decorated surroundings, they and other members will introduce people to the writings of Mary Baker Eddy, the Christian Science Journal, the Christian Science Sentinel, the Christian Science Monitor, the numerous church publications and the testimonies of faith.

"The reading room is our liaison with the community," June Austin says.

The refurbished reading room is a key element in the 100th anniversary celebration of the church's arrival in Nashua—in fact, the reading room preceded the establishment of the church in the city. But Eddy's writings did not take long to cross the border from Massachusetts, where they first took root, and where the mother church originated.

The church sprang from the teachings of Eddy, who was born in Bow in 1821. By the next century, it had spread to 74 countries throughout the world. Eddy, who was in ill health much of her life, looked to Scriptures for guidance and inner strength.

She published her insights in "Science and Health with Key to the Scriptures" in 1875; ever since, it has served as the church's principal text, along with the King James version of the Bible. "She put the spiritual message into human terms," June Austin says.

"Science and Health" is a treatise on the healing powers of the mind, working in harmony with the body, and the dominion of the spiritual over the material. It is comparable in many ways to today's concept of holistic medicine. In the age of medical technology, Christian Science is recognized as an alternative method of healing by the government; its treatment is covered by Social Security and many insurance companies.

In 1881, Eddy established the Massachusetts Metaphysical College in Boson. From it, she gained a core of disciples to establish the First Church of Christ, Scientist, in Boston, and later, at age 87, the Christian Science Monitor, an international newspaper. Its motto is "To injure no man, but bless all mankind."

All the while, she continued to lecture, to write, and spread her message of healing. It resonated in Nashua in the mid-1880s. By 1898, her message took hold. Susan R.K. Hoyt and a handful of other Nashuans met in a suite in the Whiting Block to organize the First Church of Christ, Scientist, Nashua. A charter was granted by the state on Oct. 14. In 1902, with an enrollment of five, the Sunday school was established and in 1916, after various meeting places, the church held meetings and services, in the Odd Fellows Building.

In 1928, its congregation growing, it purchased a permanent home in the Stark Building at the intersection of Concord and Manchester Streets. The handsome, historic building offered a seating capacity of 70 and it was filled for its first Communion Sunday on July 28.

One of the members who attended services there was Gladys Hinkley, who joined weeks before the move from the Odd Fellows Building. Recently, she was honored as the oldest member of the church and one of its most dedicated members, for years braving the snow and ice to walk to meetings from her apartment on Locke Street.

Now a resident of Aynsley Place, she still attends meetings twice a week. As is the way of Christian Science, she pays little attention to her age—she's in her 90s—but she attributes her long life to the church.

"I don't depend on drugs, I depend on prayer," says the woman who has never sought medical services.

The repository of Eddy's prescription for good health can be found in the reading room and its many publications. First opened in the community in 1889, it was housed at various locations on Main Street before becoming a part of the church in the Stark House. In 1955, realizing its community service to all faiths, it was returned to downtown. Through the years, it maintained a quiet presence at several storefront locations before moving to its present address, 168 Main St., where it is a haven for anyone interested in reading its publications.

Through the 20th century, the reading room and the church at the tip of Concord Street gained a firm foothold in the community. Prompted by civic pride, the church donated a small wedge of the property to the city in 1968 for the Firemen's Memorial. As the church approached the 1970s, however, the Stark House grew too small to fill meeting and Sunday school needs.

The church's plan to raze the Stark House and build a larger structure, however, met with objections from the Historical Society and the community at large. Saving the house became a cause celebre, landing on the front page and editorial pages of *The Telegraph*. Always civic-minded and rooted in the democratic process, members were shaken by the response and quickly sought to settle the matter. But the need for more space, coupled with limited funds, demanded resolution. To settle the discord, the city considered purchasing the property.

The property eventually was sold to business interests obliged to preserve its historical value. The church built a new facility north of Greeley Park at 115 Concord St. The simple brick building, dedicated on June 22, 1978, has well suited the congregation for more than 20 years. Meetings are held on Wednesday evening and Sunday morning, the schedule of services since it began.

Born in America, the Christian Science Church reflects the democratic thinking of its founder. It is run by a board of directors. There is no human hierarchy, no autonomous figures at its helm and no missionaries.

Rather the Scriptures, as interpreted in "Science and Health," are supreme and instead of a pastor, the services are led by a first reader and a second reader chosen every three years by the congregation. Wednesday evenings, after readings by the first reader, spontaneous testimonies of faith and healing are heard by the congregation.

Sundays, the same portion of the Bible and "Science and Health" is read in every Christian Science Church in the world, in 17 languages and in Braille.

In spite of working nights and going to school days, Bret Rush is completing his term as first reader at the Nashua church. The Rushes met after college while working at the mother church in Boston. The Rushes' two children, like their parents, were born into the church. Because of insurance constraints, their children were both born in the hospital. Medical assistance is a matter of personal choice, it is not forbidden, says Rush.

Laurie Berna

"Everyone is at a different stage of development," adds the Rivier College graduate student completing his master's in education.

Throughout his life, Rush has heard many testimonies of healing by prayer and he has his own story to tell.

He attended Principia College in Illinois, the church's college, and was on the school diving team. In a meet to qualify for the nationals, he lost his footing, hit his head on the diving board and suffered a concussion and other serious injuries. He was immediately taken to the treatment center, where he was attended by the wife of the college president, a Christian Science practitioner.

"Within a few days I was up and within a few weeks I was back on the diving board."

When he steps down as first reader in December, Rush wants to teach Sunday school.

His faith provides the health and energy he needs to maintain his busy schedule of school, a full-time job at Teradyne, a part-time vending machine business and his role as church reader.

He and other members of the congregation embark on the church's second century in Nashua with an invitation to visit the reading room at 8 P.M. to hear a talk on "Spiritual Healing" given by Robin Berg. Afterward, the congregation will gather for a dinner at the Holden Farm Clubhouse.

October 10, 1998

Telegraph Photo Files

The Christian Science Church donated the land for the Firemen's Bell Memorial on Concord Street to the city in 1968.

MAIN STREET METHODIST CHURCH

Few of us buying fish at the former Philbrick's Market on Main Street are aware of the pearl to be found behind the shop. Trapped in back of the brick wall of stores on Main Street is one of the historic gems of Nashua, the Isaac Spalding House.

"It is a well-built house, as solid as the day it was built," says Jim Allard, project manager for P.M. MacKay & Sons, as he clears a path through the thicket of wood and nails on the floor. The air is thick with plaster dust, for he and his crew are knee deep in the second week of a major renovation effort.

For the Main Street United Methodist Church, which now owns the building, it will mean more pleasant and accessible Sunday school and library space. For the community, it will mean the preservation of another piece of its history.

History places the Isaac Spalding House in the year 1852. It was a gracious home befitting the richest man in New Hampshire. At the time, Main Street was the city's upscale residential neighborhood lined with other grand colonial homes of the pre-Civil War era.

Spalding is Nashua's Horatio Alger story. He grew up in Wilton and at age 13 was apprenticed to an Amherst merchant. A shrewd and industrious Yankee, he rose to become a leading dealer in iron and steel, a bank president and a railroad baron.

The home he built for himself, his wife Lucy and two sons was reputed to be the first in the city with running water. Simple but elegant, it was adorned with Italian architectural influences of the day. Pillars frame the entrance, ornate plaster molding and polished woods can be found throughout the interior, and capping the roof is a belvedere encircled by a widow's walk from which to view the city.

Today only the belvedere, a magnet for pigeons, is visible from Main Street.

"I don't know what our pigeons are going to do. They had a major entrance into the building from the roof. That told us we had to do something," said the Rev. Ralph Bruce, minister of the church.

Other signs of aging such as the chunks of plaster falling from the ceiling and chinks in the fireplaces made it evident that the house, renamed the Wesley Educational Building, needed attention.

The church purchased the Isaac Spalding House in 1965. Just a few steps away, it offered ideal space needed for the expanding Sunday school. No one seems to know when the row of stores laid claim to the tree-shaded front lawn and elaborate wrought iron fence.

"The stores were there when we moved here in 1934," says longtime parishioner Laura Quimby. "We used to have lunch at the Transfer Station."

Less than a decade after the church purchased the home, the congregation faced a wrenching dilemma. It met to discuss selling the church property on Main Street and moving to the suburbs as many churches had done.

"The trustees had in hand an offer for several million dollars," remembers Phyllis Appler, wife of Dr. David, chairman of the building committee. She noted the plan called for the stores, the house and the church to be razed for a modern business complex. The indignation of the late Martha Cramer moved the congregation to reject the idea.

"My father mortgaged our house to make sure that the church wasn't lost and we're not going to sell it now," the daughter of the church's beloved pastor, the Rev. Thomas Cramer, told everyone.

Years later the Cramer house made it possible for the church to undertake the renovation of the Spalding House. Money from the sale of the house after Miss Cramer died provided the start-up funds.

"We purchased it for $136,000 and now we are investing $350,000," says the Rev. Bruce.

Nashua architect LouAnn Fornataro emphasizes that the project is one of adaptive reuse rather than restoration.

"Better not to tear down or modify if you don't have to" is the philosophy that has saved such antique treasurers as the brick oven wall in the basement. Fornataro surmises it was part of a large kitchen added to the original building.

Another discovery, found in the cellar, will be returned to its original place. It is the 3-inch thick, 7-foot paneled front door. All but one of the black-and-white

Laurie Berna

marble tiles in the foyer floor are intact.

"I can put in a new one but I'll have to rough it up a bit to look old," said Allard with a smile.

When finished, industrial fluorescent lights will be replaced by chandeliers and the glow of Nashua history will again be restored to what was once one of the grandest homes in Nashua.

April 11, 1992

Nashua Historical Society

ST. CHRISTOPHER CHURCH

It was Christmas Eve. Yolanda Santerre and her sister Dorothy Vacca could smell the damp cement as they sang in the choir of St. Christopher Church for the Christmas Mass. In spite of the surroundings—the folding chairs and the makeshift altar—the choir never sounded more inspired as it sang Christmas carols.

"There were sandbags all over and water dripping through," Gabrielle Burpee remembers of the 1950 Christmas Mass in the church basement. She and her husband Henry, a supervisor at the Pennichuck Water Works, were among the founders of the church, and like the other families seated in the basement, it was joy to see their dream become a reality—even if they were a bit uncomfortable.

"Everybody was enthusiastic. That made it worthwhile," she recalls of the occasion.

Ground for St. Christopher Catholic Church had been broken that fall. After holding Mass and CCD classes in the basement of Mount Pleasant School, the parish moved into the bare beginnings of the church.

It was the foundation from which a strong and vital congregation would emerge to celebrate its 50th anniversary in the year 2000. A Mass of Thanksgiving to mark the golden occasion was conducted last Saturday by Bishop John McCormack and a time capsule was buried by the parishioners after the service. The sanctuary was filled with families with a long history in the parish.

"There is a nice family atmosphere here," says the Rev. Richard J. Kelley. The sixth pastor, he succeeded the Rev. Karl E. Dowd Jr., who retired in June.

Families were at the heart of the church from the beginning. In the early '50s, Nashua was pulling out of the economic doldrums after the closing of the mills. The city's population had grown to 34,669, and more than 2,000 belonged to St. Patrick's Church, the only English-speaking parish serving the central and northern neighborhoods of the city. That parish had been established during the mid-1800s by Irish immigrants who settled in Nashua. It was named Immaculate Conception Church and flourished on Franklin Street. In 1909 the building was sold to the Lithuanian parish and the original parish relocated as St. Patrick's Church on Spring Street.

At the end of the 1940s, the time had come for another parish and through funeral director Richard J. Sullivan, the Diocese of Manchester purchased the land on Manchester Street in 1950. The original home, built by the Andrews family, became the rectory and by the end of 1950, the church began to take shape. Fathers

Laurie Berna

and sons built the deacons' benches and the chairs on the altar; mothers and daughters sewed the vestry robes. The Rev. Lancelot Quinn was appointed pastor of the new parish and served there until his death in 1960. In May 1951, he celebrated the first Mass upstairs in the new church and the young people in CCD classes received their first communion.

At that time, Reginald and Yolanda Santerre left the city briefly while he served in the Army during the Korean conflict. When they returned to Nashua from Panama with their 8-month-old son, Peter, the yellow brick church was waiting for them. After his discharge, Reginald became the assistant manager of the A&P store in downtown Nashua and they bought a home on Pennichuck Street, where they still live today.

St. Christopher has been their parish ever since. Their three sons served as altar boys, graduated from St. Christopher School, joined the parish Boy Scout troop and in recent years all were married in St. Christopher Church. Son Paul, a musician, also directed the church choir—the one in which his mother sang—when he was in college. Santerre joined the choir as soon as she returned to Nashua after they returned from Panama.

Under the direction of Mary Herlihy and later under organist Corrine Conlon, the group rehearsed evenings in homes of parishioners. By then, however, they sang in the sanctuary lined with pews.

"The priest did the Mass in Latin, the choir sang the response in Latin and the priests faced the altar," she says, noting today the service is in English and the priest stands behind the altar, facing the congregation.

Not long after the church was built, establishing a school became the next objective, and in 1952, the church acquired the vacant, ramshackle Shattuck Street

School building. Within a few months and after a lot of muscle and elbow grease from parishioners, it was transformed into a school for 64 first- and second-graders for the fall term. By 1957, the school included third-, fourth- and fifth-graders; sixth- and seventh-graders attended classes in the church hall. The school was run by the Sisters of Mercy.

As the parish grew, the need for a larger school became apparent, and in June 1963, Monsignor William Collins, St. Christopher's second pastor, broke ground for the new facility on the Manchester Street land.

The school opened in 1966 with 355 students, ten teachers, eight Sisters of Mercy and two lay instructors.

"Those teachers worked so hard," recalls Ann Plante, widow of Noel Plante, another founding parishioner. "Tuition was $3 a month and we paid for 10 months."

Yolanda Santerre remembers the children going off to school in their uniforms—the boys in their white shirts, dark pants and plaid ties to match the girls' plaid skirts. They all carried green school bags filled with books, and their lunch boxes. As president of the Women's Society, Santerre coordinated a crew of mothers to serve "hot dog lunches" once a week.

The highlight of the year for the Women's Society, along with an auction and a Mother's Day Tea, was a Communion Breakfast at the Nashua Country Club. "In those days we wore white gloves, hats and dresses," she recalls. The mothers also were dedicated to decorating every corner of the school for Christmas.

With their 11 children attending the school, Marilyn and James Hogan, the longtime city engineer, were deeply involved with its activities for more than 30 years. St. Christopher School prepared all the children well for their high school and college years. Today their mother, long active in the Legion of Mary outreach program, is a Eucharistic minister at the church.

Whereas the school dominated the 1960s, the 1970s began with the retirement of Monsignor Collins and the appointment of the Rev. Cornelius Goggin as pastor in September 1971. In just two decades the church had grown from 500 to more than 1,300 families.

Though he retired in 1985, two appointments the Rev. Goggin made during his term remain a vital part of the staff today. Sister Mary Leon Pennell, the parish's first female Eucharistic minister, went on to win a national award for the Visitation Program she initiated with the backing of the Knights of Columbus. John Levesque became the custodian responsible for the upkeep of the Manchester Street complex, including the church, the rectory, the education building, the school and the grounds.

Rev. Goggin also points with pride to another national award to parishioner John Keegan, voted school board member of the year by the Catholic schools' national conference.

During his appointment, Nashua and the church grew beyond the central city with two new parishes. In 1968, Immaculate Conception split from St. Patrick's to establish a parish in the south end, and in 1970, Parish of the Resurrection split from St. Christopher to build a parish in the northwest corner of the city near the Hollis border.

After his term as pastor ended, the Rev. Goggin was succeeded for a year by Monsignor George E. Murray. In 1986, the Rev. Karl E. Dowd became the pastor of the parish he knew so well. A native Nashuan, he grew up on Faxon Street, learned to play the organ as a pupil of Elmer "Pop" Wilson, and belonged with his family to St. Patrick's Church.

"Technically, I've always lived in Nashua," says the priest who studied at the College of the Holy Cross in Worcester, Mass., and St. Paul's University in Canada. He came back home after serving 14 years as the pastor of St. Joseph Church in Salem. "I knew one-third of the parish before I came," he says.

Among his many objectives was to replace the 16 clear glass panes in the church with stained glass panels, which the windows were designed to hold when the church was built. The timing in the early 1990s was not the most fortunate, however, since the city was in recession. "But people came to us and offered to pay for them," says Dowd, amazed at the parishioners' generosity.

The new windows were designed by a stained glass artisan in Lyme, Greg Goren, and gradually installed by Levesque. The window from the '50s, behind the statue of St. Christopher, depicts the modes of modern transportation. The first two panels of the newer windows, Dowd observes, are representations of Mary and Joseph, as is true in every Catholic church. On the other panels are the various saints of North America with one exception, Mother Catherine McAuley, the founder of the Sisters of Mercy.

During Dowd's stay as pastor, the school became a separate entity from the church and Mary Roy was hired as coordinator of the religious education program. The church opened a food pantry and the young people reached out to the world, taking two mission trips to Honduras. Through the Rev. Dowd, now president of the Nashua Interfaith Council, the parish became involved in ecumenical efforts in the community.

The statistics gleaned from its 50-year history show 5,541 baptisms, 4,341 first communions, 3,760 confirmations, 1,664 marriages and 1,318 funerals. Behind these figures are the stories of hundreds of Nashua families.

"We came from families who were into parish life," says Ann Plante, the mother of five children and grandmother of 11, two of whom now attend the same school their father did. "We wanted to bring our faith into our own homes and to pass it on to our own children."

September 23, 2000

TRINITY BAPTIST CHURCH

He was a teenager attending Spring Street Junior High School when the spiritual message took root in Nashua. It influenced the direction of his life in the years to come as well as his work in faraway places such as Bangladesh, Rwanda and Bosnia.

Fifty years later the Rev. Dr. Arthur Gay Jr. will share memories of planting the seeds of a new Nashua religious congregation when he speaks at the Trinity Baptist Church golden anniversary banquet, Nov. 4 at Alpine Grove in Hollis.

The following day, Nov 5, the same date as the first service 50 years before, the Rev. Steve Murray, the pastor, will mark the occasion at services in the sanctuary of the church at the crest of Lund Road. As he has done every Sunday for four years, he preaches from the simple lectern rather than a more formal pulpit to establish a closer relationship with his congregation. Sunday School before the service, however, will not be held. Instead there will be choir rehearsal and anyone who has ever sung in the church choir is invited to add their voice to the celebration. "Celebrate the past . . . Build for the future" is the theme of the yearlong observance.

The past is a story of the handful of people in search of a more evangelical worship experience in Nashua. Arthur Gay Sr. and his wife, Marguerite, were among the Nashuans who sought to fill the void in their hometown religious community. A graduate of Wentworth Institute, he worked for Nashua Corp. At the beginning of the 1940s they moved their family to Chicago to study at the Moody Bible Institute. When they returned to Nashua, they found a small group of people like themselves interested in a more Bible-centered expression of their faith.

"Truly God's words," remarked the Rev. Murray of their mission at an informal meeting of church members last Friday.

"They believed Nashua churches had become too liberal," observed Marguerite Gay, now widowed. She had traveled from her home in Rumney to join the group of fellow church members who never tired of hearing its history. At the time, Gay continued, only one small Nazarene church in Nashua offered the observance they sought.

Looking back, she noted the small band of believers came from many denominations—Methodists, Catholics, Congregationalists and the Salvation Army. At the end of the 40s, they held Bible study meetings in the YMCA on Spring Street, led by a seminarian from Gordon-Conwell Seminary. After two years of meeting they were faced with the question of whether they were prepared to undertake the

Laurie Berna

responsibility of starting a new church. Little more than two dozen people, six of them teenagers, accepted the challenge.

"The teenagers were very much a part of it," recalled Mrs. Gay, the first clerk, noting that all of them continued to work as adults for the church in missionary work, in education or as ministers.

On Nov. 5, 1950, after signing a charter, organizing a church board and affiliating with the Conservative Baptist Association—a relatively new fellowship—they held the first morning and evening service of Trinity Baptist Church in a converted barn on French Street, where other organizations rented space for a kindergarten and dance classes during the week. Until the arrival of the Rev. Harold Burchett in May 1951, visiting ministers conducted services.

The young pastor accepted the Nashua assignment for $35 a week and he and his wife resided with a member of the church. Finding a permanent home for his congregation was a top priority the Rev. Burchett quickly accomplished. When the stately Victorian home of a lawyer at 269 Main St. became available he knew he had found the right spot. The asking price for the property, however, was $25,000—more than they could afford.

"We didn't have much money but we all prayed," said Mrs. Gay.

Their prayers were soon answered; the owner reduced the price to $21,000. The bank granted a mortgage for $16,000 and five people gave $1,000 for the down payment, several mortgaging their homes to do so. In June, the house became the first home of Trinity Baptist Church. Everyone pitched in, tearing down partitions, painting, readying the building for services, Sunday School and an office. The sanctuary was designed to hold 100 seats, a sign of growth for the flourishing new congregation.

"There was a great spirit of unity. The first step had been accomplished and it was not the last one," Gay observed.

Arthur Rioux was one of the members who offered to install the seats from an old Boston theater donated by a warehouse in Massachusetts. But, remembers Rioux of the dedication services on Aug. 13, 1951, "we had to put up folding chairs; there weren't enough seats."

Rioux and his fiancée, Eleanor Wooley, were the first to be married in the church 46 years ago. Both native Nashuans, he had been raised as a Catholic and she without any religious background.

"My family never went to church. I went to different churches with my friends," she recalled. The Rioux have been active in Trinity Baptist Church for 48 years. In the early years, they served as teen directors of Vacation Bible School, still an important part of the education program.

Willard and Eva Mann were looking for a church when he started work as an engineer with Sanders Associates. They lived in Chelmsford, Mass., but at the suggestion of a relative, they started attending services at Trinity Baptist Church; 32 years ago they bought a home in Merrimack after joining the church.

"We met people we liked, like Arthur and his wife," was Mann's reason for joining. It was echoed by members who arrived in later years. The people gathered round the table in the church last Friday morning had similar stories of a church that welcomed members as they came to town: Stella Pierce, the current clerk; Jerri Dempster and Elizabeth Forney, who designed an afghan to be sold as a memento during the church's anniversary, along with a book of memories and a cookbook, "Jubilee Keepsake: Fifty Years of Faith and Fellowship."

From a box of church mementos Pierce took out a flyer for the gospel program, "Above the Clouds," presented every Sunday morning by the church on WOTW, the local radio station. Along with musical selections by a ladies trio and a men's quartet, the service was broadcast live from the church. The lyrics to the theme song reflected the spirit of the church: "Above the clouds the sun is always shining. Above the clouds, all tears are wiped away. Our loving God will lift you from sin's darkness, above the clouds into eternal day."

Other mementos hark back to 1957 when the congregation purchased 9.5 acres of land on Lund Road for $18,000. It is now the site of three buildings, housing the main body of the church, the fellowship hall and the administrative offices. By 1980, however, the congregation had outgrown the original sanctuary on Lund Road and Easter worship had to be held in the Nashua High School auditorium.

To accommodate its expanding congregation and its outreach programs, Trinity Baptist Church adopted a five-year expansion program. Its plans included renovation of the parsonage into a counseling center, administrative and youth facilities, known as the Diakona House, as well as a new sanctuary, dedicated in 1985. The latest addition is a preschool, The Treehouse Learning Center, scheduled to open in the fall of 2000.

As it has from the church's beginning, missionary work plays an important role in the church, both locally and abroad. It has held revival services led by well-known visiting evangelists and continues to organize and host an annual missionary conference.

Guided by a passage from the Bible, the congregation will mark its 50th year in the Trinity Baptist tradition. Each month it will donate food, clothing, eyeglasses, books and other items to the needy.

At the 50th anniversary dinner, the Rev. Dr. Gay, the first to be ordained in the church in 1962, will speak of the vision that he took from Trinity Baptist Church, one that has sustained him as president of the National Association of Evangelists and its World Relief. Today he is pastor of a church with a long history, The First Baptist Church in Portland, Maine, but the memories of being involved in a new Nashua church from its beginning have been a lifelong inspiration.

October 14, 2000

UNITARIAN UNIVERSALIST CHURCH

In days of crisis, we gather together for solace. Celebrations wait. So it was last week at the Unitarian Universalist Church of Nashua. Tuesday evening following the World Trade Tower and Pentagon disasters there was a spontaneous gathering in the sanctuary of the church, says John Sanders, the president of the congregation.

On Sept. 16, 2001—the date of the church's 175th anniversary in Nashua—there was no celebration. Rather, members flocked to the Sunday morning service to pray and to listen to the Rev. Stephen Edington's sermon. It was not on his traditional topic, the advent of another year, but on coping with the terrible tragedies of the week. His sermon was titled "For Us, the Living (after Sept. 11, 2001)."

"In times of tragedy, a minister has a challenging role to play in the life of his parishioners," says the Rev. Donald Rowley. The minister emeritus of the church understands the spiritual strength to be gained at the church by people trying to make sense of the bad things that happen to good people. He was the minister during the Vietnam War.

Sunday, Sept. 23, the service dedicated to the history of the church and its mission in the community went on as planned though the celebration was subdued.

Rowley and the Rev. James Norman, district executive of the Vermont-New Hampshire Unitarian Society, who entered the ministry because of Rowley, joined the Rev. Edington at the pulpit in a service highlighting the significance of the church's liberal religious presence in Nashua for 175 years.

After the service and the reception, the Nashua Historical Society opened the Abbot-Spalding House, to allow the congregation to visit the place where the founding documents of the church were signed on Sept. 16, 1826.

Through the centuries, Nashua has evolved from a rural village to a thriving industrial city. But the mission of the church has remained constant. Expressing the independent thinking of the Unitarian founders, Leonard Freeman Burbank in the first history of the Nashua Unitarian Church, wrote, "tradition and power may be hard to subdue, but the right to think is impossible to suppress."

"We do not have a single creed," says Edington. "We are open to a variety of paths of faith."

How its philosophy influenced the church's community efforts during his ministry was the topic of Rowley's talk. In addition to planting seeds for the Big Brothers Big Sisters program, he and the congregation supported a family planning organization, Fair Housing Practices and the National Organization for Women, ideas not readily accepted then in the community. Continuing on the path of his

Laurie Berna

predecessor, Edington and his congregation welcomed the gay and lesbian community to the church. The church also has offered a home to Head Start and in later years to the French Hill Neighborhood Association when both organizations were getting off the ground.

The Unitarian Church has never shied away from controversy or new ideas. In fact, it was born of a rebellion against the strict Calvinism of the early 1800s. The meeting to establish the church in Nashua was held in the home of its most influential citizen, Daniel Abbot, and ahead of the times, several wives participated and signed the official documents.

Abbot, a lawyer, was responsible for changing the character of Nashua in many ways. He was the first president the Nashua Manufacturing Co., the Nashua and Lowell Railroad and the town's first bank. He was also one of the pillars of the Unitarian Church and donated the land used for the sanctuary, the parish house and the cemetery. In fact, he is buried in the cemetery together with a host of Nashua civic leaders.

On the hill next to the church are the graves of Alfred Beard, founder of *The Telegraph*; J. Thornton Greeley who donated the land for Greeley Park; John and Mary A. Hunt and Mary E. Hunt, whose estate built the Hunt Memorial Building and Hunt Home; Thomas Laton, who built the Laton House; and Maj. Gen. John Gray Foster, whose statue dominates Foster Square. Anna Stearns was the last Nashuan to be buried there at the end of the '80s and the near $1 million bequest she left the church has been set aside to fund such projects as the new hospice in Merrimack which has a room named after Donald Rowley and his late wife, Norma.

"There is a lot of Nashua history in that cemetery," says Edington.

History books record that the oldest church building in Nashua is the Unitarian Church. The original sanctuary still stands on Lowell Street, where it was built

in 1826. The building, with its distinctive white pillars characteristic of its neoclas-
sical architecture, was moved 20 feet when the parish house was erected in 1929. In
1957, when its next-door neighbor, the Armory, burned down, an office and education wing extended its domain to Lemon Street.

The late 1950s were pivotal years in the church's history. The church and the
Nashua Universalist Church had combined congregations smoothly in 1957, three
years before the two churches joined forces nationally. The money from the sale of
the Universalist Church and its parish house and two bequests was used to build the
educational-office wing on the Armory site after the fire.

Longtime members Naomi Lyon and Robert Sampson still remember the fate-
ful day of the fire, Sunday, Feb. 3, 1957. According to Lyon, a Sunday school teacher
for many years, the children in Sunday school were going to practice a fire drill. But,
she says, "it turned into the real thing." Miraculously, Nashua firemen had kept the
flames from spreading to the church.

Sampson speaks of feeling the intense heat of the blaze through the church
windows and how almost before the ashes cooled, the church had already put in a
bid for the land since its growing parish was feeling pinched for space.

The Unitarian Church has been an important part of the lives of both Nashua
natives and each has been a member more than 50 years. Sampson's parents were
members of the church and he has fond memories of growing up in the church, of
the dances in the parish house and of youth group meetings with the minister,
Edward Cahill.

Nashua Armory fire of 1957

Nashua Historical Society

After going to college he returned to Nashua to serve in many capacities under Rowley and as president of the congregation under Edington.

Lyon came to the church after being raised in another denomination. She was attracted to the church because, she says, "they do what they believe in—they live their religion."

"The church became the center of our lives," added the mother of nine children. Her children's lives were enriched by the church in many ways, including music lessons, trips to youth conferences, singing in the choir and working for church projects. She also was involved in youth projects and was the purchasing agent for the White Wing school when it began.

However, when Lyon needed him, she says, the Rev. Rowley was always there to counsel her on personal problems though politically they had disagreements over the Vietnam war.

Rowley began his career in Nashua in 1958 and was minister of the congregation "for 29 and a half years." The church was on the brink of an ambitious new venture, starting White Wing Kindergarten and Nursery School, which opened in 1959 in the new education section.

"Cal Libby painted a bright, floral painting for the children to see when they came in the entryway," recalls the minister, noting the paintings of the late Nashua artist, a member of the congregation, are seen in many rooms of the church; the church has endowed a scholarship in his name.

During his long tenure, Rowley observes, in the true Unitarian spirit, the church gave him free rein to work in the community for the things he believed in. Among the many community endeavors, he served as president of Community Council and on the boards of the Adult Learning Center and Harbor Homes.

The guiding principle of his ministry is, he says, "moral and intellectual integrity. That is more important than beliefs—beliefs change."

In 1978, during Rowley's ministry, Jim Norman, his wife and baby daughter moved to Nashua to work for the FAA. He joined the church and was inspired by Rowley to make a career change.

"At age 45, I decided to study for the ministry," he says. "In 1983, I went to the seminary."

Of Rowley, he says, "He had more integrity than anyone I had ever met . . . and he was always ready to move in a new direction."

In 1988, Rowley retired and Edington moved to Nashua to lead the congregation in new directions.

At the anniversary service the Revs. Edington, Norman and Rowley all reflected on what it means to belong to the Unitarian Universalist Church, how it has influenced their thinking, and how the church has affected the history of Nashua in the past 175 years and will continue to be a spiritual force in the years to come.

September 29, 2001

COMMUNITY SERVICE

My Window on Main Street

EXCHANGE CLUB

The rap beat of a Kid Rock recording boomed over the park, past volleyball play-ers to the Centennial Pool, almost creating waves in the water. The hot dogs siz-zled on the grill and teen-agers came and went, their chatter competing with the deejay hit parade. Everybody was in high spirits.

The sound of happy voices was music to the ears of Exchange Club members manning the grills. Clad in shorts and sandals, the senior class of Nashua High was out in full force for the annual senior class picnic. The event put on by the club at the Amherst Street playground behind Holman Stadium followed Friday morning's graduation rehearsal.

"We do what the kids like, not what we like" said George Law, a longtime Exchange member trying to ignore the blaring sound system. "Loud music and lots of food," he said, is the menu for success.

Nashua High senior Elizabeth Bober, signing yearbooks with classmate Preethi Dayanand, offered, "it is a great way to say your final goodbyes."

By a vote of the senior class, the picnic replaced the post-prom party in the early '90s. For more than a dozen years, the post-prom party, complete with live music and a lavish buffet, attracted the partying crowd. But after the prom moved from the high school gym to a hotel ballroom, its appeal dwindled. Rather than scrap the extended celebration, the Nashua Exchange Club asked the seniors what they would like to have instead, and the picnic was the winner.

Like the business community it reflects, the Exchange Club's flexible attitude has kept the service club afloat for more than 50 years.

"Some things work and some things don't," George B. Law, a charter member and past president said philosophically. The club has also bent with the times by adding women to its membership, which it did eight years ago. This summer, a woman, Beverly Johnson, will succeed John Parolin as president.

While the club has been willing to change through the years, its mission has remained the same: encouraging young people by honoring their achievements and helping disadvantaged youths to succeed.

In 1947, when it was organized in Nashua, the objectives of the new club were made to order for a group of men in Nashua.

"A bunch of us had just come home from the service," recalled Law, remem-bering the organizing meeting in Nashua with the national club representative.

Three charter members honored by the Exchange Club are, from left to right, Charlie Caras, Dr. Boyd Weston and George Law.

"When we were in the service, we were kind of out of things and we wanted to get back in the life of the city," added Dr. W. Boyd Weston, a retired Nashua dentist, also a charter member. Service to country rang true to men who had put their lives on hold to go off to war. Imbued with patriotism, they returned and poured their spirit and their energy into their hometown.

Weston, then 26 and a lieutenant in the Navy, had come home to practice dentistry with his father. Law, then 28 and a second lieutenant in the Army, joined the family's transportation firm. Both were married with young families and were grateful to be able to resume their lives in the city where they were born and grew up.

"My father wanted me to join the Rotary Club," relates Weston, but, he reasoned, the Rotary members were older and more established members of the community; whereas the new club attracted men like himself, many of them World War II veterans just getting started in their careers. There was always room for another service organization in town and with a new club they could set the agenda.

Law's father belonged to the Rotary, too, but he also opted to join the Exchange Club. "There were 50 or 60 of us; doctors, lawyers, insurance men, real estate men, businessmen," he added, naming charter members who went on to become the city's civic leaders.

Luncheon meetings did not work out so they met every Wednesday night at the White Gobbler, once a restaurant where the Pheasant Lane Mall is now situated. They continue to meet on Wednesday nights at the old Howard Johnson's, formerly on the Everett Turnpike.

"I've made a lot of good friends and we had a lot of good times" said Law, pausing to add, "I never knew Boyd Weston before I joined."

"Just the fellowship of a group of guys," is Weston's reason the club has lasted for so many years.

The two charter members are still active in the Exchange Club, regularly attending meetings and volunteering for all the club's projects from the first, a dinner for top scholars, to the picnic last Friday.

The awards dinner for top scholars at Nashua High School was the club's first major effort after receiving its charter in the fall of 1947. It is still as popular as it was in 1948 and, with the growth of the city, has been expanded to include high schools in the surrounding towns. This year it was named the Boyd Weston Award.

Soon after the academic awards dinner was held, the group founded an awards dinner to recognize junior high athletes, beginning with Spring Street Junior High. It later grew to include Elm Street, Fairgrounds and Pennichuck junior high schools. A pep talk from a high school coach is still one of the highlights of the dinner.

When the city Little League program grew too big, the Exchange Club formed a minor league, sponsoring four teams so that more boys would have an opportunity to play. When the city needed a new scoreboard at Holman Stadium, the Exchange Club raised the funds. The club purchased TV sets for the children's wards in both of Nashua's hospitals and provided seed money for the city to build the Centennial Pool at the Amherst Street playground.

Among other additions to the city landscape is the Gazebo at Greeley Park that displays the Freedom Shrine, a collection of the famous speeches and documents defining U.S. democracy. The club has also placed Freedom Shrines in each of the city schools, several other area schools, City Hall and Nashua District Court. Providing flags and commending businesses that display them remains high on the Exchange Club agenda as well.

During Crime Prevention Week the club honors a policeman of the year and during Fire Prevention Week it honors an outstanding fireman. The club also provides the Fire Department with its Learn Not to Burn material to distribute to schoolchildren.

In its 52-year history, the Nashua club has never lost sight of its main objective: helping children. The post-prom party was the club's gift to parents who would know where their kids were in the wee hours of the morning.

A tradition of many years is The Bucky Snow Fishing Derby, sponsored with the Big Brothers and Big Sisters and the N.H. Flycasters Association. It is a fun outing for foster children and their families at a local fishing pond.

When the national Exchange Club launched its Child Abuse Prevention program, the local club, with the help of the New England district, opened a center in Nashua. To cap the club's 50th anniversary, it presented a $50,000 check to Marguerite's Place, a shelter for women and children rebuilding their lives.

Throughout the years, the Exchange Club's Golden Deeds Award has recognized outstanding Nashuans who have contributed to the betterment of the city's children. The award has taken its place among the city's annual prestigious tributes. In 1950, when the award was not yet named, the club conferred the title of honorary Exchangite on Birdie Tebbetts, the famed baseball player from Nashua. Golden Deeds award winners followed.

Early in its history the club faced the need to raise money to support its projects. "Some were a success and some were a dismal failure," wrote Law in his 50th anniversary history of the club and its fund-raisers. The first successful fund-raiser, he recalls, was a citywide exposition that started in 1950 and occupied three floors in an empty mill.

"We purchased the materials on credit, built the booths, stage and decorations from scratch," he recorded in a brief history. Daisy May and Al Capp opened the show, thanks to a member's grandmother with a celebrity connection. It was a big success and was held the following year in October at Boire Field, in three circus tents set up on the fields.

"Our timing was bad," Law continues. "We had rain, sleet and wind. Very cold. The lightly clad photo center girls froze. During the high winds we physically held down the center poles of the tent that were coming off the ground."

"We still made a good profit."

As the years went by and the city's business climate changed, the exposition gave way to another unique and profitable fund-raiser, the Ski Swap Shop. As usual, Law and Weston were there to set up the booths and do whatever needed to be done. The Ski Swap Shop is still held in the Armory on Thanksgiving weekend.

"We still rely on Law and Weston," said Edward J. Flynn III, a past president and now district director for the club. "We couldn't run the ski swap without them."

As it starts the new century, a second club, the Morning Exchange, has taken its place beside the original evening group. Its emphasis is on the opposite age spectrum, the seniors in the community. But Law, 81, and Weston, 79, will remain with the evening club and its dedication to youth.

After seeing the two men in action, Johnson, the new president, observed, "They're both young at heart."

June 17, 2000

CITY CARES FOR ITS CHILDREN

Two disgruntled 6-year-olds cornered the teacher near the door.

"Lisa, he just said a bad word," Chris blurted out.

"He said something rude to me," countered Romy.

Fighting words? Maybe somewhere else but not in kindergarten at the Greater Nashua ChildCare Centers, not even on one of the hottest days of the year. The spider mobiles hanging from the ceiling barely moved, while the papier-mache bees and caterpillars hardened on the wooden towel rack.

Satisfied that he had spoken up, Chris returned to the large tent near the center of the kindergarten room. Romy sat down in the "thinking" chair, looking very solemn. After a quiet rap session with teacher Lisa Barbera, he rejoined the tent-side groups, and the make-believe campers continued playing as if nothing had happened.

The system to diffuse explosive situations is carefully put in place in all the classes, even the younger ones. "They take a breather before they respond," explains Barbara Cleland, director of the centers. "You get them to talk about a problem and what they can do about it before striking out," she adds.

Twenty-five years of nurturing, affordable daycare for low-income families in Nashua have produced results at the Greater Nashua ChildCare Centers. The plural centers in the name was the tacit expectation of expanding in the future.

To kick off its anniversary year celebration, the non-profit GNCCC will hold an open house Monday. The reception was purposely planned during hours when the center is in session so visitors can see more than a building.

Ninety-two children, ages 13 months to 6 years, gather Monday through Friday between 6:30 A.M. and 6 P.M. year-round in the picturebook brick building on Shattuck Street. A mural of children holding hands decorates the wall of the steps leading to the entrance.

This mural was painted by United Way volunteers as were murals inside the building. United Way and federal funds meet most of the operating expenses since fees are on a sliding scale. Other grants help defray the cost of minor improvements. Cleland is currently looking for a way to finance air conditioning.

This summer a class for older siblings has been added to the curriculum. The group of youngsters ages 6 to 10 makes up the Tomodachi class. Like each of the other classes, the name is a foreign-language equivalent of the word

Laurie Berna

"friends." Tomodachi, the Japanese equivalent, occupies the third-floor room used as a multipurpose area during the year. The Spanish Los Amigos is the name of the kindergarten class; the French Les Amis, the class for 4-year-olds, and the Italian Amici, the class for 3-year-olds. The room for toddlers is simply called friends. What might serve as the GNCCC banner, many different colored handprints interspersed with the names of the classes, hangs above the entrance of the school.

Most of the preschoolers are children of single parents struggling to get off welfare and to improve their lives by working or through job-training programs. Some are from families in crisis, and they may stay for only a few weeks. Others are children placed with families or in foster homes by DCYF, or are referred by the Area Agency for the Developmentally Disabled. There is a waiting list of 50 children.

"Our children come to us with a lot of needs. They require one-on-one attention," says Cleland, adding there is a staff of 22 full- and part-time teachers.

"It's very demanding, very rewarding and takes a lot of caring" she says, leading a visitor into Les Amis class on the first floor. A band of little bodies in bathing suits files through the door, and Cleland greets each one by name. The 4-year-olds have been cooling off outside in the splash pools.

Each picks up a basket bearing a paper butterfly with his or her name on it and proceeds into the room to change. After they wriggle into dry clothes, they drop their towels by the make-believe beach set up with a large cardboard boat to carry out the beach theme in the classroom.

"They are so independent and so proud of themselves," says Cleland as she sees them dress themselves with ease.

Downstairs in the toddler room, no children are in sight since the class is on the playground. Toys, high chairs lined up against the wall and changing tables are clues to the presence of toddlers.

Parents need not worry about their offspring being toilet-trained, says Cleland.

"They will see the other children and train themselves," she assures parents. "They are so proud of themselves pulling up their big boy and big girl pants."

Smoothing the way for the parent to work or go to school is part of the school policy. Built into the program are workshops and parent-support groups. The staff is always willing to listen and to help.

Cleland holds a bachelor's degree in elementary education and a masters in early childhood education. She has had 27 years experience in the field, and as a single-parent herself, she understands the strain of raising children alone. She speaks sympathetically of one mother who drops off four little ones at the center every morning and then runs to catch a bus to work. Another parent just earned her associate's degree and got her first job, Cleland relates with pride.

Overhearing one of the center's young scholars say matter-of-factly to a friend, "when I go to college . . ." pleases her the most. It proves the GNCCC philosophy is working.

June 24, 1993

LIONS STILL ROARIN' TO GO

Imagine the raised eyebrows when the group of Nashua businessmen doff their jackets, loosen their ties and hop on the nearest chairs to roar like kings of the jungle.

"It is quite an attention-getter," says Ed Lecius. The past president of the Lions Club is describing the rousing cheer reserved for special occasions such as the club's dinner to honor the Nashua High School basketball team.

It was such an occasion in the 1970s that attracted Lecius, then a senior and manager of the high school team, to the club. After graduation, he was invited to join by downtown businessman Peter Scontsas, and five years later, he became the club's youngest president. He has just completed a second term in office.

On the flip side of the club's lighter moments are dozens of pancake breakfasts, Christmas tree sales, and road races—any fund-raiser that works.

The club motto, "We serve," has produced among other things, thousands of pairs of eyeglasses for needy Nashua youngsters, blood-sugar monitoring equipment for the diabetic children in the public schools and a clubhouse for the Friendship Club for the Handicapped.

Ask Jan Ethier, head nurse for the city schools, where she turns when youngsters fail the required eye tests and their families can't afford doctors' fees or other corrective measures.

Without hesitation she answers, "The Lions Club. They have been there forever, or as long as I've been here."

The Nashua Lions Club will celebrate its 70th anniversary next Saturday with a dinner at the Sheraton Tera. True to form, the next day it will hold a French toast breakfast fund-raiser from 7 A.M. to noon at the Holiday Inn.

"We'll just come from the party, take off our jackets and cook," said Lecius at the Monday night meeting.

Of all the pancake and French toast breakfasts the Lions have served, one has been elevated to legendary status in local Lions Club lore. The story begins with a 9-year-old boy who needed major eye surgery, which his parents could not afford. A Lions Club member heard of the youngster's plight on his CB radio and relayed it to the club. Members rallied to the child's aid with a pancake breakfast. News of the event was broadcast far and wide on the CB airwaves and one of the upcountry residents to attend was Gov. Meldrim Thompson, known for his official state pancake breakfast at his farm in Orford.

The dining room at the former Spring Street Junior High School affectionately known as the "pit," was packed and there were lines of people winding outside the door. The club raised the funds for the operation, and two of its members, eye surgeons, contributed their services for the operation.

"No one ever knew the name of the boy or his family," says Lecius, which is typical of the many youngsters the club has helped.

Further, it is the club that supplied the schools with funds to purchase vision-testing equipment. Any needy child recommended for a more thorough examination or glasses receives them, thanks to the Lions Club. For the first time, many adults referred by the city welfare department have been helped as well.

Eyes have provided the direction and vision of the International Association of Lions Clubs since its inception in 1917, when Helen Keller, both blind and deaf, asked Melvin Jones, a Chicago insurance executive, to round up a group of businessmen to assist her cause. They formed the first service club in chapters throughout the world.

Today the International Association of Lions Clubs supports the Lions Sight and Hearing Foundation, and individual clubs target areas of need on the local front.

Six years after the Lions club was born, Nashua members were welcomed into the fold. On Sept. 11, 1923, *The Telegraph* reports the visit of a national officer to organize the Nashua chapter. On Sept. 28, 20 men were inducted at a ceremony in the old YWCA on Temple Street.

Telegraph Photo Files

Clustered around the original club charter at the Nashua Lions Club meeting, from left to right are Sarah Holt, first woman inducted into the club; Phil Flynn, president; and Frances Bielawski and Evelyn Flynn, who transferred from the Hudson Lioness Club.

In its long local history, the Nashua Lions Club has built a strong record of community service and established its share of both club and city traditions, including support for Little League teams and the YWCA Swim-In, and help with Boys Club and Girls Inc. projects. The lighting of the community Christmas tree in front of the Hunt Building was begun by the Lions Club in the '50s before the city took it over. Lions Club members and their families gathered to sing Christmas carols at the holiday ceremony.

However, even the traditions that are the glue of good fellowship change. As the club begins its seventh decade, for example, it will admit women for the first time when Sarah Holt, wife of past President David Hold is inducted at the anniversary dinner. According to a directive from the national office, the Lioness Club in Hudson was dissolved last year and two members from its ranks, Evelyn Flynn and Fran Bielawski, also have joined the Nashua Lions Club. The Hudson Lionesses became the Nottingham West Lions Club.

"It's like coming home," said Bielawski, whose husband, the late Joseph Bielawski, belonged to the club for 43 years. He was the only Nashuan to serve as district governor. A bunkhouse bearing his name stands on the 35-acre site of Camp Pride, the camp for disabled children that he spearheaded on Merrymeeting Lake in New Durham. The two New Hampshire districts still support the camp, also used for two weeks in the summer by Camp Carefree for diabetic youngsters.

At the weekly Monday night meeting at the Holiday Inn, Phil Flynn, the current president, reported on his weekend visit to inspect the Camp Pride bunkhouse property and to notify members that painters would be needed for a refurbishing job.

Painting, pounding nails, even electrical and plumbing installations are nothing new for Lions Club members. With the late Nashua Mayor Mario Vagge, a former club member at the helm, the Lions built the clubhouse at 0 Orchard Heights, where the handicapped members gather twice a week for dinner and socializing.

This year the club helped repair the roof and bought a new snowblower.

As they enter a new era with women as members, the men may wonder if the Lions will continue to roar. With or without this attention-getter, however, the club's fierce dedication to a good cause will remain strong.

A piece of local history, misplaced for many years, is now in the hands of its rightful owners.

The Nashua Lions Club will ring in its 70th anniversary with a handsome brass bell—thanks to the detective work of the Kiwanis Club of Nashua.

The old bell engraved with the Lions Club name and crowned with the club's emblem was one of its treasured mementos, a fixture at weekly Monday night meetings until the end of the 1960s.

"We had the bell when I came in. That was 1963, and we met at the Country Club," remembers Norman Farnsworth, the Lions secretary for 26 years.

Soon after, Lions Club meetings moved to the Howard Johnson's restaurant, a popular meeting spot for many organizations. In fact, as a convenience, the motel set aside a closet where clubs could keep banners, bells and other paraphernalia.

When the Lions Club moved to the Holiday Inn, the bell got left behind. "Somewhere it got misplaced and we purchased another one," says Farnsworth.

In the mid-1980s, Kiwanis Club members found a dented old bell hidden behind the banners. It was scratched and topless but still usable. With a new Kiwanis Club emblem on top, it occupied a place near the president's gavel.

"One night I just happened to look at the writing," recalls Douglas Adams, then Kiwanis Club president.

Much to his amazement, the engraving, tarnished with time, read "Lions Club of Nashua." The markings on the bottom of the bell indicated that it was made by William Highton and Sons, an old Nashua company purchased by the Bronzecraft Corp. in 1944. Though there was no date on it, Adams estimates the bell was made and presented to the club in the 1930s by James Shenton, an owner of Highton and probably a member of the Lions Club.

A design engineer at Bronzecraft, Adams took the bell back to his company for a restoration job. The bell was polished and the "K" hat replaced with an "L."

Late last winter three members of the Kiwanis Club showed up at a Lions Club meeting carrying a brown paper bag. Loren Dubois, then president, William Livingston and Adams presented the bag to Ed Lecius, Lions Club president.

The bell now is safely sequestered in the home of the current president, Phil Flynn, and it is only displayed in public at special occasions such as the anniversary dinner.

Adams nonchalantly dismisses one service club's good deed for another. "We know each other and we often work together," he says.

October 16, 1993

MASONS' LEARNING CENTER

It is easy to overlook the plain storefront surrounded by upscale shops on Main Street. Yet for parents and their offspring, finding the way to its door offers an end to years of anguish and frustration.

"By the time they come here, they're pretty desperate," says Nancy Lemcke, the director of the 32nd Degree Masonic Learning Center for Children.

Children with dyslexia are the singular focus of the center. Four afternoons a week, learning disabled children receive individual tutoring in the labyrinth of rooms inside the street floor office space of the Masonic Building. Parents with siblings are only too happy to sit in the waiting room while their youngsters get the one-on-one instruction they need from caring teachers in a method designed to help them overcome the obstacles to their reading. Respected by both educators and doctors, the Orton-Gillingham Approach, a phonics-based system of learning, provides the key to unlocking the way the brain processes language.

All the parents in the waiting room tell a similar story. Year after year, they have watched their children struggle with school work—having intelligence questioned and confidence shaken—as they try in vain to keep up with classmates. The youngsters may be tested and coded in the school system but year after year the parents witness the child falling behind. Their frustration with the child's school mounts and they spend thousands of dollars and a multitude of hours searching for the cause of their youngster's dilemma without success. It is a futile battle for both parents and child.

Susan Jimenez tells a typical tale of concern, ending happily with 11-year-old son David Jimenez enrolled this fall in the center. She and her husband Jose, both retired from the Air Force, have two children older than David. The oldest son attends the U.S. Naval Academy at Annapolis, Md., and the 15-year-old son attends Nashua High School. David, the sixth-grader at Fairgrounds Elementary School, has been diagnosed with dyslexia.

German was the first language David knew best when, during his formative years, his parents were stationed in Europe. Although he was born prematurely in Germany, he seemed to develop according to normal guidelines until he started school.

His parents returned to the States after completing their service and enrolled their youngest in kindergarten. His problems with decoding letters and words emerged.

"I knew there was something wrong," says his mother, echoing a typical refrain of parents whose children are dyslexic. Although he was tested and coded by the New Hampshire school district where they lived, his parents were discouraged by the school's indifference and had him privately tested.

"The doctor recommended that we move to Nashua," says his mother.

Since second grade, he has been in a special education program at Fairgrounds. "He made more progress there in one quarter of a year than in the previous two years at his other school," she says, noting that an aide is provided by the school when he needs one.

Always on the lookout for more support for her son, Susan Jimenez heard about the center from her boss at Emory World-Wide Airlines. She works there nights, and days she is a student at Rivier College. Jack Balcom, the quality control manager of the company, is also a Mason and a member of the Merrimack School Board. A recent graduate of Rivier College, where he earned a second master's degree in education, he is one of nine tutors in the training program at the center, and there are nine professional tutors on the staff. He became familiar with dyslexia while studying early childhood education at Rivier. It was never a concern with his two children, both attending college on scholarships.

When he heard about the Masonic Center, he enlisted in its program to train tutors in the Orton-Gillingham Approach.

After 100 hours of tutoring and 45 hours of seminars, he will earn his certification as an Orton-Gillingham tutor. For others in the training program, such as Judy Beattie, a fourth-grade teacher at Sunset Heights School, it is another tool they bring to their classroom.

David's tutor, Heather Bierschend, a Milford Middle School special education teacher, is also in the training program at the center working toward a certificate in the Orton-Gillingham Approach.

She works with the teenager, drilling him to distinguish the difference in words using such vowel sounds as "ou" and "u," "e" and "ei." Of his progress, she says, "he's learned to get around his disabilities, he has learned to compensate. He is now in regular classes."

Balcom observes, "most people process reading with both sides of their brain but a dyslexic person uses only one side of the brain," adding "we have to create another learning path."

They do it so successfully that all the children attend sessions without any complaints. David says, "I like coming here," and his mother reports he faithfully does the exercises he takes home and never resists coming twice a week for hour-long sessions.

Balcom tutors the youngest client at the center, Benjamin Poole, age 6.

"He is a special case; his brother came here as a non-reader in the sixth grade," says Lemcke, noting the earlier the work with a dyslexic child begins, the better.

Balcom, recalling a session with Benjamin, says, "the first time he read a word, it was exciting. It was 'sit' and it was such a breakthrough."

A 32nd degree Mason, he is proud of the organization's support for the much-needed program, mentioning that 20 percent of children live with the learning disability in varying degrees.

"The center benefits the taxpayers, the schools and most of all the kids," says the member of the Merrimack Board of Education and a candidate for state legislature.

The 32nd Degree Masonic Learning Center of Nashua is one of 26 centers in the Northeast Jurisdiction funded by members of the Ancient Accepted Scottish Rite of Freemasonry. The New Hampshire Consistory, a branch of the Scottish Rite, provides the space, the heat and the electricity for the center, according to William Bryant, the commander in chief of the consistory. The national organization funds the staffing expenses.

The centers for dyslexia, initiated three years ago, fit into the fabric of Masonic philanthropies geared to helping children. Among their efforts are college scholarship programs and the Shriners, an arm of the Masons, supports hospitals to help physically disabled children and burn victims.

Thirty more learning centers for dyslexic children are planned during the next three years using the Orton-Gillingham Approach.

The techniques were developed by Samuel Torrey Orton, a neuro-scientist, pathologist and psychiatrist in the early 20th century. According to history he had met a 16-year-old boy who read at primary level and was convinced the boy's problem was not retardation. Rather, his problem was related to the processing of sounds in language. From Orton's research and his collaboration with Anna Gillingham, a teacher and a late reader herself, grew a language curriculum to help the dyslexic.

Lemcke, a disciple of the method, came to the center after years of working in support services at St. Paul's School in Concord. She is a graduate of the Orton-Gillingham Program of the Learning Disabilities Clinic at Massachusetts General Hospital, one of the teaching centers in the country. The director of the center since it opened in 1998, Lemcke knows the history of the 40 children in the program and often stops to visit with families in the waiting rooms.

Bill Vallieres of Derry waits for 10-year-old daughter Theresa. After tutoring at the center, he sees a big difference in her self-esteem along with her reading ability. She has come out of her shell, joining school activities, says her pleased father. Since his older three children were all top students, he and his wife, Maureen, were bewildered by Theresa's difficulties. Since pre-school, they have been troubled and sought help from her school. They took the child to San Francisco to be privately evaluated and even tried home schooling.

"We went the whole route," he says, adding their worries multiplied until they found the center.

"You couldn't pay for anything better than you get here," he marvels of the center.

November 14, 2000

NASHAWAY WOMAN'S CLUB

With the first sprigs of spring, a pair of marble benches will appear on the lawn of Library Plaza.

Each bench will bear the name of the Nashaway Woman's Club, bracketed by the years 1896 to 1996.

"They will be there as soon as the snow melts off the ground," Audrey Carragher, president of the local women's club, assures downtown sun-seekers. And if past President Madeleine Miller gets her wish, they will be surrounded by the state flower, lilac bushes, in years to come.

A gift to the city marking the club's centennial anniversary, the two elegant landmarks are designed to weather the winds of the 21st century as the club has done since it began 100 years ago.

With the advent of the electric trolley car in 1894, Nashua was connected to the outside world.

Little wonder women of comfortable circumstances began to expand their horizons, seeking new interests beyond the confines of their homes. A number of women's organizations with religious affiliations sprang up in the latter part of the 1800s. They often were the source of the volunteers who helped meet the humanitarian needs of the community.

As the 19th century drew to a close, the time was right for a broader social group directing its energies toward educating and enriching the lives of women.

"By invitation of Mrs. E.F. McQuesten and Mrs. Frank McQuesten, the following 10 ladies met at the residence of Mrs. E.F. McQuesten, Sunday afternoon May 29, eighteen-hundred and ninety-six," records the graceful script in the minutes of the organizational meeting, now a treasured memento of club history.

Twenty-five women attended the first general meeting at the Nashua Boat Club. Members adopted the native American spelling of the town's name, set dues at $3 a year and limited membership to 50, but so many women were eager to join, that the roster was expanded to 75. At the third meeting 150 women were listed as charter members, and by 1920 the club was stretched to the limit, with 400 women involved.

From its inception, the stated mission of the Nashaway Woman's Club was "to promote sociability and mental culture and to further the education of women." However, the influence of the budding suffragette movement and the growing impact of women on the well being of the community prompted them

Laurie Berna

to add another objective: "to make itself a power for good in local and national civic projects."

True to its stated purpose, the club formed study groups to pursue interests in art, literature and current events. An annual public lecture sponsored by the Nashaway Woman's Club brought to town figures of national recognition such as Lt. (later Adm.) Robert E. Peary, elaborating on his expeditions to the North Pole; Julia Ward Howe, reciting her "Battle Hymn of the Republic," and Fanny Farmer, presenting demonstrations on cooking. Booker T. Washington was a guest speaker, and Mrs. Edward MacDowell, widow of the revered American composer came to describe the MacDowell Colony in Peterborough that she was going to establish in his memory.

Never to be forgotten, however, were projects to improve the community. One of its first civic endeavors was to furnish a room at the new Emergency Hospital, when it opened in 1898. With monies raised from silver teas, musicals and other benefits, it supported the work of other women's organizations, including the Good Cheer Society's Protestant Orphanage and the King's Daughters Day Nursery and Home for the Aged.

Through its educational committee, the club established a dental clinic for children and raised money for the distribution of free milk to undernourished children in Nashua.

One of the club's most far-reaching contributions to education was the addition of domestic science and manual training courses to the curriculum of Nashua High School. The club paid for the courses, held initially in the evening, until the school department took them over.

During the Depression years, the club ran a Woman's Exchange before Christmas to help women in the community earn money with their handiwork.

"Undoubtedly it will be spent in the Nashua stores, thus doing double service," notes an article in the *Telegraph* that's in the club scrapbook.

During its 100 years, the accomplishments of the Nashaway Woman's Club ranged from the preservation of the old Man of the Mountain with the state General

Federation of Women's Clubs to planting gardens at Greeley Park, and from funding a class at the Mount Hope School to providing four college scholarships for Nashua High School girls. This year the club added a scholarship for a single mother returning to college.

"This organization does so many amazing things when they put their mind to it, and they do so without any thoughts of glory," says Carragher.

"Joining the Nashaway Woman's Club was like coming home," says Carragher, whose mother, Louise McLeod, had been president of the Pepperell (Mass.) Woman's Club.

For Betty Robbe, joining the club was also part of her birthright. Her mother, Florence Morton, was a member and served as president in 1940. Robbe joined in 1938, the year after she married.

White gloves and a hat were de rigueur at meetings, recalls Robbe, adding, "when I joined, mothers didn't work, so we all went to meetings."

For her, attending meetings was just a matter of crossing the driveway from 12 Concord St. to 10 Concord St., the club's home from 1930 to 1952. For years it had met on the fifth floor of the Odd Fellows Building, while members dreamed of having a place of their own. With a fund it started in 1901, the club purchased the Dearborn House for $10,000, a reasonable price in the Depression. Even with adding professional offices, the financial burden of maintaining such a massive building became too great. In 1952, the property was sold for $31,000 and the money deposited in local banks.

In 1959, one if its more illustrious members, Mabel Chandler, died and left the club a bequest of $30,000, and the union of the two funds allowed the group to function without fund-raisers.

Ten years later a meeting place of its own became a reality after the club contributed $64,000 to the then-Nashua Arts and Science Center. This was to assure the club a meeting place in perpetuity, in the lower level near the center's kitchen. As the fate of the center (later the Nashua Center for the Arts) became more uncertain, so did the permanence of the meeting room.

"They took our kitchen facility and put us upstairs in the big, cold Carter Gallery," recalls Joan Prue, then president.

"In 1989 we moved to the Friendship Club where it seemed warm and cozy," she adds. Since Prue is the administrator and the club takes care of the Friendship clubhouse's needs, and often caters dinners for the handicapped to whom the facility belongs, the relationship is a happy one.

Veteran members Robbe and Sylvia Jaquith seldom miss a meeting. Jaquith enjoys relating memories of the quintessential member, Mabel Chandler, arriving at a meeting in her chauffeur-driven car.

"She said it was a great day when she came to meetings," recalls Jaquith.

Through the years, thousands of Nashua women have echoed the sentiment.

March 30, 1996

NASHUA CHARITABLE FOUNDATION

There is great affection in Jimmy Stellos's voice when he speaks of Nashua. "I was born in Nashua in St. Joseph Hospital and brought up on Harbor Avenue. I still own the house," says the CEO of Stellos Electric Supply, Inc. His parents came to Nashua in the '20s and worked in the J. F. Elwain shoe factory. Except for military service after graduation from Nashua High School in 1952, he never wanted to live anywhere else.

"I started my business here in 1954 when I was 21," he says, adding that today he has 80 employees.

Although devoted to the Lions Club and St. Philip Greek Orthodox Church, he made time for a new group in town because he appreciated its objectives. In 1985, he became one of the first incorporators of the Nashua Charitable Foundation, started by architect John Carter, another native Nashuan.

"Nashua is one of the finest places to live. I wanted to give as much to the town as it has given to me," Stellos offers as the reason for joining the small group of men interested in insuring Nashua's future.

Nashua was a fine place to live for his family, he reasoned, and if the foundation had the foresight to make it so for families to come, he was for it. Today he is the vice chairman of the foundation.

Although functioning and still growing in membership 15 years later, the Nashua Charitable Foundation is still one of the best kept secrets in town. Few people know about the organization or its objectives.

For the past four years, it has entered the spotlight to sponsor a fund-raising luncheon honoring several outstanding Nashuans with humanitarian awards. This year's event will take place Thursday at the Marriott Hotel with former Mayor Maurice Arel, president of Pennichuck Water Works; the Rev. Donald Rowley, retired minister of the Unitarian-Universalist Church; and Mary Jordan, director of the Adult Learning Center, receiving the awards.

Each year after the luncheon, the foundation again fades into the fabric of the city to carry out its mission

"They're quiet movers and shakers," Shaun Marquis says of fellow members of the low-key organization. Marquis, director of Information and Referral of Greater Nashua, a pivotal agency in the city's human services network, is a knowledgeable adviser to the foundation, identifying city needs.

Through the years, the membership of Greater Nashua Charitable Foundation has grown to more than 30 people who have made their mark here in business, industry and the professions. Capitalizing on their good fortune, they aim to perpetuate the quality of life in the community that made their success possible.

"I'm a pretty lucky guy. I grew up in the family business," says Jack Law, the foundation chairman, and co-chairman of the luncheon with Marquis. "Nashua is a special place."

The native Nashuan was born at Memorial Hospital, graduated from Nashua High School in 1959 and was married in the Arlington Methodist Church in 1962. He began his business career in his great grandfather's company, Law Motor Co., and runs BSP Transportation, his own trucking company in Londonderry, with two of his three sons.

Law and Stellos are the Nashuans Carter had in mind when he conceived the Nashua Foundation.

"A lot of prominent people had come and gone. They had not helped the city, nor left anything behind," he said in a phone conversation from his home in Florida.

Carter grew up in a family committed to improving the quality of life in Nashua. His father, Eliot Carter, was the treasurer of Nashua Corp. and had started the city's Community Chest, which later became the United Way. Eliot and Edith Carter had been generous to the city in many ways including donating the funds to build the Nashua Public Library on Court Street and to support the Nashua Arts and Science Center. In fact, Edith Carter's bequest to the center was the first sizable investment made by the foundation. It is now managed by the Nashua Charitable Foundation.

"It was a small endowment of a couple of hundred thousand dollars, and today it is up to a million," Carter says.

The first meetings of the Nashua Charitable Foundation were held in his home and the "Original Incorporators" were David Hamblett and S. Robert Winer, both lawyers; Herbert Miller, owner of Millers department store on Main Street; Stellos; and Leon Brassard, owner of Heat Inc., a commercial heating and air conditioning distribution company in Hudson. Brassard had come here from Berlin.

Along with his success, Brassard became a civic leader in his adopted town. Among other community efforts, he succeeded Carter as the foundation chairman when Carter assumed the title of president.

By the time Brassard relinquished the post to Law three years ago, the foundation had the promise of bequests to secure its future.

"The purpose is to build endowments but not for a specific charity or building. We don't know how or where they will be used in the future," says Law, adding, just knowing the funds will be there allows the foundation to fulfill its mandate.

With proper money management, in 1994, the foundation had the funds to make modest contributions to agencies in town such as Marguerite's Place, the Nashua Soup Kitchen and Shelter, the Tolles Street Missions and the French Hill Association. This year, according to Scott Flegal, the organization's secretary, the foundation will be able to contribute $20,000 to the American Stage Festival and $50,000 to Home Health & Hospice Care to build its hospice facility in Merrimack.

Last year, Flegal, a lawyer in town, succeeded Winer, the secretary of the organization since its inception.

Winer, who was born at Memorial Hospital and graduated from Nashua High School, flew with the Army Air Corps in the Invasion of Normandy in World War II. After graduating from Harvard Law School, he returned home, was elected to a term on the school board and recently retired from the Board of Trustees of the Nashua Public Library after more than 40 years of service. For 15 years, the Nashua Charitable Foundation was a top priority on his list of civic duties.

A relative newcomer to town, Flegal was impressed by the caliber of members in the group and its objectives.

"I love the place," he says of Nashua. "It's a great place to raise a family and to have a business. If the foundation can perpetuate this I'm all for it."

Anyone thinking of leaving a legacy with lasting power need look no further than the Greater Nashua Charitable Foundation.

As its guiding principle, it proposes, "the test of the genuine community leader is in that person's willingness to invest some of his or her own labors in the future of the community from which that harvest grew."

May 2000

NASHUA COLLEGE CLUB

The 18th amendment had just locked the nation into Prohibition, the Charleston was creating a sensation on the dance floor and Calvin Coolidge had ascended to president of the United States after the sudden death of Warren Harding.

In Nashua, the mills were humming. "Nashua industries running full blast," was the headline on a front-page story that spring. The Nashua Exposition, a salute to the good life showcasing Nashua-made products, took place in the fall.

The city was flourishing, with population exceeding 28,000. Crowley Street school was built that year and Mount Pleasant School was on the planning board. Field's Grove opened for swimming and Main Street was widened. Along with the prosperity, the tax rate of the previous year, $24.60 per $1,000, was reduced by 60 cents.

The year was 1923. The women wore shingled hairdos and skirts that skimmed their knees. Their voices were being heard more often in every community and their votes were becoming a political force, nationally and locally.

A small group of Nashua women, most of them considered career women in their day, were in step with the times when they organized the Nashua College Club to pursue a goal they passionately believed in. Their objective was to advance "the intellectual stimulation of women and to support higher education for women."

The only qualification for membership then, as it is today, was a bachelor's degree from an accredited college.

As progressive as they were in their thinking, even they could not foresee the giant strides women would take in all walks of life during the latter half of the 20th century. Hardly could they have imagined that New Hampshire would have a woman governor, a woman state Supreme Court judge, and a woman Speaker of the House of Representatives; nationally there were also two women sitting on the U.S. Supreme Court, as well as many women college presidents and CEO's in business.

Today, Nashua College Club board member Mary Beth Carroll is typical of the modern woman. She was a vice president of Liberty Mutual Insurance Co. when she joined the club in recent years.

This spring, she resigned to work with her husband and stay at home with their 22-month-old daughter, Bryn Elizabeth.

"We need to keep the College Club going for the younger generation. They are our future community leaders," she says of her dedication to the club and its goals.

In recognition of the many women moving into high places, this year the College Club will celebrate its 78th anniversary by honoring an outstanding woman in the community, a role model for young women, one who has made her mark in her profession and as a civic leader.

The club's first Woman of Distinction Award will be presented to retired Superior Court Justice Margaret Quill Flynn at its annual scholarship dinner Monday at the Nashua Country Club.

College-educated women were few in 1923 when the club began. The careers they pursued were limited, usually to the fields of nursing and education.

Among the charter members were a number of Nashua High School teachers: Elizabeth Cornell, Martha Cramer, Anna Cross, Ruth French, Marion Lord and Helen Norwell. There were also women involved in community life: Mrs. Vasco Nuniz, Mrs. Robert Hamblett, Mrs. Harry Gregg and Anna Sterns.

"I had just graduated from college when Anne McWeeney sponsored me for the College Club," says Florence Calderwood, then Florence Connor, a member of Radcliffe's class of 1927. She was flattered that her former English teacher at Nashua High School asked her to join.

A native Nashuan, Miss Connor taught English at the junior high school on Temple Street and later social studies at Nashua High School on Spring Street before marriage to Donald Calderwood meant she had to retire, according to school department rules.

"We (in the club) had a lot of good times," recalls the 94-year-old College Club member of more than 70 years. Until recently, she was a regular at meetings.

As a member years ago, she served on the scholarship committee and she remembers, "it was an eye-opening experience sifting through all the applications." There were many bright women in need, she adds.

In the early days, College Club members met in each others' homes, as they do today. They often invited speakers and discussed books and timely topics.

They hosted bridge parties and rummage sales to raise money, giving scholarships of $100 to $200 to Nashua High School girls—a big help in paying tuition bills.

With time, the club expanded its fund-raising efforts for scholarships to sponsor special films at local theaters.

As the cost of college tuition increased, the club took measures to keep pace. In 1946, members voted on the recommendation of the scholarship committee to make the scholarships an official part of the club's bylaws.

"Beginning with the class of 1947, the College Club will award one or more scholarships to girls entering college as freshman and loans without interest to girls in the upper class," the amendment read.

By the '70s, scholarships were as much as $2,000 and the club looked for more lucrative fund-raisers.

Concerts for children proved to be the answer.

The club's annual Rosenshantz concert, now performed by musician Gary Rosen, were held at Elm Street Junior High School auditorium as they are today.

Tickets sold for the concerts raised much-needed funds for both scholarships and the interest-free loans, which Cam Moran, president of the club, calls the club's "well-kept secret"—even though the club has ledgers recording loans that date back to 1929 for $150.

The hard work that has gone into fund raising over the years has paid off: These days, annual scholarships for $2,000 to three or four graduates from Nashua High School and Bishop Guertin High School—which now incorporates the city Catholic girls school, Mount St. Mary—have totaled $154,000, Moran said.

The Rosenshantz concerts aren't the club's sole fund-raiser, as other fund-raisers have became part of its tradition. In recent years, the club has started hosting progressive dinners at members' homes, with appetizers starting at one person's house and other courses served at other members' houses. "We always end up at Ginny Nedved Cook's for dessert," says Moran.

Money from tickets sold for the dinners goes to the scholarship fund, which has also grown from membership donations and memorial contributions.

Besides its scholarship fund, another College Club tradition since it began is its reading group, the Antheneum, still meeting monthly in each others' homes.

Each member reads the book of her choice and tells the others about it.

Often several will pick the same book, such as "Angela's Ashes." At other discussion sessions, the books they read will explore a particular place or theme. Scotland was the subject of a recent gathering.

"I discovered books I had never read before," says Anne Hostage, past president of the College Club and former English teacher at Nashua High School for 20 years.

Education has proven to be a lifetime effort for members individually and the club as a whole.

One of the projects initiated by the College Club has contributed to the city's schools for more than 30 years. The Nashua School Volunteer program was conceived by Van Eresian, then a member of the College Club. She enlisted the club to sponsor the pilot program in the state.

When it began, the club compiled an index of men and women with interests and talents who were willing to share them with the schools.

From the list of volunteers, the program branched out to form teams of teachers' aides in the schools. In 1969, the Nashua College Club was presented an award by the N.H. Council for Better Education for its innovative, citywide program.

From Nashua, the School Volunteer Program—then coordinated by Ruth Ginsburg—swept the state and has since saved school systems countless dollars.

One of the Nashua Board of Education members who supported the program when it began was Flynn. Always ready to encourage efforts in education before and after she served on the school board, Flynn has been a member of the College Club since 1950.

When she is presented Monday with the first Woman of Distinction Award, she will be adding it to a long list of honors she has received from the city and the state.

Calderwood, who also expects to be at the dinner—and who recalls the many times Flynn drove her to club meetings—is glad to see the longtime member being honored.

"I can think of no one more deserving," she said.

May 20, 2000

NASHUA ELKS

It was a Sunday morning father-son ritual. After church, Carl Savage would take his small son by the hand and head for the Elks Lodge on Main Street.

"I was just about as tall as the pool table. I was 5, now I am 73," says Albert Savage, recalling a favorite childhood experience.

Memories of trips to the Nashua Elks have multiplied for the younger Savage in the more than 50 years since he became a member, following in his father's footsteps as Nashua exalted ruler, state president of the New Hampshire Elks and district deputy grand exalted ruler.

"When I became district deputy, we were the first father-son in the organization to hold those three titles."

Who better to record the history of the local lodge. After a two-year labor of love, Savage has produced a 144-page book crammed with pictures and stories about the Elks' members, objectives and achievements during the 100 years since the club was organized in Nashua.

The book was given as a souvenir to each of its 900 members, now both men and women, to commemorate the 100th anniversary of Nashua, N.H. Lodge 720, Benevolent and Protective Order of the Elks. The occasion was celebrated in September 2001, with Savage as the chairman. The three-day event took place at the headquarters, the familiar white lodge on the Daniel Webster Highway. Capping the centennial was a visit from the grand exalted ruler.

Both the national and the local Elks have left their imprint on the calendar and landscape of the nation. From Flag Day to Veterans Day observances, from Biddy Basketball competitions to Trojan Drum and Bugle Corps processions, the Elks have contributed in many ways to the American scene. Long before Nashua was named the nation's No. 1 city in which to live, the Elks Nashua youth programs were cited for 11 years as the best in the nation and Savage was involved with them all. For his efforts, he was the first to be awarded the city's Service to Youth Award, in 1969. It was just one of many awards to come, including the Exchange Club's Golden Deeds Award and the Southern New Hampshire Chamber of Commerce's Citizen of the Year citation.

Thirty years later he is still involved. By his side, as she has been for 48 years, is his wife, Marion, the girl he courted at Elks dances. She is a past president of the Emblem Club, the women's auxiliary of the Elks. Together they still organize, cook and serve at youth sports banquets. Just two weeks ago it was for the East Cal Ripken Baseball League.

Who would believe that a group that began as the Jolly Corks could become such a powerhouse in their communities?

The Jolly Corks were theatrical professionals, all men, who formed a social club in 1867. As its treasury and membership grew, they sought a more suitable name and a more businesslike arrangement.

The grace and dignity of an Elk, an animal known to avoid all combat except in protecting the young and the helpless, appealed to all and in 1868, the Jolly Corks became the Benevolent and Protective Order of the Elks of the United States of America. Some 30 years later Nashua's initiation to Elkdom paralleled the national organization, starting as a small social men's club, Entre Nous, and evolving into the Nashua Lodge of Elks No. 720.

Speaking of its beginnings, Joseph D. Killbride, the first exalted ruler, told a *Telegraph* reporter on the club's 50th anniversary, "It all started on Aug. 3, 1896. There were 30 of us ranging from 20 to 30 years old. Most of us had grown up together, and on that day we assembled at the old Lawndale Gardens in the South End to hold an old-fashioned New England clambake. We had a great time all day long and sort of hated to break up.

"Someone suggested we raise a little money, rent a room someplace and form a social club. This sounded like a good idea."

It was, but as the membership changed, affiliation with a national organization with the same outlook on fellowship seemed a more enduring route to go. On July 18, 1901, Nashua affiliated with the B and P Order of the Elks. The only prerequisite for membership for a male, 21 years old, was belief in God, American citizenship and payment of dues. Since it was a fraternal organization, not a service club, no stipulation was put on the number of meetings to attend or mandatory participation in group projects.

Elks parade down Main Street (circa 1943)

The Elks lodge offered a home away from home, a sanctuary to meet for good fellowship. From 1910 to 1961, when it was gutted by fire, the Nashua lodge occupied the third floor of 135 Main St. Fortunately, construction on a new and separate building on the Daniel Webster Highway was in the works. Since Nov 12, 1961, it has become a Nashua landmark and in its centennial year Exalted Ruler Edward Sekenski was busy with renovations for anniversary festivities.

From the early years of the 20th century, charity and patriotism played an important role in the annals of Elkdom. Washington's birthday was always reserved for lodge festivities—a dinner and a speaking contest—and since 1909, the Nashua lodge has done its share to promote the observance of Flag Day.

Members marched in morning suits, tall silk hats and canes for a Flag Day parade with Elks throughout the state in 1914, and every year after it was observed as a special day.

But in 1949, the observance once exclusive to the B and P Order of the Elks went countrywide when Harry Truman signed a law designating Flag Day a national holiday.

Putting Flag Day on the national calendar spurred greater accomplishments in another direction during the second half of the century. Beyond helping the disabled, the Elks broadened their interest in youth activities.

In step with the times, the Nashua lodge sponsored field days, Boy Scout troops and Girl Scout Cadettes.

Al Savage stands in front of Elks float in Sesquicentennial Parade.

In 1956, when the city wanted to start a basketball program for boys, the organization it turned to was the Elks. The Elks Youth Committee not only fleshed out the details but raised the money for the uniforms.

In the fall of 1956, 125 boys signed up and six teams were formed. In the second year there were 12 teams and a tradition, a banquet to honor the boys, was begun. The program was so successful that in 1960, financing uniforms and equipment, was taken over by the city but the Elks continued to put on the banquets. Today the league has 24 teams and 25 Elks still prepare the dinners, served by the wives in the Emblem Club. And a Girls Biddy Basketball League and Junior Biddy League banquets have been added to the roster.

"Whatever the sport, you name it—hockey, soccer, baseball—there is not one sport the Elks don't sponsor," says Leon Stratton, exalted ruler in 1976.

Stratton is typical of so many members who were involved in Elks youth programs before joining the lodge. The reverse is also true with the Elks youth programs providing the city with leaders such as the late Noel Trottier, who went on to serve as the parks and recreation director for many years.

Stratton says candidly it was the Elks youth program that prompted him to join. His children belonged to the Elks Trojan Drum and Bugle Corps and he was the equipment manager. In 1965, when Albert "Berdie" LaFlamme needed a feeder corps to prepare young musicians for the Spartans Drum and Bugle Corps, the Elks were the natural organization to look to for help. The Trojans grew to 110 boys and girls and by 1970 it was the largest drum and bugle corps in the state, playing for presidents and in every local event in Nashua, including the annual Veterans Day and Memorial Day parades.

In honoring veterans, the Nashua Elks made national news in the mid 1960s. A moving flag tribute to each of Nashua's veterans was initiated by Elks Boy Scout leader Roy Gannon. In the Memorial Day and Veterans Day parades, boys marched down Main Street in a double line, one with the Cub Scouts carrying the name of a deceased veteran and the other with the Boy Scouts carrying the flag given to the veteran's family in recognition of service to country. The Associated Press picked up the dramatic photo and it appeared in newspapers across the nation.

"We got calls from all over the country from groups who wanted to do the same thing," says Savage.

Today, the Elks are involved in an another ambitious veterans project. The lodge has purchased 10,000 flags to be placed on the graves of veterans of every war in Nashua, Hudson and Merrimack, and young people are being recruited to help the Elks make a permanent record of veterans buried in local cemeteries.

Observes Leo Cabana, at 85 the oldest living exalted ruler, "the Nashua Elks have lived up to their motto: 'Elks Care—Elks Share.'"

September 17, 2001

ODD FELLOWS

Every Monday night Floyd Foster unlocks the heavy oak doors on the fourth floor of the Landmark Building.

One by one, fellow members of Granite Lodge 1 of the Independent Order of Odd Fellows assemble in the grand hall, a chamber resembling the throne room of a medieval castle. As they enter, the men don starched collars like necklaces over their sports shirts.

At 7:30 P.M., the door is locked shut and the meeting begins. To be admitted, latecomers must ring a bell and recite the password to the guardian peeking through the lookout.

The weekly ritual is generations old. Nothing has changed, not even the meeting day.

"We meet every Monday and have been doing it for a hundred and fifty years," says Lee Lancaster, a past noble grand. He is compiling the last 50 years of history of the Granite Lodge 1. It will be added to the record of its first 100 years for the lodge's 150th anniversary. The official celebration, an open house at Landmark hall, is set for Saturday, Sept. 11.

History records the first meeting as Monday, Sept. 11, 1843.

The Nashua Oasis, a weekly newspaper, reported on the installation ceremony at the newly acquired headquarters, Harmony Hall, in the Exchange Building on Main Street:

"I.O.O.F.—A Society of the Independent Order of Odd Fellows was instituted in this town Monday last by P.G.M. Hersey of Boston. It is known as Granite Lodge No. 1.

"Mr. Hersey of Boston stated the objectives of the association, which were love and charity for each other—and their only secret was a means of ascertaining whether applicants for assistance were Odd Fellows or not."

As a secret society, the new organization had its share of detractors and some difficulty in finding a meeting hall. Its own history presents a candid account of the same occasion.

"Fifteen resolute young men were made members on that memorable day and began to carry on against public sentiment of bitter prejudice against secret societies, with both pulpit and press thundering anathemas and pouring hot shots into their ranks."

Misconceptions about the organization still persist, and members say the name Odd Fellow often puts them on the spot today, too.

"We are strange," quips Robert Stuart Griswold, the financial secretary, with a smile.

On a more serious note, he adds, "they were out of the norm when they were organized. It was a fraternal organization that helped people." Drinking was discouraged at meetings.

The Odd Fellow creed exhorts members to educate orphans, to bury the dead and to relieve distress. Its insignia, three linked circles, represent Friendship, Love and Truth, the three degrees members must attain to complete their allegiance to the society.

What manner of man takes the oath as an Odd Fellow and why? Ask Noble Grand Raymond St. Onge, and he will say members defy any rigid description. One of the younger members at 35, St. Onge is a Navy petty officer first class now stationed in South Weymouth, Mass.

He joined the Odd Fellows a few years ago at the urging of longtime Nashua buddy Ronald Morris, an autobody technician who's now vice grand. It was the group's show of solidarity at the funeral of Grand Master Frederick MacKay that convinced Morris to join.

"He was very impressed with what he saw of how the group came out for you," said St. Onge, adding that another member of the order, Steve LaBonty, joined at the same time.

"We are not an elite group," says Fred Benson, at 87, the senior member of the lodge. He adds that members include bank presidents, undertakers, merchants and auto mechanics.

"We only ask your name and occupation," he says, displaying the original registry listing all the members who have ever belonged. In the early days of the century there were 800 members. Today there are 55.

Laurie Berna

No questions are asked about religion or politics, and neither may be discussed at meetings. Rather the group concentrates on its own activities, such as its indoor baseball and dart league to promote camaraderie. Projects in the community include its sponsoring of the N.H. Eye Bank, initiated with the Pennichuck Lodge of Odd Fellows, another chapter in Nashua; sponsoring a Bambino baseball team, and serving Christmas dinner at the Friendship Club.

A constant thread through its 150 years is helping the widows and children of deceased members.

Passed down from generation to generation, a host of rituals are deeply ingrained in the minds of the members of the fraternal organization. Pomp and circumstance reign at degree ceremonies, often held with other lodges in New Hampshire or Massachusetts.

The meeting hall is equally imposing with its austere high-back chairs and benches covered in wine velvet fabric and its wall murals, three illustrating the degrees of Friendship, Love and Truth. The fourth wall depicts the work of the Olive Branch Rebekah Lodge, the sister group for women, established in 1886. Although they often combine for social functions, there is no talk about the two uniting.

In 1891, the Odd Fellows built the building where they meet today, and it bore their name until the early 1960s when it was sold.

In the 1850s, the lodge also acquired a large corner of Woodlawn Cemetery on West Hollis Street. Benson says it was probably given to the Odd Fellows in return for money lent to the city, not an uncommon practice at the time, when local government coffers were depleted.

Today the granite Lodge membership rolls may have shrunk but the fraternal bonds still hold strong.

"I used to bring older members to meetings. Now the younger ones bring me," says Benson.

"I don't miss many meetings," adds the member who is a past noble grand and an Odd Fellow for more than 50 years.

September 28, 1993

RED CROSS TO THE RESCUE

Everyone knows the name. We hear it mentioned on TV, and read about it in the newspaper. It is stamped on the beginner's swimming certificate in everyone's packet of childhood mementos and on the list of blood donation sites stuck on the refrigerator door.

Few organizations touch the daily lives of so many people in so many places in so many ways as the Red Cross. Like the maiden aunt a family takes for granted, the Red Cross instantly appears on the scene whenever needed, takes little credit for helping and moves on to the next task at hand.

Little wonder that the first contact a flood victim from Grand Forks, N.D., had, when she took refuge with a family in Merrimack, was the Nashua Chapter of the American Red Cross. She had driven with her children non-stop from North Dakota. Worried and cut off from home, she turned to the Nashua chapter to keep her in touch with friends and family left behind.

"We were able to tell her what was going on," says Walter "Skip" Dehart, executive director of the greater Nashua and Souhegan Valley Chapter, commenting on the strong network of chapters around the country.

"'Good people help, because help can't wait' . . . that is one of the Red Cross mottos," he adds.

The local chapter itself is still recovering from an earth-shaking event, a visit last week from Elizabeth Dole, president of the national organization, at a reception marking it 80th anniversary. "You are the heart and soul of the American Red Cross," she told supporters assembled at the Concord Street headquarters. "Without you, there would be no Red Cross."

From the Crown Hill Fire of 1930 to the Blizzard of 1996, and each year's share of fires and calamities in between, Red Cross volunteers have come to rescue Nashua neighbors and disaster victims across the country. Along with its daily roster of health and safety classes, the Red Cross has been there to administer its usual dose of solace and staples for survival in times of great duress.

The year 1917 was important in history for many reasons. For the Nashua Red Cross, it was the beginning of its identity after separating from the Concord chapter and assuming an independent status. On June 15, 1917, with Winthrop Carter as its first chairman, it established headquarters in the Temple Street School. In August the chapter was designated an official member of the Red Cross family.

It was none too soon. In 1918 a flu epidemic swept the city, calling forth all its resources, including the Red Cross. Its volunteers quickly produced masks and other needed supplies.

In the '30s, its mission was put to the test again with two major catastrophes: the Crown Hill Fire of 1930 and the Flood of 1936. Each left behind $2 million in damage. Some 400 families lost their homes in the Crown Hill Fire. Its flames also consumed three plants (Procter Brothers, White Mountain Freezer Co., and American Box and Paper Co.); two churches (Holy Infant Jesus and Crown Hill Baptist); and Holy Infant Jesus School. The Flood inundated the basements of 300 homes, closed several factories, and forced the *Nashua Telegraph* to vacate its Main Street building and to print in Milford until the high waters receded.

As a Red Cross volunteer, Stanley Morton was called into action for both. In the '30s, he worked for the Nashua Gummed and Coated Paper Co. (now Nashua Corp.), which was headed by the Carter family. Strong supporters of the Red Cross, the family gave employees such as Morton time off to volunteer in such emergencies.

At 92, Morton still has vivid memories of the city reeling from the destructive forces of nature. "Both were wild, but the fire was worse. All the railroad tracks were closed, until the fire equipment arrived. The fire departments came from Boston, from all around," says the Nashuan, remembering how the high winds spread the fire in a flash.

He remembers that during the flood, the police chief picked up victims on forays in a rowboat through water-clogged streets.

Morton was on duty at Red Cross headquarters, the Nashaway Inn on Chestnut Street, giving shelter to the homeless. Among his personal treasures is a stack of photos of both horrific events in Nashua's history, at which Red Cross volunteers worked night and day.

Sixty years later little has changed. Today, the Red Cross van is a familiar sight at scenes of tragedy in the city and surrounding towns. It provides comfort for the victims, dispensing care with a cup of soup and professional counseling while making provisions for those in need to get food, clothing and shelter.

"We don't give money. We have accounts with vendors all over town. There is never a question about paying the bills; we always do," says DeHart.

The scenario is familiar to Judy Gross. A disaster volunteer from Wilton, she worked at the Dr. Crisp School shelter during a severe winter storm when families were without power. The shelter was staffed around the clock for five days.

The Nashua experience pales, however, in comparison to one that followed says Gross, recently returned from helping flood victims in Ohio. "It's pretty exhausting while on duty but everyone was really up," she says of the responsive, well-trained volunteer crews called in from across the country. "We also did outreach to make sure we got to people who could not get to us."

"When we arrived, people were desperate and covered with mud. When we left, they had a dry place to live. You really can tell we've been there," adds the health care professional raised in the Red Cross tradition.

Helping disaster victims is a "must service" in the Red Cross book of rules and regulations, says DeHart. "Though the staff is reduced, we still have to do the job" he insists. "There is no way we could produce disaster service without volunteers."

With a $30,000 cut in United Way funds beginning July 1, on the heels of previous annual reductions, the staff has shrunk, and maintaining services has taken some juggling. Where five years ago there were six full-time staffers and eight part-timers, now there are two full-timers, and six part-timers. Julie Lastowka is director of health and safety services, and DeHart has added the role of volunteer coordinator to the many hats he wears as director.

Health and Safety Services Director Julie Lastowka, left, and Executive Director Skip DeHart.

"Prevention is a key part of the program. It is always better to prevent an emergency than to respond to it," says Lastowka, offering the philosophy behind the standardized Red Cross courses devised by experts in the field.

Through the years the local Red Cross has trained thousands of people to be prepared to handle often life-threatening emergencies. Standards, for example, mandate that cardiopulmonary, or CPR, certificates must be renewed each year and first aid certificates every three years.

The wheels of instruction spin daily at headquarters. Classes taught by Donna Hastings, Merrimack psychologist, offer mental health training for social workers and psychologists involved with disasters, while Patricia Ryan, Milford registered nurse, coordinates the certified nursing assistant training program.

Two new spokes will be added this year. One is an emphasis on involving more young people in the programs and the second is a sport safety program developed with the U.S. Olympics Committee.

To raise much-needed revenues to keep these programs on track, the Red Cross will hold its fourth annual Golf Classic on Monday, July 21, at the Sky Meadow Country Club.

If one program is synonymous with the Red Cross, however, it is the blood donor program, which was started during World War II to aid service men wounded in battle and continued in the civilian realm afterward. Today, a lifesaver for everyone, it has a momentum of its own. Though managed by the Manchester chapter, many Nashua area sites are staffed by local volunteers.

"We have gone from 50 pints to, on average, 90 and 100 units. We usually exceed our goal of 35 pints," says Lillian Anderson, coordinator for the past 15 years of the monthly blood drawing at St. Christopher Church.

"Anderson is just one of the many volunteers dedicated to sustaining Red Cross programs through the years," DeHart observes. Sitting in the living room of the headquarters at 28 Concord St., he surveys the homey setting of the chapter's base for more than 50 years. Once home to the family of Winthrop Carter, the chapter's first chairman, it was deeded to the chapter in 1941 in memory of Carter's son, Barton, who died in the Spanish Civil War.

"It is friendly and warm, what the Red Cross is all about," DeHart says.

Like a reliable old aunt, the Nashua Red Cross has made good on Clara Barton's dream of tending to the needs of the world and, after 80 years, it is still going strong.

June 14, 1997

NASHUA ROTARY

Monday at noon, Nashua's movers and shakers put work aside and flock to the Nashua Country Club for a luncheon meeting. The commitment is as strong today as it was 80 years ago.

In the winter of 1921, even when a storm knocked out the city's power for three days, closed down the mills and made traveling almost impossible, attendance at its weekly meeting was almost 90 percent. No wonder Rotary was cited for its attendance record in 1922, after its first year in Nashua, 16 years after the first Rotary club was organized in Chicago. Today there are thousands of Rotary clubs around the world.

"The Nashua Club was awarded a silver cup for the largest percentage of attendance at meetings in the past year. The cup was subsequently placed in the window of J.C. Mandelson's store on Main Street and was to remain permanently in the possession of the Nashua Club. It was a slender, graceful cup, gold lined, and bears a suitable inscription," reads the entry in its early history.

The cup has been lost but not the commitment to attend meetings nor the tradition of highlighting each weekly meeting at the Nashua County Club with a "Rotary moment." Almost 80 years later, there were myriad moments to chose from and as the club's years have mounted, memories to share by fathers and sons belonging at the same time. Not until future decades will there be mothers and daughters, since membership was not open to women until the late 1980s.

Brian Law, a third-generation Rotarian, presided at the Monday meeting at the Nashua Country Club. Over the years, fathers and sons have multiplied in the membership rolls but only a few families have reached the third generation level. The Law family qualifies even with a renegade in the family, George Law, who jumped ship to become a charter member of the Exchange Club when he returned to Nashua after serving in World War II.

There is an unwritten law among the city's service clubs against belonging to more than one since it dilutes one's efforts. Today there is a Law, Scott Law, in the Exchange Club and older brother Brian in Rotary. And both have taken the reigns of their respective organizations as president.

For father Jack Law, a member since 1969, there are two Rotary moments he will never forget. The first was his induction as president by his grandfather, Vernice "Bunny" Law, a veteran Rotarian, in 1982, and the day in 2000 when he swore in Brian.

Jack Law, Brian and three other Rotarians representing three generations gathered recently at the Law Warehouses Inc. to trade memories of their years in the Nashua Rotary. They included Philip Hall and his son Charles, both following in the steps of the late J. Lawrence Hall. For attorney William Barry III, the three-generation link is through his mother's family, his grandfather, Francis Collins, and his uncle, Francis Collins Jr. His father, William Barry Jr., also a lawyer, worked in Concord and his grandfather, the late William Barry Sr., was mayor of Nashua and a member of the Elks.

"I remember my grandfather (Collins) talking about flying to Keene in a piper cub plane to make a Rotary meeting," says the Nashua lawyer. Rotarians are expected to attend 60 percent of the meetings though for some Rotarians, such as the late Dr. Adrian Levesque Sr., a perfect attendance record was so important the club held a meeting in his hospital room when he was sick. The Nashua dentist maintained a perfect record attendance for 52 years.

But, according to Rotary rules, a missed meeting can be made up at other clubs anywhere in the world. For years Jack Law has attended meetings in Bermuda while vacationing there and the Bermuda Rotary is like a second home.

While honeymooning in Spain, Barry attended a meeting in Madrid without his bride, attorney Helen Honorow, who was not a Rotarian at the time. She, however, later went on to become president of Nashua Rotary West.

It was Barry's uncle who urged him to join after he graduated from law school and returned to Nashua to practice. One of his unforgettable "Rotary moments" was selling Christmas trees for the club soon after he was inducted.

"It was a cold winter night with the wind whipping through the field," he recalls. "It was in the same place where the Christmas tree sale is today, but it is no longer a field, it is a shopping center."

The Christmas tree sale is but one of the Nashua Rotary's vehicles for raising money to fund many service projects, locally and internationally. Internationally, through a worldwide program of providing vaccines begun in 1985, the Rotary has been credited with eradicating polio. A recent international project provided a water system in Honduras after a flood devastated the Central American country.

Locally, the Nashua Rotary has been there to fulfill community needs since 1923 when it pledged $1,000 to aid handicapped children. The list of its contributions since then touches every corner of the community. In the late 1940s, the club purchased oxygen tents for both hospitals, furnished equipment for the Community Council building, purchased machinery for the manufacture of orthopedic devices, supplied hearing aids for the deaf and aided handicapped children.

In the '70s, it appropriated $123,000 to build the recreation complex in the south end, giving the city a second public pool. To celebrate the bicentennial in 1976, it built a monument in the shape of the state of New Hampshire in Bicentennial Park near the Main Street Bridge and in 1990 it built the band shell at Greeley Park and dedicated it to the memory of Dr. Levesque, who had died that year. In 2000 Nashua Rotary contributed $50,000 to the hospice built in Merrimack, in a campaign headed by Jack Law.

Through the years Nashua Rotary has been a source of support for just about every social service agency in town including the Boys and Girls Club, Girls Inc., the Adult Learning Center, the Adult Day Care Center, YMCA Camp Sargent, the Red Cross and United Way.

"What you accomplish as a group, you couldn't accomplish as an individual," said Charlie Hall, underscoring the club's motto, "Service Above Self."

And service with a smile might well be the corollary.

"Fellowship is equally as valuable as service," says the current president of the Nashua Rotary, who grew up with the club. It was always a part of the younger Law's life whether attending a Rotary Youth conference in Canada or talking to foreign Rotary dignitaries who stayed at his house while his father was president.

At weekly Rotary meetings, fellowship begins at the door. Name badges are lined up on a bulletin board at the entrance to the Country Club room reserved for Monday meetings. Greeting members and guests as they arrive are "the freshman five," the newest members of the club.

"It is a great way for them to get to know members," says president Law.

Longtime member Roland Breault plays a medley of popular songs on the piano as members make the rounds of the buffet spread and take their seats at the tables set up around the room. In the name of good fellowship and getting to know you, members never sit at the same table or with the same crowd.

Asked to give the benediction is Max Silber, the senior member of the club who just turned 90.

Before the meeting begins, Tracy Hatch distributes envelopes with tickets for the May golf fund-raiser for everyone to sell. Hatch will become the second female president of the group since women were admitted as Rotarians rather than members of the auxiliary. During the meeting, she presides over the Presidents Day quiz, asking obscure questions about U.S. presidents which, when missed, are certain to fatten the treasury with fines. In

Before the dedication of the Adrian Levesque Sr. Performing Arts Shell in Greely Park are, from left to right, Dr. Robert Levesque, a brother; Adrian Levesque Jr.; and seated, Dr. Adrian Levesque Sr.

days gone by, members at random were fined for wearing the ugliest tie, which was promptly snipped off as the fine was paid.

Before the program on the Adult Learning Center begins, members rise to talk about the good news they have received during the week about a family member, their business or their organization. G. Frank Teas reminds everybody about the upcoming billiards competition and just as he has been doing for years, his father, Frank Teas, delivers a wrap-up of the news of the week.

With dessert and coffee Rotarians hear about the work of the Adult Learning Center, particularly with immigrant families. The speakers are Mary Jordan, director of the center, and Holly Harmon-Morse, chairwoman of the board.

The meeting lasts little more than an hour and a half but a lot is accomplished for the club. And for 80 years, the Monday meeting has gotten the week off to a good start for Nashua Rotarians.

March 3, 2001

SPARTANS DRUM AND BUGLE CORPS

There is only one sour note in the long, varied musical career of Albert "Berdie" LaFlamme. Yet the uninspiring, brief business venture ended on a triumphant chord, for out of its ashes sprang the Spartans Drum and Bugle Corps.

Under LaFlamme's leadership, the Nashua-based musicians developed into a first-rate marching corps performing with distinction across the country and in Canada.

On May 28, the Spartans Drum and Bugle Corps will mark its 40th reunion. It will begin with a reception at Spartans Hall, decked out for the occasion with displays of uniforms and trophies, videos of past performances and pictoral exhibits.

The event grand finale will be a dinner at the Sheraton Tara. The Rev. Tony Fontero, once a drum major with the corps and now a priest in the Manchester diocese, will give the benediction. To end the evening, the corps will preview its latest production, Ben Hur, marked with all the sound and fury of the Hollywood movie.

For the more than 600 alumni from across the country, the reunion will trigger a wave of nostalgia about the days of their youth strutting smartly with the Spartans in parades, shows and competitions.

The 70-year-old LaFlamme, now sharing the Spartans mantle with his sons, will be there to greet them. The hair is white but the smile and the genial manner, his secret weapons in motivating young musicians, are still the same. Past awards such as the Salem School District's "Teacher of the Year" and Nashua's "Service to Youth Award" are testaments to his lifelong rapport with blue-jean generations.

Nashua's unofficial Music Man was a 30-year-old, a father and a professional vibraphone artist when he opened the music shop over Daly's drugstore in Milford.

"The store didn't make it. I ended up selling records, which I didn't want to do," recalls the maestro. Instead of the latest Elvis and Beatles hits, he wanted customers to buy instruments and learn how to play them.

Unlike Professor Harold Hill of "Music Man" fame, it was community spirit, rather than the distractions of the pool hall, that drove the LaFlamme dream to involve local youth in the pride and excitement of a marching band.

"It was just to get a little unit to march on Memorial Day or Veterans Day. We begged our way to the first performance," he says as he recalls the fund-raising efforts.

Through the years, Nashua businessman Al Savage spearheaded many fund drives for the corps and often contributed generously himself, says LaFlamme, about his friend and golf partner.

With the first $500 raised, LaFlamme acquired second-hand uniforms from a marching band in Rockland, Maine. Mothers altered the uniforms and the corps was ready to march in style.

"Right away, it got away from us," says LaFlamme, of the corps sudden success in 1956.

At the end of the '50s, Bill Jaquith was one of the many Nashua High School musicians who also played with the Spartans. One of the corps' first jaunts was to New York City to take part in a parade.

"You could hear the drums ricocheting off the buildings," remembers *The Telegraph* controller of the exhilarating experience.

"You had to be in tune with the Spartans; it came first. Little League and everything else came after," he adds. Five- and six-hour rehearsals and weekend trips to perform demanded commitment.

In its early days, the Spartans rehearsed in Milford. More often than not, LaFlamme picked up a carload of young Nashua musicians along the way and drove them to and from Milford. He was also the teacher, choreographer, composer, arranger, administrator and corps psychologist.

With its membership expanding, the need for more space prompted the Spartans move to Nashua. A few years earlier it had its first taste of national fame with a fifth-place finish in a national competition in Seattle. Son Phillip LaFlamme, with the corps through his childhood, was a member of the troupe when they went on the trip to Seattle.

"We chartered a Greyhound bus and some of us slept on the hat rack. Along the way we stopped to see the Badlands in Missouri and other sights. In Seattle, we

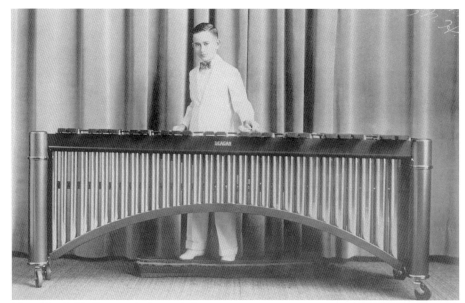

Albert "Berdie" LaFlamme playing marimba

Albert "Berdie" LaFlamme and his oldest son, Philip, giving a performance together on the marimba.

stayed at the University of Washington and went up in the Space Needle," he says, remembering the details years later.

The excitement continued when they arrive home; they had a police escort to their headquarters.

"And the whole town turned out," adds Phillip, the reunion chairman, who attended the New England Conservatory of Music. He counts among his memories performances for presidents and concerts with himself on the marimba and his father on the vibraphone. In recent years, son Peter has taken over more Spartans duties from his father, allowing the elder LaFlamme to play golf several times a week.

Peter has also followed in his father's footsteps as a teacher. A 1980 graduate of the University of Lowell, he was chairman of the music department in the Amherst school system. His father had been director of music at Salem High School.

Being Spartans-minded comes naturally to Peter. He came up through the ranks performing as a 10-year-old with the Trojans, the former feeder corps for the Spartans, and later in the senior corps. In 1990, he took over as director of the drum and bugle corps and as administrator of the building. Purchased by the Spartans in the same year, the building earns extra revenue for the corps with bingo games seven nights a week. In the '70s, it cost $30,000 a year to maintain the Spartans; today the cost is $30,000 a month, says the director.

On weekends the facility is the rehearsal hall for 80 teen musicians. In the summer they travel. "On the road they have to be up on time, show up for meals on time, know how to do their laundry, take care of themselves, look out for each other and budget their time," says Peter.

As head of the parents group, Georgie Moquin is in charge of getting the chaperones, rechristened the support staff in contemporary lingo. The Spartans is a way of life with Moquin, whose husband Dale was in the corps when they met. Now three of their four children belong.

Peter LaFlamme

"I don't play an instrument but I've always enjoyed the excitement of the corps, and I'm amazed at the hours the kids put in," she says.

Nashua High senior Jessica Loranger, the NHS Band drum major, will finish her four years in the corps this summer.

"I never traveled before I joined the Spartans," she says. She reels off the places she has been since signing on: Wisconsin, Mississippi, Tennessee and Canada, to name a few.

On the road the 80 teenagers travel on three buses now owned by the Spartans. A food trailer and a trailer to carry their uniforms and instruments are part of the entourage.

"It's a regular caravan," marvels the senior LaFlamme.

Forty years later, the house of music he built with horns, drumsticks and flags is stronger than ever.

May 1995

A GOOD BYE TO THE YWCA

For more than a decade, I've never needed robins to forecast spring. I could always depend on Polly Sherwin.

Come March, the YWCA aquatics director would breeze in the door with a packet of plans for publicizing the Swim-in. The annual fund-raiser supported the YWCA's swim program for the handicapped. It was Polly's pride and joy.

This year I know spring will be late. Punxsutawney Phil saw his shadow and I will not see Polly. The YWCA will no longer sponsor the Swim-in because it no longer has a pool. In fact it may no longer have a home.

For me, the passing of the Nashua YWCA as we knew it is like losing a dear aunt. While she was full of vim and vigor we took for granted all the nice things she did for us. Now that she is ailing we are left with a sense of sadness and a space no one else can quite fill. But memories of better days remain, memories shared by the whole family.

As do most waterproof Nashuans, my children remember paddling from level to level of Red Cross swim tests in YWCA pool sessions. My son, David, earned his lifeguard stripes in Polly's class.

One summer my daughter Laurie reigned as Miss Israel, thanks to the YWCA. We have home movies to document it. She and a bunch of other winsome maidens paraded in the Scampers Miss Universe Pageant under the shade trees in the Y's back yard. There were Miss Sweden, Miss France, Miss Greece, Miss Africa and Laurie, age 9, proudly wearing the blue and white crepe paper costume my mother-in-law had made for her. With flags waving high, the Miss Universe Pageant capped the YWCA's summer camp program for girls with an unforgettable salute to a world of diversity.

On the road to maturity my kids picked up many lifelong skills at the YWCA. Their mother benefited in less tangible ways.

Though I studied American history in high school and college, it was through the auspices of the YWCA that I received the most meaningful lesson in what it means to be an American. The patriotic feeling sparked by fireworks on the Fourth of July pales in comparison to marching down Pennsylvania Avenue in Washington with hundreds of thousands of fellow Americans in a testimony of belief.

Seven years ago in the month of April, the Nashua YWCA organized a bus trip to Washington so we could join other men and women from all parts of the country in the Pro-Choice March.

We left Nashua at dusk on Saturday night, transferred in Boston to another bus with more women, including Nuns for Choice, and proceeded through the night to the nation's capital. We arrived at dawn and gathered with busloads from everywhere for a hearty breakfast at the YWCA's national headquarters. By 9 A.M. we joined the New Hampshire contingent at the Washington Monument, crowded with marchers singing, holding religious services and getting acquainted with one another.

To walk to the steps of the Capitol Building in the company of your countrymen and women is an exhilarating experience.

As she did throughout the trip, Jan Stenbak, president of the YWCA at the time and a Peace Corps veteran, shepherded her Nashua flock through the streets of Washington back to the bus.

For the opportunity to be a blip in the pulse of democracy, I thank the Nashua YWCA.

I also thank the YWCA for another illuminating experience in my life. It took place at the Hillsborough County Prison for Women in Goffstown. One winter evening a couple of years ago, I sat in on the parenting series arranged for the inmates by the Nashua YWCA. The women met weekly with counselors to learn how to keep in touch with their children and how to help little ones deal with feelings of separation.

The YWCA also arranged for the inmates' children to take bus trips to the prison to see their moms.

The process of being admitted to the inner sanctum of a prison was unsettling and so was talking with the women—but for a different reason from what you might think. The women were not the hardened criminals I had expected. Rather

Dedication of YWCA and YMCA

Telegraph Photo Files

they were women struggling to survive in difficult environments. In spite of their problems, they were profoundly concerned for their children.

Of all of the good things the YWCA did for Nashua women, perhaps the one remembered with the most affection is its yearly November Valentine, the Distinguished Women Leaders Tribute.

From the first event in 1981, it was a time to enjoy the company of friends often not seen enough throughout the year and to hear inspiring talks by women of accomplishment, such as Congresswoman Patricia Schroeder and TV anchorwoman Liz Walker.

Above all it was a time to celebrate our sisterhood and take pride in our collective achievements.

Who will call us together for such a celebration next year?

March 4, 1996

SENIOR ACTIVITY CENTER

Today is a day to celebrate for Pat Francis, a day she can kick up her heels and shout, Whoopee! On this very day, she is eligible for a membership card in an organization she has been waiting 20 years to join. On June 22, 1998, Francis marks her 55th birthday, thereby giving her entree to the Nashua Senior Activity Center.

For 20 years, the almost native Nashuan has been director of the center. The record shows she was born in Manchester and her family moved here when she was 4 years old, but Nashua's senior population considers her one of their own, more like a favorite daughter than a peer. But that, too, will change.

"Watch out. Maybe I'll join the dance class and be in the show," says the ebullient coordinator of one of the busiest places in town. The thought of growing older doesn't daunt her a bit.

"I'm quite comfortable at where I am today, unlike some baby boomers," she says.

Maybe 20 years of mingling with an older crowd has produced a patina on her philosophy of aging. She is surrounded by people who have cultivated their zest for life, learning new skills, keeping body and mind active even though both may need little jump-starts now and then. Francis learned that the good life can outwit mounting birthdays.

John Collins is an example of someone with his foot still on the gas pedal. He turned 80 last week, but he is a relative newcomer to the center. He joined last fall at the urging of his two sons. They owned a diner across the street from the center, and met members who brought food left over at the end of the day. Impressed by the energy level at the center, they prevailed on their father to make a visit.

"I never thought of joining," says the retired president of Pennichuck Water Works. "I was not much of a card player."

Collins held several executive posts during his working years. He was the president of Public Health Engineering in Massachusetts, and he also worked with the New Hampshire Environmental Control Office. Even after he retired and after his wife died, he kept busy helping his sons with their business.

He had never considered joining the center, but when he did, he discovered—much to his surprise—that it offered much more than cards. In fact, he signed up for a writing course given by Millie Janz, a retired teacher and writer who recently moved to Nashua.

Pat Francis and Mary Barrille of the Senior Center.

"I've written a lot through the years and I enjoyed it," he says, noting the course was the frosting on the cake, with participants in the class reading and critiquing each other's work.

He was also pleasantly surprised to meet a lot of people with common interests and equally impressive histories. And with the center embarking on an ambitious plan to expand, he agreed to become one of the new members of the board.

It was during a past citywide rejuvenation effort 20 years ago that Francis was appointed director of the center. The idea for the meeting place for seniors had been proposed several years before, and though it attracted members, including other senior citizen clubs, the new senior center was forced to close due to lack of funds.

Mayor Maurice Arel appointed the Nashua Jaycees to set the center back on its feet financially, with a boost from a grant underwritten by the city. One of the Jaycees' first moves was to hire Francis. The local chapter subsequently won a national award for its successful effort to rally the community behind its plan.

In 1981, the center, housed in the old Montgomery Ward building at 221 Main St., was humming along when a fire gutted the building. A fund-raising campaign spearheaded by the seniors in 1982 raised $565,000 to build a new facility at 70 Temple St. The building, with a main hall, pool room, several multipurpose rooms and its own parking lot, opened with great promise of things to come.

Even though too young to join, Francis became synonymous with the center, and an attempt in 1990 to remove her was met with protest from the members.

During Francis' 20-year tenure, the center has become financially self-sustaining; with a budget of $180,000. It has broadened in scope, and its membership has multiplied.

"There were 250 people when we had our first mailing of our newsletter in '78. Now we send out 2,500, and it is read by 3,133 members," says Francis. "Twenty years ago we had four clubs meeting here, a pool room, whist, bingo and a dance class."

Today the newsletter lists a variety of classes from aerobics to tai chi, instruction in topics from painting to computers, discussion groups covering topics from health to taxes, and trips from Boston to Bermuda.

Many center-organized activities bring seniors into the community spotlight. One such event is the center's annual fall show, directed by Penny Tamulonis, and written by and starring the seniors. To accommodate the large audience it attracts, the production is now staged at the Edmund Keefe Auditorium at Elm Street Junior High School. Other senior performing groups, such as the Harmonica Saints and the Silver Lining choral group, are in demand at nursing homes, club meetings and the city's Summerfest programs.

With a new name, the Nashua Senior Activity Center, reflecting the dynamic attitudes of today's older and healthier population, the center has embarked on a campaign to expand both its meeting space and parking lot.

"And the nicest part about joining before you retire is you can find out about all the things you can do afterwards and try some of them out ahead of time," Francis says.

When it comes to the center, Francis takes her own advice. As of today, the Nashua Senior Activity Center's membership is 3,134.

June 22, 1998

CHANGE UNDER WAY AT
PASTORAL CARE CENTER

The smell of fresh paint permeates the corner office of the Nashua Pastoral Care Center. It is another reminder of the change in the air at the social service agency off Main Street.

"It is the first time it has been painted since we've been here," quips Carl Swenson.

The office was Swenson's until this week when he officially retired as executive director of the agency that he helped to create 16 years ago. The addition to the Church of the Good Shepherd that serves as its base of operations was built during his tenure as its guiding force.

Much like a parent gently loosening the chord, he has eased the agency into a new phase in its development. He has planned on retirement since the long-range planning committee drew up its agenda two years ago, so there has been ample time to prepare for his departure.

This week the board named Maryse Wirbal, the business manager, as his successor, but Swenson will stay on part time until April as director of the agency's Emergency Assistance (EA) program. Though her background is financial, she is learning the ropes of running a social service agency through mentoring with other agency directors and through the Leadership Program run by the Nashua Chamber of Commerce.

"For all intents and purposes I'm not here, I'm just an astral projection of myself," Swenson says with the wry sense of humor for which he is known. Almost without thinking, he adds, "E.A. is open only Tuesdays and Thursdays; we don't have enough money to keep it open any more."

The constant headache of finding money to finance the agencies programs is no longer his.

At age 64, the avid outdoorsman looks forward to having time to smell the wild flowers and the sea air with June, his wife of 43 years. After a brief respite, he intends to find another job to stretch his Social Security check.

Swenson spent most of his early working life managing construction jobs from Canada to Australia after he graduated from Dartmouth as an English major. Tired of traveling and with the help of AA, Swenson, a recovering alcoholic, bought a business in New York State only to have it hit rough seas.

New Hampshire's attractive economic environment and the New England landscape brought Swenson, his wife and three children here and after some searching

Pastoral Care Center Office on Concord Street

they found the congregation of their choice, the Good Shepherd Episcopal Church. Swenson sampled a number of careers, including photojournalism, before finding his niche as a counselor, building the framework of a social service agency.

"The strength Carl brought to the Pastoral Care Center is counseling, in the right time and at the right place" says Gary Wingate, immediate president of the board. And he soon perfected delivery of the Center's services, adds Terrence Williams, publisher of *The Telegraph*, now board president.

When they first conceived the idea in the early '80s, an established citywide institution with the breadth of Pastoral Care Center was beyond the imagination of Swenson and the Rev. Robert Schenkle, then pastor of the church. The two men talked of the church's need to address what Swenson calls the "outrageous social injustices" suffered by people down on their luck. They envisioned "a one-stop shop" for help within the church.

Today as he leaves his post behind, Swenson still decries the holes in the system's safety net. One never-to-be-forgotten "outrage" he cites was Medicaid approving payments for the extraction of a man's teeth without making provisions for dentures.

"That's considered cosmetic; I guess he's suppose to gum his food," Swenson remarks.

When he and Schenkle started the small church outreach program, there was a lot they needed to know to perform services effectively, Swenson recalls. He volunteered to answer the door and the phones. To learn more about local humanitarian efforts, he also attended meetings of Nashua Inter-Agency Council (NIAC). Then and now, the network of social service agencies is coordinated by Shaun Marquis, director of the non-profit Information and Referral Services of Greater Nashua.

"Shaun was my teacher; she took me under her wing and she taught me on the job."

The knocks on the door also made him a quick learner.

"After the first month, people started coming and they haven't stopped. We've never had to advertise, not even in the telephone book, yet people found their way to us," Swenson marvels.

The food pantry proposed by a parishioner drew people desperate to feed their families, and through the years, the numbers grew. Fortunately the community responded.

The outreach program at the Good Shepherd Church also met another need, one not addressed before. It established a source of security loan deposits that landlords require of new tenants. People living from paycheck to paycheck could manage to pay the rent but few could come up with a security deposit beforehand so the center stepped in with loans that could be paid back in small increments over a period of time.

The loan initiative was started by the center even before the state instituted a similar program to help the working poor. Today, Denise Taylor, the Pastoral Care Center's outreach director, administers the state Housing Security Guarantee Program for southern Hillsborough County. She started working for the center seven years ago as part-time manager of the food pantry and is now the full-time outreach director.

To qualify for help, people had to find a path to independence. They had to sign up for a training course in a job skill or in an education program.

Carl Swenson

Telegraph Photo Files

Today a number of the former clients are working in the community, some in the computer field, others as beauticians and still others in local businesses.

It takes time and patience to change styles of living, Swenson observes from experience. "You could not make Newt Gingrich and John Sununu into Democrats in a month," he quips.

As the services expanded and the clients multiplied, the center out-grew its first home in the Church of the Good Shepherd.

"As a denominational church, we couldn't ask for community funds," says Swenson, adding that he and the Rev. Robert Odierna, then pastor, agreed the solution was to take a more inclusive course. In June 1987, with "Father Odie" leading the way, the center was incorporated and funds were raised for its present home, an addition at the rear of the church. It was built in 1992.

"The first budget was for $50,000; in 1998, it is for $550,000," says Swenson.

"In January of '87, we had no assets except a used electric typewriter. In July 1998, we will have capital assets of $750,000," he adds.

The assets include property bought and rehabbed in the past few years for transitional housing, mostly for single mother families. A building on C Street provides homes to four families, another on Vine will soon have five units and there are nine rented sites scattered around the city.

Yvette Martin, director of Transitional Housing, Taylor, Kim Odierna and Wirbal comprise the full-time staff; there are also four part-timers.

How do you measure the success of a social service agency? By the size of its staff? Its assets, its budget? To Swenson, it is knowing how to answer each knock on the door with the right words, the right plan.

Come April, for the first time in 16 years, he can put the calls for help aside and head for the woods with his bike and canoe.

"I just saw something on TV about white-water rafting in Idaho. It looks like such fun," he says, as he gazes over the rooftops on Main Street from the Pastoral Care Center's window.

February 17, 1998

Editor's Note: In the spring of 2000, the Center moved its headquarters to 7 Concord Street. It leases the building from the First Church.

KING'S DAUGHTERS

At the beginning of the school year, all fourth-grade teachers in the Nashua school system receive boxes of goodies to share with their class throughout the year. Instead of cookies or brownies, the large brown boxes contain tidbits of Nashua history. There are memorabilia from mill days, such as spindles and swatches of material, historical games and books about the past.

Two volumes are read again and again: "Obediah Comes 14," written by the late Elizabeth Spring, a longtime Nashua librarian, relates the story of a boy growing up in Nashua in the early 1800s; "A River Ran Wild," by Lynne Cherry chronicles the growth of Nashua from Indian days to modern times.

The books and other treasures in the box are a gift from the King's Daughters Benevolent Association to the classes designated to learn about Nashua and New Hampshire that year.

It is just one of the King's Daughters' gifts to the young history scholars. Every year each fourth grade visits the Historical Society on Abbott Street and the Little Red Schoolhouse on Daniel Webster Highway South. At the start, the two field trips were funded by the King's Daughters; now both groups join to cover the costs.

Little Red Schoolhouse on DW Highway

The Little Red Schoolhouse itself is a gift of history to the city. The city's oldest schoolhouse, now on the north edge of the entrance to the Royal Ridge Mall, was restored to its original state in 1976 by the King's Daughters as the group's contribution to the city's Bicentennial Celebration.

"They wanted us to sell plates or something," recalls Roberta "Mitzi" Barrett, a member of the King's Daughters who served on the Nashua Board of Education.

Instead, the King's Daughters, assisted by fund-raisers conducted by the Nashua High School Honor Society and Nashua's fifth-graders, undertook the more challenging, more enduring project. They transformed the deteriorating landmark in the cemetery to the one-room schoolhouse of 1841. With hard work and research, they brought back to life the one-room schoolhouse that served Nashua until it closed in 1921.

Starting in mid-April there is a fourth-grade class visiting the school every day until the end of school, and each is taught a lesson in the manner of the times, by a school marm typical of that era.

In the summer, the schoolhouse is open to visitors once a week and they are treated to the same living history lesson free of charge.

April 9, 1994

Restoration Plaque on Schoolhouse

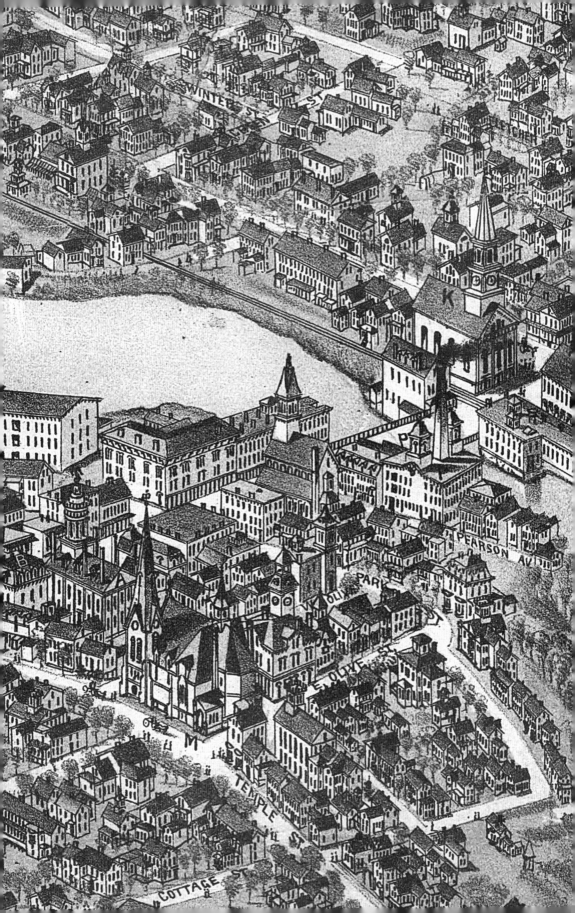